Win the
Leadership Game

About the Knowledge@Wharton Insights Series

Win the Leadership Game is the first in the Knowledge@Wharton Insight Series, the product of a partnership between Knowledge@Wharton and Wharton Executive Education. This series applies the intellectual capital of the world's most published business school faculty at the Wharton School to critical issues that shape business today and determine its course for the future.

For more information about Knowledge@Wharton,
please visit *http://knowledge.wharton.upenn.edu*.

For more information about Wharton Executive Education,
please visit *http://executiveeducation.wharton.upenn.edu*.

Knowledge@Wharton Insights

Win the Leadership Game

How Companies Can Create Unbeatable Global Teams

Jason Wingard, PhD
Editor

Editor: Jason Wingard, PhD, Vice Dean, Executive Education,
Wharton School, University of Pennsylvania
Editorial Consultants: Mukul Pandya, Editor in Chief, Knowledge@Wharton;
Robbie Shell, Managing Director, Knowledge@Wharton; Wendy Parsons,
Director of Communications, Executive Education, Wharton School,
University of Pennsylvania; Rahilla Zafar
Cover Design: Lara Andrea Taber

Knowledge@Wharton
The Wharton School
University of Pennsylvania
332 Steinberg Hall-Dietrich Hall
Philadelphia, PA 19104

10 9 8 7 6 5 4 3 2 1
ISBN: 978-1-61363-001-3

Printed in Mexico.

Contents

Contents

Introduction
Leadership Lessons for the Global Playing Field

The challenges facing business leaders today raise an all-important question. But first consider the context for these challenges—what we call the global playing field. It's a field of rapid change, rocked by seismic shifts in nearly every sector. For your organization, it could be the impact of emerging markets on the world economy, and the threats and opportunities they offer. Or the shudders reverberating through world markets triggered by recent economic crises. Or perhaps the role of new technologies in moving more power from producers to consumers. In light of these and countless other challenges in current global markets, what is the most important thing you can do to sustain competitive advantage?

Klaus Kleinfeld, former CEO of Siemens, one of the world's largest private companies, offers this answer: "If you're talking about a sustainable competitive advantage, probably the only one is the quality of people you have and the way they interact as a team." We underscore Mr. Kleinfeld's thinking with the observation that the world's most stellar global teams leverage and improve organizational processes while accomplishing tasks across functional and international boundaries. What, then, can you learn from them and their leadership to create unbeatable teams that succeed and maintain your lead on the global playing field?

Both the challenges of leadership and managing global teams call for a deep understanding of the factors that shape your organization and the markets in which you operate. But arriving at that state of understanding can be an arduous process if you rely on experience alone. It makes more sense to learn from those who have faced similar obstacles and achieved success. To that end, we are partnering with Knowledge@Wharton, Wharton's global online business journal, in a book series that offers executives the wisdom of some of today's most successful business leaders along with thoughtful analysis by Wharton's leading faculty.

This series from Wharton's Aresty Institute of Executive Education and Knowledge@Wharton represents our commitment to sharing the best of Wharton's knowledge and analysis with you on a continuing basis. Each volume in this series contains a comprehensive selection of in-depth articles and analyses around timely and relevant business topics.

Our initial offering focuses on leadership. I have edited it based on the priorities that arose during my conversations over the years with CEOs and other business leaders. The volumes that follow will offer our latest thinking in the areas of business that have direct relevance to your viability and strength as an organization. They will include such topics as strategy in a global context and innovation—not only around new products, but in creating more effective business models or designing a program with far-reaching social impact.

The first in this series, *Win the Leadership Game: How Companies Can Create Unbeatable Global Teams* examines leadership through multiple lenses, divided among nine parts. We assembled a comprehensive view of leadership both from within the organization and as it influences and is influenced by the marketplace.

Part One, "Crisis Management as a Leadership Imperative," follows the trajectory—and often the slippery slope—of leadership in times of crisis. From BP's stumbling response to the massive oil spill in the Gulf, to the hits Toyota took during its massive recall, this chapter provides an examination of leadership in the face of crisis. These articles offer practical steps leaders can take to avoid faltering when the heat is on—such as quickly offering sincere apologies when your company makes a mistake, maintaining company stability when disaster hits, preserving market position in times of turbulence, and keeping employees motivated in the face of deep cuts and layoffs.

Part Two, "Gaining A Competitive Advantage Through Targeted Team Building," focuses on the key factors that can determine success for global teams—and their organizations—and those that can drive global projects into the ground. In one such article, Wharton Graduate Leadership program director Evan Wittenberg suggests that when it comes to teams, size does matter. The optimal number for teams? Five or six is most often the right number. And in another story, Wharton professor Nancy Rothbard argues that when faced with making hiring choices, organizations should consider career history and the ease, or difficulty, with which new team members can be acclimated to corporate strategy and culture. The articles in this chapter take a wide view of teams, including how the values of your employees can be a deciding factor in your success, as Mexican companies have learned based on the influence of religious devotion in the styles and work practices of their employees.

Part Three, "Technology as a Competitive Differentiator," demonstrates the truth of Andy Grove's prophetic words over a decade ago: "Technological change is going to reach out and sooner or later change something fundamental in your business world." In the span of 60 seconds, four million web searches take place, more than 500,000 pieces of content are shared on Facebook, 100,000 products are searched on Amazon, and 40,000 tweets are created. Both small start-ups and large corporations that fail to understand the social data phenomena may soon find themselves out of business. And the speed of technological change is nowhere more evident than in the race to gain marketshare with new products and new applications. In "Sprint's 4G Advantage: Game Changer or Not Enough to Call Home About?," Wharton public policy and business professor Gerald Faulberger points out that despite Sprint's strides in the area of customer service, the company can lose marketshare unless it develops innovative and exclusive applications for its hot-selling HTC Evo 4-G.

Part Four, "Leveraging Strategic Opportunities in Emerging Markets," advises business leaders of both the challenges that are currently shaping emerging markets, and the bountiful opportunities that these markets offer. There are stories, for example, that examine the current market-driven pain and possibility in Russia, pointing out that while the country's turbulent transitions since the demise of communism 20 years ago persist today, its oil-rich economy has fueled demand for consumer goods. Africa is also highlighted as a market with enough consumer power and opportunities for suppliers to give China and India a run for their money.

Part Five, "Entrepreneurship in a Complex Global Marketplace," looks at the enormous impact that entrepreneurs like Fadi Ghandour, founder of Aramex, the Dubai-listed global logistics firm, can have on the business community. Arguably the region's best-known mentor, role model and angel investor for many young Arabs, Ghandour tells young business leaders that entrepreneurship is not just about creating mega companies like his. Smaller companies, he counsels, can create jobs and value—and wealth for their employees. His advice for young entrepreneurs: "Go and do it."

Part Six, "Accelerating Innovation through Inventive Management Practices," examines how creative approaches to management can drive growth, inspire teams, motivated and get products to market faster, and help organizations move toward what Deloitte's John Hagel III calls "the edge"—where passionate, change-driven employees collaborate with others on the kinds of innovations that keep core business models fresh and constantly evolving. As Wharton management professor Adam Grant says, an innovation as simple as a five-minute interaction with employees can increase work productivity and create a happier team. The key is in ensuring that your team knows their work is meaningful and that what they do will have a positive impact on others.

Part Seven, "Driving Social Change through Creative Leadership," explores the social impact of global business—from the ripple effect of the economic crisis on the poor in Africa to innovative partnerships such as the Coca-Cola Company's work with the World Wildlife Fund to provide expertise to communities and governments in their attempts to tackle water scarcity and pollution problems in some of the world's most vulnerable regions. A number of articles follow the path of individual business leaders whose vision has helped to lift people out of poverty through such innovations as microcredit and access to renewable energy.

Part Eight, "Preparing for Succession and Executive Transition," focuses on the importance of succession planning, and the impact a change of command can have upon a company's identity and future success. The stronger the corporate culture, the less that the boat will rock—except in cases where the CEO's personality is closely tied to the brand, such as Apple's Steve Jobs. There is also danger in going outside the firm for the new CEO. Wharton management professor Katherine Klein points to the learning curve inherent in bringing in an outsider. "A CEO who comes in from the outside is very dependent on those left in the company for orientation, perspective, and information. That's potentially problematic."

Part Nine, "Key Lessons from the Multinational CEO," takes a close-up view of a dozen international top executives to illustrate the challenges and opportunities of leading on a global playing field. Hu Xiongqing, president of Akiyama International, talks about the complexities of a mergers and acquisitions growth strategy and the lessons Chinese companies have learned about mapping out global strategy, adjusting to an international legal environment, overcoming obstacles to reform, and bridging cultural differences. Roger Farah, president and chief operating officer of Polo Ralph Lauren, explains how his company emerged unscathed even as many of its competitors went belly up during tough economic times. He credits the company's success to a major push into the Asia-Pacific region and a combination of "left-brain" discipline and "right-brain" creativity. ■

—Jason Wingard

PART 1

Crisis Management as a Leadership Imperative

Under the Hood of Toyota's Recall:
"A Tremendous Expansion of Complexity"

In the wake of complaints about sudden acceleration problems that have led to the recall of millions of Toyotas over the past year, the automaker has faced criticism over everything from the design of its cars to the failure of company executives to acknowledge and address the issue head on. Perhaps most damaging is the hit to Toyota's overall reputation for quality. Wharton management professor John Paul MacDuffie recently sat down with Takahiro Fujimoto—an economics professor from the University of Tokyo and a leading authority on the Toyota production system and automotive product development—for his views on what caused the crisis, how Toyota has handled it, and how other car companies should react to Toyota's predicament.

An edited transcript of the conversation follows.

John Paul MacDuffie: I'm John Paul MacDuffie from Wharton's Management Department. We are here today with Professor Takahiro Fujimoto from the University of Tokyo, perhaps the world's leading authority on the Toyota production system and automotive product development. He's also a colleague of mine with the International Motor Vehicle Program, an international consortium of researchers who provide insightful research into the industry. Taka, welcome to Wharton.

Takahiro Fujimoto: Thank you very much.

MacDuffie: You have studied Toyota and its production system for a long time. Can you tell us what surprised you about the recall crisis, and if there was anything that didn't surprise you?

Fujimoto: I was surprised to see that Toyota was the first to be caught in this trap of what we may call complexity problems. Society and the market are making stricter and stricter demands on all the cars and vehicles in the world. So this could happen to anybody. But I was a bit surprised that this happened to Toyota first, because Toyota executives had [issued] a warning about [being] in a very difficult situation regarding complexity. So they knew that this could happen to anybody.

MacDuffie: Toyota had always been one of the best at managing complexity, right?

Fujimoto: Right. So they were probably a bit overconfident that they could handle these kinds of complexities better than other companies. Ironically, as a result they probably took in way too much complexity. It was [beyond] their capacity.

MacDuffie: I know that one of Toyota's primary explanations for these problems is how rapidly they have grown in the last decade. As you think about everything you have learned, does that seem to you like a good root cause of the problem? Or are there other factors as well?

Fujimoto: It's really true that Toyota was growing very rapidly. But other companies, like Hyundai, were growing even faster than Toyota. So the growth itself was not the only cause. Growth multiplied by other factors was probably the real cause of the problems—other factors like the number of production lines, production facilities, number of models sold in the global market, and the growing complexity of each individual vehicle due to social pressure and market demand. All these things multiplied together created explosive expansion of the workload for handling quality problems. Although Toyota usually had the capability to handle these kinds of things, even they couldn't really handle this tremendous expansion of complexity.

MacDuffie: I know there's a saying at Toyota that a problem is a treasure. You want to find problems because each problem provides an opportunity for improvement. Under that philosophy, hiding a problem would be the worst thing. When you look at how Toyota has handled this crisis, do you see them living up to that philosophy of revealing problems and focusing on them to resolve them?

Fujimoto: Yes, to my knowledge they are not trying to hide the problems. But when a very complex problem happened, they were not sure to what extent this was a responsibility for the company, and to what extent other parties were responsible. So their attitude was, "Wait a minute. This is complicated." They were sure that they were not the only party responsible for this problem.

But it is also obvious that Toyota was at least partly responsible for many problems that were popping up one after another. Probably what they should have done was to deal with it as quickly as possible—[such as send] a senior person to America as quickly as possible and then have [the company] apologize for whatever [it felt was their] responsibility. So a partial but thorough apology, and definitely a quick apology, was what they had to do. But they probably hesitated to come to the U.S. because they were not sure to what extent they were responsible for those problems. Then people saw that as, "Gee, Toyota is escaping from responsibility for this problem." This is not what Toyota meant— but the way they handled the initial problem was very bad, I think.

MacDuffie: Yes, for a problem that appears in the factory, even if it's complicated, you have more control [over it] and more access to full information. But when a customer says something to a dealer, it is more ambiguous. It seems that Toyota had trouble taking that kind of information and recognizing a problem that definitely needed its focus and attention.

Fujimoto: Right. I think this can happen to any company which is confident of its quality. This has happened to other companies in the past, too. When you're very confident of your quality, this is a source of arrogance.

Back in the 1990s, I saw some of my friends complaining about how Toyota treated people when there was a problem. You know, they go to the dealers and then the dealer reports to Toyota about these problems. But [the customers] tended to get a reaction from the company that said, "The product must be good. We are confident of the quality of the products. So logically it must be your driving problems." That made many people very angry. I noticed these kinds of things were happening at first sporadically, but then more frequently. I was always warning that arrogance is the number one enemy of the Toyota philosophy. But they didn't take this seriously until big problems happened. And it was really sad to see that.

MacDuffie: Clearly what's happened has damaged the Toyota brand and reputation. Do you have some advice or recommendations for Toyota president Akio Toyoda on what would be the best way to help restore that reputation?

Fujimoto: Ironically this is really a long-term race, like an obstacle race, of handling growing complexities that we cannot avoid. Toyota was one of the frontrunners in making very complex products, like hybrids or luxury cars, at very high volume and then growing the volume. They were taking on all kinds of complexities, and they were the frontrunners in handling that complexity. Then they took on too much complexity and they stumbled. But this is a race that you are not allowed to retire from because there are customers waiting for you. So Toyota will have to stand up and go again. There is no excuse for them, and there is no room for them to retire.

They will have to just keep on building capabilities. That is the only solution in the long run. In the short run, they have to persuade people that, even though they made a big mistake this time, they will go back to find the root cause and do the Toyota Way of finding and solving problems. Later, they need to come back to make sure that everybody is convinced that this will not happen again.

MacDuffie: Sounds like "back to basics."

Fujimoto: Back to the basics.

MacDuffie: So not a change away from the Toyota Way or the Toyota Production System?

Fujimoto: Right.

MacDuffie: But "back to basics" to build capabilities to handle the new demands.

Fujimoto: Right. I think the Toyota Production System or the Toyota Way as a philosophy is still a good way to handle customers' needs quickly and accurately. But the headquarters in particular made a deviation from the Toyota Way. I'm not talking about production people, because I'm constantly visiting the production sites, almost every week. There are no signs of decreasing capabilities on their side. We have to understand that, so far, all of the problems picked up in the Toyota recalls are design quality problems rather than manufacturing quality problems.

MacDuffie: Yes, I think that's an important distinction.

Fujimoto: Of course it's true that production sites have problems. I go there and I see many, many problems there. But those production problems...and quality problems that we see now in the news are not directly connected. In this kind of situation, people tend to pick up all kinds of bad news about Toyota, and of course this is a big company, so you can easily find 10, 20 items of bad news.

The danger is that people tend to connect the two problems. "This happened and that happened, so there must be causal relations between the two." But this is not the case. There appears to be no connections between the design problems and the Toyota production system or Toyota Way.

I would probably say middle managers, particularly at headquarters, started to deviate from the Toyota Way by being arrogant, being overconfident, and also they started not to listen to the problems that customers raised. Toyota is a problem-finding, problem-solving company. This culture is still there in the factories and in product development centers. But in some parts of the headquarters, someone started to say, "Hey, this is our problem. I am responsible for finding my problems and solving my problems. It's not [for] you [outside Toyota] to find our problems."

Sometimes I'm critical of Toyota. But they get angry. They always say, "We want to find problems. So please, give us any clues on the problems you see." But if I actually say, "This is a problem for you," they say, "This is none of your business. We have to find the problem. Not you." This attitude was growing for some time, I think, in some parts of headquarters. That was very dangerous. It is a good time to correct this kind of attitude and go back to the basics of the Toyota system.

MacDuffie: You mentioned complexity earlier and you talked about the demands of society and also the demands of the market. I know we have talked before about how a car is an expensive, heavy and fast-moving object in the public space, and that is why all these demands face an automaker. Could you say more about that, elaborating on the complexity issue?

Fujimoto: Right. I don't say that a car is a special thing. A car is very different from a PC, for example, or an Internet product and other digital products in a sense that it's heavy and it's dangerous; it's fast moving as you said. This is why society is very strict in dealing with these products, because these products were born with original sin....Because of cars, people are killed and then air pollution happens and it's noisy and oil is consumed heavily. So there are many bad things about the car. But there are many good things about the car. That's why we see 700 million cars on earth. So we have to solve all kinds of problems. And [the auto companies] can't stop innovating. They don't have the luxury of stopping innovations. Because of social pressure and constraints—such as regulations and customer requirements getting higher and higher—the complexity is getting higher and higher. What was okay 10 years ago is not okay now. For example, some of the things that are part of the Toyota problem now were not a big problem 20 years ago. So customers and society are fussier and fussier about what they expect from cars.

MacDuffie: And that creates tremendous demands on the designers, right?

Fujimoto: Right, it's a nightmare for the designers. You have to take on all these constraints. It's like solving gigantic simultaneous equations involving structures and functions. For example, with the Prius recall, the problem resulted because Toyota tried to improve fuel efficiency and safety and quietness at the same time through a nice combination of very powerful regenerating brakes, plus the latest antilock brake system, plus the hydraulic braking system.

But the relationship between the three kinds of brakes changed with the new design, and then drivers could have an uneasy experience when there was switching between the different brakes a little bit....Toyota failed to see this problem in the right way, at least in the beginning.

MacDuffie: If all these things are happening to Toyota, would you say we can expect other auto companies to have problems with these issues as well? These challenges must face all auto makers.

Fujimoto: There are some specific Toyota things like arrogance....But this complexity issue—nobody can escape from that. Everybody is in the same race. Toyota was ironically one of the frontrunners when they stumbled. A big failure happened there. But we are all in the same race. So smart companies, rather than laughing at Toyota, say, "Oh, this could be our problem, too." Some CEOs started to say, "Check all kinds of potential quality problems because this could happen to our company." And that's a very healthy reaction.

MacDuffie: I guess that if Toyota is very good at recovering from this—that would be the optimistic view—then perhaps they gain some advantage in dealing with these issues ahead of other companies, if the other companies don't proceed.

Fujimoto: Right.

MacDuffie: Could you say which of Toyota's competitors you think might benefit from this recall situation?

Fujimoto: The companies which are truly quality driven. In this kind of situation, a frontrunner stumbles so people tend to say, "Hey, this is a great chance to gain market share in an easy way." That's very dangerous, I think. That company may become the next victim. So rather than this, they have to say, "Hey, this is the time when quality is very important, and in particular, safety is number one. And complexity is going up. So we have to be very careful not to dissatisfy customers." If they focus on their quality and safety, and make customers happy, then the company will grow and gain market share. The companies sticking to this kind of philosophy will, I think, be winners.

MacDuffie: I know it would be a sweeping assessment at this point, but do you see the U.S. automakers being in a position to do that well? This is a kind of opportunity for them.

Fujimoto: Right. If they see this as just a short-term marketing opportunity, that's very dangerous. But if they see this as a great opportunity to look at their own quality—improve the design quality and manufacturing quality at the same time—and make more customers happy, there is a great chance for them. ∎

Published: March 31, 2010 in Knowledge@Wharton

Managing Talent During a Period of Crisis

Given the uncertainty surrounding the current economic crisis and their own deteriorating balance sheets, many companies have not hesitated to make cuts in their workforce without realizing that in most cases, such measures will not solve fundamental problems and will more likely worsen the labor climate and worker motivation. To help companies avoid this kind of mistake, Simon L. Dolan, professor of human resource management at ESADE, and Ramón Valle Cabrera of the Pablo de Olavide University have written *Managing Human Resources: How to Attract, Retain and Develop Successfully Human Capital During a Time of Transformation* (Madrid, McGraw-Hill, 2007). The authors recently spoke with Universia Knowledge@Wharton.

Universia-Knowledge@Wharton: In terms of managing human resources, how do companies usually react during times of crisis? What are the principal mistakes they often make?

Ramón Valle Cabrera: The most normal reaction is to look for ways to cut costs, almost always in the area of labor. In some cases, companies also cut their productive capacity in reaction to contracting demand. The main mistake that many companies make is to decide about adjustments without first analyzing where these adjustments can and must be made. They look for the greatest quantitative adjustment rather than identify those areas where they can intervene and make improvements. Crisis requires global analysis.

UK@W: What are the key challenges that senior human resource managers have to deal with in times of transformation?

R.V: Without doubt, the first one is to design flexible systems. Flexibility is a necessary condition for adapting oneself to change, and organizational flexibility implies flexibility in people—in every one of them. Second, it means encouraging and stimulating entrepreneurial activities within the organization. Third, it means learning a great deal about your organization's skills, about the distinctive elements of your company.

UK@W: Are human resource departments prepared for the kind of situation we are dealing with today? How could they prepare themselves?

R.V: You can't generalize, but our experience in Spain tells us that [human resource managers] have a ways to go. The short term and the immediate future are what dominate the behavior of people who manage human resources. They must play a much more strategic role, and they must integrate themselves more into the decision-making bodies. The strategic orientation of human resource policies determines the success of the organization. These policies must incorporate a vision of the organization as a whole, and [managers] must interact with their colleagues. They must realize that the old methods and principles of managing personnel don't help us solve new problems.

UK@W: What are the short-, medium- and long-term consequences of dismissing workers based on corporate performance?

R.V: Clearly, [such cuts] provide temporary help when it comes to operational costs. But over the medium term, those things that are going badly will return. Those employees who stay are affected by the [personnel] decisions that are made. The working climate deteriorates and motivation drops off. If you don't make a thorough analysis of the situation—including your marketplace, the competitiveness of your product and your skill at making innovations—these kinds of measures cannot solve the problem all by themselves. Many studies have shown that those companies that take into account the long term when they make these decisions get better results. These companies look for creative solutions, and they get results. For example, in the insurance sector there are companies that have not fired anyone, and have increased the value of their shares three times more than if they had chosen to let go of workers as a strategy for reducing costs. The explanation: When you decide not to lay-off or fire anyone, you have to look for more innovative solutions, and when you're successful doing that, that leads to an improvement in the economic performance of your company.

UK@W: What recommendations does your book make regarding attracting and retaining talent?

Simon L. Dolan: The first thing is to realize that they are the employees who will play a strategic role because they are the ones you will strive to retain. Attracting and retaining those people can be achieved by offering them competitive working conditions when it comes to personal development and salaries. In Spain, we're getting close to having a scarcity of talent, according to the Professional Perspectives Index 2007 of the Institute of Labor Studies (IEL) at ESADE (the business school). Companies will have to take steps to deal with this scarcity. To take advantage of all of the sources of highly qualified professionals, human resource departments will have to get used to looking for new talent anywhere in the world.

That means they need to be sure that the jobs they offer meet the needs and aspirations of different ethnic groups and nationalities, of women and of older workers. In addition, they have to develop a distinctive culture. The task of each manager is to guarantee that the people who are on his or her team are motivated and encouraged.

In addition to best practices in human resources, you have to guarantee that intangibles (for example, the values that people have) are well aligned with the mission and the vision of the company.

UK@W: You talk about attracting and retaining talent, but how can a company create talent within its workforce?

S.D: You create talent in the company by expanding learning—promoting interactivity among your employees so that they share knowledge. You create incentives for entrepreneurial activities, by generating commitment to the organization, and through a good training plan. In addition, you create a culture of competitiveness and innovation so that this talent stays alive and active.

You have to get people in the company to believe that things can always be better. According to a recent study by the Hay Group, the consulting company, the main reasons why talented people are attracted to Spanish companies are professional development (20%), leadership in the sector (14%) and innovation (13%). These factors outweigh other concepts that had traditionally been considered the determinants, such as [wages and other] compensation. In the study, only 7% [said that compensation was the most important factor].

UK@W: These days, what does the word "talent" mean within the company?

S.D: Inevitably, "talent" is connected with training, and it also means something beyond that. Talent is more than just technical knowledge. It is also about behavior, skill at adapting and leadership skills.

UK@W: In uncertain times such as these, do you believe that it is a good for people to change where they are working or is it better to "bear with" their uncomfortable situation and dissatisfaction until [economic] conditions normalize?

R.V: In uncertain times, when expectations about finding alternative jobs decline, the only people who tend to change jobs are those who have advanced qualifications and professional training. In any case, companies pay a high price for having dissatisfied workers, and they should be concerned with changing that situation.

UK@W: How would you characterize the sort of employees a company needs? Does having the right employees enable a company get through a crisis?

S.D: Human capital in a company must be measured by its capacity to add value, and by the degree to which it possesses the sort of knowledge that determines your competitiveness. When you have identified those sorts of employees and you manage them the right way, there is a greater likelihood that you will overcome the crisis than your competitors will.

When we manage talent correctly, we are in better shape to deal with a crisis. Talent has to do with a feeling of fluidity and when we put talent to work, there are five characteristics of that flow: challenge, goal, feedback, control and concentration. A company that develops confidence and generates these conditions motivates its talented personnel to produce more than it has ever produced.

UK@W: How would you describe the condition of talent in Spain? Is Spain behind other countries?

S.D: Spanish companies have made a major effort to incorporate human resources into their new initiatives but a great deal remains to be done. They started from behind when it came to understanding that having a talented workforce is a key to competitiveness, and that managing it means making changes in the way you manage.

From the viewpoint of general management, the data tell us that six out of every 10 senior managers believe that they must improve the recruitment, motivation and development of their employees, especially if we compare ourselves with North America and countries in Europe. Chief executives hope that their human resource departments can lead the way, but this is rarely the case because HR departments rarely enjoy the confidence of senior management.

Some areas where companies can change and become more agile, intelligent and responsive to changes in the market include teamwork, knowledge management, and improved synergies and interactivity between various departments [within the corporation]. The great engines of organizational change have been mergers and acquisitions, as well as new commercial strategies that originate in a need to adapt to a new focus of the marketplace. Eighty-seven percent of all senior managers in Spain agreed that the sound management of their human capital and talent is a strategic priority. ■

Published: October 15, 2008 in Universia Knowledge@Wharton

BP's Slippery Slope: The Dangerous Disconnect Between Rhetoric and Reality at a Time of Crisis

BP's flawed handling of the environmental crisis in the Gulf of Mexico is creating an identity crisis for the company. The gap between its stated commitment to environmental responsibility and its slow and stumbling reaction to the oil spill disaster exposes its top management as tone deaf and seemingly indifferent to the deep damage being done to the company's brand. Two management professors—Hamid Bouchikhi of the ESSEC Business School in France and John R. Kimberly of the Wharton School—wrote about BP's equally faulty treatment of the 2005 explosion at the Texas City, Texas refinery in their book, *The Soul of the Corporation: How to Manage the Identity of Your Company*. Now they offer six steps that BP should have taken this time around to mitigate the damage—and that other companies should consider when it's their turn to cope with crisis.

* * *

Its logo implies beauty, sunshine, a concern for "green" and a love of nature. However, the recent events off the coast of Louisiana raise major questions about BP's stewardship of the environment and its commitment to behaving in ways that are consistent with its emphasis on social and environmental responsibility. In 2007, we wrote about how BP's handling of the explosion at the Texas City, Texas refinery in 2005, in which 15 workers lost their lives, was at odds with the company's efforts to construct an image of a green and socially responsible corporation. Three years later, we find ourselves writing about BP again.

Here is how we see matters to date: BP's response to the disaster has made a bad situation worse. Not only has the company been unable to stop the flow of oil into the Gulf of Mexico and onto the shores of Louisiana and other states, it has consistently underestimated the scope of the problem. And in so doing it has outraged the American public.

The company's leadership has seemingly been oblivious to the fact that every company has an identity, a set of things that differentiate it more or less clearly and more or less consistently from its competitors. And they seem to be oblivious as well to the fact that when there is a substantial gap between rhetoric and reality, between the image an organization constructs of who it is and how it actually behaves, there can be a huge backlash.

When times are good, when profits are rolling in, an organization can construct an image for the outside world that may, in fact, be somewhat fanciful. It is when the going gets rough, in times of crisis like the one that BP is now facing, that we discover the organization's true identity—who it really is—through the way it behaves. To the extent that the constructed image aligns with the way it behaves, we can speak of authenticity. But when there is a gap between the two, however large, questions inevitably get raised, both for those inside the organization and those outside, about who the organization is, really. In this respect, BP is digging itself a huge hole.

The explosion that sank BP's Deepwater Horizon rig on April 20 took 11 lives and has released millions of gallons of oil into the Gulf, causing untold damage to marine life and many miles of shoreline. The company's response thus far leads us to ask a central question, "Who is BP, really?" Is it the responsible steward of the environment that the image the company has worked so hard to project would have us believe? The company's initial slow response to the crisis, its CEO's relative invisibility and its consistently serious underestimation of the magnitude of the spill have certainly raised large doubts in the minds of all concerned: employees of BP, environmentalists, the businesses along the coast that depend on the Gulf, coastal residents, and officials of the affected states and the federal government, to say nothing of the millions of customers who fill their gas tanks with BP products every day.

Playing Down the Damage

Where has the company's leadership been in this crisis? Tony Hayward, BP chairman and CEO, did not appear at the Senate Energy and Natural Resources Committee hearing held on May 11, sending his representative instead, Lamar McKay, president and chairman of BP America.

On May 19, Hayward attempted to play down the extent of damage to the environment in a statement on Sky News: "We will mount, as part of the aftermath, a very detailed environmental assessment but everything we can see at the moment suggests that the overall environmental impact will be very, very modest." Most recently, he has denied that there are any oil plumes, directly contradicting researchers from three universities who are working on the spill.

Furthermore, BP managers are suspected of repeatedly ignoring warnings about the risks of deep sea oil drilling and possibly, according to a government report, of using gifts and other ethically questionable tactics to neutralize drilling regulators. The picture is getting uglier by the day, and the company's behavior is only making things worse.

So what can we learn from this tragedy thus far? As of this writing, BP managers have certainly not displayed much in the way of empathy in elaborating on the circumstances of the blowout and the toll on human and marine life, or in acknowledging the actual and potential suffering of the communities affected by the spill. Circulating settlement agreements among coastal residents that reportedly offer $5,000 in exchange for not suing the company can hardly be seen as a gesture of empathy (the company has halted that process). Taking responsibility for the consequences in carefully crafted legal language—"where legitimate claims are made, we will be good for them"—will never be mistaken for empathy no matter how much BP is willing and able to pay.

In the heat of the moment, BP managers may have forgotten that the whole purpose of investing as liberally as they did in building a corporate identity is to establish emotional connections with stakeholders, internal and external, and shift the transactions with these stakeholders from a purely instrumental plane to an emotional one. When corporate branding efforts are aligned with how the corporation actually behaves, its claims about who it is are validated internally and externally, and can generate enough trust and goodwill to elicit from its stakeholders understanding, even forgiveness, in times of crisis.

Is BP eliciting this type of reaction? The evidence so far does not suggest a positive answer, thus putting years of branding efforts at risk. In the meantime, public anger is mounting steadily, as witnessed by former Labor Secretary Robert Reich's call for receivership for BP, putting the futures of both Tony Hayward and the company in doubt.

What Should Have Been Done

How could BP managers have handled the crisis in a way that is more consistent with the official emphasis on BP as a socially responsible and good environmental citizen and that might have avoided—or at least minimized—the public relations disaster the company now faces?

With the obvious benefit of hindsight, we would suggest the following lessons, not just for BP executives, but, more importantly, for leaders in other companies who might at some point face their own crises.

- First, BP executives should have been more alert to the significance of the company's identity in the minds of the public. Top managers should have been mindful of the fact that everything they say (and do not say) and do (and do not do) in this time of high public scrutiny sends messages about who BP is.
- Second, they should have reacted quickly. As Toyota recently learned the hard way, there is a need to be proactive immediately. Almost any delay sends an unfortunate message.
- Third, they should have appreciated the symbolic value of being physically present, on the ground, as close as possible to those affected by the spill as quickly as possible. The message of real concern this sends is unmistakable.
- Fourth, they should have tried to balance legal/economic language with emotional/empathic tones in their public statements.
- Fifth, they should have acknowledged the company's moral responsibility before dealing with legal liabilities.
- And finally, they should have had the courage to put the interests of the company's shareholders and managers after those of the environment and the communities affected by the spill.

The product recall by Perrier in 1990 immediately following the discovery of traces of benzene in some of its water bottles in the United States is a case in point. Although the Food and Drug Administration found no immediate risk to consumers, the company's managers decided on a worldwide recall, on the grounds that a premium brand such as Perrier could not afford to do otherwise. While the recall hurt the company's sales and market share badly, its broad and dramatic action showed that it cared more about its customers' health and its reputation with them than about immediate sales and profits.

When are BP managers going to show that they too care as much about the environment and the communities as they do about profitability? Only when they do will there be consistency between the image they project and who BP is, really, and only then will there be a long-term payoff from the company's substantial investment in image-making. ■

Published: June 9, 2010 in Knowledge@Wharton

DuPont CEO Ellen Kullman's Four Principles for Moving Ahead during Turbulent Times

The impact of the financial crisis began to hit DuPont about a month after the collapse of Lehman Brothers in September 2008. Sales volume slid, good customers cancelled orders and employees were gripped by fear and uncertainty.

As the environment worsened and sales fell by up to 50% in some units, DuPont CEO Ellen J. Kullman ordered two traumatic restructurings. Perhaps more importantly for DuPont's future, Kullman also concluded that the company faced a "new reality" requiring fundamental changes if it were to remain successful.

Her challenge was balancing the need for immediate action to maintain the company's financial stability during the crisis, while focusing on strategic objectives that would preserve the company's leading market position in the future. Among the highest hurdles: Motivating employees to work on the things they could control and avoid becoming paralyzed by the market's volatility.

Speaking at the recent 13th Annual Wharton Leadership Conference, co-sponsored by the Center for Human Resources and the Center for Leadership & Change Management, Kullman described how she changed the company's thinking about its business model, while reinforcing its 200-year-old culture of innovation. "The question is, given the megatrends in the world and given the new economy, what changes do we have to make to continue to be successful? There is no playbook for what we are experiencing today," said Kullman, 53, a 20-year DuPont executive who became CEO in January.

In April, DuPont announced first-quarter earnings of $0.54 per share, 59% lower than a year earlier, reflecting a severe decline in industrial demand due to the global recession. The company increased its 2009 fixed-cost reduction goal to $1 billion and reduced capital spending by $200 million in an effort to preserve cash and better position the company for economic recovery.

Kullman's first step was "understanding the dynamic relationship between what should not change...and what has to change—and having absolute clarity on that." Deciding what would not change was easy: the company's commitment to science and innovation as primary drivers of growth since its founding in 1802 as a maker of black powder. Deciding what to change was far more difficult.

Kullman identified three trends that would transcend the current crisis and provide a strategic framework for the company's annual $1.4 billion investment in research and development—increasing agricultural productivity, reducing dependence on fossil fuels and protecting lives.

Four Principles

But organizing the company to respond to these long-term trends during a period of extreme uncertainty required strong leadership and specific initiatives "to change the way we think," said Kullman, who joined DuPont in 1988 as a marketing manager for medical imaging, and was named executive vice president and a member of the office of chief executive in 2006, and president in October 2008. Prior to joining DuPont, Kullman, who has a B.S. in engineering from Tufts and a master's in management from Northwestern, worked at GE.

She shared four leadership principles that she has implemented to guide DuPont through the financial crisis since October 2008.

The first principle: Focus on what you can control. Kullman realized she needed to shift the company's attention from what was going wrong to the immediate action required to protect DuPont's financial position as revenues fell dramatically. "Last October, I saw a lot of people who looked scared and didn't know what to do," she said. So, she directed DuPont's management to "figure out those...things we can do something about, and get about doing them."

"We realized that what we had to protect...mostly was our financial stability and flexibility, so we had to focus on cash. We're a company that spent 207 years focused on earnings and the cash seemed to show up. All of a sudden, it's a new world and we had to adjust every single business person's mindset around the notion that earnings are nice, but cash is more important," Kullman said.

To preserve cash, she issued four financial directives: Maximize variable contribution dollars, drastically reduce spending, zero-base capital expenditures, and significantly reduce working capital. Maximizing variable contributions required "a tremendous amount of coaching" to teach the sales force how to think about pricing in a downturn and how to engage with customers who "didn't want to talk."

Promoting DuPont's innovations—901 new product launches last year and a record 500 in the first quarter of this year—proved an effective way to generate sales and increase variable contributions. "There's nothing like a new product, a new innovation that allows you to go out and talk to that customer," she said.

One approach involved finding new markets for existing products, such as selling an engineered polymer designed for India's railways to China. "We needed to get our people in India working with our people in China," Kullman said. The interaction resulted in an $18 million order. Another involved introducing improved versions of widely used products, such as Kevlar for bullet-resistant vests and Nomex for fire-resistant suits. DuPont is hoping that U.S. economic stimulus programs could create a market for upgrading the equipment of "fire-fighters...police, and even the military."

The second of her leadership principles for the crisis has been to "adopt a new trajectory by rethinking your business model." For DuPont, that meant "getting people to think differently" about a business model that had always measured success based on plant capacity and capital investment: "We invent, we build, we make, we sell," Kullman said. The change has involved developing service-based models providing new ways to engage with customers and monetize products. Although it is difficult to get people who are very successful to embrace change, she has found that they are willing to try new models when markets are in disarray and when there's uncertainty about what will work in the future.

Kullman led a new trajectory 11 years ago when "we decided to take our safety capability and see if we could create a business out of it." It wasn't easy. "We spent 200 years trying to figure out how to create a very safe environment for our people. We have lots of methodologies...but we didn't know how to sell it, how to create a contract around it. Believe me, the lawyers were really concerned about our liability."

The new venture started as a pilot with a small team that brainstormed with Wharton faculty and "made a lot of mistakes" in initial customer pitches over six months before "figuring out a value proposition that played." The service was a logical extension of DuPont's industrial businesses because "our sales force is calling on plants that have serious issues around safety [in which] we can help." Result: In addition to annual revenues in the hundreds of millions of dollars, DuPont's safety and protection business creates "relationships with customers around the world that we can leverage" across all of the company's business lines.

More recently, DuPont's applied biosciences unit developed a high-performance plastic polymer, grain Hytrel, made from renewable agricultural sources that addressed the auto parts industry's need for sustainable products. As a newcomer, DuPont was able to win business from a demanding global parts maker, Denso Corp., by providing "real innovation" in sustainability that "they think is important to their future."

The ability to address broader customer needs through high-value services—going beyond the traditional "make-sell" business model—is critical in deciding which new technologies will receive funding, Kullman said. But how do you incite the change required for new trajectories in a global organization with 60,000 employees in more than 70 countries? Kullman recommends a viral approach, starting with a small pilot program in one area, generating interest, and communicating its success to other parts of the business. "If you try to change everybody at once, you're changing nobody, so you really have to start in one area, or a couple of areas, and show success."

Getting Employees' Attention

Kullman's third crisis leadership principle: Communication is key. "I'm a firm believer that there is a direct correlation between growth and the success of our communication. When we have an aligned team that understands" very clearly what the goals and the tradeoffs are, "that's when things can absolutely happen," Kullman said.

"The first step is really getting their attention, and that's a very hard thing to do with all the noise" in the world today, she said. But getting through to employees is vital because their natural tendency is to "hunker down," hoping the crisis will pass and "everything will go back to normal."

In announcing two restructurings within five months since December 2008—unprecedented at DuPont—Kullman insisted that her leadership team "get out in front of the troops" with a consistent message. "It's not something they can delegate." She personally went to plants in Germany and Ohio where there were layoffs and "answered very tough questions about the deal [employees] thought they had with DuPont."

If company leaders aren't willing to "get out and communicate on the really tough issues, then the credibility our organization has in the decisions we are making is always going to be called into question," Kullman said.

There is a risk that business leaders will grow tired and stop communicating after delivering the message five or six times. "We think they've heard it and move on to another message, [but] all we've done is confuse them. It takes 15 or 16 engagements [for employees to understand] that this is what we need to do and this is where we need to go." Economic uncertainty has made the task more difficult, "but I think maintaining that communication—the strength and alignment around it—is more critical in today's environment."

The last of her four crisis leadership principles is to maintain pride around the company's mission. "There's nothing like a bad economy to get people confused about what their mission is. They start thinking their mission is to reduce cost. That's a tactic, that's not our mission," Kullman said.

During informal weekly meetings with employees, Kullman said she was amazed that the "number one question was about whether we are going to stick with our mission." She quickly realized that "people are scared [and] people want direction." Making sure that people understand the mission—and linking their daily activities to the company's broader purpose—is essential to reducing fear, maintaining morale and keeping employees motivated, Kullman said.

DuPont's mission is "sustainable growth," defined as increasing shareholder value by reducing the company's environmental footprint—and that of its customers, Kullman said. The mission includes "denominator strategies," such as reducing waste and fossil fuel usage at its chemical plants. It also involves "numerator strategies," such as inventions supporting biofuels, photovoltaics and other forms of renewable energy, or hurricane-resistant building materials that help save lives.

"It's really critical that we maintain the focus on the mission and keep reminding people of it. People have a lot of pride in the mission and they want to understand that the mission is not going to change, even though the world around it has changed tremendously. You've got to capture that heart and soul," Kullman said. "That's how we're going to be successful." ∎

Published: June 24, 2009 in Knowledge@Wharton

Leadership Strategies for Dealing with the Crisis

Against the backdrop of the worldwide financial crisis, Madrid Expo Management, the largest conference for European managers, took place at the end of May. Organized by management training firm HSM, the event offered business leaders and experts in human resources, marketing, finance, psychology and politics the opportunity to discuss strategies for managing companies and personnel during the ongoing global recession. High on the list of priorities, they said, is developing executives who are flexible and able to bring people together around a common goal.

Anders Knutsen, former chief executive of Bang & Olufsen, who is considered one of the top twenty business leaders of the twentieth century, assumed his role at the company during a time when the electronics firm was undergoing a serious crisis that had brought it to the brink of bankruptcy. "It is consumers who define the market," Knutsen told the forum audience. "They constantly choose between low prices and high quality, depending on the importance they give to the particular service. Companies have to choose: Either compete for the lowest price, or look for solid value, good design and markets where people can make an effort." When it is time to think up a new campaign, Knutsen offers the following advice: "Be brave! If you have nothing important to say, that's unfortunate. But if you have something [to say], say it. Be distinctive. Let yourself look and be accessible; maintain contact with your customers to establish solid relationships and alliances."

According to Knutsen, "Customers show themselves to be more open during periods of crisis. They look for alternatives to previous styles of consumption. This brings a significant opportunity for those companies that can offer something unique, and which support the worldwide interest in protecting the environment in the future. Although I would like to think that [such] values are universal, there are many different ways to capture the attention of customers. I don't believe that the geographical component is as important as the common values shared by cultures." He added: "Marketing is based on the presentation of values, and the stimulation of [other people]. The more enthusiastic your messages are, the more you will impress people. Everything involves innovating and deciding how to proceed and how to guarantee that everyone moves in the same direction. The more, the better!"

Leadership Challenges
According to Paul Schoemaker, a strategy specialist and research director of Wharton's Mack Center for Technological Innovation, "Managers must develop a capacity to move toward those changes that will occur in the future, and introduce an element of flexibility in their strategies. This is the only way to move forward in times of uncertainty. It is also necessary to have organizational

skill and to control external changes in real time." In his view, "uncertainty is an opportunity for those who are prepared. Managers tend to be protective about what they have, and they hope that over time, uncertainty will end and things will work out. A better strategy is to take advantage of uncertainty. The best opportunities arrive in times of crisis, not in times of stability." What is the key to making the most of those opportunities? "Except in the case of historic fluctuations, managers must resort to their imaginations, paying attention to indicators of weakness, and making comparisons with other sectors, while listening to outside experts and those within their own company."

Schoemaker noted that if companies re-think their strategies, they can also avoid suffering the avalanche of layoffs that is occurring everywhere. "A better strategy would be to promote growth and, as a result, new business. However, too frequently, managers focus on what worked in the past, and they don't succeed in adapting their strategy to the new reality. Companies are dynamic by nature. Nowadays, for example, we are witnessing a process of creative destruction while in other times, we've seen the ability of big and small companies to reinvent themselves." In addition, he said, "leaders can learn from their mistakes in this crisis. Some are excessively confident. Others ignore relevant facts, and some feel insecure and uncomfortable in a situation rife with confusion. The role of the leader becomes more relevant in times of crisis. A leader must be capable of tolerating mistakes, both his own and those made by others. He must learn from them and overcome them. When all is said and done, what doesn't kill you makes you stronger." According to Schoemaker, the qualities that make a true leader include "having curiosity; skill at anticipating events and changes; the ability to face the unknown; and personal charisma when managing other people and gaining their trust."

Bill George, former chief executive of Medtronic and a professor of management practice at Harvard Business School, offered similar views. "The crisis puts true leaders to the test. This is when you know where they are and who are the good ones, and when they demonstrate their bravery, intelligence and capacity to bring together on a single team those people who are going to support their leadership. I believe that the keys to being a real leader in times of uncertainty are to be genuine, authentic and capable of confronting real situations and adapting to them. [Leaders] should face problems and recognize that they are in a crisis and change direction in order to adapt to conditions. If they don't act that way, they will certainly fail."

How can a manager take advantage of the opportunities that the current global crisis presents? According to George, "First, we need to know what caused the current global crisis. I believe that it was the focus on short-term results rather than on the long term. We took on too much debt, both consumers and institutions. And we were not conservative in our financial behavior, to the point that we lost sight of what was important for companies: creating lasting value for our customers, employees and shareholders. I believe that we now recognize that [focusing on] the short term is a mistake, and that these are the times to choose intelligent leaders who can guide us when conditions are difficult. I believe that companies with this class of manager will have the opportunity to overcome the crisis, and will wind up being the winners. Many people believe that markets will return to what they were once the recession ends. Nevertheless, [I believe] that's not going to happen; the companies that succeed will be those companies that know have to deal with the needs of their customers and consumers."

Jeffrey Immelt of General Electric and Indra Nooyiof PepsiCo are two examples of chief executives who have done an extraordinary job in recent years, he noted. "The chief executives who are acting with the same mindset as in the twentieth century—by exercising absolute control without being transparent— probably should be replaced," George said. "We have seen big changes after the baby boomer generation: Now, there is a new generation of leaders who are less than 45 years old. These new leaders are more aware of the needs of people, and they have figured out how to cast aside the old hierarchies. I am optimistic. I believe that this new group will do an excellent job if it focuses on creating value over the long term for shareholders, employees and customers." But is it easy to pursue that path? "Many leaders wind up losing the basics of their beliefs; their values and their principals. I believe that when they stop being motivated, it is because they feel pressured. They cast aside their beliefs and they are seduced by money and recognition. If you manage to become aware of this, and admit your mistakes, and face reality, and recognize that these habits have led to an awful lot of problems, then you will be able to re-take the right road and recover your motivation. If you don't do that, the best thing that can happen is that you resign your position."

George has been considered one of the 25 most influential business leaders because of the way he managed the medical technology firm Medtronic for the past two decades. According to George, "We must have leaders who know who they are, who have a high level of knowledge of themselves, and are faithful to their beliefs. This means an authentic person who knows how to delegate to others so that they, too, can evolve and wind up being leaders. These are the qualities that I believe we need in the leaders of the twenty-first century. They must know how to work with their partners toward a common mission, and must establish [corporate] values. They should also recognize that their task consists in serving their customers and employees to create a spirit of collaboration within their organizations. I believe that if leaders are autocratic and dictatorial or if they show themselves to be too worried about their own status, then they cannot do a good job of leading."

According to George Kohlrieser, a professor at the IMD business school in Switzerland and an expert in leadership, "We are living in a propitious time for change. We have to understand that nowadays many people are thinking only about their survival, which limits their creativity and their search for opportunities. Survival is always the most important goal for the brain, so the leader and employees look for a way to defend themselves and do not look at external opportunities. Few conditions are more destructive than this sort of mental and emotional impotence. Leaders have to be resistant and positive, and they must focus on opportunities. They should put a limit to complaining, since that only leads to despondency. This is the time to learn, to develop one's talent for finding innovative and creative ways to do things. Leaders should focus on positive factors and on opportunities that exist in any time of crisis, because this is when employees can become more resistant and more determined to find ways to make progress."

Kohlrieser adds, "Those leaders who let themselves be overcome by panic, who have closed minds, little resistance and poor communications skills; those who are distant and not inspiring—those leaders don't work out. The world will never go back to being the same, so we need chief executives who understand how to benefit from globalization, and how to tackle the crisis of capitalism [as well as how to tackle] sustainability, climate change, [the emergence of] a different type of capitalism [and] the battle for talent; how to manage financial value; and how to guide people toward common goals. The leadership skills of the future will require the greatest possible degree of collaboration for effectively overcoming limitations. This change in leadership skills will help employees adopt a more activist attitude about risk-taking and tackling change. Other challenges include creating efficient teams in different countries, who have access to virtual communication; using influence without resorting to authority; searching for innovation; coaching; developing skills at adaptation; appreciating complexity from various points of view; rapidly learning through dialogue; and gaining the confidence to take action even in cases of ambiguity. This is where two true opposites exist, such as the search for growth and the quest for cost reduction. Communications skills are more important than ever, especially in the case of virtual leadership. Leaders need to be more and more effective when it comes to making themselves understood."

Psychological Efforts

Amidst so much uncertainty, ExpoManagement also looked at how to manage the crisis not only from the corporate point of view, but from the personal perspective. According to Mario Alonso Puig, professor of surgery at Harvard University and a member of the New York Academy of Sciences, people need exercises for controlling their anxiety so they can relax during the recession. In his view, "Any decision we make is closely related to the way we perceive things. So it is critical to focus our minds on what we want and what we have. It does not make any sense to wear ourselves out by dealing with things that we cannot change. You have to move from 'that's the way it is' to 'it must be' that way, because that means moving from being a victim to becoming the main figure."

According to Alonso Puig, "In a crisis, you can distinguish with special clarity those leaders who believe in people and call for commitment, from those leaders who are not able to create that feeling of belonging and confidence in the possibility of emerging stronger from the crisis." He adds, "The great ideas emerge from passion or from necessity. In a crisis, people urgently need to find a way out. However, many people give up when they face adversity. Especially when times are hard, a leader feels a profound loneliness so it is essential for him to depend on people who have his total confidence; who permit him to express his emotions; and who enable him to feel as if people are listening to him. When a person shares his feelings with others, he has a clear perspective when it is time for him to make decisions." ∎

Published: June 3, 2009 in Universia Knowledge@Wharton

Crisis in Haiti: Where Do We Go from Here?

The earthquake that rocked Haiti on January 12, 2010, caused unimaginable death and destruction, a reminder to everyone that catastrophes are usually unforeseeable and therefore almost impossible to prepare for. Yet ironically, scientists almost two years ago warned Haiti about an impending major earthquake. The Haitian government lacked the resources to follow up on the report, which raises the question of whether any country or region of the world, rich or poor, can take meaningful steps to avoid the destruction caused by catastrophes of any kind, from earthquakes and hurricanes to terrorist attacks and pandemics. Knowledge@Wharton asked professors Howard Kunreuther and Michael Useem, authors of a new book titled, *Learning from Catastrophes: Strategies for Reaction and Response*, and professor Morris A. Cohen, to talk about the challenges of dealing with such crises.

An edited transcript of the conversation follows:

Knowledge@Wharton: Thank you all for joining us.

Howard, let's start with you. As I noted, although scientists predicted an earthquake in this area almost two years ago, the Haitian government was unable to act on the warning. If they had been able to respond, what could they have done?

Howard Kunreuther: That is an excellent question. I think that we are dealing with a situation in Haiti where, as you indicated, poverty has really dominated the scene. So one of the key questions that comes up with this Haitian earthquake is: What could have been done in the way of preparation? You had houses that were really poorly designed. To design better houses requires a great deal of money and resources. It would have been extraordinarily hard for Haiti to have prepared for this without a great deal of assistance from the rest of the world.

Knowledge@Wharton: Mike?

Mike Useem: I would just add the idea that big problematic developments—disasters of one kind or another; hurricanes, earthquakes, tsunamis, rare events that are sometimes referred to as "once in a century"—don't sit at the front of people's consciousness. They are not in front of a legislative body thinking about the budget for this year. We know that these events are out there, the forecasts are there, but one of the great challenges is becoming better at being able to translate an assessment of high-consequence but low-likelihood events into what we do now. [In the case of] Haiti, which is very short on resources, even had they been more aware of [the earthquake warning], and even if they

30

had additional resources, points of intervention weren't feasible. But prior to even thinking about allocating resources to improve housing stock, to bolster construction of schools and the like, it is critical that we find devices to help people in legislatures and executive offices better prepare and plan so that they know how to think about these low-likelihood but hugely-consequential events.

Knowledge@Wharton: Morris, what are the supply chain challenges that relief efforts face in such situations? And are there any lessons that we learned from the tsunami that would have been helpful in Haiti?

Morris Cohen: We are seeing, unfortunately, as this tragedy unfolds that the big bottleneck is essentially a logistics problem, that it is not even a question of shortages of resources. There is lots of drinking water. There is lots of food. But it's impossible to get it to where it is needed. This is an incredibly complicated supply chain problem and we saw the same thing with the tsunami. We've seen it in other natural disasters. The world has recognized this and there have been attempts to develop better response techniques, better deployment—prior deployment—of resources. It is ironic. These events are once in a century, once in two centuries, so we can't predict them. But with certainty they will occur. We have to be prepared.

We don't know where or when they will occur, but we have to deploy resources in advance of them. I think that's a very important issue. Having the right resources, having the right processes in place—even in a more advanced or developed environment—would have been an enormous challenge. In Haiti, it is compounded by the fact that it was already an environment that was hurting in this regard. So the challenges of getting the resources to where they are needed—on time and with the clock ticking—may, unfortunately, become even more difficult before they get easier.

Knowledge@Wharton: What has been the role of the media in showing the extent of this tragedy and also encouraging people to use Twitter and other social media to donate money to the relief effort?

Kunreuther: I think the media always plays a critical role here. In the case of Haiti, what has happened—certainly in the United States; I can't speak about other countries—is that people have been extraordinarily sympathetic. The Obama administration has played a very, very creative and very important leadership role here in getting people to think about things. In the spirit of the comments that Mike and Morris have made, there is this myopia here that we have to at least reflect on. People are willing to give money now. There is an opportunity for large contributions to come from the private sector and hopefully from the government. We are seeing some of that now.

But if it doesn't happen [to a greater extent] in the next few weeks, there will be another crisis that will then dominate the scene, and we are going to be forgetting Haiti in the way that we have forgotten the tsunami and other problems. The problem is in terms of how you are going to deal with the short run, but at the same time try to get large contributions for long-range planning so that Haiti can be in a position where it can really change. I think there is a challenge here, but there is also a tremendous opportunity.

There was a very, very interesting column that David Brooks wrote in terms of poverty and how to deal with it. We need to do things that can really reflect the long run. The media can play an important role here. But keeping it on the media's agenda is going to be extremely difficult after a period of three or four weeks—at least from past experience.

Knowledge@Wharton: That was my next question. I wonder what Morris and Mike think about the idea that the public has a very short attention span. It is clear what is needed in a country like Haiti is long-range thinking. Is there a chance that life could actually get better in this country now that global attention is focused on the challenges? Or is that just wishful thinking?

Cohen: There was an interesting article in *The Wall Street Journal* over the weekend that talked about major disasters that have occurred in cities in the last 300 years—Lisbon, San Francisco and other places—which have led to the rebirth of these cities and [the influx] of major investment. But the betting seems to be that this is not going to happen in Haiti. Haiti has been a problem case for the world for a long time. Will attitudes change sufficiently because of this disaster? Even with Twitter, not that much money has been donated compared to other disasters. We are talking about peanuts, compared to what is needed. The media is bringing it to our attention, but the response that is needed is much, much greater than what has happened. There is an enormous gap still there.

Useem: This disaster is one of enormous scale. We have to remind ourselves that several million people are directly affected. Death tolls could rise to over 100,000 at least. But having said that, in our recent past we have been through some events of comparable magnitude. The earthquake in China, for example, back in 2008 is estimated to have killed about 70,000 people. With the tsunami back in December 2004, the estimate of loss of life there was somewhere around 280,000 or more. Katrina itself killed 1,300, but well over 1.5 million people were evacuated, and we know the enormous consequences that persist to this day of that disaster and its scale. I think we all appreciate that the media right now has taken extraordinary risks—personal risks—on the part of reporters and crews that have gone with them to report to us as graphically as they can what it means to be in Port-au-Prince now, under a pile of rubble, still with some life left in you. The flow of cash, the extraordinary outpouring of support generated by the media, has been notable.

But as my two colleagues have implied, we often soon forget. It is not a media problem. It is a more general problem for leaders of organizations—those in elected office, those responsible at the U.S. Agency for International Development, the World Bank, the U.N. agencies, etc. It would be helpful—after this immediate crisis has ended, at least in terms of emergency services—to take a step back and ask what we can do as reporters, as teachers, as organizational leaders to better prepare internationally for the kind of disasters that are out there. Morris said it well just a few minutes ago: An earthquake like this, we don't know when it's coming, but we know it will come sooner or later. There is a long list of such low-probability, but high-consequence events that I think we all need to become better at thinking about and being prepared for.

Knowledge@Wharton: If we could probe a little bit deeper into the media, including social media like Twitter and Facebook, for example. One thing that is very striking this time is that in previous catastrophes, the highest amount of money the Red Cross raised through social media was about $3 million. This time, within days of the earthquake, I think it raised $20 million—much of it through text messages. Now we have all heard about the "wisdom of crowds" concept. There is something to be said about the "altruism of crowds," and what that shows about the way the media is changing.

Kunreuther: Let me raise the issue that Morris partly brought up when he indicated that [the donations] make up a larger amount of money certainly than we have had in the past, but they aren't the kind of money that is really needed. And so maybe you can use Twitter and Facebook as a signal of the [desire] people have to really use these [methods] to generate much larger funding. One current example of this is that the World Economic Forum is going to use Haiti as a key issue in the conference next week at Davos. The fact that they want to use that as an issue for people to think about is an opportunity to really raise not just millions, but billions, of dollars from the private sector and from groups that could afford this [level of giving]. There is an opportunity here for altruism at a broader level. So I think if we can use Twitter and Facebook as a way of saying, 'Look, there are things that are needed at a bigger level in order to do the kinds of reconstruction that are necessary,' then I think you have a chance. It's an uphill battle given everything we all know about Haiti to do the kinds of things that are necessary.

Let me use one example that I think is an instructive one from the 1923 earthquake in Tokyo that destroyed the entire city. Frank Lloyd Wright's Imperial Hotel was the one building that managed to at least stand, and it didn't even stand completely. The government was really very concerned. They had tried to develop a plan but never really implemented it. But there is one thing that they did do, and we know about Japan today versus where it was in the 1920s. They developed reconstruction standards and they made sure that buildings that were designed, that were rebuilt, met those standards.

The challenge is going to be whether, in a country with abject poverty, one can have enough money so that international organizations will be able to [take the steps] that Japan did. Japan was a richer country and was able to do things in a variety of ways that [may not be possible in] Haiti [in terms of redesigning] the city. But that's what people are looking for. That's the short-term challenge, as we have all said. Can you have a strategy and plan that can be implemented [if you] have enough money to do it? Twitter and Facebook are not going to be the [sources] for that kind of money.

Cohen: One thing the media has done more and more—and this disaster illustrates it—is [show that a catastrophe] is no longer something that occurs in a distant place that we can't imagine. We see it in real time. We can experience it. And so the altruistic response is there. But I absolutely agree with Howard that the long-term solution is not tens of millions. It is tens of billions. And where is that going to come from to invest in Haiti?

My bigger concerns right now are long-term issues. We can redesign the building codes. We can invest in infrastructure. But I think we are facing a crisis between now and, let's say, the next two weeks, where you could have riots in the streets. You could have widespread disease. You could have all kinds of issues occurring. And it's not clear to me how that is going to be alleviated. The U.S. Army is on the scene, but in order for them and everyone else—the U.N.—to address this problem is on an order of magnitude like the invasion of Normandy. You are going to need an army to invade the country and occupy it in order to solve this problem. If not, then people are going to start dying in greater numbers through disease and starvation. I don't see the answer to that immediate problem at this point.

Knowledge@Wharton: How developed is the insurance market in Haiti? How much do you think insurers might be liable for, or is there no insurance market there?

Kunreuther: We have not heard very much, and we study insurance. I've heard very, very little about any insurance in Haiti. My guess is—although we can check that out and others who are hearing this Podcast can comment on this—is that there is very, very little. This is one of the challenges in the emerging economies. You don't have the institutions that really exist as we do in the developed world for dealing with insurance. And so my guess is that there would be very little insurance. Most of these homes were very, very poorly constructed. There isn't an insurance company I could imagine that would have been willing to provide the kind of coverage that would be necessary to help on the rebuilding. So I think we are really talking about new money coming in. I do want to add to what Morris has said and I know Mike and I have chatted about this in the context of our own book on *Learning from Catastrophes*, that the very short run has to be dealt with. Everything we are talking about, with regards to the long run, pales if we don't get this country to the point where it is able to survive and cover these problems. If we don't do that, everything is going to go by the wayside because everyone is going to have to put out fires over the next few weeks or months or possibly years. All the good intentions, and even maybe the money that is raised, could [be wasted]. But on the insurance side, it would be very interesting to hear a little bit more on what actually exists. My guess is there is very little.

Useem: To add to that, the immediate consequences are in front of us everyday right now, including the catastrophic impact on life and limb. In the weeks ahead, the problems are going to be different, but they are going to be, in some respects, no less severe. Of course, when disasters do strike of this scale, it is the most vulnerable populations—the very poor, children, those who are in need of medical care already—who are most affected. So I think the second order consequences of this particular earthquake playing out over the next several weeks are going to be not in terms of direct threat to life, but in terms of economics and social existence. And, of course, the economy has been just about stopped in its tracks here. Once we get through this immediate search and recovery phase and then start worrying about simply reconstructing housing and beyond, there is the whole issue here of how to get this economy, which was not in great shape to begin with, back on its feet. It is a way of saying that the world has a long-term obligation to hang in here. We do worry that after media attention backs off, these more far reaching problems—social, economic, and beyond—will not be addressed. I think there is an opportunity for social entrepreneurs with the benefit of the web these days—everything that goes with that, including Twitter and well beyond—to develop ways to involve thousands, maybe millions, of people around the globe in not just immediate relief for Haiti but in longer-term investment in Haiti.

Knowledge@Wharton: Mike, following up on what Morris said earlier about the necessity for perhaps an invading army to enter and solve the problem: Very often after a catastrophe of this type, especially if there is the leadership of a very poor country involved, you have giant relief agencies that come in and try to make things happen. To what extent is this really desirable and what does it say about leadership and, indeed, the idea of sovereignty in this global economy?

Useem: You know, there is such a lesson here from the Haitian experience. And that is that in the immediate aftermath of the earthquake itself, many of the

U.N. representatives on the ground who are partly responsible for distributing relief were themselves killed and their whole operation put out of commission. It is akin to the fact that some of the nerve centers for New York's response that should have been able to pick up quickly as 9/11 began to unfold back in 2001, some of them were actually in the buildings directly impacted by the two attacks early on 9/11. It is really a statement that when it comes to large-scale disasters, we are generally underprepared organizationally to respond in a systematic, comprehensive way. No surprise, and no blame here to be allocated. It is just a reality of life. As we have watched, in fact, the United States come to control air traffic at the Haitian airport in the vacuum that is left there, [it seems to me that this is] symptomatic of the fact that many organizations, many agencies are simply filling the vacuum with very good motives to help the country at least get through this crisis. Longer term, you raise a great question. At some point the U.S. is going to have back out of their seats [and give] sovereignty back to the hopefully soon functioning government of Haiti.

More generally though, here is a statement to make. This is, as we have already said, not the first disaster of this scale—for sure not the last. It is beyond any community's capacity or any country's capacity to adequately respond. Isn't one of the lessons here that—as a universe, as a globe—we have to develop better mechanisms, better organizational schemes, stronger forms of commitment on the part of people privately through the United Nations and other vehicles to be ready to assist and to have a scheme for intervention without it having to be quite so ad hoc as it has been.

Cohen: What Mike says underscores the fact that one of the key challenges here is coordination. There are many agencies and entities that are prepared and even on the scene that have been less effective than they possibly could be. The finger pointing has already begun. The French have accused the Americans of invading Haiti. And the sovereignty issue has been raised. But the ability to coordinate these things on a global level is an enormous challenge. The United Nations has developed new processes and procedures for disaster relief. There has been a lot of progress made in the Red Cross in figuring out how they can deal with these contingencies. But if you look at the scale of what happened in Haiti, it is not anything close to what they were prepared to do. No one agency—not even one country—has sufficient resources to solve this problem. So the problem of coordination is there and real. And, yes, we need to figure out how to solve it in a better way. But I don't see the answer to that, at least in the short run.

Kunreuther: The one point that I would add to what my colleagues have mentioned is that this really is going to have to fall at the end of the day on the Haitian government. In some sense, they could see this as an opportunity, with the leaders saying that they could change things in a way that will benefit them—whatever their values are, and hopefully they are positive. They could take the role of helping to coordinate with international organizations and serve as a case study of how a country has managed to find opportunity [arising out of the devastation]. There is a chance for something like this to happen. But if the leaders feel that it is business as usual and that they have to fall back on where they are, it is really going to be extraordinarily difficult—no matter what the U.N. does or what the World Bank does or any of these international organizations. It really has to be a partnership. One of the open questions—and I think there is probably a lot of discussion going on right now with the government—is to see the challenges, but also the opportunity to take that leadership role and coordinate in such a way so that things can happen which otherwise would not.

Knowledge@Wharton: Mike and Howard, in your book, do you discuss some of the behavioral biases that cause bad decisions to be made about the likelihood of disasters?

Kunreuther: Biases? Interesting word. Let me start. Mike and I have talked a lot about this and it is an area that both of our centers have been concerned about. I think there are two biases that we have actually been talking about. One of them is this notion of a short-run bias and the idea of myopia, feeling that I can't really think more than the next year or two years ahead. There may be very good reasons for that, and there may be a whole reward system and incentive system that encourages that.

So there is a myopia bias—an "it cannot happen to me" bias. Then there is a bias where, in many, many situations, people say, 'Look, here are the pleasant reasons for living here. I don't want to think about a disaster.'

And then the last bias, which is the one that, of course, has happened right after the earthquake—what we call an availability bias. The minute that disaster occurs, it is on everyone's agenda for a short period of time [during which] Twitter and Facebook and a variety of things are going to mobilize a set of activities.

And, so, we have these three kinds of combinations. It is a combination of these that make it really, really difficult to deal with.

Useem: Another short coming to add to that is just who we are. We tend to hate bad news coming up from below. We don't want to hear it if it reflects poorly on us, for example. It is pretty well documented now in the current financial crisis that many of the problems that took down companies like AIG and Fannie Mae were problems that people could see. That is, those on the front line recognized that the subprime mortgages were shaky, that everything was going to be okay so long as everything was going up. But if there was a tipping point reached and a systemic decompression so to speak, that there would be big problems forthcoming.

People in the trenches often saw exactly those problems. As they sought to communicate upwardly the warning signs, the resistance was pretty everywhere at the top. Not because people are perverse and don't want to face problems, but it is the nature of who we are. We don't like bad news. If you want the extreme example that, I think, sums it up as well as any I have ever seen, consider the Challenger launch in January 1986 and its problems with the infamous O-rings that cracked under cold conditions, which described the launch conditions that particular early morning at the Cape in Florida. The problems with the O-rings actually were known by the maker of the O-ring, at least with the engineers who were most directly in contact with those particular parts of the booster rocket in which they were located.

Despite efforts to bring those concerns upward, top management did not absorb that information. Now in defense of top management, there is lots of bad news that comes up everyday. And we have to become mindful of the fact that some criticism, some bad news, we cannot and should not take into account. Other information, though, we should. So when it comes to behavioral biases, I would simply add the need for a device that would help us be better at, I call it, peripheral vision, as one of our colleagues has written about, in which you can see the warning signs. The fact is that indeed there were warning signs in Haiti about the prospect of an earthquake, but they were ignored by everybody including myself. I didn't pay any attention to those, of course, didn't put money into something that might have averted that. I think that particular behavioral problem is one of the major sources why we seem to stumble into these low-probability, high-consequence events too little prepared.

Knowledge@Wharton: How can someone, or the world, prepare for such events? In fact, can you prepare? Does your book say anything about that?

Useem: The great hurricane that hit Myanmar, the great flooding in Mozambique, the Katrina experience, 9/11 experience, the Challenger disaster: It is not that we want to dwell on these terrible, terrible circumstances and ordeals that people have gone through, but in our view we must remember most the need to stay vigilante and be focused on working with bad news and risky circumstances. If we want to do something for the people of Haiti along with all the things that millions of people are doing now in terms of immediate relief, it would be to describe the lessons of Haiti as graphically and in as much detail as we can, and communicate those lessons so that they will help all of us be ready for the next Haiti-like event.

Kunreuther: One of the challenges that we have had in all of these low probability events is that we are able to put this below our threshold level of concern by saying this is a one in two century event. People say, 'Well, the probability [of something bad happening] is sufficiently low that we can ignore it.' That is a major problem in terms of not putting it on the agenda. So one of the reasons that we have all been talking about longer term is that we may get people to think about things in a different way. I'll just use one little example that we have used in even a class experience.

You tell an individual there is a 1 in 100 chance of a flood, earthquake or hurricane occurring next year and you need to take some steps to protect yourself. You ask people what they would do or how much they would pay. The 1 in 100 sort of looms as a relatively low event.

If you change the time horizon and think long-term and tell the individual that if you live in this house for a 25-year period, the chances are greater than 1 in 5 that you will have at least one flood, earthquake or hurricane, the reaction is extraordinarily different. People pay more attention to it. They think about things in a different way. And so a challenge I think that we are facing is that when you have these events, let's think about these things on a longer-term basis. Present information in that way and think of strategies. We may be able to do a better job of preparing if people feel that this event is more likely to happen than that "it won't happen to me" event.

Knowledge@Wharton: There has been a lot written about new approaches to mitigation and preparedness and emergency response and all that. What does this book—your new book—offer that goes beyond that, or that you feel would be especially helpful to know about given what has happened in Haiti?

Kunreuther: What we found very exciting is that we have tried to put together in this book a group of people who were part of a global agenda council associated with the World Economic Forum who had experience around the world. And so this is not a book by us. We are authors or editors of 20 people who have written from their perspective—not only about natural disasters but about the financial crisis, about pandemics, about other kinds of disasters where there are principles here that we felt really are important.

The principles are in the context of what are you going to do before hand? How can you think about what will happen afterwards? How do you put these together? The experience is that we have gotten a much broader perspective from people with different backgrounds, including meteorology, the financial sector and so forth. We view this book really as something that is not just a do-it-yourself kind of thing for natural disasters, but really how do you think more broadly about a variety of these low probability events?

Useem: The thrust of the book is really a product of a moveable seminar. Twenty people. We met several times at some length people who were experts on financial crises, on pandemics, on physical crises like we see in Haiti. And with that in depth understanding in different areas of what went wrong, we looked for the common themes that seemed to explain why in all these cases things went wrong. We can diagnose what went wrong. That is certainly the right step to take in looking now at how to make it right before this kind of disaster happens again.

So, for instance, we observed in all these different settings a lack of readiness on the part of people to swiftly intervene, to know the drill, for many different units to be ready to orchestrate public and private relief together—things that Morris alluded to earlier. Just to sum all this up, in the end we identified half a dozen—we call them guiding principles—that anybody concerned with disaster, avoidance, or disaster recovery ought to be mindful of.

This is almost a chestnut from the field of leadership and leadership development: There is no better time to have leadership—and all the principles that go with that—in place before you need it.

Number two, leadership is not natural. It is not a natural skill that most people bring to the table. Therefore, looking ahead, once we can get beyond Haiti, our book does suggest that it would be a great time to take the tsunami, the events in Haiti, the disaster in Myanmar, Challenger, the implosion of AIG, and with that collective experience work with these principles and build others. And then going all the way back to new social media, I think we have an opportunity for these ideas to be communicated far more extensively than they have been in the past. So in the same sense that President Obama built some of this success with the grass roots through social media, I think with these ideas, these principles now are pretty clear, at least to our group of 20 , as to what is really vital going forward. I think we have better devices, if you will, for these ideas to be communicated out.

Knowledge@Wharton: Since the book is titled *Learning from Catastrophes*, could you suggest a couple of things that you hope people will learn from catastrophes from your book?

Kunreuther: One of the key lessons of *Learning from Catastrophes* is that this is not an isolated event in the sense that only one country is involved. We are in an interconnected world. We have interdependencies. We have a whole variety of things that really impinge on all of us. And to the extent that we see these as global risks, rather than risks for the country, and I think the media, and the variety of what we have today, communicates it in that fashion, we have a better opportunity of bringing all of us together to think about that. And so I would say the interconnectedness—and the notion that we have been stressing from the very beginning of trying to think more broadly, and trying to think long-term, and coordinating these activities, both in the short-term and long-term—are the lessons we would like to see coming out of this book.

Useem: I think I would add to that, Howard, the idea that catastrophes have been here since people have been here on earth. The scale of the catastrophes we have seen, though, in recent years in some respects has become more significant, in part, because of population growth, the concentration of people in areas that ordinarily would not be inhabited because of urban pressures and all that.

And, thus, as we look ahead the next 10 or 15 years, again going back maybe to what Haiti can help us do now, we see the vital importance of becoming more mindful of the fact that low probability, big deal events are going to happen. I think Morris said it so well. They are going to happen. We don't know where or when. And, therefore, within our country and certainly even more importantly within the world community, our conclusion is that we have to develop devices, if you will—mechanisms to build leadership and commitment to prevent the disasters that are avoidable. Some disasters are—to use a tennis phrase here— unforced errors. Other disasters are not. Whichever way they come, we certainly want to be prepared to have in place relief and recovery. Again, there are many specifics to go with that. But I think the summary line is organization and pre- paredness for what lies ahead.

Cohen: On an optimistic note, I think we have seen the development of better tools for the allocation of resources and for planning for these types of low probability events based on contingencies. In many ways, what we are dealing with here is analogous to a real option. Society has to make investments in advance of these disasters. What I have seen—even in the more mundane levels like in supporting mission critical products in after sales and so on—is that the effectiveness of mitigating is primarily determined by the decisions you have made prior to its occurrence. And we all know that. We are seeing better tools. It's not that we can forecast it. And it is not that we can prevent it. We have to figure out, given that it is going to occur, how will we respond? And the decisions that we make about how we respond—99% of them are made prior to the event. That requires better decision-making tools. As I said, optimistically, we have developed better tools. We are making better use of information. I think the technology and the will to use these tools are improving. ∎

Published: January 20, 2010 in Knowledge@Wharton

PART 2

Gaining a Competitive Advantage Through Targeted Team Building

How Group Dynamics May Be Killing Innovation

To come up with the next iPad, Amazon or Facebook, the last thing potential innovators need is a group brainstorm session. What the pacesetters of the future really require, according to new Wharton research, is some time alone.

In a paper titled, "Idea Generation and the Quality of the Best Idea (PDF)," Wharton operations and information management professors Christian Terwiesch and Karl Ulrich argue that group dynamics are the enemy of businesses trying to develop one-of-a-kind new products, unique ways to save money or distinctive marketing strategies.

Terwiesch, Ulrich and co-author Karan Girotra, a professor of technology and operations management at INSEAD, found that a hybrid process—in which people are given time to brainstorm on their own before discussing ideas with their peers—resulted in more and better quality ideas than a purely team-oriented process. More importantly for companies striving for innovation, however, the trio says the absolute best idea in a hybrid process topped the Number One suggestion in a traditional model.

"Manufacturers prefer 10 machines with good output over one very good machine and nine really defective ones. You would rather have 10 good salesmen than nine poor salesmen and one superstar. In those areas, what matters is the total cumulative output, the total picture," Terwiesch points out. "When it comes to innovation, however, what really matters is not getting many good ideas, but getting one or two exceptional ideas. That's really what innovation is all about."

Although several existing experimental studies criticize the team brainstorming process due to the interference of group dynamics, the Wharton researchers believe their work stands out due to a focus on the quality, in addition to the number, of ideas generated by the different processes—in particular, the quality of the best idea. They say the research is also distinctive in its study of how teams select the most promising initiatives that come out of the brainstorming phase.

"The evaluation part is critical. No matter which process we used, whether it was the [team] or hybrid model, they all did significantly worse than we hoped [in the evaluation stage]," Terwiesch says. "It's no good generating a great idea if you don't recognize the idea as great. It's like me sitting here and saying I had the idea for Amazon. If I had the idea but didn't do anything about it, then it really doesn't matter that I had the idea."

'The Boss Is Always Right'

Forty-four University of Pennsylvania students were recruited to help test how the two processes fared. The undergraduate and graduate students were divided into groups of four and asked to employ the hybrid process and team process separately to come up with student-friendly new product concepts for a hypothetical sports and fitness products manufacturer and for a hypothetical home-products manufacturer. Teams were given 30 minutes to brainstorm using the traditional group process. To test the hybrid model, they were asked to spend 10 minutes generating and ranking ideas individually and 20 minutes discussing those thoughts as a group.

The ideas generated by both methods were evaluated independently, by three separate panels asked to evaluate the product ideas on their business value; attractiveness to potential customers and overall quality based on the feasibility of actually building the product; the idea's originality; the size of the potential market for the product, and the extent to which it solved a particular problem. The students came up with a total of 443 ideas—including a trash can that reduces the odor of the garbage inside it, a water bottle with a built-in filtration system and a waterproofing system that allows for reading in the shower.

Business leaders trying to integrate innovative ideas into their office culture can learn from the structure and intricacy used to generate and evaluate the ideas, suggests Terwiesch. He and Ulrich are also co-authors of the book, *Innovation Tournaments: Creating and Selecting Exceptional Opportunities*, which suggests that companies should use coordinated competitions to filter the most exceptional proposals. He says an online system that creates a virtual "suggestion box" can accomplish the same goal as long as it is established to achieve a particular purpose. "People like having a process because they understand that it's fair. In a typical brainstorming meeting, it's not fair and everybody knows it: The boss is always right," Terwiesch says.

Imposing structure doesn't replace or stifle the creativity of employees, Ulrich adds. In fact, the goal is to establish an idea generation process that helps to bring out the best in people. "We have found that, in the early phases of idea generation, providing very specific process guideposts for individuals [such as] 'Generate at least 10 ideas and submit them by Wednesday,' ensures that all members of a team contribute and that they devote sufficient creative energy to the problem."

The results of the experiment with the students showed that average quality of the ideas generated by the hybrid process were better than those that came from the team process by the equivalent of roughly 30 percentage points. The hybrid method resulted in about three times more ideas than the traditional method. In addition, the quality rating was higher for the top five ideas produced through the hybrid process—and the difference in quality between the team and hybrid methods in terms of the best idea was much higher than the average difference in quality, suggesting that "in an innovation setting, examining only [average] quality as opposed to the quality of the best ideas is likely to underestimate the benefits of the hybrid approach," the authors write.

Terwiesch says notions spawned through an individual brainstorming process are valuable thoughts that must not be "killed too early because of group dynamics. Your initial thoughts are very vital to the company because they are your unbiased opinion."

Self-Censorship and Build-Up

There are several reasons why people are less likely to offer an unbiased opinion in a purely team-based brainstorming process. Employees might censor themselves to go along with the status quo or to avoid angering a superior. Putting several people in a room together is bound to create a lot of conversation; if everyone contributes, there is less time for individuals to share all of their ideas. Some people may think less critically about a problem because they are happy to let others do the heavy lifting.

"We're fighting the American business model where everybody is [creative], which is just not the case," Terwiesch states. "We find huge differences in people's levels of creativity, and we just have to face it. We're not all good singers and we're not all good runners, so why should we expect that we all are good idea generators? But it's not politically correct to say so, even though there is more to being a good businessperson than generating ideas."

In addition to idea quality, the researchers also tried to measure one of the predispositions of group dynamics that they believe creates a roadblock to innovation—build-up, or the tendency of people to suggest ideas similar to one that has already been proposed, and embraced by, the unit. They found that ideas built around other ideas are not statistically better than any random suggestion.

Build-up, Terwiesch believes, "is a social norm showing that you listened. If a group is working together on an idea that's already on the table, you're wary of coming in with your own agenda because you might be seen as selfish and not a team player. So you build on the idea that is currently on the table."

But that kind of thinking is what keeps the team from doing the kind of "sky's the limit" thinking that leads to the development of a product or process that hasn't been seen before. "Instead of searching the world broadly, we are all kind of searching only in this little sphere," Terwiesch says. "In innovation, variance is your friend. You want wacky stuff because you can afford to reject it if you don't like it. If you build on group norms, the group kills variance." ■

Published: May 12, 2010 in Knowledge@Wharton

Is Your Team Too Big? Too Small? What's the Right Number?

When it comes to athletics, sports teams have a specific number of team players: A basketball team needs five, baseball nine, and soccer 11. But when it comes to the workplace, where teamwork is increasingly widespread throughout complex and expanding organizations, there is no hard-and-fast rule to determine the optimal number to have on each team.

Should the most productive team have 4.6 team members, as suggested in a recent article on "How to Build a Great Team" in *Fortune* magazine? What about naming five or six individuals to each team, which is the number of MBA students chosen each year by Wharton for its 144 separate learning teams? Is it true that larger teams simply break down, reflecting a tendency towards "social loafing" and loss of coordination? Or is there simply no magic team number, a recognition of the fact that the best number of people is driven by the team's task and by the roles each person plays?

"The size question has been asked since the dawn of social psychology," says Wharton management professor Jennifer S. Mueller, recalling the early work of Maximilian Ringelmann, a French agricultural engineer born in 1861 who discovered that the more people who pulled on a rope, the less effort each individual contributed. Today, "teams are prolific in organizations. From a managerial perspective, there is this rising recognition that teams can function to monitor individuals more effectively than managers can control them. The teams function as a social unit; you don't need to hand-hold as much. And I think tasks are becoming more complex and global, which contributes to the need for perspective that teams provide."

Each Person Counts

While the study of team size is one of her areas of concentration, Mueller and other Wharton management experts acknowledge that size is not necessarily the first consideration when putting together an effective team.

"First, it's important to ask what type of task the team will engage in," Mueller says. Answering that question "will define whom you want to hire, what type of skills you are looking for. A sub-category to this is the degree of coordination required. If it's a sales team, the only real coordination comes at the end. It's all individual, and people are not interdependent. The interdependence matters, because it is one of the mechanisms that you use to determine if people are getting along."

Second, she says, "what is the team composition? What are the skills of the people needed to be translated into action? That would include everything from work style to personal style to knowledge base and making sure that they are appropriate to the task."

And third, "you want to consider size." The study of optimal team size seems to fascinate a lot of businesses and academics, primarily due to the fact that "in the past decade, research on team effectiveness has burgeoned as teams have become increasingly common in organizations of all kinds," writes Wharton management professor Katherine J. Klein, in a paper titled, "Team Mental Models and Team Performance." The paper, co-authored with Beng-Chong Lim, a professor at Nanyang Business School, Nanyang Technological University, Singapore, was published in January 2006 in the *Journal of Organizational Behavior*.

In an interview, Klein acknowledges that when it comes to team size, each person counts. "When you have two people, is that a team or a dyad? With three, you suddenly have the opportunity to have power battles, two to one. There is some notion that three is dramatically different from two, and there is some sense that even numbers may be different from odd numbers, for the same reason. My intuition is that by the time you are over eight or nine people, it is cumbersome and you will have a team that breaks down into sub-teams. Depending on the group's task, that could be a good thing or that could not be right. There is a sense that as a team gets larger, there is a tendency for social loafing, where someone gets to slide, to hide."

Ringelmann's famous study on pulling a rope—often called the Ringelmann effect—analyzed people alone and in groups as they pulled on a rope. Ringelmann then measured the pull force. As he added more and more people to the rope, Ringelmann discovered that the total force generated by the group rose, but the average force exerted by each group member declined, thereby discrediting the theory that a group team effort results in increased effort. Ringelmann attributed this to what was then called "social loafing"—a condition where a group or team tends to "hide" the lack of individual effort.

"After about five people, there are diminishing returns on how much people will pull," says Mueller. "But people, unless they are not motivated or the task is arbitrary, will not want to show social loafing. If the task is boring and mundane, they are more likely to loaf. If you tell executives this, they say, 'One of the things I'm worried about is loafing and free riding.' Whereas social loafing is decreased effort in a group context relative to individual context, free riding is rational and self-interested. If a person is not going to be rewarded, they say, 'I'm going to free ride' and they don't participate as much. The two concepts are hard to distinguish, but they are just different ways to measure similar outcomes."

The Number Six

Evan Wittenberg, director of the Wharton Graduate Leadership Program, notes that team size is "not necessarily an issue people think about immediately, but it is important." According to Wittenberg, while the research on optimal team numbers is "not conclusive, it does tend to fall into the five to 12 range, though some say five to nine is best, and the number six has come up a few times."

But having a good team depends on more than optimal size, Wittenberg adds. For instance, when Wharton assigns five to six MBA students to individual teams, "we don't just assign those teams. We make sure they can be effective. We have a 'learning team retreat' where we take all 800 students out to a camp in the woods in upstate New York and spend two days doing team building and trust building exercises. I think this is what people forget to do when they create a team in a business—spend a lot of time upfront to structure how they will work together. We get to know each other and share individual core values so we can come up with team values. But most importantly, we have the students work on their team goals, their team norms and their operating principles. Essentially, what are we going to do and how are we going to do it?"

In the work world, says Wittenberg, it has been "reinforced that five or six is the right number (on a team). At least for us, it gives everyone a real work out. But frankly, I think it depends on the task."

Recent research by Mueller would seem to support Wittenberg's notion that preparation for team success is vital. In a recent paper, "Why Individuals in Larger Teams Perform Worse," Mueller channeled Ringelmann's theories on large group efforts and tried to explain why the title of her paper is true. For decades, researchers have noted that mere changes in team size can change work-group processes and resulting performance. By studying 238 workers within 26 teams, ranging from three to 20 members in size, Mueller's research replicates the general assertion that individuals in larger teams do perform worse, but she also offers an explanation for this conclusion.

"Understanding the reasons why individuals in larger teams in real work settings perform worse may be one key to implementing successful team management tactics in organizations, since research shows that managers tend to bias their team size toward overstaffing," she writes. In addition, "individual performance losses are less about coordination activities and more about individuals on project teams developing quality relationships with one another as a means of increasing individual performance. Because research on teams in organizations has not examined team social support as an important intra-team process, future research should examine how team social support fits in with classic models of job design to buffer teams from negative influences and difficulties caused by larger team size."

But is there an optimal team size? Mueller has concluded, again, that it depends on the task. "If you have a group of janitors cleaning a stadium, there is no limit to that team; 30 will clean faster than five." But, says Mueller, if companies are dealing with coordination tasks and motivational issues, and you ask, 'What is your team size and what is optimal?' that correlates to a team of six. "Above and beyond five, and you begin to see diminishing motivation," says Mueller. "After the fifth person, you look for cliques. And the number of people who speak at any one time? That's harder to manage in a group of five or more."

Diversity: Bad for Cohesion?

Klein's recent research has looked at another confusing area when it comes to teams—the value of diversity. Various theories suggest that diversity represented by gender, race and age leads to conflict and poor social integration—while various other studies suggest just the opposite. "The general assumption is that people like people who are similar to themselves, so there is a theory to suggest that a lot of diversity is bad for cohesion," says Klein. "But there is also a theory that says diversity is great, that it creates more ideas, more perspectives and more creativity for better solutions."

In their own research, Klein and Lim find a distinct value in having some similarity between team members. The authors describe how "team mental models—defined as team members' shared, organized understanding and mental representation of knowledge about key elements of the team's relevant environment—may enhance coordination and effectiveness in performing tasks that are complex, unpredictable, urgent, and/or novel. Team members who share similar mental models can, theorists suggest, anticipate each other's responses and coordinate effectively when time is of the essence and opportunities for overt communication and debate are limited. Our findings suggest that team mental models do matter. Numerous questions remain, but the current findings advance understanding of shared cognition in teams, and suggest that continuing research on team mental models is likely to yield new theoretical insights as well as practical interventions to enhance team performance," the researchers write.

Wharton management professor Nancy P. Rothbard has a similar theory on what she calls "numerical minorities"—including gender, race, age and ethnic groups. "Often times, a numerical minority can appear to be less threatening because it's not unexpected that someone who is different from you has different viewpoints. But if they are more similar to you and they disagree with you, some groups find that more upsetting. It can raise the level of conflict on a team. That's not necessarily a bad thing, if the conflict doesn't get in the way of being able to think through a problem and do what needs to be done."

Klein has also looked into what factors determine who becomes important to a team. The single most powerful predictor? Emotional stability. "And the flip side is neuroticism. If someone is neurotic, easily agitated, worries a lot, has a strong temper—that is bad for the team."

Within a company, individual teams often begin to compete against each other, which Wittenberg finds can be troublesome. "One of the problems is the in-group, out-group problem," he says. "Depending on how we identify ourselves, we can be part of a group or separate from a group. At many companies, the engineering group and the marketing group are very much at odds. But at the same time, if you talked about that company vs. another company, the teams are together, they are more alike than the people at the other company. Teams are sometimes more siloed within a company and they think they are competing with each other instead of being incentivized to work together."

When it comes to creating a successful team, "teams that rely solely on electronic communication are less successful than those that understand why communication in person is important," says Wittenberg. "Email is a terrible medium....It doesn't relate sarcasm or emotion very well, and misunderstandings can arise. There is something very important and very different about talking to someone face-to-face." ∎

Published: June 14, 2006 in Knowledge@Wharton

Is This Madness? How Losing by Just a Little Can Help a Team—or Company—Win

Yesterday was the first day of "March Madness" in the United States, a two-week period in which 64 college basketball teams vie for the National Collegiate Athletic Association championship in a tournament that rivals the World Cup in fan frenzy.

It was also the deadline for an estimated 37 million Americans to place bets on the outcome of the tournament—not just the ultimate champion, but the winner of every game in every round. For a fee, participants in the betting can compete with pools of co-workers or other informal groups to see who has the most accurate picks. The winners get the pool of money generated by the entry fees.

That means an entry with just a few bad picks in the first round of the tournament is probably doomed to fail. But what if one of the betting participants could know in advance which teams would be leading at halftime in those first-round games? The logical move in that situation is to pick the team that's winning, right?

Maybe not. According to recent research by a pair of Wharton professors, teams that trail by a little at the half actually have a better chance of winning the game than the squad in the lead.

Wharton marketing professor Jonah Berger and Devin Pope, a professor of operations and information management, found that teams which were slightly behind at the half won more often than they lost. Their research paper, which is based in part on the results of more than 6,000 recent college basketball games, is titled: "When Losing Leads to Winning."

But Berger noted that these findings could just as easily apply to the workplace, because they suggest that employees—like basketball players—should be more motivated and thus perform better when they are close to, but just short of, an important goal.

Close Enough to Taste It

"Take any situation where someone is so close to a goal that they can almost taste it," Berger noted. "The fact that they're almost there makes them work harder." Thus, in the corporate world, where goal setting is an important management tool, Berger said it's a good strategy to pick milestones that are within reach, such as passing a close competitor in sales.

Focusing on goals that are close and achievable may be more motivating than lofty but unrealistic goals, according to Berger. "You want to pick a target that's close, where you are almost there but not quite."

Pope, his co-author, elaborated: "A lot of tools are used in the workforce to motivate people, such as wages, bonuses, etc. While surely these things can have motivating effects, one should not underestimate the potential importance of psychological motivation as well. This paper shows that the psychological impact of being behind by a small amount can cause significant increases in performance."

Motivational behavior is not Berger's usual academic focus. Usually, he delves into topics such as social contagion, viral marketing and decision-making issues like those explored in Malcolm Gladwell's best-selling book, *The Tipping Point*. But Berger began to think about the issue of motivation while coaching youth soccer. "As the coach, I always had to say something at halftime. And I always tried to be motivating. But I noticed that regardless of how much I emphasized that we needed to work hard, the players always seemed more motivated when we were behind."

When Berger came to Wharton, Pope mentioned an interest in similar issues, so they began to look for statistical evidence to back up the idea that trailing slightly could be a motivator. Earlier research into major sports shows that a team taking an early lead in a game tends to win two-thirds of the time. The reasons are self-evident: The unit jumping to a quick advantage is likely a more talented squad, and the trailing team must make up extra ground to win.

But Berger and Pope decided to look at how smaller halftime deficits affected the outcomes. To do that, they collected the results of 6,572 college basketball games played between 2005 and 2008 in which the difference at halftime was within 10 points.

As expected, the data showed teams with big halftime leads usually went on to win. For example, a college squad that is leading by six points at halftime is the victor about 80% of the time. But there is a significant deviation from the expected result for a team that is losing by just one point at the half. Using the rest of the data to control for expected performance, the trailing team ought to win about 46% of the time, according to Berger. But, in fact, those teams won 51.3% of the time.

Why does this happen? Berger and Pope believe that the answer lies in how losing affects people's drive. "Being slightly behind can be good because of the psychology of human motivation," Berger said, adding that the score provides the players with a reference point for working just a little harder. "If you're behind, you get a little more motivated. You work harder and because of that, you are more likely to succeed."

Indeed, there was no advantage to being far behind at halftime. The researchers note that their findings jibe with earlier research showing that animals run faster when they are closer to a food reward and that people work harder at a task when it is closer to completion, not when the goal appears to be distant.

Second-half Surge

Consistent with the notion that being slightly behind is motivating, the basketball data show that the effort of the trailing team seems to be greatest right after the half. Teams that were trailing by one point at the half outscored their opponents by an average of 1.2 points in the second half—and half of that average boost came in just the first four minutes of the 20-minute period. The researchers found no evidence to suggest that teams with a one-point lead were easing up.

But how to translate these findings into the business world, where there is not a large scoreboard hovering over the players' heads? Here, Berger and Pope suggest that the role of managers as motivators looms larger—to set goals that are understandable, achievable and within reach.

They also conducted a secondary experiment in which people were paid to compete in a short, simple game that involved typing letters on a keypad. Midway through the game, one group of participants was told that they were close behind, slightly ahead, far ahead or far behind. A control group was not given any information at the break. Just as the real-life basketball results had suggested, the group that exerted extra effort was the one that had been told it was only slightly behind midway through.

"First, merely telling people they were slightly behind an opponent led them to exert more effort," they write. "Competitive feedback that they were slightly behind not only increased effort in general, but did so more than being tied, slightly ahead or receiving no competitive feedback at all. Second, while being behind boosted effort, it did so only when participants were not too far behind."

Additional research showed that motivation is closely tied to self-confidence. In another sample group in which participants played the keyboard game, they were also evaluated for their self-efficacy—that is, their belief in their ability to accomplish goals. The researchers found that people with higher self-efficacy were the most capable of exerting extra effort in the second half.

Stop to Take Stock

Berger and Pope see these finding as useful to other fields—not just business but also in academic settings. For example, they suggest, a team of researchers involved in a competition should focus on the ways that they are slightly behind the opposing academic teams. They also recommend what they call "strategic breaks"—in which managers cleverly design the timing of breaks to allow employees to stop and take stock of their efforts.

The concept, according to Berger, is similar to how skilled coaches might cleverly use timeouts to control a game. "You obviously want to call time out when the other team is on a run so that [the opposing players] don't gain confidence," he said. "But you also want to call time outs in a way that motivates your own team—for example, when they are just slightly behind their opponents."

Wharton marketing professor Maurice Schweitzer recently co-authored a paper called, "Goals Gone Wild," documenting, among other things, how overly ambitious goals set by managers led to scandals at firms such as Enron and Sears when employees felt compelled to cheat in order to reach the lofty targets. Berger said that this finding is one more reason why managers would want to focus on more achievable goals. "What these examples show is that the goals were set too high. Monetary incentives made employees extremely motivated, but the goals were so unreasonable that they didn't have the ability to meet them— so they cheated."

The goal of the research, Berger noted, was not so much to gain insight into sports but to open a window into human motivation. "The psychology of these situations is the same, whether it's sports or business or academics. [It's about how] we motivate employees or researchers, and how we use competitive situations to help them succeed." ∎

Published: March 18, 2009 in Knowledge@Wharton

"Locals," "Cosmopolitans" and Other Keys to Creating Successful Global Teams

Global teams are like oceans: Depending on how they are navigated, they can link the world together or split it apart. When global teams work, they tap into a company's top talent, exploit local expertise, unite far-flung groups and ramp up worldwide production. When they don't, they are divisive, spark massive miscommunication and drive global projects into the ground.

"In any team, there are lots of barriers to effectively working together, and there are ways to make teams more effective through selection, through design, through leadership," says Wharton management professor Nancy Rothbard. "The challenges are really exacerbated in global teams where you have even greater potential barriers, especially when there are different cultural norms."

Working across international, cultural and organizational boundaries poses daunting challenges on a variety of levels. Time zone differences can make meetings difficult. Language and cultural differences sometimes lead to communication problems. And a variety of less obvious differences trip up global team members in ways they rarely expect.

Despite such difficulties, global teams—in all forms—are here to stay. Whether it's a small task force within a single company, a cross-border partnership or a multinational coalition of leaders spanning several organizations, global teams have become an essential element of modern business. "They're often a necessity," says Rothbard. "You may need those diverse cultural perspectives to solve a cultural problem....We need to find ways to make these teams work effectively. We need them to get the work done as the world becomes a more global place."

When done right, global teams can be an asset, unlocking tremendous value for companies that use them. "Global teams are able to take advantage of people not being in the same place at the same time, in order to get the work done," says Batia Weisenfeld, a management professor at NYU's Stern School of Business. "Projects can be progressing 24 hours a day. You'll be doing software development in Silicon Valley and then the software testing is being done in India while those people [in California] are sleeping."

Global teams can also ratchet up creativity and innovation by tapping into unique skill sets and multiple points of view. Weisenfeld points to one New York advertising firm as an example. The firm's New York office developed what was supposed to be a worldwide advertising campaign. But the campaign probably wouldn't sit well culturally for Asian consumers, the company's Asia office advised. So team members in Asia tweaked the campaign to accommodate local tastes. In the process, they improved the campaign so much that headquarters ultimately replaced the original campaign with the Asian version.

Unlocking Value

Despite such potential, global teams pose challenges that must first be overcome.

One of the most common issues is time. When team members are scattered across several time zones, simply scheduling a meeting can be difficult.

Consultant Ana Reyes is a partner of New Worlds Enterprise LLP, lecturer in the Penn Organizational Dynamics Program. Reyes once experienced a timing and communication snafu when working as a consultant for a large multinational corporation. The company, which had offices in several U.S., European and Asian locations, usually held global teleconferences in the morning New York time. Since team members in Asia attended the meetings in the evening, they usually used their personal phones at home. When it came to scheduling a meeting via videoconference, however, things became very complicated. Asian team members didn't have videoconferencing equipment at home, and discovered— weeks, unfortunately, after their meeting was scheduled and the agenda was set—that they couldn't use the video equipment in their office building because it was locked at night. "To get the video conferencing, they had to hire technology support and security for the building," Reyes says. In the end, the company decided it would be easier to just fly people to New York.

Organizations often assume that global team members are willing to meet when it's convenient for headquarters, says Catherine Mercer Bing, CEO of ITAP International, a Newtown, Pa.-based consulting firm that "works at the intersection of business and cultural issues." The unfortunate result for some team members: Every meeting takes place in the middle of the night or at the crack of dawn.

"It becomes [demotivating] for those team members who always have to be available at 4 a.m. or some other off-work hours," Bing says. Her suggestion: Start global conference calls by asking what time it is for everyone involved, to make everyone aware of other team members' situations. Also, change meeting times frequently so that everybody has a chance to attend a meeting during the day. "Rotate," she suggests. "It makes it fair. It makes team members feel more equitable."

Tackling cultural differences can be much more of a challenge. When global teams include more than one culture, team members carry unspoken assumptions that can lead to inadvertent misunderstandings. After all, the type of information people share and how they share it is culturally based, says Rothbard. "Hesitation in voice in one culture might signal discomfort with what is being shared. In another culture, it might just [mean they're] being deliberative. What people mean, and how [others] interpret what they mean, is very subtle. The speaker might have no idea that their words are being interpreted in a certain way."

Depending on a person's cultural background, fellow team members might seem to be speaking too loudly or softly, interrupting too much or being too reticent, demanding a ridiculous amount of information or being oddly ambiguous.

"Everybody is programmed by the cultures they grew up with," says Reyes. Studies have shown that people from Latin American, Middle Eastern and Mediterranean countries speak several decibels louder than other cultures. In many of these countries, interrupting is considered an acceptable way to exchange turns in conversation. "These communication patterns...become annoyances that people can't figure out, so people often ignore [them]. And best practice is to talk about them."

Cultural differences also impact the way global teams communicate information to others outside of the team—another possible source of conflict. Bing once worked with a global team with members in the U.S. and Spain. Consistently throughout the project, the Spanish team members would copy their superiors in emails about what the team was doing. Members of the U.S. team misinterpreted the move as attempts to undermine team efforts. "The U.S. [team members] were saying, 'You guys are trying to get us in trouble,'" Bing recalls. "But part of who gets copied is a cultural decision." The misperception ultimately caused so much conflict between members that the team missed a project deadline.

Cultural differences even creep into the technologies companies use, creating additional challenges for interaction, Reyes says. "Culture is really pattern-based ways of organizing space, time, human activity and the material environment. So technology—any kind of technology, whether it's a robot or a technology system—[involves] human practices that have been disembodied and put into a machine."

Barriers to Sharing Knowledge

While cultural differences may stand out as an obvious stumbling block for global teams, differences in other areas also drive teams apart, experts point out. "Each person is likely to be situated in a very different context so their assumptions may be different," says Weisenfeld. "Some of those may be cultural, but they can also be legal or societal."

For example, when organizations in Europe restructure, one of the first things to come up in discussion is labor unions. This is not as much of a concern in the U.S. as in Europe, where labor laws are different, Weisenfeld says. "Those become taken-for-granted assumptions. It's not cultural. They're not about people's values. They're about people's taken-for-granted assumptions about the way things work."

Wharton management professor Martine Haas has made a career of studying team interaction in large organizations, looking for factors in addition to culture that may lead to a team's success or failure. "When you talk about global teams, most of the research is about cultural issues, but there are a lot of [other interactions] that happens in global teams," she says.

Haas has found that a mix of "cosmopolitans" and "locals" are a key to team success. She defines "locals" as team members on the ground who know a lot about the country they represent. "Cosmopolitans" are team members who have lived in several countries and may speak multiple languages. Having worked on projects in different parts of the world, cosmopolitans have a birds-eye view and may be able to see the global implications of a team's actions. But only a local might be aware of what consumers in a particular country want from a new product, or understand the subtleties of a new environmental regulation the local country just put in place. "It's good to have both of these on the team because they bring different things," Haas says. "Teams that have both of these in them are most effective."

Haas also identifies four sets of differences that can drive global team members apart: cultural, geographic, demographic and structural. Cultural barriers, discussed earlier, stem from a team member's birthplace and background. Geographic barriers refer to the actual location where the team member resides. (These two can be different if, say, the team member is an American-born expat in charge of a company's Beijing office.)

Demographic barriers refer to factors such as age, tenure and education level of a team member. Structural differences refer to a team member's position in the company hierarchy or a particular business unit. "All these kinds of differences reduce the likelihood that you're going to share knowledge," says Haas.

Not all differences are created equal: Haas has found that structural differences play a stronger role than demographic ones, and geography plays a stronger role than culture. In fact, structural differences play a stronger role than either geography or culture. So managers from two different countries who work in the same company division could find it easier to share information than people from the same cultural background who work in two different departments or satellite offices. "The reason is that structure and geography have more powerful effects on how team members understand and communicate about their tasks than demography and culture," Haas says. "As a result, they can encounter more communication problems when they try to communicate across structural and geographic differences than across demographic and cultural ones."

So what can managers and companies do to make global teams work better? Our experts offer a few ideas and suggestions:

Try to meet at least once face-to-face, says Weisenfeld. "There is evidence that when people have even just one face-to-face meeting, it makes virtual teams work much more smoothly."

Choose team members carefully. Find the right balance of locals and cosmopolitans, Haas suggests. Don't overlook soft skills such as interpersonal communication abilities, Rothbard adds. "Often the technical skills get prioritized very powerfully over teamwork skills," she says.

Keep the team small if possible. "Teams optimally work most effectively when you have five to seven individuals," says Rothbard. "As you get larger than that, it becomes more challenging. You need to be very careful as you start going above that number. You need to be clear that you are adding value... I'm not saying you can never go above that number. You just need to make sure that you know there's a tradeoff."

Consider cross-cultural training. According to Reyes, best-practice companies "train in cross-cultural communication, project management, teamwork and stakeholder management" and they "provide guidelines and support for chartering teams, selecting communication and collaboration technologies, and building and maintaining trust in globally diverse settings."

Be explicit upfront about how the team will operate, making no assumptions that some things should be obvious or understood. Bing worked with a team once that called a meeting and forgot to include one member on the email. The man thought he had been fired. The reality: Nobody had sent out an email list of who was on the team. "Who's on the distribution list? How will we communicate with each other? What technologies will we use? Just establishing appropriate protocols is important," Bing says. "Come up with a team culture that says, 'We all agree that this is how we're going to work together.'"

Be conscious of time. That means not only time zones but expectations of how long tasks should take, how long meetings should be and when they are expected to start and finish. This is especially important if the team is composed of members from different cultures who have varying concepts of time, Weinsenfeld remarks. If the meeting is at 10 o'clock, for example, team members from Germany could show up at nine while those from Brazil might not dial in until eleven. "If the meeting is one hour, you can be sure that people will miss each other," she says.

Consider how the team is organized. Be aware of conflicting interests of team members. Reyes suggests forming sub-tasks to pull the group together and counteract the tendency to splinter along cultural or geographic lines. Teams are easier to manage if everyone is reporting to the same individual, Weisenfeld notes.

Don't overload team members. Haas says her research has shown that a team's effectiveness is compromised if its members are too overloaded with tasks. These can be tasks for the team itself or external projects that team members have to complete in addition to their work on the team.

Give the team autonomy. Being autonomous is one of the key factors to a global team's success, Haas has found. Teams that have no control over their budget, are beholden to outside interests or have little authority to make decisions about tasks and resources struggle to meet their goals. Without autonomy, Haas says, a global team's scheduling efforts, cross-cultural dialogue and efforts to increase information-sharing could well go to waste. "How good is the team if they don't have the ability to act on what they know?" ∎

Published: September 2, 2009 in Knowledge@Wharton

Siemens CEO Klaus Kleinfeld: "Nobody's Perfect, but a Team Can Be"

Corporate leaders must build international organizations to compete in today's economy and be prepared to defend globalization at home, according to Klaus Kleinfeld, chief executive of the German electrical and engineering conglomerate Siemens AG.

Speaking at a recent Wharton Leadership Lecture, Kleinfeld said U.S. concerns about the sale of port assets to a Dubai-based firm, and French resistance to the sale of yogurt-maker Danone—which French officials called a "national treasure"—highlight growing fears that globalization comes at the cost of jobs in developed countries. Those fears could spark a backlash against globalism and limit future economic growth, he warned. "The common people—the voters—do not understand what's going on and see a threat," said Kleinfeld. "We, as leaders, need to be responsible for explaining the positives of globalization."

Siemens, with sales last year of $91.5 billion and locations in 190 countries, operates a range of businesses, including power, transportation, automation and controls, healthcare, lighting, and building technology. Germany, where Siemens operates out of joint headquarters in Munich and Berlin, has benefited as a net exporter in an increasingly global economy, Kleinfeld suggested. "But people do not connect the dots. Business needs to do the explaining more than ever before. If we don't, in a democracy things swing according to what the common man thinks—and that's scary."

Siemens was a pioneer in extending the German workweek from 35 hours to 40, with no additional pay, in 2004. Unions grudgingly agreed after the company threatened to move plants to Hungary. This spring, unions have targeted Siemens and DaimlerChrysler AG for strikes this year by workers seeking a 5% pay increase.

At 48, Kleinfeld, is a marathon runner who is viewed as a youthful and outspoken business leader in Germany and a person who is in touch with American business culture after a three-year stint in Siemens' U.S. headquarters in New York.

During his Wharton lecture, Kleinfeld stressed his conviction that increased labor flexibility will ultimately benefit German workers. "If people want to compete, they have to adjust and understand what the world is like," he said. "I can only hope that more and more people understand that only if we are competitive will we have secure jobs and be able to offer new jobs."

With 460,000 employees worldwide, including 70,000 in the United States, the 159-year old company is the world's eighth largest private employer. Siemens' German operations employ 165,000 and are costly to run, Kleinfeld noted, but they are not a drag on the overall corporation. "The teams in Germany are among our most intelligent. They bring our products to world markets at a fast pace. You should never change a winning team." He said customers from all over the world come to Siemens facilities in remote parts of Germany to learn about cutting-edge products. "Whether I have additional costs, or not, doesn't matter as much as the speed to market and the quality of the design. We're not talking about a pure cost game."

Siemens is expanding rapidly in Asia, the Middle East and other parts of the globe, including the United States. In 1995, Germany represented 43% of sales, but that figure dropped to 21% by 2005, while the percentage of German employees declined from 57% to 36% in the same period.

The company's global expansion has raised concerns about "offshoring" in Germany. "Offshoring is a funny thing for an international company. Where is your shore?" asked Kleinfeld. "My shore is as much in India and China as it is in Germany or the U.S." Siemens will continue to migrate to developing regions where new sales are growing. "I really see more international businesses, or fragments, run out of those growth regions like India and China," he said.

The company "is going to invest in almost all of the opportunities we see that make sense for us," noted Kleinfeld, who added that Siemens is not limited in its expansion by finances. The biggest constraint is a lack of qualified people to lead businesses in these new markets. Indeed, his lecture was titled "Next Generation Talent Management."

"In today's world, knowledge travels faster than ever before, so if you are talking about a sustainable competitive advantage, probably the only one is the quality of the people you have and the way they interact as a team," he said, adding that leaders within Siemens are evaluated on general management abilities, such as analytic skills, and on personality traits, including self-discipline and the ability to speak out for what they believe in. In addition, Siemens looks for rising executives with a specialty, such as a background in math or engineering, a second language or industry expertise. "What I want to see is an individual who has the passion to do a deep drill to understand something to the very bottom."

Exporting German Engineering

Kleinfeld earned a PhD in strategic management from the German University of Wuerzburg in 1992 and a master's degree in business administration and economics from the University of Goettingen. He joined Siemens in 1987 in the company's corporate sales and marketing division. He later founded Siemens Management Consulting and was executive vice president of the company's medical engineering group in 2001, when he was appointed chief operating officer of the company's U.S. businesses in New York. A year later he was promoted to chief executive of U.S. operations. In 2004, he moved back to Germany and in early 2005 was appointed chief executive of the company. Within months, he sold off Siemen's troubled mobile handset business to BenQ of Taiwan.

Kleinfeld noted that the firm was founded by an entrepreneur, Werner von Siemens, and is rooted in electrical technology. "Electricity was so cool, and it still is today. It is really what led us into all the businesses we are in now." Within a few years of its founding, the company opened offices in London and began building a telegraph system for Russia. "We were formed as an international company, but around German engineering values, and we were able to export that" throughout the world, said Kleinfeld.

He acknowledged that the conglomerate structure has fallen in and out of vogue three times during his career, but said it works for Siemens. "To be successful as a conglomerate, you need to be successful in each of the single businesses, from medical to transportation to communication. You have different competitors in each business, but you need to be better than those competitors."

At the same time, the conglomerate structure provides synergies that can boost the performance of individual businesses. For example, following the September 11, 2001, terrorist attacks on the United States, Siemens researchers who were working on pattern recognition in the company's medical business saw opportunities for the same technology in the security sector. The company's building systems division is now developing pattern recognition products.

Another example of the benefits of a conglomerate, he said, is illustrated by Siemens' 2005 acquisition of the Flender Group, a German-based manufacturer of industrial drive systems. Demand for Flender products is up sharply because Siemens' sales force is now carrying the company's products in 190 countries instead of just 20 where Flender had distribution networks on its own.

The conglomerate works well when dealing with clients that have their own complex structure, he added. He points to airports as a growing business segment with complicated needs, from security systems to baggage handling, cooling and heating, and communications, all areas in which Siemens has expertise. Siemens has even built its own simulated airport near Nuremberg to develop and test airport products, including parking guidance, baggage transport and check-in systems. "We can help our customers understand where the path of technology is going," he said. "That increases value for the customer given the speed of change that's occurring" in that area.

"Control Freaks" Need Not Apply

Managers working in the global economy must always think internationally, but act locally, Kleinfeld stated, and he laid out some principles for successful leaders, although each came with a caveat. First, he said, leaders need to "raise the bar" and challenge themselves to deliver outstanding performance and mastery of details, but they must also delegate. "You cannot run the organization as a control freak."

He encouraged self-starters, but only if they also rely on senior managers to protect them from ill-advised schemes. "With entrepreneurial freedom comes the responsibility to think about what's the utmost negative consequence. If you dig a hole in the ship below the water line, you risk the entire ship sinking. That kind of entrepreneurial behavior is not a good idea."

Respect for colleagues and the ability to talk and listen to other members of a team is critical, especially in the age of e-mail. "You don't have the right not to respect the individual even if you are letting that individual go," said Kleinfeld. "There are people who get lust out of firing people. Those are sick individuals and I don't want them in our organization." ■

Published: April 19, 2006 in Knowledge@Wharton

Hiring from Outside the Company:
How New People Can Bring Unexpected Problems

As life-long employment fades and the workforce becomes increasingly mobile, many companies look to hire skilled, experienced workers to improve productivity quickly. Those workers, however, often bring baggage from prior jobs that can negate the benefits of their prior experience, according to new Wharton research.

Companies might be better off investing in training fresh recruits with little experience in an industry so the companies can have more control over how the new workers adapt to their new employer's corporate strategy and culture. The research found that training may be more productive than paying a premium to hire experienced workers who might come from a different sort of corporate environment.

"Human resources managers will want to [hire] people who worked in a related industry or firm for the skills they bring. That makes sense from a human capital perspective, but we question whether that's all they bring with them. Do they bring other experiences...positive or negative?" asks Wharton management professor Nancy Rothbard, co-author of a paper titled Unpacking Prior Experience: How Career History Affects Job Performance. Rothbard wrote the paper with Gina Dokko of New York University's Stern School of Business and Steffanie L. Wilk of Ohio State University's Fisher College of Business.

Drawing on psychological theory, the authors examined employment applications and hiring records at two call centers for a major property and casualty insurance firm. The authors set out to assess not only the impact of bringing in skilled and knowledgeable workers, but also cognitive and behavioral responses that developed during [the new workers'] previous employment.

When More Experience Means Less Success

In interviews with managers early on in the project, Rothbard and her colleagues discovered that the issue of cross-corporation baggage kept coming up. A senior human resource manager told the research team, "We tried to hire from our competitors and paid a premium for the experience—but those hires were the least successful." Another manager quoted in the paper said: "People are weighed down by the baggage they bring in."

Rothbard says executives at the insurance company told of hiring a talented and highly trained adjustor from another insurance company. While the hiring company provided high-end insurance with a strong emphasis on customer service, the adjustor came from a company that was more focused on keeping costs down. Rothbard says the adjustor just could not help himself from "nickel and diming" customers on their claims, even though that attitude conflicted sharply with the firm's strategic direction and culture.

"It was so embedded in his ideas about how to do the job that even at this other firm, where management tried to instill the other set of values, it didn't translate," explains Rothbard. "He had the skills to get up and running quickly in the [basics] of what an adjustor does, but...he was ultimately not adaptable to the strategy and norms of the new firm. His experience tended to trap him."

Rothbard describes employment "baggage" as a set of norms and experiences that shape the workers' response to their jobs as much as, if not more than, the industry and occupation-related skills and knowledge they bring to their work.

According to the paper, "Habits, routines, and scripts that contribute to performance in one organizational context may detract from performance in a different organizational context. That is, the relationship between prior related experience and performance may not be wholly positive. Indeed, despite the common assumption that prior related experience will improve performance, past research findings have been mixed about the effect of work experience on performance."

Rothbard and the other researchers were intrigued by the notion that the norms and values employees pick up in the culture of one firm are not easily shed as they cross organizational boundaries. "Those kinds of transfers really are not discussed at all when we talk about mobility of the workforce. We assume people are cogs that can be plugged in and they will perform similarly in different environments."

Incidentally, Rothbard says, managers in certain industries may find the research particularly important. "For example, consulting firms have very large differences in culture and strategy and mission. It can be very difficult to overcome the years of acculturation you get from one firm."

The transition between companies is an increasingly important issue for employers and workers. In the late 1970s, Americans were estimated to have an average of seven employers during their working years. By 2005, the U.S. Bureau of Labor Statistics found the average American worker born in the later years of the baby boom had 10.5 employers by age 40.

The research team reviewed the work history of more than 7,200 employees and applicants to explore the relationships between prior experience and productivity. Their findings show a strong relationship between prior experience and knowledge and skills on the job. At the same time, however, the models indicate that prior experience does not always signal increased productivity.

A Factor in Reviews: "Cultural Fit"

Beyond those results, the researchers were able to examine employment reviews to delve into the question of individual employee adaptability and the impact on productivity. Supervisors rated employees on adaptability. The researchers found that people who were more adaptable did not reflect a negative relationship between prior experience and effectiveness on the job.

The authors also looked at "cultural fit" within the organization. For employees who felt they fit into the culture of the firm, the negative effects of prior experience in the occupation are not pronounced. For employees who said they did not fit well into the organization, there was a significant indication of the negative effect of prior "baggage."

Rothbard says the research findings are important not only in light of the increasingly mobile workforce, but also because so many companies are in a constant state of change themselves. "If your business has changed, you need to consider trying to retool people, not just in terms of their skills, but in terms of their values," Rothbard suggests. "Not that people can't shed these things. But it may take more training and socialization than you" first expected.

According to Rothbard, companies may want to use a mentoring program to help employees from similar companies readjust to the culture and mores of their new firm. "I know it seems odd that if you hire someone with experience to then say, 'Here's your mentor,'" Rothbard acknowledges. "But maybe they need a mentor for the values of the company, not so much the skills needed for the job."

Rothbard says that when companies hire employees with experience, they tend to rely on that experience as a substitute for training. "Maybe they pay more for those people and invest less in training, but we suggest that might be a mistake. You really need to think carefully about your training and socialization to mitigate the negative effects of the trouble people have transferring the way they think about how the job is done."

Finally the researchers used the data to gain insights into the role of cross-company transfers of skills, as well as cultural baggage, on long-term careers. The research indicates that the advantage of prior task-relevant knowledge and skills diminishes the longer an employee stays at the new firm.

"Over time as individuals become socialized into the new firm, the amount of prior work experience they brought with them matters less for the skills they demonstrate on the job," says Rothbard. "However, the negative direct relationship between prior work experience and performance does not diminish as much, suggesting that the norms and values people bring with them may persist quite substantially."

The new research findings should help companies develop hiring and training strategies that fit well with their own culture, Rothbard adds.

"If you have a strong culture and a clear strategy in doing things that differ from your competitor, you may want to think carefully about whether you want to hire for experience or whether you want to hire people with less experience and invest more in training them in your model," Rothbard advises. "If your competitive advantage is the culture of your company, you want to be careful about bringing in people with a long tenure in their occupation or industry and think about how that prior experience is going to bring positives as well as negatives to the firm." ■

Published: September 3, 2008 in Knowledge@Wharton

PART 3

Technology as a Competitive Differentiator

"Act Now, Apologize Later": Will Users "Friend" Facebook's Latest Intrusion on Privacy?

With more than 400 million users, social networking giant Facebook theoretically has a lot to lose if it sidesteps privacy without consumers' consent.

But each time the company introduces new features that make users' personal information available to an increasingly wide circle, the site continues to grow. In 2007, for example, it introduced "Beacon," a system that tracked users' online purchases and reported them back to their profiles and made the information visible to their friends. The goal was to create more opportunities for targeted advertising. The problem: Facebook never asked users for their permission to record and publicize their browsing activities. Following a groundswell of resistance from its member base, Facebook CEO Mark Zuckerberg issued an apology and the company shuttered the service.

Flash forward to today, and Facebook—now the largest social networking site—has once again become the center of a debate over online privacy as the company pushes norms and raises a few hackles along the way. This time, industry observers are eyeing its newly announced "Open Graph" plan—an attempt to link Facebook users to other parts of the web by sharing their "likes" and other activities across a number of different sites. Days after Zuckerberg unveiled Open Graph at Facebook's f8 conference for software developers on April 21, privacy groups banded together and petitioned the Federal Trade Commission for an investigation.

Experts at Wharton say that despite vocal opposition, Facebook is increasingly defining the parameters of online privacy through new features and its ever-changing policies. "Facebook's approach is to 'act now, apologize later,'" notes Wharton legal studies and business ethics professor Kevin Werbach. "It has repeatedly pushed the envelope on privacy, sometimes clearly going too far." This time, will the company ultimately face a backlash from users and regulators?

The "Open Graph"

According to Zuckerberg, Facebook's latest initiative will put "people at the center of the web" by connecting them with sites like Pandora, an Internet radio service, Yelp, a local business review and referral network, and content-driven sites like CNN and IMDB, the Internet Movie Database. All it takes to make these connections is clicking a "like" button on a site when users are logged in to Facebook. Anyone with a Facebook account can visit Pandora, for example, and see what songs their friends are listening to, or check CNN to read stories their friends liked. The benefits to partner sites that enable these "like" buttons are obvious: increased traffic from recommendations across Facebook communities. And, according to Wharton experts, Facebook benefits by becoming the center of what's known as the "social web," where status—and any potential

71

monetization—is based on personal connections and recommendations rather than search engine results.

Unlike the bumpy Beacon launch, Facebook argues that it has found the right balance between being useful to customers, linking together social profiles and gathering data that could be valuable to advertisers. Facebook's Open Graph approach features plugins that can be included on any site so users can "like" or recommend content, and personal data is controlled by Facebook and not shared with the partner site. However, a user's recommendations show up as public information on their Facebook profiles. Users can change their privacy settings to determine which recommendations are visible. Nonetheless, critics such as privacy advocacy group Electronic Frontier Foundation (EFF) say Facebook makes it hard for users to restrict the information they share.

"Facebook's privacy settings are very confusing," says Peter Fader, a marketing professor at Wharton. "And the fact that Facebook changes frequently makes it worse. Due to [the potential for] monetization, Facebook prefers users opt out. It's better for the user [to be able to] opt in. The controls could be much clearer."

Experts at Wharton are quick to note that, in the past, Facebook has been able to push features and change privacy settings without much impact on the site's meteoric growth. While some bloggers and commentators closed their Facebook accounts in response to the recent changes, Facebook's continued expansion makes it unlikely these protests will have much impact on the company. "It's doubtful whether a user boycott would be successful," notes Kendall White-house, director of new media at Wharton. "If you managed to get a million people to close their accounts—which would be quite a feat—that only represents one-quarter of one percent of Facebook's user base" and would be unlikely to compel the company to change direction, he says.

Shawndra Hill, a professor of operations and information management at Wharton, says there is a cost to users when it comes to all of these privacy changes and new features: The time that it takes people to understand what changed and how it affects them. "What's important is that Facebook try to understand why people keep some things private. Facebook can't blindly make everything public."

Whitehouse says the risk to Facebook isn't users leaving in droves but, rather, how the company's seemingly cavalier attitude toward privacy could taint its image among advertisers and corporate customers. "The danger for Facebook is that it might become the next MySpace," he notes, adding that while MySpace still commands a large audience, the site isn't as attractive to many corporate and enterprise customers as Facebook or Twitter. MySpace is often eschewed as a place to promote major brands, "unless you're a musician or a pop culture film," says Whitehouse.

On a blog post following his keynote at the f8 conference, Zuckerberg argued that connecting sites and services together seamlessly will have "profound benefits....We're really proud that Facebook is part of the shift toward more social and personalized experiences everywhere online."

Privacy: A Moving Target

However, Wharton experts say there may be problems along the way. Facebook isn't only benefiting from the propensity of Internet users to share details of their lives, but also defining privacy online. Meanwhile, Facebook has to balance user demands with those of advertisers—the key to making money—and the law.

"The challenge with online privacy is that people care very deeply about it, but have a difficult time articulating where to draw the lines," Werbach says. "It's difficult to set rules for services that no one has experience with over time and at scale. As the world becomes increasingly interconnected, many domains that were once private become public. On the other hand, that can't mean that the deep human values associated with privacy should be abandoned."

Hill says that users don't necessarily understand what they give up in privacy when they join Facebook. Meanwhile, Facebook's ability to share information outside of its network can be worrisome if users aren't schooled on what they should keep private.

In addition, Facebook is perceived to have an ethical responsibility to protect user privacy, but the "extent of legal responsibility is totally up in the air," says Andrea Matwyshyn, a legal studies and business ethics professor at Wharton. According to Matwyshyn, the larger problem is that no one—legislators, users or social networks—agree on a common privacy definition. "Until there is some consensus, companies will keep pushing the edge on privacy. Facebook is testing the waters."

The EFF has tracked Facebook's evolving privacy policy. In 2005, the company told users that "no personal information that you submit to Facebook will be available to any user of the web site who doesn't belong to at least one of the groups specified by you."

In December 2009, Facebook stated: "Certain categories of information such as your name, profile photo, list of friends and pages you are a fan of, gender, geographic region, and networks you belong to are considered publicly available to everyone, including Facebook-enhanced applications, and therefore do not have privacy settings."

In April 2010, Facebook's privacy policy noted: "The default privacy setting for certain types of information you post on Facebook is set to 'everyone'. Because it takes two to connect, your privacy settings only control who can see the connection on your profile page. If you are uncomfortable with the connection being publicly available, you should consider removing (or not making) the connection."

That final change is what riled up 15 privacy groups, which in late April petitioned the FTC to investigate Facebook. The complaint revolved around "material changes to privacy settings made by Facebook that adversely impact the users of the service." Facebook "now discloses personal information to the public that Facebook users previously restricted...and now discloses personal information to third parties that Facebook users previously did not make available," the groups said in their complaint. "These changes violate user expectations, diminish user privacy and contradict Facebook's own representations."

Facebook has maintained that it cares about privacy and giving users control over their data. Werbach agrees, but says the definition of privacy is changing by virtue of users' actions: Users may say they want everything private yet share the most intimate details of their lives. Given that fact, Facebook's approach of act first—and apologize later if needed—makes sense.

"Facebook has a culture of constant iteration and experimentation on its core service. It makes a lot of mistakes, but it's good at fixing those mistakes or further evolving quickly. That has been the story of all of Facebook's prior privacy intrusions, [including] Beacon," says Werbach. "From my perspective, Facebook cares a great deal about privacy, but it thinks about it differently than most privacy experts. Facebook doesn't start with privacy principles; it tests concrete user experiences on real users."

David Hsu, a management professor at Wharton, agrees that Facebook may be just reflecting societal changes with privacy. "People have been acclimated to sharing more and more information," says Hsu. "It's a change in mentality that's provocative and problematic as privacy is redefined."

A Backlash?

The problem with that approach, according to Werbach and other experts, is that it's dangerous for Facebook. Ultimately, consumers could change their views of privacy and deactivate their Facebook accounts.

Werbach points out that these flare-ups have occurred before, but were resolved either with an apology from Facebook—as in the case of Beacon—or because users just became used to feature changes. "Facebook has generally been successful at recognizing the difference between sustained user outcry and uncomfortable adjustment to a new feature."

Matwyshyn notes that while consumers can control their privacy settings, it's almost impossible to keep up with Facebook's changes. "Things that are too confusing simply aren't used," adds Whitehouse, indicating that while Facebook's privacy controls are highly specific, their complexity effectively undermines their value.

The perception of control is important, however. "When I talk with my students about Facebook and privacy, they often come back to the issues of control and community," says Werbach. "As long as they feel they have control over their information, they are comfortable sharing it. And they think about Facebook as a distinct environment that largely overlaps with their physical communities such as the university and their families. Taking features such as 'likes' out to the public Internet breaks that 'magic circle.'"

Eric Bradlow, a marketing professor at Wharton, says that any concerns about the Open Graph are likely to blow over. Facebook is "thinking of clever ways to utilize the social graph" and users are likely to play along, because they have the control not to participate if they choose, he notes.

Fader agrees that critics are overstating the privacy concerns. Once everyone makes their likes, recommendations and affiliations public, worries about that information being public will fade, he says. However, he believes the site's convoluted opt-out procedures are ultimately detrimental. "Facebook does make it hard to opt out. It should be totally upfront about this stuff and make it easier to change your settings. Facebook should be bending over backwards to do that." Why? "It's just good business," says Fader. "Facebook has created a deep connection with the customer base that exceeds everybody else, [including] Google and eBay. While that may give Facebook carte blanche, there's no gain in abusing it."

High Stakes, High Profits

Experts at Wharton say that Facebook's Open Graph initiative—as well as the privacy debate it has sparked—boils down to the balance between making money through targeted advertising and keeping users happy. "Eventually, [Open Graph] can lead to recommendations and targeting, which allows for Facebook to monetize" the user information it has, says Bradlow. Hill agrees. "Facebook has the best data by far in social networking. [It] has geographic information, behavior, the sites you click on and groups you like. That's powerful for target marketing."

For now, Facebook has not indicated how it plans to use any data collected through the Open Graph. Werbach predicts that the social web will have a big impact on advertising, but it may take time. "Going from social graphs to effective advertising in practice is harder than it seems, and it raises a whole additional layer of privacy concerns," says Werbach. Many advertisers are still in the experimental stage with social media, and they don't want to be involved with privacy flaps.

Matwyshyn notes that Facebook is currently aggregating a massive amount of user data, but that doesn't necessarily mean that advertising is the Holy Grail. "The master plan may be to aggregate information and develop big revenue streams in data resale," she says.

Whatever business models Facebook develops, experts at Wharton suggest that the company may not be invincible in the long run. It's possible that privacy problems, user backlash and the need to generate revenue will create a toxic stew that erodes trust. "People stay with Facebook because they feel locked in, but they may lose trust over time," says Matwyshyn. "It could be an ideal time for a competitor to come in and harness that trust deficit." ∎

Published: May 12, 2010 in Knowledge@Wharton

Tarnished Brands at Bargain Prices: Will the Tech Sector's Latest Growth Strategy Pay Off?

Companies throughout the tech sector seem to be on a buying spree of late. Oracle, which specializes in database management systems and related corporate software, has completed 67 acquisitions in the last five years. Hewlett-Packard has added Palm and 3Com to its portfolio since last fall. And a bevy of other deals—or attempted deals—ranging from Microsoft's pursuit of Yahoo to information infrastructure company EMC's acquisition of Iomega, a producer of networking storage hardware, have been proposed or completed recently.

In many of these recent instances, the target company has lost some of its brand luster or market strength and the acquiring company, attracted by a bargain-basement price, thinks it can do a better job of running things. For example, Palm bet big on one device—the Pre smartphone—to turn around the company's fortunes. But the move didn't pay off: In February, Palm cut its revenue forecast; in March, it reported a quarterly loss of $22 million; and in April, the company cut its forecast again. On April 28, HP announced that it had purchased Palm for $1.2 billion, looking beyond the company's problems to see an opportunity to use Palm's well-received WebOS mobile operating system to compete with Apple's iPad.

Other recent examples: Sun Microsystems was losing money—$2.2 billion in fiscal 2009—amid a revenue slide and various restructuring efforts when Oracle came calling in April 2009. Oracle said Sun was unproductive and too decentralized, and outlined a repair plan when it closed the $5.6 billion deal in January to buy the computer company. And Microsoft made a $44.6 billion bid for Yahoo in early 2008, hoping to gain more search engine market share to better compete with Google. But Microsoft ultimately settled for a partnership with Yahoo rather than a merger.

"Palm, Sun and Yahoo were all at inflection points," notes David Hsu, a Wharton management professor. "Acquirers are trying to airlift the brands, technology and know-how and embed them in a different setting to maximize success."

More than typical M&A activity, these deals—and others like them—show that the technology industry has matured, say experts at Wharton. Once companies reach a certain size, acquisitions are one of the few ways to grow and keep the innovation cycle going. As technology companies find it increasingly difficult to move the revenue needle by acquiring startups, larger acquisitions of former superstars have become the focus.

"The technology industry is evolving. You can see it mature," says Saikat Chaudhuri, a Wharton management professor. Andrea Matwyshyn, a legal studies and business ethics professor at Wharton, agrees: "Tech companies are demonstrating the patterns we see in industries with more longevity."

The goal of these more mature takeover strategies is to gain market share, enter a new market or acquire intellectual property that can head off a competitor. Some technology companies, such as Cisco Systems and Google, tend to buy smaller firms. An increasing number of acquisitions within the industry, however, more closely resemble leveraged buyouts in which the objective is to find value, make the target more efficient and reap the rewards, says Hsu. But these acquisitions come with the usual risks and challenges associated with bringing any new arrival into an acquiring company's fold.

The big difference between what's happening in the tech sector and a traditional leveraged buyout is that there is little to no debt involved in the recent tech deals. "Microsoft, Oracle, Apple and others have a ton of cash," notes Hsu. "To take the leveraged buyout approach [and turn around a company] you have to be able to finance it. Technology companies have the resources." Indeed, HP had cash and equivalents of $14.1 billion as of April 30; Oracle had $9.3 billion as of February 28, and Microsoft had $8.1 billion ($39.7 billion, if you include short-term investments) as of March 31. "For many of these companies, it's like they have money burning holes in their pockets," says Wharton management professor Lawrence Hrebiniak.

Making the Deals Work

The master plan behind many of these purchases is to increase share in a particular market to better compete against a stronger competitor. HP bought 3Com to go up against Cisco in networking. Its acquisition of Palm was about acquiring the intellectual property to sell corporations a variety of mobile technologies. Karl Ulrich, an operations and information management professor at Wharton, notes that each deal has its own story line, as the HP examples show. "Any particular acquisition will be motivated by an idiosyncratic mix of factors," he says, which range from intellectual property and brand cachet to operational expertise and price.

Whatever the story line is for the purchase itself, the acquired company has to fit into the buyer's larger corporate narrative, or else problems will develop. Experts at Wharton give both HP and Oracle credit for being able to pull off multiple acquisitions without any big disasters. Wharton experts note that HP has had a history of making acquisitions work. Mark Hurd, its CEO, has been adept at acquiring companies, cleaning them up and stitching them into the company's product portfolio, says Chaudhuri. In a conference call last month, Hurd noted that "all of our acquisitions have a pretty extensive filter in terms of [being] strategically sensible [and] financially sensible."

As for Oracle, in many respects it pioneered the approach to acquisitions that is now becoming prevalent in the tech sector. Oracle has acquired a series of former competitors—PeopleSoft, Siebel Systems and BEA Systems, to name a few—and some of the targets were struggling at the time they were bought.

Oracle's acquisition of Sun puts the company into the hardware business. Traditionally, Oracle has sold database applications that run behind the scenes at big companies. With Sun, Oracle is looking to offer complete systems and compete with the likes of IBM. "These companies are fierce competitors trying to move up from the No. 2 or No. 3 spot in a market and challenge the leader," says Chaudhuri. "These deals are strategic moves designed to buy specific pieces of a product portfolio."

The challenge for the acquirers is that they have to integrate their targets and then create a new market or product category. "HP isn't going to win by adding what everyone else has," says Hsu. "These [mergers] are really successful or they go up in flames. Companies need to have a plan as to whether they can integrate relevant knowledge and divest what was holding back the company. This is basically the leveraged buyout industry. An acquirer comes in to reorganize, make managerial decisions and create some value. It's the same idea here."

The Dangers Involved

While shopping for struggling technology companies can be full of potential, dangers lurk at the checkout counter. "All companies have to do the due diligence, understand what they are acquiring, know the IP and see if it fits," notes Hrebiniak. Indeed, experts at Wharton say these acquisitions raise a host of issues. For instance, some of these damaged brands were on the decline for a reason. Sun was innovative, but failed to make money from inventions such as Java. "Sun had visionary types who didn't know how to implement their technologies," says Chaudhuri. "Sun wasn't practical and lacked operations expertise. They were all technology dreamers."

The challenge to the acquiring companies is to right the ship, change the culture and keep the strong parts. If those tasks are not completed, buyers get stuck with a "value trap," or a purchase that looks like a bargain but never lives up to its potential. The risks involved with these acquisitions are part of the reason why companies such as Cisco tend to focus on smaller purchases that can easily be folded into operations. "If it's a struggling company, there's probably a reason why it's struggling," Hsu says. "There were poor choices by management, poor choices on product development and personnel issues." For instance, HP will have to take Palm's assets and strip out the behaviors that led to the company's struggles. "It wasn't always the case that Palm struggled. There are definitely assets there in the domain of intellectual property."

Gaining market share in search is what sparked Microsoft's original interest in Yahoo. Microsoft CEO Steve Ballmer said repeatedly that he wanted economies of scale in search to compete with Google. Since that initial effort, Microsoft launched the Bing search engine and is now integrating its search partnership with Yahoo. However, companies can't be blinded by the allure of a head start when it comes to dealing with integration challenges. Culture clashes, departing personnel and the inability to innovate are all risks, says Hsu.

Oracle CEO Larry Ellison has said he is confident that he can innovate with Sun. He told Reuters that Sun management "made some very bad decisions that damaged their business and allowed us to buy them for a bargain price." But he noted in a separate interview with *Wired* magazine that Sun had good engineers and technical managers. Chaudhuri describes the purchase of Sun as a "high risk, high reward deal." Oracle's core business has been software, and it has to prove that it can also sell servers and integrated hardware systems that compete with entrenched players like IBM. The challenge is not merely to make Sun more efficient: Oracle has to harness the best parts of Sun and use them to disrupt the existing market landscape.

"There are two steps to ensure a successful acquisition," says Chaudhuri. "First is the easy part with [implementing] the cost synergies. But companies need to go beyond that and innovate. Tech companies have never been about cost synergies. It's about the innovation that leads to new technologies."

Incomplete Endings and Murky Returns

One thing is certain: The acquisitions will persist as the technology industry continues to mature. IBM CEO Sam Palmisano said last month that the company plans to spend $20 billion on acquisitions between 2011 and 2015. Dell CEO Michael Dell said early this month that his company will continue to look for acquisitions. And other players show no signs of slowing down, either.

It's possible that the real returns on recent and future tech acquisitions will never be completely known, Wharton experts say. In leveraged buyout situations, a company may return to the public markets after becoming more efficient as a private firm. Investors in the revamped company can then measure performance every quarter.

Technology companies, however, often lump acquisitions into established units, so it's almost impossible to track sales after a deal closes. For instance, 3Com became HP's networking unit, which is combined with its enterprise server and storage unit. For its part, Oracle lumps its enterprise applications acquisitions into one division. "You can see the rationale for these acquisitions and you can see the prices paid," notes Chaudhuri. "But you don't know whether these companies remain also-rans. The verdict is out." ■

Published: June 9, 2010 in Knowledge@Wharton

Do You Know Where Your Kids Are?
Disney's Rich Ross Probably Does

Rich Ross is a morning person. This may be an asset in many professions, but Ross was starting out in the entertainment business—a field that's never been known for early risers. So back in 1986, when he showed up for his first day as a short-term freelancer at a fledgling cable network called Nickelodeon, he walked down a long, dark hallway where just one office light was on. As it happened, the woman sitting in that office, eating an oversized breakfast muffin, invited the rookie to sit down and join her. And for most of the 22-plus years since, she's been a mentor and boss as Ross, now the president of Disney Channels Worldwide, rose through the new world of cable television and ushered in a revolution in programming aimed at young viewers. His breakfast partner, Ann Sweeney, now runs the conglomerate's television group.

Ross told the story recently during a Wharton Leadership Lecture that stressed the career-making power of serendipity, personal connections and team-building. "The people around you are the people most able to help you with your career because they know you best," he said. "People close to you, people who might be in this room, are the ones who can help."

As president of Disney Channels Worldwide, Ross,whose office is in Burbank, Calif., leads the corporation's burgeoning universe of kids programming—94 channels available in 163 countries and 32 languages. He also has responsibility for Disney's 42 owned-and-operated radio stations.Even in a dour economy, Ross has been in the midst of launching a new channel and web site, Disney XD, aimed at six- to 14-year-old boys.

How does Disney manage in a world of illegal downloading and competition from free-of-charge YouTube sensations? Ross said it's as simple as making good shows. Early in his tenure, he pushed for creating original movies and content aimed at the "tween" demographic. "Tweens"—short for between—are the niche demographic betweenchildhood and adolescence that was first identified by the network. It's a big business market today, which means Disney is already competing with a number of other players.

"Disney had been making movies, but they were movies based on Dickens novels," said Ross. "No offense to my English major, but I don't think kids were running out for 'Old Curiosity Shop.'" He led the development of such popular-culture touchstones as the "Hannah Montana" franchise, "High School Musical" and "'tween" music sensations the Jonas Brothers.

Any Platform Will Do

At a time when traditional media companies, from newspapers to local broad-casters, are faltering, Ross said Disney has prospered by emphasizing quality content while not being picky about what platform could be used to display that content: "We can't leave our heads in the sand....People are getting [entertainment] in different ways. My boss made one of the first deals with iTunes for content. And people [said], 'Wow, are you crazy, what are you thinking?' But if we can make things available on something that people love, which clearly they do, and set a price point that makes sense, then that's a good business model."

Ross considers himself "very lucky to work for a company that puts content first, because that's where everyone comes. People are not buying diluted versions. They want the real thing. And we're lucky that we can do it....We've been given a mandate by our company: Eyes open. We're launching Disney XD in the middle of God-knows-what in our industry, and I've never gotten more support" from top executives.

In betting on content at a time when many in the media are settling for aggregation, Ross also relies on expertise about how young people navigate the dizzying array of devices for media consumption. "The multiplicity of options is astounding," he said. "What you often find is girls and boys differing. You walk into a girl's bedroom, she will have the computer open, she's IM-ing, the schoolbook is open, a magazine's on the bed, phones, the whole shebang. And [if] you turn to the girl and ask her about one of the interfaces, she'll tell you what's on it. Girls are very good at multitasking." As it happens, Disney's programming has skewed towards girls. "Boys are very linear," Ross said, noting that they tend to focus on one thing at a time—games, chats, TV or anything else. Disney XD will take advantage of some of these insights to craft an audience around boys in the tween demographic.

Ross's path to Disney was an unlikely one, shaped by serendipity and mentoring. As a student at the University of Pennsylvania, he worked summers at the William Morris talent agency, thanks to some family connections to people in the entertainment field. His mother, for example, had gone to summer camp with a woman who became Merv Griffin's bookkeeper. After earning his BA in the bleak job environment of 1983, Ross talked his way off the waiting list at Fordham Law School and earned his law degree in 1986—even though he wasn't particularly interested in being a lawyer. Instead, he wound up working his way out of the William Morris mailroom with a skill he had used to earn extra money in college: typing.

An array of jobs followed: That freelance assignment with Nickelodeon turned into a seven-year run. "I started in the talent department," Ross said. "I did celebrity booking. It was 20 years ago. I got Madonna, and it was like, how long is she going to last?" Further promotions turned him into a casting director—something he had never done before but which became a field of expertise. Ross said he would ask to meet the young actors' parents in an effort to gain critical insight into their kids. He eventually led the network's new European channels as a London-based vice president.

Watching Murdoch

Ross then followed mentor Sweeney to News Corporation's new FX channel, working for Rupert Murdoch, a man Ross described as a visionary. He occasionally got a ringside seat to observe the media baron in action. At one meeting, he recalled, Murdoch leaned over to an aide and asked him to look into the possibility of structuring a complex deal to acquire rights to show the Olympics in Asia on what was then his new Star TV satellite network. The aide returned with an answer 20 minutes later. "And it dawned on me—there was no Google at the time—that the guy had actually gone and called [International Olympic Committee chairman] Juan Antonio Samaranch and gotten an answer."

After three years at FX, Ross followed Sweeney to Disney, which had been an uninspiring television also-ran. Upon his arrival, he said, Sweeney told him that he had six weeks to create "a programming solution for this network. I looked around and that's where we came up with the tween strategy." Since then, his bailiwick has steadily expanded, encompassing the radio stations, CDs, toys and other gear. Last month, a slew of Ross's Disney talent performed for the first family at a kids' inaugural concert in Washington.

Though he spoke passionately about mentoring, Ross said the key to assembling a good team involves a certain contradiction: "One is find people you like. Two is do not find people just like you....You can't hire carbon copies of yourself. People talk about diversity in front of the camera. It's an imperative with me to have diversity behind the camera. And not just in skin tone or gender or whatever. It's in every way."

Ross predicted that despite the recession, demand for television content will stay strong. "Though we live in challenging times, now more than ever, kids and their families still need connections," he said. Professionally, it also helps to work at the most famous name in entertainment, one whose modern incarnation is a globalized entertainment firm that can be both comprehensive and nimble. "What I ask people is, 'Do you really want to bet against us?'" ∎

Published: March 4, 2009 in Knowledge@Wharton

Sprint's 4G Advantage:
Game Changer or Not Enough to Call Home About?

Sprint has a hot-selling phone with the HTC Evo 4G and a fast, next-generation data network, the first in the business to be up and running. The company is hoping to capitalize on that status to overcome a painful spate of customer defections and close the gap between itself and industry leaders Verizon Wireless and AT&T. But the jury is still out, experts say, because of problems Sprint has had in recent years with customer service, the short period in which it may have first-mover advantage and the lack, so far, of a blockbuster application that would keep it ahead.

Early in June, Sprint said sales of the Evo, the first mobile phone with so-called fourth-generation (4G) network capabilities, beat the wireless carrier's launch day record, previously held by the Palm Pre and Samsung Instinct. "It is terrific to see customers react so positively to this device," said Sprint CEO Dan Hesse in a statement. Sprint's 4G service, offered through a partnership with wireless startup Clearwire, is based on the WiMAX (short for Worldwide Interoperability for Microwave Access) telecommunications protocol. WiMAX promises access speeds of one to six megabits per second (Mbps), compared with 3G speeds ranging from 400 kilobits per second to two Mbps. The Evo 4G, which is manufactured by the Taiwan-based HTC Corporation, can use the speedy WiMAX network as well as current 3G networks.

The new-generation phone and network are intended to address capacity problems with the current wireless infrastructure, which is straining under the demand to provide increasingly more data services. The 4G technology will open the door to a wide range of new applications involving rich media such as video, ultimately allowing smartphones to assume more of the functionality of laptops.

The stakes are high for Sprint, which is looking to turn around years of customer losses. By being first with a 4G phone, Sprint can highlight its operating improvements and build some momentum before other carriers enter the market. Verizon is developing its 4G network—based on technology called Long Term Evolution, or LTE—in 2010 with a phone planned for sometime in 2011. AT&T is due to test its LTE system in 2011 with a more aggressive rollout planned for 2012.

But experts at Wharton, noting that Sprint has a limited window of opportunity to make gains on Verizon and AT&T, say that the company needs more than just a head start—and one new smartphone—to pull off a comeback. "Evo has done well so far," says Kartik Hosanagar, an operations and information management professor at Wharton, adding that "devices can certainly help bring in customers." But, he notes, "one needs a complete game changer [like the iPhone was in the United States for AT&T] to have a dramatic impact on market share."

Gerald Faulhaber, a business and public policy professor at Wharton, agrees that Sprint's new phone and faster 4G network may not be enough to put the company on top. "Sales for the Evo have been brisk, but Sprint has to tell people how WiMAX changes everything," says Faulhaber. "It's faster, but Sprint needs a new application to do something wonderful that consumers couldn't get elsewhere." But Kevin Werbach, a legal studies professor at Wharton, gives Sprint a fighting chance. "If Sprint can deliver on the promise of 4G as a faster, more robust mobile data infrastructure before its competitors, it could carve out a strong market niche," he asserts. "To do so, however, it needs a phone to get those iPhone, Droid and BlackBerry users to switch. That's where the Evo comes in."

Fighting a Reputation for Bad Service

Sprint also has to overcome its image problem. The company has been working to reverse a reputation for bad customer service going back to 2007 and early 2008, when the company experienced a series of high-profile snafus. It often dropped customers who called service help lines, sparred with a woman who complained about an erroneous $14,000 bill in a dispute that landed on YouTube and took heat for sending disconnect letters to U.S. soldiers serving overseas over roaming charges. Sprint eventually settled these spats, but not before drawing plenty of bad press and losing a lot of customers. As of March 31, Sprint had 48.1 million subscribers, down from 53 million at the end of 2006. Verizon had 92.8 million subscribers as of March 31, followed by AT&T's 87 million, according to figures from the companies.

Since the string of high-profile complaints, Sprint has been working diligently to lure customers back. It has lowered prices on its family plans and now offers money-back guarantees if new customers don't like the service. In mid-June, Sprint said that its customer satisfaction scores, as measured by the 2010 American Customer Satisfaction Index, had improved more than those of any other company over the last two years.

Though on the road to recovery, Sprint hasn't quite turned the corner. For 2009, the carrier lost 1.13 million net subscribers, an improvement on the 4.58 million customer defections in 2008. And while it has cut that number even further this year, the company is still in the loss column, down 75,000 net customers for the quarter ending March 31.

Saikat Chaudhuri, a management professor at Wharton, says that the industry's history should give Sprint hope. "The good thing about this industry is that with every new generation of technology there's an opportunity to make a comeback," notes Chaudhuri. "It's not guaranteed that if you do well in one generation that you'll continue to do well." Indeed, the telecom sector is chock-full of comebacks, Chaudhuri adds. For instance, the Droid handset put Motorola back in the game after being a no-show in the smartphone market. And Palm briefly resurrected itself with the popular Pre device—only to have that success stall later.

How Valuable Is the First-Mover Advantage?

The key question is how resourceful Sprint will be in capitalizing on its head start in 4G. Experts at Wharton say that a first-mover advantage is real, but that there are multiple variables that determine its impact over the long run.

Rahul Kapoor, a management professor at Wharton, recently published a paper in *Strategic Management Journal* which found that a firm's first-mover advantage from a new technology is greatly affected by the "ecosystem" in which the technology operates. In other words, a given innovation does not stand alone—a number of players need to build on the core innovation. "4G is a much improved technology from 3G, but it isn't just about Sprint," asserts Kapoor. "First-mover advantage is dependent on other players in the ecosystem." For instance, Kapoor says, Sprint "needs content creators, developers and others to offer products and services to make the best use of 4G. If those adjustments aren't synchronized, there will be less of a first-mover advantage."

The Evo is powered by Google's Android operating system and its app marketplace. New applications designed specifically to take advantage of 4G would rely on the army of Android software developers. Sprint needs to "hit that sweet spot where it nails the hardware, software and infrastructure to compete," says David Hsu, a management professor at Wharton. The problem? The company must "create a value proposition that will move me away from an existing service," Hsu adds. "The competitive landscape is fierce and Sprint has no leverage on the Android side because it's a common platform" on multiple phones and carriers.

What Sprint really needs is a compelling new use for a phone that can utilize 4G speeds, notes Hsu. Features like video chat and real-time video could get new customers to join Sprint, he says, but it's unclear how large the demand is for those services. Sprint's Evo offers video chat, but Apple's iPhone 4, its newest 3G model, just introduced FaceTime, a similar feature that allows two iPhones to host a videoconference over Wi-Fi. (Wi-Fi provides coverage for a range of 300 to 400 feet; Evo's system, WiMAX, permits access for up to 30 miles.) "For Sprint to succeed big with the Evo, it needs to convince users that data-intensive services like video chat and live streaming are compelling," says Werbach.

Faulhaber acknowledges the need for differentiated services if Sprint is going to make a comeback based on 4G, but says that the company needs an entire package to woo customers from AT&T and Verizon. "Technology itself never gives you a competitive advantage," says Faulhaber. "Most consumers want to know about the service or what Sprint is providing. It's about the new and exciting, not the technology. What is Sprint delivering to people?"

Some analysts believe that Sprint's Evo can now compete with Apple's iPhone 4 and Verizon's flagship Android devices such as the HTC Incredible because of its faster network, unlimited data plans and key new features, such as video chat. "The main advantage of the Evo in our view is the potential for true unlimited data usage for heavy users, particularly in 4G markets," Deutsche Bank analyst Brett Feldman said in a research note.

The Competition Isn't Far Behind

But those advantages may prove ephemeral because Sprint doesn't have much time before its rivals introduce their own 4G services, say experts at Wharton. Sprint's 4G lead may last only a year or two at best. Verizon's 4G technology, based on LTE, will be faster than Sprint's network when it launches in the next year. "I don't believe any first-mover advantage for Sprint is sustainable in the long run," asserts Hosanagar. "First, it will take a lot more than a 4G network to change Sprint's poor brand image. Second, there's the issue of technological uncertainty [WiMAX versus LTE]. It's not clear if Clearwire/Sprint will stick with WiMAX. A switch to LTE may not be trivial."

The picture is similar on the device side of the equation. Sprint's phone had the limelight for about two weeks. Then, on June 7, Apple CEO Steve Jobs unveiled the iPhone 4. Preorder demand for the device was so strong that Apple and AT&T were straining to keep up. Apple said that it sold more than 600,000 iPhone 4 devices in one day. In addition, Verizon plans to introduce a new Motorola Droid smartphone on July 23 to follow up on the strong sales of its HTC Incredible. (The new model will be an advanced 3G phone; Verizon's 4G entrant will not be unveiled until next year.)

Bob Brust, chief financial officer of Sprint, conceded that the competition among new devices is strong. Sprint has plans for follow-up 4G smartphones beyond the Evo. Speaking at an investment conference earlier in June, Brust said Sprint is in "a competitive landscape which we hope will be mostly fought with service, network quality and handsets." Faulhaber notes that Sprint has had trouble competing on all three of those fronts, however. "Sprint hasn't managed to get the customer service or coverage right," says Faulhaber. "And devices may not be that big of a deal. Sprint was the first one to have the Palm Pre and it didn't do much with it."

The challenge is to put all the moving parts together to become a true contender. "The smartphone battle has so far been a story of Apple versus everyone else," Werbach states. "The iPhone is the clear market leader, although Research in Motion has a solid position [with the BlackBerry] and Android devices are coming on fast. In the minds of users, the iPhone's Achilles heel is the carrier partner, AT&T. That creates an opening for Sprint and others, such as Verizon, if they can marry good service with a good device."

Chaudhuri agrees. "With the right branding and pricing combination, Sprint can come back," he says.

The Elephant in the Room

But the elephant in room with Sprint's 4G plans is the company's bruised image, Wharton experts say. "Companies with a reputation for poor service have a real problem," notes Faulhaber. "These reputations last and it takes years to [recover from] that." Indeed, J.D. Power & Associates in March rated Sprint last in wireless customer care among the major carriers, but its score of 721 on a 1,000-point scale was better than the 704 it got last year and wasn't far behind AT&T's score of 733 this year. Verizon and T-Mobile led the rankings with scores of 753 and 752, respectively.

Hsu says Sprint has made strides to overcome the image problem. Besides focusing on more family-friendly pricing and money-back guarantees, it has launched a number of subsidiary brands that are putting the parent company in the background. Sprint has used the new brands (including Assurance Wireless, Boost Mobile, Common Cents Mobile and Virgin Mobile, which it recently acquired) to concentrate on prepaid phone service. This type of service targets lower-margin customers who pay for minutes in advance instead of signing long-term contracts billed each month. The prepaid market isn't as profitable as targeting higher-end markets, Hsu points out, but Sprint may have other motives. "Sprint is big on this Evo device, but the company has been creating other businesses and brands in case Sprint does not do well over time," Hsu notes. "It's not impossible for the Sprint brand to come back, but it makes sense to obfuscate it in case something goes wrong."

Chaudhuri cautions, however, that having all of those subsidiary brands may make it necessary for Sprint to refocus. "What customer does Sprint really want to go after?" asks Chaudhuri. "I want to see more strategic clarity." Kapoor and Faulhaber assert that the launch of Evo and 4G service may allow Sprint to talk more about the improvements it has made to the business, including its gains in customer service as well as its differentiated pricing plans. "Sprint can use this 4G opportunity to enforce multiple messages at the same time," says Kapoor.

The one wild card is timing. Experts at Wharton say there are no rules about how long it takes for a company to turn around a poor reputation for customer service. On the bright side, Sprint's launch of the Evo at least gives it a chance to change the conversation. "The Evo is a good start for Sprint," says Hosanagar. "But it will take much more than one Evo to turn around its image." ∎

Published: June 23, 2010 in Knowledge@Wharton

Going Mobile: How iAD and AdMob
Move Apple vs. Google to a New Playing Field

What spending in the mobile advertising industry lacks in heft, it more than makes up for in buzz. Witness Google's recent purchase of AdMob, which brings together the two largest mobile ad networks, and Apple's recent efforts to gain a stronger foothold in the market.

On May 21, the Federal Trade Commission signed off on Google's $750 million acquisition of AdMob, a move that originally created antitrust fears because the two are the biggest players in the market of bringing ads to consumers' smartphones. Fears of dwindling competition were quashed in part due to Apple's own attempts to become a stronger player in the sector. Following an unsuccessful bid to buy AdMob, Apple in January purchased Quattro Wireless, the third largest mobile ad network, for $275 million. Last month, Apple introduced iAd, a service that places ads inside applications running on the company's mobile devices, including the iPhone and iPad.

In a statement permitting the Google/AdMob deal to move forward, FTC officials said they had "reason to believe that Apple quickly will become a strong mobile advertising network competitor," and that any competition lost because Google and AdMob are no longer jockeying to place ads on the former's Android platform will be made up for by rivalry between Android-enabled devices and the iPhone, where Apple will be using its iAd network exclusively.

The battle between two major players could represent a tipping point for mobile advertising, Wharton experts and others say, and suggests that the sector could become a significant money-maker in the future. "Mobile advertising is likely to be the next big thing," says Wharton marketing professor Eric Bradlow. "People are increasingly using their portable devices as computers and will have the same expectations for targeted ads as they do on the web today. What exact form those ads will take is unclear, especially with [the growth of] geo-targeting," or the ability to target a consumer based on where he or she lives, or is spending time at a given moment.

AdMob, one of the largest mobile ad networks, services billions of personalized ad impressions (views). The company reaches 160 countries and provides a suite of data and analytics services to help marketers track the traffic their ads receive. The company was founded in 2006 by Omar Hamoui who, in a past interview with Knowledge@Wharton, compared AdMob's services to the way Google handles ads on the Internet. While iAd will be specific to Apple products, Quattro—which offers similar services to AdMob—said at the time of its purchase that the company will continue to offer its network on all devices and platforms.

The motive behind Google's and Apple's acquisitions is clear: Define the market while the industry is young. Mobile ad spending in the United States, including text messaging-based formats, reached an estimated $416 million in 2009, compared with almost $24 billion that was spent overall for online advertising, according to eMarketer, a New York-based business information service. But the company predicts that spending on mobile ads will grow to $1.56 billion in the United States by 2013.

Meanwhile, the mobile ad land rush heightens the competition between Apple and Google, two companies that are already going head-to-head on mobile operating systems (Google's Android vs. Apple's iPhone OS) and the applications that go with those platforms, Wharton experts note. "Google's acquisition of AdMob is a smart move when you consider that Apple is also looking at mobile advertising," says Andrea Matwyshyn, a legal studies and business ethics professor at Wharton. "Google views advertising as core to its self definition. It couldn't cede mobile advertising to Apple."

Two Different Strategies

The companies' approaches to mobile advertising will be heavily influenced by their overall business strategies.

Apple is entering the sector with an eye to how it already markets other aspects of its product line—charging higher prices, but promising more bang for an advertiser's buck in terms of innovation and the opportunity to reach a coveted consumer audience. The company is constrained in the number of consumers it could reach with iAd because the service is limited to those who own its mobile devices. Google's Android operating system, however, is already offered on a number of different smartphone brands, and the ranks continue to grow. During the first quarter of this year, for example, phones running the Android system outsold the iPhone for the first time, according to NPD group, a research company.

"Apple won't be able to sustain the same reach with just a couple of devices, and advertising is fundamentally a medium about how many consumers you can reach," says Noah Elkin, a senior analyst with eMarketer. "But the profile of iPhone users is so attractive to advertisers that Apple is betting on being able to sell an advertiser on having access to this audience—that the cost may be a little more, but they are ultimately getting more in return."

Bloomberg BusinessWeek reported that Apple is expected to charge about $10 per 1,000 times an ad is displayed and $2 each time it's clicked on by a user, which works out to about $30 per 1,000 impressions. AdMob charges $10 to $15 on average and is paid for either ad impressions or clicks, as opposed to both, the magazine reported.

During the introduction of iAd last month, Apple CEO Steve Jobs demonstrated the type of media-rich promotions the company is hoping to bring to mobile devices. As an iPhone screen was displayed for the audience, he clicked on a banner ad for the movie Toy Story 3 that stretched across the bottom of a search results page listing entertainment news. The ad took up the phone's entire screen and included video clips, a game and a way to search for theaters showing the movie.

"The idea of ads as content has been...bandied about by advertisers for a long time but has never really been brought to fruition because consumers just see them as ads," Elkin states. "Apple's proposition [is] that it's going to create ads, but people will want to click on them because they are getting something valuable in return."

Matwyshyn says it should be interesting to watch how Apple and Google compete and shape their respective strategies for mobile advertising. "Apple's approach is less predictable," she notes. "If Apple comes up with something uniquely innovative with promotional opportunities, it could be perceived as a benefit by consumers, and Apple could gain users." At the same time, Apple could alienate users if it comes on too strong with mobile advertising.

Although Apple is hoping to cash in on the allure of its customer base, users of the Android platform have a similar profile, Elkin says. They are affluent enough to afford a smartphone and tend to be highly engaged with the devices.

"Google controls close to 70% of [computer] search; that's the core part of their business and I think they recognized that, with the iPhone and the growth of mobile apps, app stores and ad-supported apps, Apple has really hit on something," Elkin notes. "They realized that in addition to [focusing on] search on mobile devices, there was this important display ad medium, whether it was on websites accessed through a mobile browser or apps that are supported by display advertising. [Mobile advertising] was a market they couldn't ignore."

The AdMob acquisition gives Google "the dominant position in the mobile advertising space," says Kartik Hosanagar, an operations and information management professor at Wharton. "This not only opens up a new growth opportunity for Google but also has great synergies with Google's existing offerings. Google can now offer advertisers a single platform to access the lion's share of search and mobile ad inventory."

In a blog post, Susan Wojcicki, vice president of product management at Google, wrote that growth in mobile advertising "is only going to accelerate," and publishers, developers, marketers and consumers should all benefit. The combination of AdMob's network with Google's Android operating system, search advertising, analytics and DoubleClick, which serves online display ads, offers a powerful ecosystem to advertisers, says Hosanagar.

Meanwhile, Apple is trying to leverage its market advantages to take hold of a similar opportunity. "There's a lot of money to be made here," says Kendall Whitehouse, director of new media at Wharton. "Apple is already a content gatekeeper on its mobile platforms, and moving to advertising is a straightforward transition....Apple's vertical integration with the iTunes store, mobile devices and the Mac gives it a strong hand in moving into advertising."

But Elkin points out that both companies' models have advantages and limitations. "Having an open platform is an advantage; it makes it easier for partners to work with Google [including] handset partners and ad networks.... The downside of it, and this is where Apple's value proposition lies, is not having control over the experience from beginning to end. Of course, having so much control has its downside, too, in terms of what the consumer ultimately gets and also the perception that you're not really free to do what you want, whether you're an advertiser or a consumer."

Despite the companies' different approaches, it is doubtful either will cede control of the mobile advertising space, Hosanagar says. "Given Apple's penchant for control over its full ecosystem, I doubt Apple is going to watch someone else extract all the ad dollars that will be generated on its platforms."

Why Mobile Advertising

How big is the growth potential for mobile advertising? Big enough to be a potential game-changer for the companies, Wharton experts say.

"Mobile advertising certainly represents the biggest growth opportunity for Google," says Hosanagar. To date, Google has mostly been a one-trick pony, with most of its revenue deriving from Internet search advertising. With the purchase of AdMob, the company's future growth could revolve around mobile advertising.

The combination of Google and AdMob will derive revenue from five primary sources, according to Caris & Co. analyst Sandeep Aggarawal. The merged companies will service mobile advertisements and deliver ads within mobile applications, paid search results on mobile phones, text messaging ads and recommendations to download particular applications.

"There are close to four billionmobile phones globally vs. only 1.2 billion computers," Aggarawal wrote in a research note. "Google generated $1.00 in paid search revenue per PC in the installed base in 2003, [a figure] that reached $21.50 by the end of 2009. Even if Google can generate $1.00 per mobile phone in the installed base by 2013, it can be a $4 billion revenue opportunity." In addition, the ability to better target users with mobile ads means that Google's advertising partners could more easily convert clicks to actual purchases. "What you see in the Google and Apple moves is the importance of data and analytics," says Steve Ennen, managing director of the Wharton Interactive Media Initiative. "With mobile advertising, you can see what users are actually doing [behaviorally]."

It's unclear whether the relationship between Google and Apple will be further strained by their respective forays into mobile advertising. Google's services power multiple features on the iPhone, ranging from search to YouTube to Google Maps. While those features may continue, Apple may move to control more of the advertising revenue derived from those services. "On the advertising side, both Google and AdMob make significant revenue from iPhone and apps," Aggarawal wrote. "We believe that Google's and AdMob's combined revenue [from] Apple is around $150 million to $200 million."

While both Google and Apple see mobile advertising as a future growth market, the industry is still emerging. United Kingdom-based Juniper Research estimated in June 2009 that mobile advertising will be a $6 billion market worldwide in 2014. However, that sum will only account for 1.5% of the global spending on advertising in 2014.

"Both acquisitions are about the ecosystem and the move to mobility," says Ennen. "This moves beyond just smartphones to the iPad and other devices."

Wharton management professor David Hsu agrees, noting that interest in mobile ads will grow along with the rapidly expanding smartphone market. "Moves like Wal-Mart discounting the iPhone 3GS to $97 will have a substantive impact. And that's just the hardware side," he says. "The carrier fees for data access are still not necessarily accessible by the majority of the population, but that's likely to change. People will become more accustomed to accessing data on the go, and it's on those platforms that mobile ad networks become quite important."

AdMob founder Hamoui was in Hsu's classes as a Wharton MBA student when he came up with the idea for the ad network. "That was in 2006 and, just a few short years later, Apple and Google are fighting over the company," Hsu says. "I think that shows how quickly movement within the space is [happening] with respect to its development."

A Challenge of Location and Context

Advertising within mobile applications will be "as big as [its ability to be] contextual and targetable," Bradlow notes. By harnessing the data related to location and customer habits available from smartphones, Google and Apple can do a better job of positioning ads as a helpful tool for consumers, rather than nuisances that get in the way of a search or the use of an application.

But the companies may find that the mobile ad market is more complex than that of traditional Internet advertising. For one thing, ads are only one way to generate revenue in the mobile arena. "The reason advertising was so successful on the web was that it was the only game in town for monetizing content," says Whitehouse. Mobile users are already paying to load their phones with applications, ringtones and music; bombarding them with ads as well may be perceived as too pushy, he adds. "People will tolerate some mobile advertising, but there may be barriers to user acceptance at the beginning. Marketers will need to make sure their ads aren't too intrusive."

Matwyshyn suggests that mobile advertising could overcome some of those roadblocks by combining promotions with a social networking component that would "encourage consumers to make a decision on one vendor over another."

As an example, she pointed to Groupon, a website offering markdowns on restaurants, attractions and services that are activated only after a certain number of consumers commit to purchasing. Those who have already signed up for the site are encouraged to invite friends to do the same in order for everyone to earn the day's discount.

The more Google and Apple understand their users, the more intimate mobile advertising will become, notes Hosanagar, who describes mobile advertising as "a combination of location and context." Companies are getting more adept at delivering ads based on a user's location, but are still learning how to offer discounts within the context of a consumer's activities at that location. "It does not help to show an ad from a neighborhood restaurant or salon if they are not relevant to my current context," Hosanagar points out. "Am I sipping coffee at a cafe? Or in a meeting with colleagues from work? Or looking for dining options? The context part can be inferred from the content being browsed—something Google does well—and also from user-specified updates like those on [location-based social networking sites like] Foursquare. At the end of the day, being able to combine location with context will drive consumer response in mobile advertising." ∎

Published: May 26, 2010 in Knowledge@Wharton

PART 4

Leveraging Strategic Opportunities in Emerging Markets

Playing on a Global Stage: Asian Firms See a New Strategy in Acquisitions Abroad and at Home

Asia has become the world's hottest arena for mergers and acquisitions.

European and American companies are seeking a larger presence in the world's fastest-growing economies even as Asian companies with strong local currencies and ample credit are pushing to enter new markets or consolidate existing ones at home. During the first quarter, Asian M&A activity more than doubled from a year earlier while activity in the United States and Europe declined, according to merger-market tracker Dealogic.

With Asian emerging markets catapulting out of the global recession much faster than developed markets, "the economic situation is a catalyst," says Wharton management professor Saikat Chaudhuri, noting that the trend started earlier due to "emerging markets' globalization as these players [began to] look for new opportunities to grow. Asian firms want to become global players. This is the next step in their evolution."

Wharton management professor Harbir Singh, vice dean for global initiatives, says M&A appetite varies among countries. For example, the worldwide economic slowdown affected China more than India because its manufacturing exports were hurt. In addition, because the Chinese yuan is pegged to the dollar, Chinese firms have not had the currency boost to help them buy aggressively.

Overall, M&A activity in Asia is moving rapidly toward equality with more established U.S. and European takeover hotbeds. For the first quarter of 2010, Dealogic reported that Asia Pacific M&A, excluding Japan, jumped 126% to $141 billion and accounted for a record 23% of announced global M&A volume. It was only 10% a year earlier and 13% in the first quarter of 2008, according to the data. Add in Japan, where most of the M&A activity is inside the country, and Asia Pacific volume totaled $166 billion, up 79% from the year earlier and more than the $162 billion total for Europe, which declined 3%. The U.S. market, the world's largest, fell 11% to $220 billion in the quarter. Asia's totals were boosted by the inclusion of the single biggest deal in the quarter—British insurer Prudential PLC's $35.5 billion acquisition of American International Group's Asian life insurance business. Dealogic's methodology assigns activity based on where the acquired operation is located. Even excluding that deal, activity in Asia grew while Europe and the U.S. shrank.

Change in Strategy

For many years, Asian companies were reluctant to embark on international acquisition as a strategy. They didn't have the capital or borrowing capabilities to make big purchases. And government restrictions in countries like India, China and Japan often made it difficult for firms in the developed world to acquire Asian companies.

But a few Asian companies showed that big international acquisitions could work. India's Mittal Steel started making overseas acquisitions in 1989; in 2006, when the company acquired Europe's Arcelor, it became the world's biggest steelmaker. China's Lenovo Group became a household name after it acquired IBM's PC business in 2005.

Since 2000, Asian M&A as a share of the worldwide market has grown from 10% to 26% last year. Some of the growth in share reflects a decline in the overall market. Indeed, 2007, when there was $728 billion in activity, remains the record for Asia. Last year, Asia accounted for $625 billion in activity, according to Dealogic.

Farhan Faruqui, head of global banking in Asia Pacific at Citigroup, told The Wall Street Journal that he expects Asia will steadily increase its global share of M&A activity and will frequently represent one third of global activity in the future. "Dialogues with clients suggest that M&A volume will be substantially higher in Asia this year," he adds.

According to Wharton management professor Lawrence G. Hrebiniak, Asian companies view acquisitions as a way to outgrow their rivals. They can increasingly take advantage of their strong local currencies and available bank loans to make acquisitions, both inside their countries and overseas, he suggests. "A lot of companies have cash, and higher interest rates in developing markets strengthen their currencies" relative to the dollar and the euro. For example, from last November to mid-April, the dollar has declined 7.6% against the Indian rupee, 5.6% against the South Korean won and 6.6% against the Indonesian rupiah.

Stronger currencies give Asian companies a cushion in their acquisition strategy. "Mergers fail because people pay too much of a premium," Hrebiniak says. "If your currency is strong, you can get a bargain." Asian companies face the same issues as other companies in making mergers succeed, he adds, but "a strong currency absolutely helps. Things are cheaper." The currency advantage is particularly significant when an Asian company is bidding against a Western company that has to borrow or issue stock in its home currency and then make an acquisition in a market with a stronger currency.

Asian companies used to regard M&A as "risky," says Singh. "Now it's seen as an acceptable mode of growth." One reason is that as companies have grown, "in some industries, there's no other choice." Wireless telecommunications is a classic example where "it's clear that the economies of scale are such that you can't have hundreds or even tens of companies." Other industries such as specialty chemicals and pharmaceuticals also have been consolidating because of global economies of scale, he says.

Another trend boosting the acquisitiveness of Asian firms is investors' acceptance of conglomerates, says Hrebiniak. "In the U.S., we don't like diversified firms. We devalue diversification. Asian countries value growth by acquisition."

Widely diversified companies such as India's Tata Group and South Korea's LG Corp. are among their nation's most powerful, he adds.

Singh also points to cultural changes, noting that in Asian markets there has been increasing acceptance of working for global companies headquartered elsewhere—an acceptance that has strengthened the willingness of Asian companies to be acquired and to make international acquisitions.

Finally, changes in developed markets make companies more willing to be acquired, Chaudhuri states. "Targets come cheaper and with less resistance if Western firms are hurting." That explains the fact that "Asia players are buying into developed markets. When business is going well, companies are more hesitant to be bought."

Managing with Uncertainty

While Western companies are buying in Asia, Asian companies are also moving to consolidate their home markets and to reach overseas into new markets. In some cases, they are buying troubled outfits cheaply in an effort to learn how a foreign market operates.

There is some evidence that Asian companies may have more success with acquisitions than Western companies have had, according to Chaudhuri. He points to an A.T. Kearney study concluding that Indian companies were less likely to overpay for acquisitions than most acquirers. "They may be more prudent because they don't have as many resources," Chaudhuri says.

He speculates that executives from India and other developing Asian countries may have more success than Western managers because they are used to handling vast cultural differences in their home markets. Wealth variations in India or China are much greater than they are in the West. In India, in particular, "there are so many cultural divides," including language, religion and caste. "An Indian company may not know how to manage French culture, but it understands how to manage cultural differences."

Chaudhuri says it is also possible that building a company in the developing world—and dealing with imperfect information and constant change—gives a manager experiences he or she wouldn't get in the developed world. "Western companies have trouble managing with uncertainty. Asian firms may be more adept at this," he suggests.

The growth in Asian M&A is contributing to moves by Western banks to expand rapidly in the region. On April 20, J.P. Morgan Chase announced it had poached a top banker from HSBC Holdings to head its corporate banking business in China, which comprises both investment banking and treasury services. The same week, Credit Suisse said it had hired J.P. Morgan's top investment banker in India to head up its own investment banking operation there.

Nevertheless, the growth of Asian M&A is likely to have its rough patches. Many studies have determined that between 40% and 60% of all acquisitions turn out to be failures in terms of boosting market value of the acquired company by more than the amount invested. Acquisitions of Asian companies and by Asian companies face the same hurdles as M&A activity elsewhere, says Hrebiniak. "They have to think about the strategic reasons for making an acquisition—the logic of it. If they're trying to achieve economies of scale in manufacturing, they have to integrate pretty rapidly. Crushing two companies together is hard."

India-based Tata Motors' painful experience in buying two British automakers from Ford may frighten some Asian acquirers. Tata, which says it is among the top five commercial vehicle manufacturers in the world, acquired Jaguar and Land Rover from Ford for $2.5 billion in 2008. So far, the transaction has been a failure, with both luxury car and SUV sales plunging in the recession. The acquired companies contributed to Tata's first annual loss in seven years and Tata's debt rating has repeatedly been downgraded. Earlier this year it named a German auto-industry veteran to turn around the car operations.

In addition, legal barriers can hinder acquisitions in some countries. Even in the U.S., ownership of television stations is restricted to U.S. citizens, and foreign firms cannot own more than 25% of an airline. China has many restrictions on foreign ownership, according to Chaudhuri, and the Chinese government can also trip up domestic companies when they try to make overseas acquisitions. A plan by a Chinese company to buy General Motors' iconic Hummer SUV line fell apart under murky circumstances. Sichuan Tengzhong Heavy Industrial Machinery Co. said in February that Chinese regulators hadn't approved its $150 million bid for the unit. Neither the company nor the government disclosed any reasons for the regulators' stance at the time. As a result, GM closed down Hummer, a brand that until a couple of years ago was one of the automaker's biggest money makers.

Such missteps are to be expected in acquisitions, experts say. "Asian acquirers tend to be long-term focused," says Chaudhuri. "If they are buying access to markets, they will give autonomy to their target. They are trying to learn from the firms they acquire. They aren't aggressive on meeting cost targets right away." So long as their home economies and home currencies are stronger than those in Europe and the U.S. they will have an advantage in bidding. "They can afford to do it if their price premiums are lower." ∎

Published: April 28, 2010 in Knowledge@Wharton

"Walk the Market": Tapping into Africa's 900 Million Consumers

When multinational companies want to tap into the massive pent-up consumer demand in emerging markets, the first countries that they usually think of are China and India. But what about Africa, asks Vijay Mahajan, author of *Africa Rising: How 900 Million Consumers Offer More Than You Think* (Wharton School Publishing). Though often overlooked in global corporate growth strategies, he argues, Africa as a whole has enough consumer power to give China and India a run for their money.

Having returned from various fact-finding missions, he uses his new book to dissect the vast, complex markets of Africa, starting with a look at the home-grown entrepreneurs who have overcome political, economic and social barriers to grow and innovate. For multinationals, particularly those facing shrinking revenues from other emerging markets affected by the global economic downturn, the lessons are timely.

The topic isn't entirely new for Mahajan, a marketing professor at the University of Texas in Austin. In 2006, he was co-author of *The 86% Solution: How to Succeed in the Biggest Marketing Opportunity of the 21st Century* (Wharton School Publishing), a look at how companies can reach the vast majority of the population in countries with a per capita gross national product of less than $10,000. In an interview with Knowledge@Wharton, Mahajan talks about Africa Rising.

An edited transcript of the conversation follows.

Knowledge@Wharton: What is the market opportunity that Africa offers? And why do so many companies tend to overlook it?

Vijay Mahajan: Your first question is the heart of the book. Like most of us, I did not realize until I started working on the book that the population of Africa—at about 950 million—is comparable in size to the population of India. And if you look at growth rates, the population could be equal in size in a few years to the population of even China.

The next point is about market opportunity. Are there consumers in Africa who have the resources to buy products like consumers in India and China do? The fact is that the GDP of Africa—that is, looking at the continent as if it were a sort of United States of Africa—is actually higher than India's. If all the countries in Africa combined forces, they would be the 10th largest economy in the world, one notch above India, and ahead of the other big emerging economies, Brazil and Russia.

In terms of market opportunity, the data I was collecting was so intriguing that it drove me to visit Africa and to speak with a range of companies there, from local entrepreneurs to U.S. and European multinationals. And at the end of the day, I was convinced that the market opportunities in Africa for all kinds of products are similar to the market opportunities that you see in places like India.

Why has Africa been ignored? That has puzzled me. When I travelled from Southern Africa to Northern Africa, I was surprised that I didn't see more U.S. or Western European companies than I did. One U.S. multinational with an exceptionally big presence is Coca-Cola. It has been there more than 90 years. Another company with a big presence there is Unilever, the Anglo-Dutch consumer goods producer. So while there are some multinationals, it's not to the same extent as what I saw in India and China when I was researching my previous book, *The 86% Solution*.

The other thing is that here in the United States and in other developed countries, we get nothing but bad news about Africa in the press. Not to criticize CNN, but you know how badly the Africa that is portrayed in the media like CNN is. The CEOs I was interviewing were so happy that, for the first time, a professor from America was interested in learning about what they were doing.

But it could just be a matter of time. When I started working on The 86 Percent Solution 15 years ago, I used to hear the same stories from many Indian and Chinese entrepreneurs.

Knowledge@Wharton: Africa is clearly a large market, but it is obviously not a monolithic market. How is the market structured across the different countries?

Mahajan: The market is not different from any other developing country. After speaking with a lot of advertising agencies, multinationals and local entrepreneurs, I decided that there are three major groups in Africa, which I refer to in the book as Africa 1, Africa 2 and Africa 3. The terminology is actually taken from an Indian entrepreneur mentioned in the book.

Africa 1 comprises between 5% and 15% of the population of each country. These people could be from anywhere in the world. They may be senior government officials, expats, people working for [non-government organizations], people working for large, international banks. This segment was not as interesting to me as the others.

The segment that really was interesting is what I call Africa 2. People in this segment are neither poor nor rich; this segment comprises average people living from month to month. They may have some savings. And you can guess that these people are civil servants—hardworking nurses, hardworking teachers and so on—or work in the hospitality industry.

This segment has very high aspirations. These people believe Africa is going somewhere, and they are upbeat. I spend a lot of time in the book on what a big opportunity Africa 2 is. The size of this group is between 35% and 50% of a country's population, the equivalent of between 350 million and 500 million people. Divide that number by 5, which is the average size of a family in Africa (in the U.S., it is 3; in India it is 4)....So there is a very viable Africa 2, which is really going to drive the economy and the consumer markets.

Now, Africa 3—the remaining 35% to 60% of an African country's population—is the one that is struggling. These are the stories that you typically hear about. But that number is not any different from other developing countries. After all, there are 700 million people in India and 750 million people in China who do not have access to a toilet. What's interesting about Africa 3 is that many of them work for Africa 2 and Africa 1, as maids and the like, and they aspire to perhaps one day be part of Africa 2.

Knowledge@Wharton: Would you be able to give a few examples of innovative, home-grown firms or burgeoning sectors that have identified opportunities in Africa?

Mahajan: One example of a remarkable firm is a company in Kenya called Mabati Rolling Mills. The name is the Swahili word for the rolled metal roofing that many Kenyans use for their houses. For people in Africa 2 and Africa 3, one of their main goals when they save some money is to build a house. So they build one room at a time, which may take years to complete. And they need a roof— that is, the 20 to 30 roofing sheets they need, which they will slowly buy, two or three at a time. You will often see people transporting the sheets on top of a taxi or balanced on two bicycles. Mabati's entrepreneurs saw that need and the company is now the dominant manufacturer of the $180 million metal roofing market in Kenya. It's also continuously updating its product lines, and now exports to around 50 countries world-wide.

Then there's the film industry. For example, Nigeria's Nollywood makes more movies than India's Bollywood in India and Hollywood [in the U.S]. The quality, of course, is questionable. And many countries do not have cinemas, so every Nollywood movie is available only on tape, not even DVD or CD.

Another burgeoning area is cosmetics or personal-care products, keeping in mind that African women are not any different from women anywhere else. While many multinationals have not tailored their products as much as they could to suit African consumers, locals have, and so you will see a lot of local hair products.

There's also a big market for used, or second-hand, products. When you or I change our mobile every two or three years, we do not even think about where it might end up. Actually, the used mobiles from Europe and the United States often go to Africa.

And interestingly, death, too, has a role to play. Although it may not be openly admitted in many of these countries, death is often a celebration. Many people use their savings if someone close to them dies, and they host a wake or what have you. You can imagine when a whole community is invited. So some companies have been set up to cater to those occasions.

Knowledge@Wharton: You mentioned Coca-Cola and Unilever. What are multinationals doing to serve the underserved markets in Africa?

Mahajan: In the last chapter of the book, I talk about "ubuntu," a Zulu word meaning, "I am because you are." In other words, we are in this together. Desmond Tutu uses the word to evoke harmony. And I tried to give it a business twist. The way I see it is that companies cannot exist unless they take care of their employees and they take of their customers.

A case in point is Coca-Cola. It has distribution centers in almost every nook and cranny of the continent, whether it means transporting their goods on buses, on donkeys, on bicycles or by whatever means. Why not use that network to distribute condoms? So Coca-Cola has been working with NGOs like Population Services International, based in Washington, D.C., to help deliver condoms to parts of remote parts of Africa.

Unilever, meanwhile, is involved in HIV initiatives that I saw in Southern Africa, which are very different from other initiatives. There they have focused on the orphans of families where both the parents have died because of AIDS. Unilever helps to find adopted mothers to raise these children.

Beyond ubuntu, something else that you see at successful multinationals in Africa is a very clear understanding of consumers. They know that they have to do more on this continent [than in other developing countries] given the spectrum of the consumer they have to deal with.

Knowledge@Wharton: Given your marketing background, what struck you most about marketing in Africa?

Mahajan: I often saw kids buying a bottle of Coke, which is expensive, and they would put the bottle right in the middle of the table so everybody can see it, and they would have enough glasses out to share that Coke with friends. It is an aspiration product. Aspiration also is an important element that I saw in many of marketing campaigns.

Another thing to keep in mind there is that Africa has a young population. A little more than 40% of the population is younger than 15, compared with about 30% in India. That's why the use of sports in advertisements is very predominant. So is music.

Knowledge@Wharton: What about pricing strategies? Do they address Africa 1, Africa 2 and Africa 3?

Mahajan: Something I had seen in other developing countries was the predominance of the "lowest coinage strategy." So when you and I buy a bottle of water here, we pay whatever we need to pay—sometimes $1 or at airports we might be paying even higher. You would find that bottled water there from multinationals, such as Nestle. But the local entrepreneurs have developed products that they sell at the lowest monetary unit, which, for example, in Nigeria is 5 naira. But the water might not be sold as it would be in developed countries, and many times it may not be filtered water. It may be the tap water, but they sell it in a small plastic bag.

Now, who is buying that? In many cases, it could be people standing in front of a mosque or a church or a temple and asking passersby for money. Because it's so hot, they cannot go the entire day without water. Some entrepreneurs figured out that that they could sell water to these people, at the lowest currency.

Knowledge@Wharton: What are the major hurdles that you found, political or otherwise, that companies face?

Mahajan: When I was there, I made a point of not talking to any politicians or any chambers of commerce. I figured that politics is not any different than in India and China, and I wanted to avoid that. Putting aside all the rules and regulations, I wanted to see how companies are able to still get close to Africa's 950 million consumers.

I saw some very creative solutions. For example, one of the most interesting companies that I studied was Innscor, a fast-food restaurant chain from—of all the places—Zimbabwe. But the interesting thing I discovered about this company was how they are able to cope with their country's turmoil by, for example, expanding into other parts of Africa.

Then there's its crocodile farm, the largest in the world. I asked Innscor's executives: "You have the restaurants and you also have a distribution channel used by multinationals to ship their products, so why this crocodile farm?" The answer was that because of the political situation, they realized that they would not have access to foreign currencies. So the crocodile farm, you can guess—the skin is sold to Europeans and the meat to Chinese.

Knowledge@Wharton: You referred to China and India. In both countries, there is an overseas diaspora that gets actively engaged in the development efforts of the homeland. Did you find the same sort of phenomenon in Africa as well?

Mahajan: Yes, diaspora is involved in Africa. According to estimates based on formal and informal remittances, Africa gets about $40 billion a year, the same amount that India gets. And there are organizations, such as one in London called Recruit Africa, which has been set up to help African emigrants find jobs. But in the book, I make a plea to the African diaspora to really get more involved.

Mo Ibrahim, the founder of mobile-phone company Celtel, is part of the diaspora. He was originally from Sudan, educated in Alexandria, got his Masters and PhD in England while working for British Telecom, and then started the mobile phone company in Kenya. And it is a fascinating story—how he dealt with no electricity, how he provides customer service to all these rural areas, and so on.

He is just one example of many from the diaspora who are returning home to start up companies. The university in Ghana, Ashesi University College, was started in 2002 by a Ghanian, Patrick Awuah, who was part of the diaspora. He was a former software engineer at Microsoft and has created a very nice undergraduate university.

The person who was the head of Coca-Cola in Africa when I was finishing the book, Alex Cummings, is part of the diaspora. He is from Liberia, came to the United States to get his education, and now he has been promoted to chief administrative officer for the entire company at its global headquarters in Atlanta.

There are an estimated 100 million Africans living away from home. But the immigrants who are still connected to their homes—like the immigrants from India and China—are sometimes very innovative. I've been seeing some very clever ways that the diaspora is involved in talent, in helping their families to start businesses back home.

Knowledge@Wharton: What advice would you give to companies that want to tap into Africa?

Mahajan: The advice that I am going to offer is not any different than what I would offer for India and China. I met with some very interesting Unilever executives when I was in Harare, Zimbabwe, and they told me that if you really want to understand Africa, you have to go on "consumer safari." You have to go and see with your own eyes what is going on. A Coca-Cola executive in Kenya also gave me the same advice. And that's not always the case. Many companies, they said, manage their Africa businesses from their headquarters in Europe. If the top management is not there, they do not really understand the market themselves, and they do not get involved with the local institution. So the good advice that I was given was to "walk the market."

I would encourage companies to turn to that diaspora for help in penetrating those countries. To my great surprise or ignorance, I found out that the number of immigrants from Africa to the U.S. is close to 1.1 million, which is slightly less than from India. Also, 10% of the population from North Africa is in Europe now. So you are talking about 100 million North Africans, and 10 million of them are in Europe, sending a lot of money back home. There is also a lot of talent there.

Another thing I would suggest is to think about making acquisitions. There are many local entrepreneurs who are running remarkable companies, just like China and India. For example, there's a supermarket chain in East Africa called Nakumatt. It's just like a U.S.-style supermarket, but customized and it is growing very rapidly. If somebody wants to go into retailing, I would see Nakumatt as a very nice candidate that they could leverage to really penetrate those markets.

The situation in Africa is not any different from India and China. You have to really get to know that continent and see for yourself what opportunities exist there. ∎

Published: July 15, 2009 in Knowledge@Wharton

China's Growing Talent for Innovation

As a business innovator, China has a wealth of advantages. These include a huge, adaptable population with an affinity for improvisation and reverse engineering; low-cost labor, operations and overhead; and mature industrial clusters ready to supply a variety of parts, components and subassemblies. These elements are creating a strong culture of innovation, one that companies from developed economies soon will either profit from, or compete against, as China moves beyond labor-intensive, low-value-added consumer goods.

Already, many large multinational corporations (MNCs) have set up R&D centers in China, and the government is encouraging the development of design capabilities among its workforce. But China is not an easy place for outsiders to be innovators. Companies from developed economies looking for R&D partners in China must learn to operate within an industrial structure quite different from their own, and take great care in selecting whom to work with and how, experts caution.

MNCs are likely to find that the best opportunities for harnessing Chinese-style innovation lie in two areas: discrete, targeted pieces of larger products and products for home-market consumption.

In this article, part of a special report on Chinese manufacturing, experts from The Boston Consulting Group (BCG) and Wharton look at how companies can profit from Chinese innovation, what drives this innovation, and what challenges they face in sourcing R&D in China.

Global Recession's Role

Jim Andrew, a senior partner and managing director in BCG's Chicago office and head of its global innovation practice, says that in the current recession, companies need to ensure that they are getting full benefit from every dollar they spend—including their investments in innovation. Andrew sees growing innovation in low-cost countries such as China and India as one way for companies to increase the cost-effectiveness of their innovation spending. "The crisis in the developed markets has accelerated the move to developing markets because they are lower-cost and now have a track record," he says, noting that the changes afoot are redefining the innovation landscape. "We will look back on this time and say it was an inflection point with regard to the speed at which certain innovation activities were scaled up in China and India in particular. There is really a step-function change in the rate at which some of these activities are growing."

Innovation in China before its economy opened up was limited to design institutes that were part of government departments, says David Michael, a senior partner and director of BCG's Beijing office. Some of institutes have since been repurposed for new commercial goals. Such is the case with the state-owned oil company PetroChina, which has a large network of design institutes within it, according to Michael.

MNCs now realize that China has tremendous development capabilities, including the ability to size up opportunities and rapidly bring products to shelves at low cost. The availability of well-educated talent is particularly attractive, Andrew says. "You can access that talent to do a lot more of the "R" (research) that is increasingly relevant not just to China's domestic markets but to developed markets." For MNCs that set up R&D centers in China, "It is more about accessing talent rather than some unique source of innovation," Michael notes. That makes innovation in China substantially different from that in other global hubs such as the Silicon Valley. "There is low-cost engineering talent in China, but that's different from saying that there is a whole fountain of innovation we can tap into," he adds.

This raw engineering talent is a valuable resource for companies from developed economies. The best way for MNCs to tap into Chinese design skills is by sourcing select pieces of their product, Michael says. As is true for contract manufacturing, much of the advantage of Chinese R&D is in low-cost labor— but for brains, not brawn. "When Western or world-class business practices line up with low Chinese costs, new types of companies develop to take advantage of this opportunity," he notes.

In health sciences, for instance, some Chinese companies are already responding to Western research needs with low-cost services. Michael offers WuXi PharmaTech in Shanghai's Waigaoqiao Free Trade Zone as an example. WuXi, a leading provider of contract research work for the global pharmaceutical industry, has become adept at setting its engineers to work on Western pharma projects. "It's run by people who understand the needs of Western pharmaceutical companies and know how to leverage local engineering talent to do the work."

This kind of division of labor is common in such East-West partnerships. Western companies typically tap into Chinese design for parts or modules, Michael says. One global energy company gets "a lot of its design for oil exploration and drilling facilities in China at the local oil companies' design institutes," he notes. Microsoft and other Western and Korean gaming and software development companies have a network of local software developers. Michael also points to Perfect World, a Chinese gaming software writer that "is booming in the 3-D world." It may not be a household name in the United States or Europe yet, but Perfect World is a leader in the country's online game market, according to Morgan Stanley Research.

Development Attitude and Disruption

Such industry specialization is common. Corporate R&D in China tends to focus on specific industries and on product development rather than basic research, says Marshall Meyer, a Wharton management professor whose research focuses on China. "You see successes in China in machine tools and lasers, but it has been a combination of development and marketing more than basic research."

Chinese companies have been good at the "D" (development) part, Andrew says. "You could grow very large very quickly by playing in existing markets if you developed new products that were just a little better than everybody else's. But with increased competition everywhere, it takes products and services that are more innovative and targeted to needs that are not already being met." One recent example is a soybean blender that produces a popular soy milk drink. Joyoung Co. in Jinan, China's Shandong province, manufactures the blender, which has become "a big hit product." The blender has no fancy technology—just a plastic body with an electric motor, but its "fundamental concept is what local consumers want," he says.

More dramatically, according to Michael, Taiwanese computer manufacturer Asus used its development capabilities to "single-handedly invent the netbook segment of the PC market." Producing computers stripped down in functionality and priced at $300 each, Asus "has completely disrupted the global PC market."

As existing markets become saturated, however, China must invest more in the "R" part of R&D to compete differently or to expand into fundamentally new markets, Andrew says. And while piracy has eroded profit opportunities in China's traditional gaming software industry, Michael points out that it has not similarly affected online games. "People are paying for the experience of playing games with each other, and that turns out to be profitable despite some piracy."

Longer-term, the capacity to innovate seems likely to grow. "The culture is very, very good at devising quick and often effective solutions to problems," Meyer explains. "I see a lot of improvisation." An increasing demand for a Chinese language card in computers, for example, prompted Lenovo years ago to create one for its products. Chinese white-goods manufacturer Haier found that potato farmers in China were using their washing machines to clean produce, so it designed a heavy-duty, special-purpose machine that can be used outdoors and will "wash your clothes or your potatoes," Meyer notes. Electronic and electrical manufacturers often design products that work with "very heavy-duty power supplies because of the poor quality of electricity" in the country.

Nor are Chinese innovators focused entirely on their domestic market. According to David Jin, managing director and head of BCG's Shanghai office, some Chinese companies have already tried to out-innovate large MNCs—and succeeded. In one highly publicized case in 2006, Chinese electrical products maker Chint won a lawsuit over its patent for a circuit breaker against the Chinese unit of the French company Schneider Electric. "Usually, it is the other way around," Jin says, alluding to Western companies accusing those in developing countries of patent infringements. Many high-tech operations are succeeding abroad as well. China Medical Technologies, a supplier of in-vitro diagnosis and treatment systems, competes with MNCs and commands a market share of more than 90% in at least one product segment and 70% in another, according to a July 2008 report from Citigroup Global Markets.

Choosing a Business Model

For companies in developed economies that want to harness Chinese innovation, Wharton and BCG experts say it's important to select the right business model. These models range from plain-vanilla purchasing through a series of one-off orders, to joint technological collaborations through supplier development programs, to taking an equity position in Chinese suppliers, says David Lee, partner and managing director in BCG's Beijing office and a supply chain and procurement specialist.

No one-size-fits-all formula exists for such partnerships, Lee adds. He has seen several MNCs invest in their suppliers, but "a lot of them don't like the idea," in part because of potential management disagreements. Some Chinese companies "are reluctant to change the way they have worked historically," he says, adding that the handling of human resources and material waste, in particular, could be points of friction. However, many of them have begun reining in waste of materials in manufacturing processes and increasing wage levels have got them to focus on lean manufacturing and productivity enhancement, he adds.

Many MNCs have rolled out supplier development programs, transferring pieces of technology and attempting to transfer their best practices to Chinese partners. But this, too, is unfamiliar territory for some. Companies from developed economies typically haven't had to worry much about quality control in their home markets "because suppliers themselves take the initiative to invest in quality-control processes," Lee says.

Markets are so competitive and dynamic in China that innovation is likely to continue relentlessly. Companies are being pressured for ever more gains in productivity. And where Chinese manufacturing wages were relatively flat for many decades—allowing wage productivity to grow—labor markets have tightened and wages have started rising, Michael points out.

The challenge going forward will be to accelerate productivity growth ahead of any inflationary pressure on wages, he says. The available labor supply in the medium term will not be as large as it was in the past—although the global economic slowdown has idled millions of workers for the moment. But the release of large blocks of talent through the restructuring of state-owned enterprises is almost complete. At the same time, rising farm incomes—at least until very recently—had constrained the supply of migrant rural labor to the industrial centers, Michael explains. That gave labor more leverage. Ultimately, as labor increasingly absorbs more manufacturing resources in the long run, companies will have to push even further for innovative solutions with "a focus on driving more productivity increases in Chinese operations." The global economic downturn will likely slow the pace of these trends—and even reverse some—in the short term. But over the mid-term and beyond, expect China to build upon its already substantial innovative capabilities in manufacturing and services.

Innovation and Intellectual Property

Does porous intellectual property protection have a negative impact on innovation? Not necessarily, says Harold Sirkin, senior partner at BCG in Chicago and global leader of the firm's operations practice. When you innovate, "you're creating a brand, and that's a different kind of intellectual property (IP) than a patent." IP protection is growing less important to innovation, even in the West, Sirkin notes. "The world has gotten so small that even if you invent the next iTunes, you can't rely on patent protection," he notes. "It's readily copied now, everywhere. A lot of the [market appeal with] iTunes and the iPod is about [their] installed base."

However, innovation and protection of IP have long been connected, and China has duly noted that linkage in its attempts to transform itself from a low value-added manufacturing center to recognized innovation leader, particularly as lower-cost countries compete for China's core business. Mike Chao, a Principal at BCG in Beijing, notes that, "The IP laws have always been there, but what's changed in the last 20 years is how they have been interpreted and enforced. There's a big difference between policy and enforcement." One notable example is the software industry, where Chao battled piracy with Microsoft China for over five years before joining BCG. After strong lobbying by Microsoft in partnership with the US government, China declared in 2003 that the government would only use legal software. That announcement was followed by two additional decrees requiring that PC manufacturers only preinstall genuine software and Chinese enterprises only use legal software. "While that's absolutely a step in the right direction, there's still work to do in terms of bringing up the levels of enforcement and awareness to comply with the policies," Chao says.

On another front, however, he notes the Chinese government's tendency to provide research grants to projects that have the same time frame as the tenure of bureaucrats, thus sacrificing long-term horizons for short-term gains. "Innovation requires a long-term approach, and companies need to know their hard work won't just be stolen right away." Therein lies the difference between betting the company on the "R" or the "D": "Research is never a sure thing, but development can consistently result in realizable output," Chao explains. "With the recently announced government stimulus programs, there is hope that more funding will go to the companies that can actually productize that research and bring it to market." Academic institutions that have traditionally received such grants have "not had a great track record in commercialization," Chao points out.

Evolving IP policies, however, will not necessarily be the savior to spurring a wave of innovation in China. "At the end of the day, the market will force you to innovate and differentiate, and if your company isn't doing that, someone else will." Chao points to the PC industry as an example. Prices of notebook computers dropped 13% on average in China last year, in large part due to pressure from netbooks, other low-cost offerings, and a general lack of differentiation. "Asus saw an opportunity to disrupt the industry with the netbook, and now PC companies are dropping prices and scrambling to catch up." Innovation is and has always been the key to competition. China's ability to do so effectively will undoubtedly determine its future in the global economy. ■

Published: June 3, 2009 in Knowledge@Wharton

Taking the "R" out of BRIC: How the Economic Downturn Exposed Russia's Weaknesses

Last June, when Russia's president, Dmitry Medvedev, gathered fellow BRIC heads of state—Brazil's President Luiz Inácio Lula da Silva, India's Prime Minister Manmohan Singh and China's President Hu Jintao—in the central Russian city of Yekaterinburg for the group's first-ever leaders summit, he called for those present to "create the conditions for a fairer world order...a multi-polar world order."

Medvedev's rhetoric is a giveaway to how, at least in some quarters, the BRIC concept, first put forward in 2003 by analysts at investment bank Goldman Sachs, has evolved from one of economic shorthand to one of political posturing, primarily against American superpower dominance. In a similar gesture, Medvedev dedicated significant air time at the summit to calling for a diversification of world reserve currencies away from the dollar—a point about which China, which holds some $2 trillion in dollar-denominated reserves, remained silent.

Ever since BRIC was first postulated as a way to group those large, fast-growing emerging markets that, at the time anyway, were expected to be the main engines of world economic growth in coming years, observers have wondered which other countries might have BRIC characteristics. Certainly, there is an ever-growing list of countries being promoted for their BRIC-like qualities to attract international business and investment interest. Goldman Sachs, in a 2005 follow-up to its first BRIC report, put forward its so-called "N11"—or Next 11—group of BRIC aspirants, including Bangladesh, Egypt, Indonesia, Iran, Mexico, Nigeria, Pakistan, the Philippines, South Korea, Turkey and Vietnam.

But now many experts question whether the once promising BRIC label has begun to lose its luster—especially in the case of Russia. Last year, Russia's economic performance was the worst among the BRIC economies by a large measure: For the whole of 2009, its real GDP is expected to have declined by at least 8% and some quarters by more than 10%. That compares to Brazil's smaller real GDP decline of 5.5%, while China's and India's GDPs grew by 8.3% and 6.5%, respectively. Russia's performance is even worse when compared to 2008, which takes into account the bursting of the oil-price bubble in the middle of that year.

Oil and Other Risks

Russia is the world's largest producer of oil and gas, which is the primary source of its power but also a significant source of economic risk. According to Witold Henisz, a management professor at Wharton, oil and gas are "both a blessing and a curse" for the country. Unlike other major emerging economies, such as Korea, Russia hasn't had to aggressively seek its revenue. And because it has never made a clean break from its feudal past, economic—and political—power lies in the hands of a few. This has reverberated throughout the country, Henisz says, bringing with it a "tendency toward centralization, control and coercion."

Although the severity of Russia's economic decline has been due to several factors, Ira Kalish, director of global economics at Deloitte Research, says that the obvious beginning was the bursting of the oil-price bubble in mid-2008. This sharply curtailed export revenues and made the country's foreign debt obligation loom much larger than it had when oil prices where heading toward $150 a barrel. Then the worldwide credit crunch squeezed the government's debt position even further and, in turn, percolated into Russia's domestic financial sector, leaving several large institutions in need of bail-outs. Rising interest rates to support a collapsing ruble completed the vicious cycle, leading to even tighter credit and further declines in foreign currency reserves.

Still, while oil prices fell by more than 70% from their 2008 peak, they recovered during 2009 to an average price for the year that was above that of 2007 and well above the average of most of the last decade, when Russia's economy was still growing at a healthy clip. Furthermore, although about 65% of Russia's export earnings come from oil and gas, the sector accounts for only about 20% of overall GDP. Other more oil-dependent economies, such as Kazakhstan or Saudi Arabia, suffered much smaller GDP declines over the same period.

So why has Russia done so poorly compared with its BRIC counterparts, as well as other oil-rich emerging economies?

The reason is "a combination of corruption, poor governance, government interference in the private sector, and insufficient investment in the oil and gas sector," says Kalish. These problems and others—such as erosion of civil liberties—will continue to stymie growth unless they are tackled aggressively, according to experts.

Even if there were the will to change, solutions are not obvious, says Wharton professor of legal studies and business ethics Philip Nichols. Consider corruption. "In most countries, the mistrust generated by corruption leads to disengagement from government institutions and the creation of relationship-based networks," he says. "In Russia, you do find these networks and they are quite strong, but they are not as pervasive as in the other BRIC countries. In fact, [in Russia,] in the absence of trust it seems that people often turn to the government for direction. And so it seems that corruption...has the odd, and indirect, effect of further concentrating power in the government."

Nonetheless, Nichols also sees some change in the right direction, including among the country's small and mid-sized enterprises (SMEs), which he has been studying over time. "In the early 1990s, [SMEs] mostly talked about the deal they were working on and maybe the next deal, but rarely looked ahead," he notes. "Now, they talk about their businesses in terms of years. They understand that this requires a sustainable, trustworthy business environment, and that they themselves need to act in trustworthy ways."

More Red Flags

As for the future business environment, Russia's Ministry of Economic Development put forward some fairly optimistic economic growth forecasts at the end of 2009 for the 2010-2012 period. Growth in GDP would be as high as 3.1% in 2010 and 3.4% in 2011, assuming oil prices continue to climb, and GDP growth would rise back to pre-crisis levels by 2012 as foreign investment returns and the domestic economy rebuilds stocks.

The forecasts were quickly dismissed by others, including leading Russian economists. The immediate prognosis for the economy is highly dependent on external factors, argues Sergey Aleksashenko, director for macroeconomic studies at the State University-Higher School of Economics in Moscow. Furthermore, too rapid a recovery—which might occur if there is another oil price surge—would be bad for the Russian economy, he says. That would lead to a strengthening of the ruble and foreign currency reserves, an influx of speculative capital, inflation and the strong likelihood of another collapse and an even more severe recession than the one that took place in 2009.

Another red flag that Aleksashenko raises is that Russia's government could be disinclined to follow the healthiest path for recovery—that is, a long steady one—ahead of presidential elections in 2012, when former President Vladimir Putin (currently prime minister) is hopeful of a return to the top job.

This highlights the most persistent problem for Russia: its institutional weakness, something that was evident in the dithering over last year's stimulus package, which at 4% of GDP was large by international standards but which was not implemented until late spring because of worries about stoking inflation further. Thus, in the first half of 2009, according to a report by the Economist Intelligence Unit (EIU), Russia had the humiliating distinction of joining the Ukraine and Zimbabwe as the only countries suffering from both a double-digit output decline and double-digit inflation.

Since the fall of communism two decades ago, the Russian business landscape has gone through a turbulent transition that is still nowhere near complete. Corruption, bureaucratic morass and the often arbitrary enforcement of rules have taken their toll. Yet its oil and gas riches are so vast that very large companies still are willing to pump in billions in foreign capital for huge projects—including BP, Exxon Mobil and Royal Dutch Shell—despite having been burned on several occasions. "Just by virtue of its size, it deserves continued attention from the investment community," says Henisz.

Inflows, Outflows

But Western companies, on the whole, are wary and have been more inclined to seek less volatile environments for their investments, as was especially evident during the downturn. A case in point: Carrefour. In October, the French retailer—the second largest in the world after Wal-Mart—pulled up stakes in

Russia, citing bleak short- and medium-term prospects for growth. The move was a surprise given that just months before in June, it had cut the ribbon on its first hypermarket in the country.

That episode underscores not only the fragile investor confidence in the country, but also the difficulty that Russia faces in developing other industries that can reduce its heavy reliance on oil and gas. Outside that sector, the opportunities are "very limited," Henisz notes. "Russia does have the capacity [to develop other sectors]—there are a lot of engineers and the education level is high. But we're not seeing many entrepreneurs who can develop large service or manufacturing companies. There's a massive gap between the small entrepreneurs—who want to stay off the tax and political radar screens—and the oligarchs."

With oil and gas clearly continuing to be a dominant force, Medvedev's new world order for BRICs is perhaps best illustrated in early 2009 by the "oil-for-loans" deal between Russia and China, when the latter arranged for its China Development ment Bank to lend $25 billion to Russia's Rosneft and Transneft oil companies to build pipelines and secure oil deliveries for the next couple of decades. Russia has been looking to diversify its markets away from the West, while China has aggressively sought to secure energy resources from as many sources as it can.

The oil-for-loans deal also underlines the potential for friction between these two BRIC members. While the BRIC summit was getting under way in Yekaterinburg in June, there was a simultaneous gathering in the same city of the Shanghai Cooperation Organization, made up of Kazakhstan, Uzbekistan, Tajikistan and Kyrgyzstan, as well as China and Russia. While the meeting may have been billed as a further display of independence from the West, Russia and China have competing interests in how these energy-rich countries bring their oil and gas to market. China—which pledged $10 billion in economic stabilization loans for the Central Asian countries at that meeting—has the upper hand.

Another destabilizing factor is the effect of concentrated ownership in the hands of a few billionaires, and the risk of capital flight from this small group, which has happened on more than one occasion and leaves the economy open to sharp and volatile outflows of capital during hard times. In the final quarter of 2008, as the financial crisis deepened after the collapse of Lehman Brothers, $164 billion flowed out of Russia's capital account.

The shortcomings of Russia's ruling political and business elite are by now well known. What's more, the warning signs of more economic trouble ahead are growing—for example, the increasing rate of non-performing loans on Russian banks' balance sheets. Experts say that strong leadership would be required now to stabilize the financial situation and, more than anything, to encourage foreign investment and management expertise to help steady Russia's economy. But the prospects of that happening soon are slim. For the time being, according to Henisz, "the path forward is looking a little darker" for Russia. ■

Published: February 17, 2010 in Knowledge@Wharton

Rural Calling: Can Nokia Sustain Its First-mover Advantage?

For the past three years, Yellakandula Urmila of Bhongir village, near Hyderabad, has been banking with SKS Microfinance (MFI), India's largest lender. She first bought a loom to weave silk saris with a US $150 loan from MFI in 2007, which helped triple her family's monthly income to US $100. Then three months ago she took out another loan for US $26 to buy a Nokia 1200 mobile phone with a prepaid Bharti Airtel connection, which she will have paid off in June. "It's been a life-changing and time-saving experience," says Urmila, affectionately patting her gleaming silver handset and recalling how she used to have to walk a mile to a wire-line public phone booth to call clients about orders. "Deals are now wrapped up in minutes," she says.

Wooing rural consumers like Urmila while teaming up with local organizations have been a key part of the global strategy of the US $55 billion Finnish handset multinational since 2006. "Partnering with local stakeholders is a cool thing," says Gireesh Shrimali, professor of information systems at the Indian School of Business in Hyderabad. "It is a neat innovation, which creates buzz and brand equity for Nokia."

That is one of the reasons why India is the company's second-largest market with 2009 net sales of US $3.7 billion, putting it behind China (with US $8 billion), but well ahead of the UK in third place (with US $2.5 billion). In the decade since it first set foot in India, Nokia has captured nearly 60% of the country's US $5.6 billion handset market and has a 62% share of GSM-based phones, according to research firm IDC. India—and in particular, rural India—has been good for Nokia.

"We saw the rural opportunities ahead of competition," states D. Shivakumar, Nokia India's vice president and managing director. Though Samsung, LG, Sony Ericsson and Motorola have also been selling handsets in India, telecom observers say Nokia has stood out from the rest by having formally forged a company-wide "social inclusion" policy in 2006 to encompass low-income consumers in its growth strategy, essentially using India as a laboratory for that strategy.

Today, rural consumers account for 25% of Nokia phone sales in India, and the target next year is 30%. With mobile phone penetration in the rural market almost doubling to 20% over the past year—to approximately 150 million, according to the Cellular Operator Association of India (COAI), a trade association—Nokia has been aggressively pursuing an even more targeted expansion strategy in smaller towns and villages. "There's an insatiable hunger for mobile phones permeating all layers of society," says Pankaj Mohindroo, president of the COAI. "And Nokia has been developing the rural market with appropriate products for a long time, unlike other players."

But now, Nokia's first mover advantage in rural India is being chipped away.

Both home-grown and foreign rivals are muscling in on Nokia's rural territory, beating it down on price. All eyes now are on Nokia, as it rolls out innovative services that can be sold alongside its handsets through a range of partnerships.

New Frontiers

It was a matter of time before the handset market, especially at the lower end, was beginning to commoditize just as service providers were developing the infrastructure to reach consumers in the heartland. "It was a given that the fast-growing telecom market in urban India would reach a saturation point after a decade," says Romal Shetty, an executive director at consulting firm KPMG. "Some companies had the foresight to look at new frontiers."

On the heels of India's rapid economic boom, the mobile revolution had an impact on both urban and rural penetration. Urban teledensity—which refers to the number of phone connections per 100 people—has exploded from 65% in 2008 to more than 90% today (with cities like Mumbai and Delhi at more than 100%), while teledensity in rural areas grew from 14% to 30% over the same period.

Nokia has been in the thick of this growth. A year after setting up a manufacturing facility in Sriperumbudur, near Chennai, in 2006, Nokia rolled out seven phones in India. Its goal was to target emerging markets at prices ranging between US $45 and US $120. Nokia manufactured 300 million devices between then and October 2009, half of which were exported to 60 countries. "Nokia has been proactive as the market leader," says Anshul Gupta, principal analyst for handsets at research firm Gartner in Mumbai.

Nokia was the first mobile phone maker to set up a satellite R&D center in India as it began tailoring products for the rural terrain. The phones look as sleek as high-end models, but are also sturdy to withstand rough usage. They have seamless keypads to protect them from dust and special grips to make them easier to hold in India's humidity. Some phones—Nokia 1200 and Nokia 1208—also double up as flashlights because of rural India's frequent power outages. Nokia has also embraced the country's plethora of languages, with interfaces in Hindi, Marathi, Kannada, Telugu and Tamil.

Along the way, Nokia has learned important lessons that are crucial to any MNC's survival in the hinterland. One of them relates to customer service. Its after-sales service includes some 700 care centers in urban India. But it's a different matter in rural India. Nokia has more than 300 vans staffed with sales representatives who regularly criss-cross the countryside. It also set up low-cost collection points like chemist shops, where distributors and micro-distributors collect the phones and take them to the nearest care center.

But according to Nokia, customer service in rural markets such as India's can be just as—if not more—important before rather than after a sale. "Consumers always worry about anything going wrong with digital products and must always be assured that care or service is just a call away," says Shivakumar. "We needed to build care ahead of sales to provide a sense of trust and peace of mind." Now the vans are divided into two groups—one to provide support and repairs and others to travel around with Nokia partners, ranging from Idea Cellular to SKS Microfinance, to promote their products and services while catering to novice mobile customers. "The rural market is still an area for a first-time user," says Shivakumar.

Getting Crowded

As all this happens, service providers have been slashing call rates and expanding their networks. That has had a cascading effect on the overall affordability of mobile telephony. Rates have plummeted from 32 cents a minute in 1998 to less than a cent today, cutting the average revenue per user from US $60 to US $4, one of the lowest in the world.

Equipment makers have also felt the squeeze. "It was evident four years ago that revenues would decline for pure-play mobile device companies," says Aditya Sood, CEO of the Center for Knowledge Societies, an innovation-focused consulting firm in India. "The downward pressure on markets and handset costs crashing to less than US $25 were expected."

Nokia is now facing competition across all its product segments, says KPMG's Shetty. The big confrontation is at the low end, where a number of players are wooing entry-level users. Chinese phones costing US $20 have flooded the market, and a slew of local and foreign competitors—like Simoco, Kyocera, Intex and Karbonn—are aiming to do the same. Micromax Mobile, too, is a challenger. Since it launched two years ago, it has become the third-largest GSM phone vendor, with 6% market share, after Nokia (62%) and Samsung (8%).

These changes offer Nokia another big lesson—competing on price isn't the only avenue it can take as pressure intensifies in its rural markets. So rather than discounting prices on existing products, Nokia says it prefers to focus on providing additional services. "Just [selling] a device will not take you into the future," says Vipul Sabharwal, Nokia's national sales director.

This is where Nokia Life Tools comes in. Launched last autumn in India, it bundles a handset with a service for farmers so that they can get access to crop prices and weather forecasts as well as English lessons for a monthly fee beginning at 65 cents. Nokia claims Life Tools has attracted nearly one million users using just one service provider—Idea Cellular, the telecom arm of conglomerate Aditya Birla Group. It expects faster growth as it expands the tool using other service providers.

The success of Nokia's rural value-added services, according to Sabharwal, is based on a range of key performance indicators (KPIs) including volume, the number of outlets that sell the offering, the returns to the service provider and visibility. But he says there are greater KPIs that might not show up on its top or bottom line. As he sees it, Nokia in rural India is not just a brand, but a "vehicle for social and economic transformation."

Yet partners like Idea Cellular are cautious. Its chief marketing officer, Pradeep Shrivastava, notes that while value-added services like texting, music and caller ring back are popular with consumers, Life Tools has yet to gain traction. "The application currently does not have the 'ecosystem' for consumer education, subscription or servicing," he says. "At this juncture, these solutions are not attracting new subscribers." Another snag came in March when wire agency Reuters called off its partnership with Nokia to provide Life Tools with real-time news feeds.

Nokia has also been caught napping and failed to move with important trends, such as the popular dual Sim-card phones, which lets users move back and forth between providers without having to change handsets. Such phones offer one reason why local player Micromax has been able to gain market share with its product portfolio: 23 of its 26 models offer dual SIM cards. Mohindroo of the COAI says around 25% of all GSM mobile phones offer a dual-SIM today, "but Nokia hasn't yet launched one." A Nokia spokesperson concedes it has been slow on that front, but its own version of a dual-Sim will hit stores later this year, along with a US $10 phone.

With Nokia ramping up its value-added offerings, competitors are readying for a fight. Samsung plans to roll out smart phones that allow users to download maps, games and music, and access interactive features online. LG and Sony Ericsson are expanding their music and games applications.

Perhaps the fact that competitors are being driven back to the drawing board should be looked at as a good thing at Nokia, says CKS's Sood. "In the telecom business, success will be defined when more players start doing what Nokia is doing," he says. That's when Nokia will have to work even harder to find new ways to woo rural India. After all, imitation, as they say, is the best form of flattery. ∎

Published: May 6, 2010 in India Knowledge@Wharton

Decoding the DNA of Brazilian Multinationals

In recent years, companies from emerging economies—especially the BRIC nations (Brazil, Russia, India and China)—have challenged the hegemony of multinational giants from the U.S., Europe and Japan in what has been called the "third wave" of globalization. Brazilian multinationals, with their own unique attributes, are leading the charge. Last year, the Boston Consulting Group ranked 14 Brazilian companies among the world's 100 "new global rivals."

Nowadays, Companhia Vale do Rio Doce (in the mineral sector), Petrobras (in petroleum) and Embraer (in aerospace) are the strongest and most recognized companies outside Brazil's borders. These firms have moved abroad as a result of changes in the internationalization process that began in the 1990s, when there was a considerable increase in foreign direct investment (FDI) in Brazil. This occurred in other Latin American countries, too—but in the case of Brazil, the trend was especially strong. During that decade, the annual average investment volume was US $1.048 billion. By 2006, the volume of investments had risen eight-fold to US $8.20 billion.

In addition to investments, there is a lesser-known globalization process within the companies themselves, "whose management model is based on an inventive combination of organizational competencies and management systems." That is the conclusion of a recent study in the Universia-Business Review, titled "The road moves forward: The path of Brazilian multinationals."

Colonial Roots

The authors of the paper—Alfonso Fleury, professor of engineering at Sao Paulo University; Maria Tereza Leme, dean of the Getulio Vargas Foundation (FGV-EAESP), and Germano Glufke, professor at the FGV-EAESP—studied 30 corporate headquarters and 68 Brazilian subsidiaries, and engaged in 12 in-depth case studies in order to identify the genetic make-up of these multinationals, and the factors that explain their competitiveness in global markets. They argue that you have to look deep into the country's Portuguese colonial period for the origins of "Brazilian-style management." According to the authors, that heritage consists of the following:

- A centralization of decision-making in upper levels of management, with a misalignment between responsibility and authority.
- Short-term vision, focused on short-term results and on solutions for dealing with crises.
- A lack of strategic planning and significant gaps between strategy and operational execution.
- A reactive management style which place a high value on creative improvisation.
- An interest and admiration for managerial practices imported from other countries.

The situation that predominated until the end of the 1980s was characterized by a domestic market that was protected by the government and strongly influenced by its political decisions. "This contributed to the creation of a parochial mentality; an approach to business that was not very entrepreneurial and was dependent on local institutions and, as a result, excessively directed toward the country itself, so that it lost sight of the global perspective," the authors write.

It was not until the 1990s, with the arrival of the government of Fernando Henrique Cardoso (1995-2003), and then that of Lula, that there was a series of significant changes aimed at the stabilization of the economy (and the control of inflation), as well as the opening of the market. These governments "opened up the market to foreign products and expanded the level of its global competitiveness," the researchers note.

The Basis for Internationalization

As elsewhere in Latin America, the beginnings of this decade were marked by the prospect for trade deregulation within the so-called Washington Consensus—a combination of economic prescriptions whose goal was to promote economic growth in the region. During that period, for example, there was the privatization of state enterprises such as Petrobras and Embraer; the consolidation of the capital goods sector, with mergers and acquisitions such as the beverage company Ambev/InBev; the de-nationalization of the durable goods sector, a process in which various companies were acquired by foreign multinationals—including Sabó (auto parts) and Weg (electrical equipment), which wound up being more competitive and better positioned for international markets.

In practice, the result of this entire process was the stratification of Brazilian companies into leading companies and those that followed them. "Among private companies, those that stood out were the ones that really developed competency at surviving and prospering competitively in the turbulent domestic market, fighting hand-to-hand against the subsidiaries of multinationals," the authors write. In the case of the state-owned companies, "the privatization process injected new competencies (especially in finance and marketing), which complemented their strong competencies in production and technology, and established new horizons for taking action."

At the same time, the creation of the Mercosur trade agreement (which includes Argentina, Brazil, Paraguay and Uruguay) in 1991, served as a new realm for experimentation, and contributed to developing a vision, among administrators and entrepreneurs, of a more globalized world. On the other hand, the researchers note, "the managerial development programs offered by Brazilian institutions gained new status abroad, and won significant positions in the specialized international rankings." These changes laid the foundations for the process of internationalizing Brazilian companies.

A Broad Profile

These days, Brazilian multinationals have a presence in a broad range of activities no longer limited to the exploitation of natural resources so characteristic of companies in emerging countries. Apart from companies in that sector, there are outstanding providers of basic supplies, such as petrochemical maker Braskem; construction materials providers such as Tigre and Duratex; and Odebrecht and other firms that focus on technical services for engineering.

Brazil's process of internationalization was generated independently. The companies made their own decisions and developed their own strategies. "There was not any cooperation among the companies in the industrial sector; or between them and financial institutions (as in the case of Spain); and there was no assistance from the government (as in China)." Nevertheless, privatized companies stand out among the biggest multinationals in the country.

Like most other firms that serve multiple markets in Latin America, Brazilian companies were late to internationalize themselves—waiting, in many cases, for decades after the companies were established. "There were small movements in the 1980s, but the process did not intensify until the end of the 1990s." In the beginning, Brazilian multinationals made Latin America their goal. This was the most natural route because of the geographic distance and the cultural and institutional differences between Brazil and regions outside Latin America.

Unlike the first multinational companies that made it a priority to seek new markets or access to new resources, companies that were "late movers" in emerging nations such as Brazil were involved in "a mix of activities that take place simultaneously and, from the beginning, also encompass a search for assets that is strategic and efficient. There is also a range of ways that these companies became international, including new acquisitions as well as joint corporate shareholdings and alliances."

Some of these players have been motivated to expand by the recent formation of "networks of global production." As the authors note, such networks, "by requiring an international presence, induce companies to make the effort at globalization. Typical examples are Sabó, Embraco (which manufactures refrigerator compressors), and companies in the information technology sector."

Management Model

The trend toward trade deregulation and the questioning of prevailing business models began, thus uprooting the foundations of the parochial management style. As a result, numerous Brazilian companies learned about the challenges that they had confronted throughout their history. They developed a new managerial model that served as the basis for their internationalization. Among the competencies they acquired, the researchers note, the following stand out: Organizational flexibility as a function of the characteristics of the market and the economic situation, versus the Brazilian tendency to establish hierarchies and centralize; and active waiting, or constantly monitoring conditions and preparing yourself so you can give immediate answers, as opposed to the traditional approach of focusing on short-term planning and intuition.

In addition, many companies developed first-class production processes, strongly influenced by Japanese models. They acquired world-class technical skills and, in some cases, new strengths in R&D. They have learned to focus on their customers, and developed new competencies in international finance and risk management. As for human resource management, these multinationals are the most advanced companies in the country, although they continue to have lots of problems addressing personnel issues that are the result of globalization.

In the laborious road toward internationalization, multinationals have been acquiring other skills such as marketing and international innovation, as well as competencies in running international networks; that is to say, "intrinsic corporate skills for managing, utilizing and exploiting inter-corporate relationships," the authors write. Finally, they add that such firms have also learned to adapt themselves to the demands of institutions and markets, and have attuned themselves to issues concerning social responsibility.

Beyond this new managerial style, which has yet to mature, are the specific advantages of Brazil, aside from its natural resources. Among these, note the authors, are institutional conditions, specialized labor forces, and access to technological knowledge. Some companies have also benefitted from their relationships with the government. Others "have taken advantage of characteristics of the domestic market to develop their own skills, which have enabled them to move into global markets."

Embraer stands out among the multinationals that have changed their managerial model, having transformed itself from a state-owned company into a market-focused company with "long-term planning and a business model sustained by multiple inter-cultural collaborations," which include risk-sharing partnerships, joint ventures and aquisitions. The company currently operates regional plants and offices in North America, Europe, China and Singapore.

Another case, the authors note, is the 'intra-entrepreneurial' culture of Odebrecht, "a company that is in an expansionary phase. It has established its own managerial practices, such as the Odebrecht Entrepreneurial Technology, the company's fundamental principles. This system of planned delegation grants autonomy to subsidiaries so that they can adapt themselves to local conditions."

The Road Ahead

According to the authors, the quality that stands out as unique among Brazilian multinationals is their managerial model. Traditional roots, such as hierarchical structures, continue to play a role within many companies. During the internationalization process, these characteristics have been revealed in different ways. One example is the adoption by some companies of mechanisms for avoiding uncertainty and risk; that is, their preference for making exports over making foreign direct investments, and their emphasis on choosing those foreign markets that are similar in appearance. Another example is making individualized—rather than cooperative—decisions to internationalize. A third is the trend toward an ethnocentric positioning, which gives priority to managers at corporate headquarters, to the detriment of local managers.

In that regard, the study points out that managers at the headquarters of Brazilian companies provide incentives for the entrepreneurial spirit in their subsidiaries, but they do not make any great effort to integrate [the various divisions], and they give little autonomy to their subsidiaries. "In this context, subsidiaries take the initiative, especially those that operate in competitive markets and are supported by networks of international companies." These characteristics, write the authors, "seem to be very favorable [for Brazil] because they reveal the skills that Brazilian administrators have for adapting to new cultures, and their ability to produce creative and innovative responses to conditions that could not possibly be more turbulent."

The authors conclude by noting that the foundations of the Brazilian managerial model are still in a developmental phase, even if those foundations are quite visible. "How quickly they mature will depend how quickly leadership acts, and on the demonstration [of other leading companies], which can bring new groups together on the same journey." ∎

Published: March 24, 2010 in Universia Knowledge@Wharton

Sheikh Nahayan Mabarak Al Nahayan: "There Is No Substitute for Education If We Want to Have a Better World"

When the United Arab Emirates (UAE) became a nation in the early 1970s, there were few signs of the Islamic Golden Age that put the Middle East at the global forefront of education and intellectual innovation hundreds of years earlier. The small nation of just a few million Emiratis, in fact, had neither a formal education system nor a university to call its own. Flash forward to today, however, and the UAE has a primary and secondary school system for both boys and girls, and new private and public universities have sprung up across the emirates.

While national investment in schools and universities continues, the UAE sees a larger role for itself as a promoter of peace and economic development through education, according to Sheikh Nahayan Mabarak Al Nahayan, the UAE's minister of higher education and scientific research who is also chancellor of two of the nation's three government-sponsored higher education institutions (United Arab Emirates University and Higher Colleges of Technology) and president of the third (Zayed University). In an interview with Knowledge@Wharton, Sheikh Nahayan discusses various UAE education initiatives, the impact of technology in and outside the classroom, and what he would envision to be an ideal education system.

An edited transcript of the conversation follows.

Knowledge@Wharton: Sheikh Nahayan, thank you so much for joining us today.

Sheikh Nahayan Mabarak Al Nahayan: It's a pleasure to be with you.

Knowledge@Wharton: You have taken such a vital leadership role in education initiatives such as the Festival of Thinkers and Education Without Borders. I wonder if you could tell us a little about your philosophy of education and how these initiatives contribute to it.

Sheikh Nahayan: Thank you. First, these student gatherings—we call one the Festival of Thinkers and the other Education Without Borders. We also have another that is called Women as Global Leaders. The reason I support these initiatives and these gatherings is that [the world is] getting smaller and smaller. It is not just that we're saying it; it's literally becoming "a village" to the extent that when there's disease, environmental crisis, conflicts or financial crises everybody gets affected. There are no boundaries and no barriers between countries. You cannot isolate yourself from what's going on in the world. Since the students are going to be the future leaders of this world, it is good to interact.

And what amazed me during these conferences is the interaction between students based on human principles. They don't think of what religion they are or what background they come from, what culture, what country. With the purity of human principle comes an action. They interact with each other and relate to each other on issues which concern [the entire] world, whether it is environment, which we've seen, and now we're going through swine flu, which in a few days spread like fire in the forest around the world. The financial crisis in the United States in no time affected everybody else in the world. So nobody is immune. These conferences will contribute to creating this interaction between the future leaders of this world. We live in an age where we are fortunate to have technology and the Internet to maintain this link and to also make the world smaller. We know what's going on now if somebody falls from a tree in a remote area of China.

I think it is only through education that we can eradicate poverty. We can eliminate diseases. If we invest now in education the world will be a much better place for our children and grandchildren. And actually it costs less. If we wait until the problem arises and we try to solve it, then it is too big. The cost would be much higher. If we invest in education in a third-world country in particular and also where there's lack of education, lack of health care, they will be able to culture themselves. They will be able to protect the environment. It will also create new markets [which] will sustain the economic development and growth all over the world. But the world has to realize that together we can do many things. And we all are affected. We all should be concerned. That's why we invest in education here and that's why I think the quality of life, the sustainability of our growth and economic development, will solely depend on human resources in education.

Knowledge@Wharton: How do you view the role of technology in education? I believe you initiated mobile technology used in education. What is your thinking and strategy?

Sheikh Nahayan: We started it because we should break the barriers that you only can study in a confined area or you have to study with a big computer that you cannot carry, or in a lab. It should be easy, as easy as texting or talking on the phone. The mobile [technology] could be anywhere else. People very much feel friendly with the technology. They can use it easily. [Because of such] technology...for the first time in human history the individual has been empowered. Now, if I have a cause or an issue I want to present to the world, literally in a few hours it will be all over the world. So if I have a good cause, I can get to people. If I have a problem, my government cannot stop me. My students can't stop me. My people can't stop me. I can get through. That's also why we have to empower them. We can use this technology to enhance the quality of life for people who are less fortunate than us because through it they can educate themselves. They can interact with the world.

I remember we were in a village in Pakistan where we go hunting. We introduced the GSM [global system for mobile communications] service there and it has changed their life. Why? Because before the farmers used to cut their crop, wait until the people came from the city to purchase their crop, and sometimes leave it too long. If they need medicine, they have to go all the way to the city. Now with GSM, collectively they interact with each other. They say, "Okay, is your crop ready? My crop is ready." Then [they] call the people from the city to come and take it. It became more efficient. The quality of life became better. If they need something from the city collectively, they interact with each other and they order what they want. So that has made their lives much easier and trading much easier.

So that's what happened to one village. Imagine what happens to many villages if we introduce the technology. And the technologies are becoming very friendly for users. You don't need to have electricity. In this village, they use small gadgets you wind to create energy for recharging the phone. We have to invest in human resources because no matter how much money we will have in the near future we will lack human resources. You might have the best hospital in the world, with the best equipment. You will not have the people to man it. You might build it, but it doesn't mean you'll have anyone to run it. So we have to invest in the human. That's our future. And the comparative advantage of any nation [will be] the quality of education.

We have to create a good education system and use it as an investment for the future. Here in the UAE we are very close to India. India is very close to us. We have 1.4 million Indians who work here, who work in different professions, labor or whatever. To my amazement, the fact is that the whole of India is over 1 billion. Non-Resident Indians (NRIs) number maybe 20 million or 25 million. [The state of Kerala has] spent a third of its budget on education. It has no illiteracy....Here, two-thirds of [NRIs] are literate and they own the professions. They earn every day hundreds of millions [in income], literally. Isn't that an investment? You don't have to maintain it. You don't have to supervise it. You just have to invest in the human intelligence and the human brain. There's a saying that you need energy to fuel it, you need someone to man it. The return on investment is very high. So from whatever way you look at it, there is no substitute or alternative for education if we want to have a better world in the future.

Knowledge@Wharton: Could I ask one last question? In trying to create the education system of your dreams, not just in the UAE, but in this region, what is the toughest challenge you have faced, a leadership challenge you have faced? How have you overcome it and what have you learned from it?

Sheikh Nahayan: At first you have to be working for a goal and not be worried about your own position or your own job. For that reason, I will see where the best practice is and how many we can learn from and get the best, regardless of where they come from. I try to bring the best people to train. I'm not claiming that I am a genius at doing it, but maybe I can bring the best people. I am not looking for a person interested in fame. As long as I'm contributing to making a better world for my people, and for this region of the world hopefully....

We face difficulties. And I think difficulties and problems make it more interesting and more exciting. We should thrive. I believe my intentions are good and have nothing to hide. So I can face these challenges. Sometime people use religion against you if they lose their job. Every time you bring change, the change curve always goes down first before it starts going up. So you have to have a commitment and the assurance and confidence that you will stick to this change until it starts getting better.

I have just been talking to some people. Somebody said, "Oh, no, we've been making a few changes again and I'm sure it's going to create an issue." But when you're in charge, you can take on these issues. And in the end you say, "If I am in this position, this is my responsibility." I should be honest and do what I think is right after studying the issue. If I'm wanted, then I'll do it. If I'm not wanted, then I leave. So I'm never afraid of losing my job. I never wanted to get anything from my job. I just wanted to do what is good and help countries that will invest more in education to make [the world] a better place for everybody.

Now of course we will see in Pakistan—if you read the latest reports— protests and militias are springing up because the government cannot provide education. The many people who are now in these militias have nothing to [learn] because the people in charge of them have nothing to [teach them about] what's going on in the world....[It's] isolationism, fundamentalism. But if we want to spend money and build a school for them, their parents would rather see them in school. And we [should] try to give incentives to these people to go to school....

Look how much it cost us for one incident. 9/11 to me has created a new era, like before Christ and after Christ. Now you talk "before 9/11" and "after 9/11." It is disgraceful, and of course everybody deplores it. But look how much it has cost us. Had we tended to the Afghanistan problem after the Russians left it in chaos, [the terrorists] would not have had the [ability] to organize them- selves—[for example, if] we had a Marshall Plan like they did for the Germans after the Second World War....So the Taliban became stronger. Had we invested even then in the infrastructure, in education, we would not have this. There's no word in the dictionary that can [capture] the importance of education for the individual, the families, the community, the country and the world. ∎

Published: August 19, 2009 in Knowledge@Wharton

PART 5

Entrepreneurship in a Complex Global Marketplace

Innovation "Out of Necessity": Entrepreneurship During a Downturn

During a recession with fast growing unemployment, looking for ways to incentivize entrepreneurial activity and enhance corporate liquidity has become a strategic focal point for Spanish companies. Ignacio de la Vega, director of the IE Business School's Center for Entrepreneurial Management and president of the Global Entrepreneurship Monitor (GEM), which analyzes entrepreneurial conditions in 43 countries, spoke with Universia-Knowledge@Wharton about the current economic crisis and its impact on entrepreneurship. The GEM 2008 Global Report, which was recently released, is sponsored by the Ministry of Industry's small and midsize business division and the Banesto Foundation for Society and Technology.

Universia-Knowledge@Wharton: What has been the impact of the global economic crisis on entrepreneurial activity in Spain? What differences are there compared with previous crises? In what ways will entrepreneurial activity evolve in 2009?

Ignacio de la Vega: Starting from 2000, we have measured the macro-climate and environment in Spain very carefully at our organization. We began with an entrepreneurial activity rate of 4.55% that year, and we see an extremely important turning point between 2000 and 2001, when the rate climbed to 7.78%. If we think about what was happening at that time in the market, we see that it was a period of boom, when the Internet bubble in Spain was at its decisive moment. There were lots of opportunities to start companies and, unlike the current situation, when entrepreneurial activity did not bear fruit it was not because of a shortage of work opportunities but purely because of the particular opportunity. In 2002, we practically returned to the levels of 2000, with a 24% drop in the rate of entrepreneurial activity, which is an accurate reflection of the overall economic climate. Then the Internet bubble burst, and there was a serious crisis in the technology sector—a sector crisis, not a systemic crisis like today—and there were the attacks of September 11...and finally, optimism declined along with the rate of entrepreneurial activity.

Ever since then, we've been experiencing rising economic activity, until this year with some isolated declines, but that reflects the growth of our economy since 2000. Analysts began to notice the crisis in July 2007, but at that time it was a crisis in financial markets that had yet to spread into the real economy. In July 2008, at the time of our annual study, the financial crisis already had a very important impact on the real economy and we were expecting successive declines in the rate of economic activity in coming years. Given today's challenging conditions, including the climate of pessimism, scarcity of financing and so forth, the rate [of entrepreneurial activity] will continue to drop. Nevertheless, we have been living through a new era ever since 2000, and an amazing drop-off in job opportunities—the unemployment rate is over 15%. Obviously, entrepreneurial projects are a very important source of development that takes place "out of necessity." For the same reason, the decline will not be as steep as in the 2000-2002 period because, since there are fewer job opportunities today, many unemployed people will have to look for refuge in self-employment.

UK@W: What barriers are today's entrepreneurs facing?

De la Vega: There are three fundamental barriers at the moment. The first is psychological. Given the problems in the market, starting a business appears to be very risky, especially in a country like ours, which has a culture where there is a clear fear of failure and risk. We find ourselves in a tense position, halfway between the need to find means for income and professional activity, and the psychological fear of failure and risk. In my view, the need [for income] will win out.

Once that barrier has been overcome, the second big barrier is [a shortage of] financial resources. Fewer financial resources are coming from the two principal sources for financing entrepreneurial activity: First, debt, which you get from financial institutions, and public support is not functioning at this time. Second, it's not coming from informal investors, either; especially when it comes to the smaller companies we're talking about, where [entrepreneurial] activity has fallen by 13%. The figure of the 'business angel' was already weak in Spain [before the crisis], and in the current situation, those people who are liquid expect to make money [on their investments], and those who have already invested [their funds] don't have any more cash to invest. Our 2008 report already reflects this situation; it shows there has been a significant increase in the number of entrepreneurs who develop a business project and contribute 100% of the financing. Nowadays, given the rate of unemployment, a normative change is going to permit people to capitalize up to 60% of their unemployment subsidies and dedicate it to entrepreneurial activity. This will add some fuel to the system.

The third barrier is real demand. Demand has shrunk a great deal, and it is very hard to find [business] opportunities in many sectors. Competition between companies is already well established and, in an attempt to survive and grow, many companies are becoming more aggressive. That occasionally means lowering their prices, and taking competitive positions in the marketplace that make it hard for someone who does not have these competitive advantages to enter the market.

UK@W: How are people dealing with those obstacles? What concrete measures are they implementing, and what's your assessment of them?

De la Vega: The solutions involve laying out public policies that are more efficient than those we have today; that includes making it a clear responsibility of financial institutions to get more involved in the system, and really bring to the market some of the rescue measures for small companies that have already begun as commitments by the communications media to develop some optimism within the system. As long as we do not see the light [at the end of the tunnel], we won't be spending. When demand contracts in the ugly way it is contracting today, entrepreneurial activity becomes paralyzed. Companies leave the market, and it is very hard for others to enter it.

The Spanish government has limited resources. For example, its monetary policy is determined by the EU. However, there are some things it can do. It has tried to inject confidence in the market with its bank rescue plan, but it has had some mediocre results because many banks are not participating or are doing so only by dribs and drabs; that way, banks are not required to provide liquidity to the market. The problem is if the small companies don't get any liquidity, and they turn off the flow of credit, and then even if they sell less and many of them don't get paid when they do sell, they wind up not being able to take care of their [debt] obligations—not making nominal payments, payments to suppliers, and so forth. The vicious circle tightens, and it is very harmful. To remedy this situation, you create a rescue plan for small companies that basically consists of providing them with some 10 billion euros, but there is the problem of communication here. Financial aid is available through the ICO (the Ministry of Economics' Official Credit Institute), but the catch is that this operates through financial institutions that have a maximum level of requirements when it comes to [providing] guarantees. As a result, small companies continue to lack access to that financing.

There is a need for more aggressive solutions such as if the government were to strongly guarantee help through the ICO for small companies that have a certain degree of insolvency. There are 3.5 million small companies, of which 80% have financing problems. On the other hand, you could jointly create a public bank to develop projects aimed at smaller companies, although that is also difficult to communicate given today's community norms. The solution definitely involves injecting liquidity and confidence into the system. Some banks do that, but with complex criteria and in sectors of activity that are not subject to so much risk. In addition, the criteria for solvency are especially high, leaving out strong companies that could survive and that, at best, have a cash flow problem.

Starting from there, there are lots of other measures: A fiscal agreement for the serious reduction of taxes so that small companies can delay some tax payments—so that they can spread out payments of VAT (Value Added Taxes); and for social security liquidations, something that they can do now but which will have an extremely high cost when there is a bank guarantee.

UK@W: Experts talk a lot about innovation and exports as two good tools for getting around the crisis. Do you believe that the right policies for addressing those subjects are getting off the ground today?

De la Vega: Innovation is not just about developing innovative R&D in technology. That is just one sort of innovation that is possible for a very specific sort of company. Many small companies don't fit in that category. The sort of innovation within reach of small companies often involves some technology but, especially, it involves an innovative business model. For example, a neighborhood supermarket faces a very trying situation such as declining revenues, higher costs for all sorts of things including logistics, and so forth. For this sort of entrepreneur, innovation could mean trying to generate additional value for customers with classic solutions such as discounting, or it could mean looking for more innovative products, since competing simply on the basis of price has become so difficult.

You have to invest in R&D and have a public policy [to support that], but people need to know this is about long-term investment. It doesn't make sense to say that [R&D] is a [short-term] solution to the crisis. If we begin to invest seriously now and, for example, create a Ministry of Innovation, perhaps we can diversify the business model of the country in ten years. The reality is that the government's R&D funding has been squandered; on occasion, it was used for buying new machinery and other initiatives that are not really R&D.

As for exports, diversified companies are more sustainable, according to the textbooks. But we are talking about small companies exporting and, at times, that is an oxymoron, a contradiction in terms. Ultimately, it is a problem of competitiveness. In order to export, you need to be competitive, and in this country we have a very troubling situation in that regard. At times, the origins of that problem are in public policy; we have trouble exporting because we have exhausted our options for exporting in many sectors. In addition, we start with an unfavorable scenario in many low-cost markets in that salaries in those countries are up to eight or 10 times lower than in Spain; absenteeism is practically zero there; quality control requirements are very lax, with no controls, etc. Things that we do not require of companies of [non-European] origin [such as China] are requirements for our companies [in the EU], and this makes our competitiveness deficit even a bit deeper. You have to start from the root of the problem: We need to educate our companies, provide them with resources so that they can be more competitive. And we all need to play with the same rules.

UK@W: The database for your report includes 50 countries. What is the profile of the typical Spanish entrepreneur? Has it changed a great deal in recent times? If so, why? How does it differ from that of neighboring countries?

De la Vega: Our rate of entrepreneurial activity is a bit lower than in English-speaking countries, but higher than in the countries surrounding us. The profile of the entrepreneur is becoming more uniform, but the interesting thing is the change that has occurred in the last two or three years; the typical entrepreneur is maturing and aging. The average age has gone up by almost four years, and it is approaching forty [years of age]. These days, an entrepreneur coming into the market needs more professional baggage—more knowledge of the sector and so forth. This is very common among entrepreneurs older than fifty. This is related to the concept of becoming an entrepreneur 'out of necessity'—starting at that age because your professional career in Spain has come to an end even though that shouldn't be the case. In addition, today's entrepreneur has a higher level of training, and education now provides an additional competitive advantage. Today's entrepreneur also invests more [in his or her business], and the average cost of an initial investment in a project has gone up. The entrepreneur contributes part of the funding from his own pocket, which means that there are fewer and fewer [external] sources of funding.

In times of crisis, the ratio between male and female entrepreneurs evens out. This is something positive, and it obscures a reality of our environment. In families where there are not workers, the woman often develops her entrepreneurial project on her own. This can even happen, at times, in traditionally masculine business sectors. Declining activity in sectors such as real estate, construction and automobiles means that male entrepreneurs are disappearing and female entrepreneurs are being created in the service sector. Traditionally, Spaniards invest in the service sector because it is more welcoming, and it has minimal risk. However, we also observe that over the past twelve months, there has been a significant increase in the industrial sector of renewable energy.

UK@W: Do you believe that the crisis will change business habits in Spain?

De la Vega: For some years, you've already been seeing a certain change, but this is a little like R&D in that it is a long-term process. Nowadays, few Spanish college students want to become entrepreneurs. We need a profound change that begins with training, a change in values and society. So long as the communications media do not recognize the entrepreneur, rather than the speculator, as the person who generates value, things will go poorly for us. This change was beginning to occur before the crisis, building on the boom. Now we are moving in the right direction. In addition, the government is very interested because small and midsize companies generate more than 80% of all new jobs. The responsibility belongs to all of us—the people, the government, the business schools, the universities and so forth. What kind of country do we want to be in the future? ∎

Published: February 11, 2009 in Universia Knowledge@Wharton

Shai Agassi, Israel's Homegrown Electric Car Pioneer: On the Road to Oil Independence

If there's a poster child for Israel's entrepreneurial spirit, start-up Better Place is one strong candidate. Since launching the company in 2007, Shai Agassi— a 41-year-old Israeli entrepreneur and former executive of software giant SAP— has been shaking up the auto industry with his vision for mass adoption of zero-emission vehicles powered by electricity from renewable sources. Starting off with $200 million of seed money, Better Place has since been setting up networks of service stations for electric cars, helping to wean drivers from their environmentally unfriendly gas guzzlers. John Paul MacDuffie, a professor of management at Wharton and co-director of the International Motor Vehicle Program, joined Knowledge@Wharton to interview Agassi from the company's headquarters in California about what it takes to develop an oil-independent future.

An edited transcript of the conversation appears below:

Knowledge@Wharton: You've often said that your inspiration for launching Better Place came to you at the World Economic Forum in Davos during discussion about ways to reduce the world's dependence on oil. But the story of how Israel's president, Shimon Peres, helped you turn that idea into a business is not as well known. Could you tell us about that?

Shai Agassi: I was [at] the Young Global Leaders Forum. I was challenged to think of a problem and then try and solve it. I started with thinking of how...you run a country without oil. I then prepared a white paper and presented it to a number of governments, [and lastly] I presented it to Shimon Peres. Peres was the only leader who jumped [at] the challenge in the sense of saying, "If it's something that you're serious about, let's go figure out a way to do it." He dragged me by the hand to every government office in Israel and a number of large industrial companies.

At the outcome of this journey that he led me through, we [set several] conditions, which were: If you find the money—$200 million—and if you find a car company that would agree to build a mass production line of electric vehicles according to the model that we described—the switchable battery car— then Israel would be the experimental site to deploy and run the model. And he, true to form, helped me find Renault and convince [chairman and CEO] Carlos Ghosn in a meeting that it was the right thing to do, and then worked diligently in Israel to get it done. I offered to do it as a government agency and he challenged me to quit my job and do it as a company, which is what Better Place ended up becoming.

Knowledge@Wharton: How difficult was it to get the support of all the other constituents in government and industry, including the other auto companies? What kind of issues came up that you had to address?

Agassi: It wasn't easy. [People] had a hard time accepting it because there was a risk of betting on something that would not end up being successful. And there was almost no incentive for politicians to make decisions that are big and robust and breakthrough and disruptive. Most of their decisions are continuous developments of things that were agreed to by previous generations. There's always somebody else to blame.

We were lucky enough to have at the time Prime Minister [Ehud] Olmert, who basically said, "If you find the money, I'll fight Israel." What most people don't realize is that he has probably one of the most key individuals who is directly responsible to him—in this case the director general of the prime minister's office—to work through the entire bureaucracy of the government. All branches of government touch on our project and he needed that one person to unify the entire government.

Knowledge@Wharton: You have been speaking to other governments as well about reducing oil dependence. What is your pitch to them and how does your experience with other countries compare with your experience in Israel?

Agassi: You have to remember that nobody had done it [before] so it was really hard to convince somebody to be the first one. It's a lot easier to say, "We'll take the Israeli model and repeat it," than it is to be Israel in this case. And in most cases when I talk to governments, the common answer I got was that it's very good that the young generation is thinking about these big problems. And that was it. Nobody was willing to be crazy enough to follow through this model with us regardless of what we asked. And most of the time, we didn't ask for any money. We didn't ask for any budget. We basically said, "Just work with us and we'll get it done." But it was the fear of being caught or being observed as crazy by the media, which put politicians in the position that they wouldn't move.

Knowledge@Wharton: You were quoted recently—I think it was at a *Wired* magazine forum—saying that China is going to be a very important market for electric vehicles. Can you tell us a little bit about what you have been doing in China to make your case for your network [of electric-car recharging stations]?

Agassi: China is now the largest car country in the world. It's the largest producer of cars as well as the largest consumer of cars. It [grew] by almost 20% in the last year. The Chinese have no incentive to protect their existing car industry because they were always looking to leapfrog the global car industry. And they've learned that it's impossible for them to do it with the internal combustion engine because they won't get to the level of quality that the Germans or Americans have gotten to after a hundred years. But suddenly in this new world of electric vehicles, they have the ability to not only leapfrog, but also lead forever in this market. Now, from a historic perspective, you have to remember that the U.S. has built its entire middle class on the car industry. Not only did people become middle class by buying [cars], but also a lot of the people became middle class by working in the car industry or its derivatives.

China is observing that same model to create its own middle class in a country that will most likely end up with the same kind of transportation layer of the West. That means China will need to add somewhere around 400 million to 500 million cars in the next decade or two. And so you start to understand that there is a huge industrial effort [which will mean] that China can take over the backbone of the world's manufacturing. And by doing so, [China will] actually pick the market. If they go electric, everybody has to go electric.

Knowledge@Wharton: Another interesting case is India. India already has an electric car, the Reva. And [in July], another new car company called Bavina said that it's going to make electric cars in southern India. Since India imports 40% of its oil, it would seem to be a strong candidate to join your network. What efforts have you made there?

Agassi: India is interesting in the sense that it's not a question of the electric car. It's a question of the electric infrastructure for the car. In India, decisions for infrastructure are taken in a very different way than the Chinese model, which is basically centralized, top-down and very rapid execution from the moment a decision has been taken. When we look at India, we see great opportunity, but we're not sure [about the] speed of execution, whereas the Chinese are already in execution mode, not analysis mode.

Knowledge@Wharton: Would you care to comment on Japan and your efforts there?

Agassi: You're seeing sort of three couples around the world—China and Japan; the U.S. and the rest of the Americas—Canada and South America; and France and Germany. On each of the continents, you see one party moving really fast—[for example] China in the case of Asia—and one party reluctantly following its OEMs. In the case of Japan, it was [stuck] behind the Prius [hybrid] model that Toyota has led. It's hard to defend the hybrid and we're now seeing Japan racing to catch up with electric vehicles, [while] China is moving on. And you're seeing the same thing in America.

But the starkest example is what's happening in Europe, where France led the conversion to electric due to the development of nuclear power in the past and Renault's position on electric. Germany was held behind by the OEMs, [and] mostly by Daimler and VW. Now that Daimler has bought into [California-based electric car maker] Tesla, and VW announced a partnership with China's BYD, you're starting to see the German government moving to catch up [with] the French regulation and position on electric vehicles.

Knowledge@Wharton: You were able to convince Carlos Ghosn that Renault and Nissan should join in the endeavor. How did that come about and how have the other car companies reacted?

Agassi: President Peres and I met with Ghosn in Davos in 2007. I don't think we convinced Ghosn. He already had the vision that the future of Renault-Nissan is electric. A lot of people tell the story as if I convinced him. Ghosn was more convinced than I was that this was the future, so he deserves the credit. He was an exception in [believing] that hybrids just don't make sense long term—its dual-drive train, its cost structure is counter-intuitive to everything that was done in the industry. So he took it to the extreme and said, "If we go more electric, let's go all electric."

The problem was that a lot of other CEOs were trying to defend their legacy instead of building for the future. And they did not understand how fast this shift would happen. But we're explaining it to them....The main problem we had was trying to explain to some of the car CEOs, the car industry leaders, that an opportunity is lurking in 2011, 2012 as the "house was burning" and they didn't see how they were [even] going to get through the next quarter or the one after. It was not conducive to getting business done. Now that hopefully a lot of them are getting out of this situation ...it's easier to convince them that they've got to build for something in the future.

John Paul MacDuffie: To pick up on that, I am curious to hear your story for the Americas in terms of who is fast and who is slow, just to complete the world survey.

Agassi: One of the things that happened in America was that while we were changing the guard in the White House, Congress and the Senate were relentless in their push for the right incentive plan. So what you're seeing is that in the U.S., we put a lot of money both into the manufacturing and the consumption sides of the equation. We put [Department of Energy] money to [facilitate the] change toward electrification with $25 billion of the budget, about $7,500 toward every electric vehicle at the federal level. Some states are doing more. We're seeing a lot of programs in the current proposed energy bill at the House and the Senate, including financing for mass production, buying batteries [and so on]. So there's a whole collection of bills that have been put through the House and the Senate which are coming into fruition and creating a fantastic [opportunity] for electrification.

I'm starting to see it from the manufacturers in Canada, and in particular in Ontario, where Premier [Dalton] McGuinty is leading this effort. [Similarly] in Brazil and some of the other South American countries, their understanding is that if they don't catch up with electrification, they will be left with the old industry, while the U.S. uses its money—hundreds of billions of dollars—to shift and rebuild the car industry before it's too late.

MacDuffie: Of course, there are several new entrants in the electric car space in the U.S., like Tesla and Bright Automotive. Have you been in contact with them? Which do you think have promising manufacturing and business models that might coordinate well with your thoughts and your network?

Agassi: It's important to understand that we're solving a very different problem than these guys, as much as I have a ton of admiration for [Tesla chairman and CEO Elon Musk] and the role that the company has played in galvanizing the public's perception that a great electric car can be produced. And [Tesla's] Roadster has been a fantastic demonstration of what technology means in the world of electric cars.

We are trying to solve a different problem, which is: How do you run an entire country without gasoline? To do that, you really need to get a plan that scales at very high volume and low cost. And so while most of these guys have targeted high-end, $80,000 to $120,000 cars, we're targeting cars that are below $20,000. We're targeting the car that will be in that $10,000 to $15,000 range, but still give you everything you would get from a middle of the road Chevy Malibu, instead of trying to go to the highest high-end car possible.

If you look at volume, at producers that can produce at the very least 100,000 of these kinds of cars per plant, there are very few players like that in the U.S. All three of them [Tesla, Bright, and Fisker] are well known as U.S. domestic makers.

Now the reason I'm saying 100,000 a plant at the very least is that we need something that is replicable, which can then go from 100,000 to a million to 10 million over a period of about 18 months to 36 months, because we have a very short period of time to solve this problem. If you don't get very quickly to a million and then to 10 million, we will not be able to solve the problem of how to live without oil.

MacDuffie: That was one of the things about scaling that I wanted to ask you, so thank you. It seems that one of the ideas that has captured the public imagination most is the battery-swapping stations. Do you think that drivers will be comfortable with leasing their batteries versus owning them? In the early period of the hybrids, there was worry about whether these batteries will have longevity and so maybe leasing looked like a nice way to deal with that concern. But it seems like those concerns are not as strong today. Do you have any sense yet of what the consumer reaction to that idea will be?

Agassi: That was one of the key misunderstandings about our model. We do not lease the battery. We as the operator, Better Place, remain forever the owner of the battery. The consumer does not lease the battery. What the consumer buys is kiloliters. We don't sell kilowatt hours and we don't lease batteries. We're not a financing organization. We're an organization that provides a service, which is unlimited driving at a price on a per mile basis. And we buy kilowatt hours and buy batteries to provide that kind of service through infrastructure, which we put around an entire region. From all the surveys that we've done with consumers who have seen our switch stations, more than 80% said they would rather own a car without owning the battery or they don't really care about who owns the battery.

MacDuffie: From the perspective of the different vehicles from different manufacturers that would potentially use one of these swapping stations, what's your sense of the likelihood of the OEMs agreeing to standardization [so that] there's one battery type? If a charging station had to stock multiple types of batteries for different manufacturers, the logistics of managing those inventories gets more complicated to avoid running out [of the batteries] or having surpluses at a particular location.

Agassi: For one, we do not assume standardization. We assume that there will be multiple types and sizes of batteries. And we believe that the early movers will most likely decide to go with batteries that are unique to them. As a result, when we start in a region, we will need to decide which cars we service, and continue to service those cars for longevity. The design of the switch station has been one [that deals] with multiple car types and multiple battery types.

At the same time, you have to remember that once the infrastructure is in place, car makers have an incentive to use the batteries that were used by somebody else [given that the volume is already high] in that region. Otherwise they're the ones who are going to need to take care of stocking the extra batteries if volume [is low]. It's the same model that you want with retailers. If you're starting your first shops, then you need to court the original makers to give you some goods to sell; otherwise, the store is empty. But once your store is serving people, it's your shelf space that becomes more valuable than the actual goods from the makers.

MacDuffie: So it's really a pull over time toward standardization when the scale is there and the customers are there?

Agassi: Let me put it this way and you'll get it very easily. We see that model today with gasoline. In the early days of gasoline, if you didn't have oil, you couldn't open up a gas station. The minute you got oil, you went out and you installed gas stations. And then you sold the oil at whatever refining level you had across all these gas stations. Once the gas stations are in the right locations and people like them...they use these stations. If somebody says, "I have a new fuel"—let's say a zero-carbon, very cheap, no-emission, no-pollution fuel—they're more at the mercy of the gas stations than the other way around. They need the gas stations to stock [the new fuel] before people buy the cars that use that fuel.

MacDuffie: I like that analogy. So let me ask a question that's more about battery technology. Do you think it will be stable enough for whatever kind of model—whether it's for recharging or battery swapping—in the infrastructure you envision? What's the risk of it becoming obsolete by a big change in battery technology or some other change that would make the infrastructure problematic?

Agassi: One of the things I believe is that huge breakthroughs in science don't happen as miracles. What we'll see in mass production in five to 10 years' time has to be in the lab right now.

[In] very few cases can we get from 200 kilowatt hours per kilogram to 300 kilowatt hours per kilogram. That's a 150% to 200% improvement over what we have today, which means we probably are going to see [a similar improvement] in about five to seven years' time if that's what is in the lab. That means we're going to see a battery that will do roughly 250 miles to 300 miles on good days at the same size and for the same cost as what we have today.

The interesting element is if you get to that kind of battery, would you put that battery in your car? [What if] you—seven years from now—have a swapping infrastructure across the region [and can] only buy half that battery at half the price and have a price advantage that is more distinguished and gives you a better business model? The answer is most people would rather pay half as much per mile and have a 120-mile battery than those who would buy a 250-mile battery and pay twice as much per mile driven.

MacDuffie: So the emergence of that kind of greater range doesn't necessarily invalidate the plan for the infrastructure [and] current battery technology?

Agassi: Remember the early cell phones—the bricks—that had a big battery attached? When that battery technology improved, we didn't keep the same talking time and the big brick. We reduced the size of the phone and put a half a battery in there. Okay? And we kept on doing the same thing again, again and again. It's not that we couldn't keep [the old phone]. Imagine today if we took a brick like the original Motorola phone and put a battery inside. You'd be able to talk forever. But who would buy that phone?

MacDuffie: Let me ask what is a kind of geography question. So far, you've had a lot of enthusiasm from Israel, but also from other places that are relatively concentrated geographies, like Denmark and Hawaii. Is there any sense that that's the most logical starting place for this model in terms of getting critical mass quickly and [needing] fewer long trips in a proximate geography, hence less need for spacing the recharger or battery-swapping stations to support long trips?

Agassi: Are you saying that it's unfair that we picked the best places to start?

MacDuffie: No, I'm just wondering if you see a natural fit for relatively smaller geographies as a place to prove this, or if you plan to prove it in large geographies at the same time?

Agassi: I just want to remind you that our third location is Australia. So we went big as well. The rationale in picking Israel and Denmark is obvious. It's a single-cell model, if you want to think of a cell-phone metaphor. Israel is almost like a one-and-a-half cell, if you think of a cell as a radius of about 100 miles from the middle point of the country. And Denmark is not different than that. With the same kind of 100-mile radius from Copenhagen, you reach most of the country. You need half a cell to cover the rest of the country.

   The issue is that we can only see multi-cell organisms. If you think of the West coast of the United States, it's basically four cells and a long freeway connecting them. Think of L.A./San Diego as one-and-a-half cells. San Francisco is a full cell. And then Portland is a half cell and Seattle is a one cell. What you see is that you've got four cells and a 1,500-mile highway connecting them. That's one of the models we'll be looking at proving. So we're always in the position that once you've done it in one country, it's very easy to replicate in other countries regardless of size.

MacDuffie: Could you say a bit more about Australia because it is a [location] with vast expanses of very low density. How are you thinking of tackling a country like that?

Agassi: We don't need to tackle all of Australia. That's the beauty of it. We don't need to do 100% of the cars on day one. Australia has three very big cells:

Melbourne, Sydney and Brisbane. All you need to do is cover each one of those cells that are very dense urban centers. If you think about them, there are extremely profitable cell-phone models in each one of those.

So the same thing [applies] to us. We have very dense coverage in those [cities] and then one freeway that connects them that runs, I think, about 1,000 miles. And that highway gets a switch station every 25 miles, which effectively gives you comfort that you won't get stuck when driving from any of these cells to any of the other cells.

You don't drive 1,000 miles every day. But when you do, you're within coverage. And so you really get an environment where you've got three major, highly profitable centers and a very good connection across all of them.

MacDuffie: You've used the cell phone—product, business model, industry, evolution—[as an] example several times. Did that enter into your thinking early on as sort of a stimulus to your vision?

Agassi: It did. It's actually more exiting minds right now than entering. One of the mistakes that we made is we thought of ourselves too much as being a cell-phone company. We're more like an energy company or a modern oil company in the sense that we sell the same product, we sell miles to drivers. We're more [like] a company [in] infrastructure, which buys its assets and through that, sells a service—effectively a comfort of driving miles only with sustainable ways both for the economy and [the environment].

MacDuffie: One more general question about the different parts that Better Place is involved with. As I understand it, a lot of the automotive value chain would change under your vision, including design, production, distribution and the way that energy is consumed. How far along are you in figuring out the incentives for each part of the chain to [encourage them to] participate in the model?

Agassi: For car makers, it's pretty obvious. They have a ton of capacity. They're looking at a non-sustainable business model as it is today. We're proposing to them a much better business model—a highly profitable car that drives for a long period of time with very low warranty costs, and some incentives to work with us and provide us with cars.

We're providing an incentive for the gas-station owners to leverage their space by [installing] switch stations inside. We're providing great incentives for the utilities in the sense that we're buying excess capacity [from them], in particular in renewable excess capacity. We're selling them standby power whenever they need it so they've got a great customer who is intermittent and is willing to share its storage, which is a very big pain for them right now. For governments, we provide a way to [rectify] trade balance issues in terms of not importing any more oil.

Finally, the consumer gets a cheaper car with more convenience, with the ability to drive indefinitely, without noise, without pollution, without killing their future and their kids' future. Overall it's one of the biggest value generators, mostly because we're taking out the implicit and the explicit cost of oil.

Knowledge@Wharton: What message would you like to give high school students about the cars and car industry of the future? And how can they get involved with Better Place?

Agassi: First thing they have to remember is that their first car will be electric. The young generation today understands that we don't have enough oil in the ground and we don't have enough of an atmosphere to sustain them until they die if we don't switch early. And the earlier we switch the easier it is going to be to recover from what we—our generation and the generations of the past—have done to this planet, and the abuse that we've [inflicted on] natural resources. And so the first thing to remember is your future is electric.

The second thing is that this is one of the most exciting times in this industry. We will have a billion electric cars on the road sometime around 2025 because we will have a billion people [driving] and there's no way they can be [driving] gasoline cars. Between now and 2025, a billion new cars need to be added and there will not be any industry that will be more exciting than this one. If you think of an industry that will make a billion of something, [with an average price of] $20,000, you're looking at a $20 trillion industry rising up from nothing today within the span of 10 to 15 years.

Those are the kinds of [things] that made Silicon Valley a great place to work and made biotechnology a great place to work and made the Internet such a fun place to be part of in 1995. If they're looking for something that will be the next big industry, there's no doubt in my mind that the electric car is the next big thing and that $20 trillion is just the core of this industry. There'll be batteries and services, innovation and new product technology. Everything will be reinvented and they've got to think of a way to get into this industry while they can.

Knowledge@Wharton: Is there a way students can get involved with Better Place?

Agassi: We have probably about 15,000 to 20,000 unsolicited resumes. There's always a way to get our attention if they want to and they work hard. I'm sure that down the road when they're done at Wharton, we'll look at their resumes. ∎

Published: August 13, 2009 in Knowledge@Wharton

Lord Swraj Paul: How to Forge a New Business with Perseverance, Determination—and a Little Bit of Luck

Punjab, India-born Swraj Paul overcame personal tragedy to become one of Britain's wealthiest businessmen. Having toiled in his father's small foundry in India in his early years, he went on to graduate from the Massachusetts Institute of Technology before emigrating to the United Kingdom to found Capparo Group—a steel-to-hotels conglomerate that today has an annual turnover of nearly 1 billion euro, where he continues to be chairman.

Though based in the U.K. since the 1960s, he's most widely remembered in his home country for what many believe was a turning point in corporate governance in India in the 1980s. As what could be called the country's first "corporate raider," he challenged the traditions of India Inc. and bought stakes in two local corporate giants, beginning a new era of transparency and financial reporting standards.

Back in the U.K., Lord Paul made history by being the first Asian to be appointed deputy speaker of the House of Lords, the upper house of Parliament, in 2008 after receiving a life peerage in the House of Lords as the Right Honourable Lord Paul of Marylebone. An active supporter of the Labour Party, he has, however, found himself embroiled in recent political turmoil, including investigations into allegations of politicians inappropriately claiming expenses. His name was cleared earlier this year.

Lord Paul met with Arabic Knowledge@Wharton to discuss a range of topics, from how business and politics have a lot more in common than many people think to why he doesn't like to give advice to fledgling entrepreneurs.

An edited transcript of the conversation follows.

Arabic Knowledge@Wharton: You were born in Jalandhar, India, in 1931...

Lord Swraj Paul: That's right.

Arabic Knowledge@Wharton: ...and your father ran a small steel foundry there. Could you tell us about your early days and your introduction to the steel business?

Lord Paul: As you said, I was almost born into this, [in] the factory, because a typical family business in India in those days was a very small business. You had offices on the ground floor, you lived on the first floor and the factory was in the backyard. That was all that I saw while growing up. Then, of course, I studied in India, went to MIT [Massachusetts Institute of Technology], where I did mechanical engineering and metallurgy. I came back to the family business, but in Calcutta because by that time [it] was there. Calcutta was the hub of the steel sector in those days. In 1966, I ended up coming to the United Kingdom.

Arabic Knowledge@Wharton: What brought about that decision?

Lord Paul: It was about one of those very unfortunate things. My daughter was ill so I brought her there for treatment. Unfortunately, we lost her after about 22 months in and out of the hospital…

Arabic Knowledge@Wharton: Sorry to hear that.

Lord Paul: Living with somebody whom you know is going to die—she was suffering from leukemia—was a very shattering experience for both my wife and me. I took what you call in India the sannyasa [a state of detachment from materialism] and went into meditation and reading philosophy, biographies, etc. I stayed in London was not because I wanted to work, but because I wanted to stay for the rest of my life where our daughter died. That's how I ended up in Britain.

After getting over [her death]—perhaps partly the meditation helped and being inspired by other people—I thought, "Let me start a little something to keep myself busy," because it was becoming difficult to keep myself occupied. I started a little business. Since then, God has been kind.

Arabic Knowledge@Wharton: Could you describe the kind of Indian businesses that were in the U.K. at that time? How typical was your venture among them?

Lord Paul: Mine was a little bit different. Right from birth, I have been looking at industry, getting involved in industry. My training as an engineer was in industry. In those days, most Indian communities [comprised] workers from India, and then some East African Asians started coming, and they were mostly in the corner shops. There was nobody really in industry. I didn't know anything else but industry. I started a little plant that needed very little money because I didn't have the money. I leased the plant, so it was exploring a completely new field for an Indian, and right in the heart of the manufacturing industry. People felt that was strange—"How on earth is he going to make anything out this thing?" But we worked through it and managed.

Arabic Knowledge@Wharton: Could you describe some of the barriers that you faced and how you overcame them? And what lessons can one learn from your entrepreneurial experience?

Lord Paul: First, I never came across a barrier, or if I did, I did not worry about it. I just said, "My job is to get on with what I want to do." Maybe that was because of my training at MIT, which taught me a couple of things: One is never compromise on excellence, [the other is] never give up. There was no way I was going to give up just because there were barriers. Once you've determined that you are not going to let any barrier get [in your way], you stop seeing them. If they come, you steamroll over them.

I'm sure people felt strange that here in the heart of British industry, which wasn't doing well at that time, somebody comes from India, of all people, and wants to set up a company. They looked [at me] with skepticism. But I found [what] was lacking in Britain in industry at that time: A consistency in quality and on-time delivery. I saw the gap and said, "I am going to make sure that I deliver something that is consistent with what I promised. I don't want to build a Rolls Royce, but whatever I want to build, it must be consistent." Second, on-time delivery was rare.

[Because] it was a very small plant, it encouraged me to build something bigger. It looked like a dream, but while running from pillar to post, I was able to raise money and we built the plant. Then one thing just led to another. In the end, it was in the hand of God, which had a lot to do with it. If you can combine hard work and integrity and hope for luck, it works.

Arabic Knowledge@Wharton: There also may be an element of ingenuity in figuring out what was preventing on-time delivery at other plants, but you were able to find the solution. Could you describe how?

Lord Paul: Part of it was that from the 1960s onward, there were a lot of industrial problems in Britain. The attitude of managements was, "Them and us." There was such a gap between the workers and management that the industrial relations were awful. I wanted to carry the workers with me. I didn't have many workers, but we tried to develop a culture in which you became part of them. That was partly the reason perhaps why I joined the Labour Party.

Arabic Knowledge@Wharton: But it's also probably the case that in Britain, perhaps even more than other countries, business tends to be an "old boys" network. How difficult was it for you, almost like a pioneer in this area, to thrive in that environment?

Lord Paul: You're absolutely right. Britain was always an old boys network, whether in business, civil service, politics, etc. But they recognized the perseverance and determination to succeed of another person. And who would not like to get his material on time and be competitive? I always told the customer, "Don't buy from me as your main source. Try me as a second source." I never went to a customer and said, "Hey, you're buying this and this from this big company. I would like to replace it." I said, "You want to make sure that this company is supplying you, but they could [run into] problems. Why don't you try me as a second source? You give them 90% of your order; all I am looking for is 10%.

Once you are able to step in, performance matters. The most interesting case I had was when I built a plant. I chased one company for two years for an order. Every year, they promised me [business]. Even then, I used to sit on the bench, not even a comfortable chair, waiting for an appointment, and they purposely made me wait. As luck would have it, two years later, I ended up acquiring the group that owned that company. When I went to visit the [managing director], he said to me, "I know we thoroughly misbehaved. If you want me to resign, I'll do so." I said, "No, you stay right there....[But] as long as you're working in my group, don't be so ridiculous to anybody." He turned out to be a very good manager.

Arabic Knowledge@Wharton: Another story I remember, perhaps from about 30 years or so ago, was when you decided to invest in some Indian companies—DCM Limited and Escorts Limited [DCM was a goods conglomerate and Escorts a transportation parts manufacturer]. What were your objectives and what lessons can be learned?

Lord Paul: You are a very young man. It was long time ago, in 1982.

Arabic Knowledge@Wharton: I had just entered journalism at that time and I remember it being front-page news.

Lord Paul: That's right. In 1982. In India, people forget. It was the late Indira Gandhi who wanted to open the economy, not anybody else. She did start in a much more cautious way, because she was a cautious person, a person who was very pro-India and very Indian. In my view, she was the greatest prime minister India has had up until today. The credit of opening the economy or planting the seed for that goes to the late Mrs. Gandhi. Then she had another idea in mind. She wanted to [get] non-resident Indians more interested in India. Up until that time, Indians and the Indian government treated non-resident Indians as if they came from the moon. They didn't want to have anything to do with them.

Both Mr. Rajan Nanda of Escorts and Mr. Bharat Ram of DCM were going around the world asking people to invest in their companies. Nobody knew in India, including me, that these people owned nothing of their companies. Nanda had less than 5% of Escorts. Ram had DCM Escorts had less than 10%.

When I saw that gap, I said, "What on earth are they are talking about? I am DCM, I am Escorts. Let me buy the shares." I ended up buying 7.5% of Escorts and 13% of DCM, so I held more shares than them. If you studied their balance sheets, there was so much of abuse, such as jewelry for women. They felt threatened and they tried to stop [me]. They went to Rajiv Gandhi, they went to [other] politicians, etc., and I ended up losing money.

Nobody should get the credit for forcing India's economy to change except Swraj Paul. But Indians are very poor at giving credit. They only know how to praise the government in power irrespective of the power, irrespective of the government. They will only give credit to them. But I do think I [helped show] the ordinary shareholder that there was abuse taking place....India is still not as transparent as one would like it to be, but it is certainly far more transparent now and I do think I deserve some credit for that.

Arabic Knowledge@Wharton: You're absolutely right. Nobody gives you credit. That was also the first time that corporate governance became front-page news on the business pages.

Lord Paul: No, I mean my reward is really [with respect to] the ordinary person of India. That was 1982...but even today, if I go to any village, people come to me and say, "Lord Paul, can I have your autograph? Lord Paul, it's nice to meet you." What better reward can you get? I don't need a reward from the Indian government. I don't need a reward from the village. The poor man is my constituency and that is what my life mission is.

Arabic Knowledge@Wharton: How at the different stages of the business did you need different leadership skills? How did you acquire those skills, which might have helped you succeed in a previous stage, but did not become a barrier to succeeding at the next stage?

Lord Paul: One thing I learned a long time ago is that you should never do the same job for more than five years, irrespective of what job you're doing. Whether in business or politics, [after] more than five years, you become useless because you can't come up with new ideas. Business and politics all need new ideas. Even when I was running the business, I always concentrated on a different aspect of it. That's why in 1996, when I turned 65, I told my son [Angad Paul], "Now you look after the business." I wanted to devote time to several passions. One is education....

I was in China one-and-a-half years ago [and left] impressed. In India, we need to pick up speed. In 1996, I told [my three] boys, "Now you run the business." They said, "Papa, why don't you remain chairman? We won't bother you." And they haven't. I let them get on with life. I don't interfere with them. They rarely talk to me. But they are driving the business. I don't. I am not necessarily going to like all what they do. But I know they are certainly better trained than I was. They have much more knowledge available to them than I had [at their age]. They are doing a marvelous job. My two grandsons just joined the business.

A long time ago, I was at MIT and I was speaking to students and one young student asked me, "What advice do you have for students who are graduating?" I told her, 'I'll give you one bit of advice. Never ask an old man for his advice because his frustrations come with it. Make your own mistakes because you will learn far more from your mistakes than [by asking me for advice]." I have followed that principle. I've made lot of mistakes in my life. But every time, those mistakes made me a better man.

Arabic Knowledge@Wharton: Can you tell me about the biggest leadership challenge you ever faced? How did you deal with it, and what did you learn from it?

Lord Paul: ...I have never been a big leader, nor do I aspire to be a leader. I am a worker...I enjoy what I do and I even tell my children now, "You can't choose what you have to do necessarily, but you can certainly learn to enjoy what you do, and unless you enjoy what you do, life is very boring...."

First, I want to like whatever I have to do. ■

Published: July 13, 2010 in Arabic Knowledge@Wharton

Huawei Technologies: A Chinese Trail Blazer in Africa

Walk into a bookstore in Beijing and you will find shelves filled with books about Huawei Technologies. As one of China's fledging multinational companies and a major force in the international telecommunications equipment industry, Huawei is rewriting the rules of competition in a global industry. Moreover, it is the first non-state-owned Chinese company to successfully expand its operations internationally, some observers say, and it has become a model for other Chinese companies and a source of national pride.

Despite the challenges facing the global economy and the telecommunications industry, Huawei achieved contract sales of $16 billion, representing a 45% year-over-year increase, with approximately 72% of its revenues coming from international markets. In less than a decade, Huawei has penetrated almost every market around the world, investing heavily in its business and technology product lines, which includes fixed networks, mobile networks, data communications, optical networks, software and services, and terminals.

According to an industry insider, Huawei segments the telecom equipment industry into three major categories: Internet switches, fixed line networks and wireless networks. "Huawei is currently the number three global company in wireless networks and number two in fixed line and switches," says founder and CEO Ren Zhenfei. "But Huawei's goal is to become number one in all three segments." Its competitors include both well-known European and American companies, such as Alcatel-Lucent, Cisco Systems, Nokia Siemens Networks and Ericsson Telephone Co., as well as lower-cost Chinese competitors such as ZTE Corp.

Huawei currently serves 270 operators in about 100 countries, including 35 of the world's top 50 telecommunications companies. As of March 2007, Huawei had more than 83,000 employees worldwide, of whom 43% are engaged in R&D. The company reports that it dedicates at least 10% of its revenues to R&D and is now the fourth largest patent applicant worldwide, with more than 20,000 applications filed by 2007. Last year, Huawei won 45% of all new Universal Mobile Telecommunications System and High Speed Packet Access contracts, making it the top supplier in this area. Huawei is also now one of the top three suppliers in the global GSM market; by the end of 2007, it had shipped base stations with total capacity of 700,000 carrier frequencies, serving more than 300 million GSM users worldwide. (GSM is currently the most popular second-generation standard for mobile phones.)

It is hard to understand Huawei's success without considering its humble origins and distinctive corporate culture. In 1988, Ren, a former People's Liberation Army (PLA) officer, founded the company as a third-party reseller of telecom devices in Shenzhen, China. Five years later, Huawei achieved its first breakthrough when it launched its C&C08 digital telephone switch, which had the largest switching capacity in China at the time. By initially deploying in small cities and rural areas, the company gradually gained market share and made its way into the mainstream market. From 1996 to 1998, Huawei experienced exponential growth, coinciding with the boom in China's telecommunications industry. After winning its first overseas contract in 1996 with Hong Kong's Hutchison-Whampoa, Huawei expanded to Russia and Africa. In Africa, Huawei began operations in 1998, starting in Kenya, and has now become the largest CDMA product provider in the region. During the same year, Huawei hired IBM consultants to gain expertise in management strategies in a concerted effort to learn industry best practices.

First, the Countryside

As a follower of Mao's thought, Ren has drawn much inspiration from the PLA's military strategy—reflected in Huawei's business strategy, organization and corporate culture. For example, Huawei has relied on a well-known Maoist strategy of first focusing on seizing the countryside, then encircling and conquering cities. Huawei followed this strategy, achieving its first breakthrough in 1993 when it aggressively marketed its digital telephone switches in smaller towns before expanding all over China. Later, Huawei utilized this same strategy by first targeting the underserved markets of Russia and Africa before moving into Europe.

Military culture is also epitomized in Huawei's rigidly hierarchical organization, where emphasis is placed on hierarchical management rather than on individual employees, who are viewed as easily replaceable foot soldiers. Like that of many other East Asian firms, Huawei's corporate culture relies heavily on rhetoric and propaganda. The introductory article of Huawei's basic law reads: "Love for our homeland, fellow citizens, work and life is the source of our cohesion; responsibility, creativity, respect and solidarity represent our company's quintessential culture."

Other aspects of Huawei's culture are characteristically Chinese. Resilience and hard work, qualities valued in traditional Chinese culture, are emphasized at Huawei as a way to gain competitive advantage. Another classic East Asian trait, putting the group before the individual, can also be seen. Huawei expects its employees to place their personal lives second in order to serve their company loyally. Its approach to business, referred to as "the way of the wolf," is characterized by reliance on instinct, extreme resilience and employees' willingness to cooperate and sacrifice themselves for the sake of the pack.

Huawei's strong identity, however, has not prevented the company from adopting Western tactics. In the mid 1990s, most Huawei managers were sanguine about the prospects of the firm. However, Ren was aware that Huawei had severe growth limitations, mainly due to the lack of organizational expertise and the absence of a viable long-term strategy. He set out to change the company into a solutions provider. By 2000, when the communications industry slowdown was noticeable, Huawei was already in the midst of a restructuring process that gave the firm its competitive edge against local rivals.

According to an industry insider, "Ren recognized that the best way to overcome Huawei's limitations was to learn from leading Western companies." Thus, from 1998 to 2003, the company hired IBM for management consulting services, modeling itself after the American company. Under IBM's guidance, Huawei significantly transformed its management and product development structure. Ren prioritized R&D and supply chain management by adopting IBM's Integrated Product Development (IPD) and Integrated Supply Chain (ISC). After discovering Huawei's return on investment in R&D was one-sixth that of IBM, Ren stipulated mastery of IBM's IPD methodology. Furthermore, Huawei adopted ISC since supply-chain performance was far below potential. According to *The World of Huawei*, Huawei's on-time delivery rate in 1999 was only 50%, compared with 94% for competitors; annual inventory turnover was 3.6%, compared with 9.4% for competitors. Adopting ISC entailed winning over suppliers and partners, many of whom had little appetite for Western management practices.

While working with Huawei, IBM was completing its own strategic change from a hardware vendor to an IT solutions provider. Ren drew from IBM's experience, also realizing that the future of Huawei was not in manufacturing what others invented, but in creating excellence in both research and service. This strategy, which may be conventional for leading Western firms, is unusual in China. Although Huawei management possessed vision before hiring IBM, it was through the experience, insight and methodologies gained from working with IBM that Huawei managed to adopt new management practices and become a global player.

Nowhere is Huawei's presence and strategy more evident than in Africa, a continent it entered for the first time in 1998, where it successfully dispelled the "made in China" image of low cost and low quality. Beginning in the 1990s, Huawei shifted its role from a manufacturer to that a complete solutions provider. Today, Huawei creates some of the most sophisticated telecommunications equipment in the world and, according to the company, is "not making it cheaper—it's making it better." Armed with its combination of a corporate culture marked by Communist roots and leading Western business practices, Huawei has executed a strategy composed of superior pricing, customer service and brand awareness to penetrate and dominate the African market, one in which few multinationals have been successful. Huawei has established a reputation as the preferred low-cost, yet high-quality mobile network builder. Its sales in Africa had topped $2 billion across 40 countries by 2006.

According to the former head of Huawei's operations in West Africa, Wilson Yang, Huawei's profit margins in Africa can be up to 10 times greater than those it realizes in China. Huawei manages to achieve tremendous margins while still pricing itself only 5%-15% lower than its major international competitors, Ericsson and Nokia. Furthermore, Huawei is cautious not to price itself too low so that it will not be seen as yet another low-cost Chinese provider. In contrast, Huawei's main Chinese competitor in Africa, ZTE, consistently prices 30%-40% below European competitors and, consequently, its products are perceived as being of inferior quality.

Huawei's pricing methodology can also be traced back to its experience with IBM, a company that helped Huawei learn the importance of turning R&D into cash and of approaching product development from both technical and business angles to ensure investment returns. This represented the transition for Huawei from a low-cost volume competitor to a value-added leading enterprise.

Learning from the Master

Another factor behind its African success is its attention to superior customer service. In 2000-2001, Huawei faced a confluence of challenges: IT investment dried up, profit margins shrank and the market faced oversupply, leading profit growth to evaporate. IBM consultants stressed increasing profits through better supply-chain management, stronger R&D and more integrated corporate structure. However, Huawei was also learning a key strength of IBM: unparalleled service. Ren appreciated the value of this concept under looming adversity. Unmatched attention and commitment to service eventually came to dominate the firm's global strategy.

Indeed, superior service was a distinguishing feature of Huawei's business model in Africa and its core competitive advantage. Yang explains how this aspect of Huawei's business model ultimately led to global growth: "Three years into its Africa experiment, Huawei still had only 20 employees on the ground and very few contracts. However, our existing clients noticed the unparalleled responsiveness of management and personnel. We brought a Chinese attitude to both work ethic and relationship building in Africa. The result was that clients soon realized they could rely on Huawei 24 hours a day, seven days a week. We emphasized close relationships to foster that reliability and soon began to realize collateral benefits. All of a sudden, our reputation for superior service and higher quality gained us introductions to decision makers in new markets, faster network building and advanced notification of competitive bids. This enhanced Huawei's ability to price safely below the competition."

Huawei is also using its business in Africa as a training ground for establishing itself as a global brand through three distinct channels: policy, local investment and marketing. Huawei leverages its resources and products to connect with developmental policy throughout Africa. In May 2007, at a forum held in conjunction with the 2007 annual meeting of the African Development Bank Group (ADBG), Huawei set out a vision for Africa that is centered on "'bridging the digital divide and enriching the lives of Africans." Huawei prides itself on giving back to the African community; one of the ways it does this is through donating educational communications equipment to schools.

Huawei has begun to establish regional training centers in African countries such as Nigeria, Kenya, Egypt, Tunisia, Angola and Guinea. By August 2004, Huawei had invested more than $10 million dollars into its Nigerian training center. Recently, Huawei opened a new training facility in South Africa, its fifth training center on the continent. There is a sixth center currently being built in Angola. The company now provides training for up to 2,000 people annually. Such local investments by Huawei help bolster the local economy with job creation and localized management while improving the company's image in the eyes of local consumers, businesses and potential partners.

Huawei is asserting its brand potential in Africa by means of smart marketing strategies and "going green," including optional use or solar and wind energy. It actively promotes its GSM base stations as among the most eco-friendly in the business, claiming that it cuts energy usage by 47% compared to regular towers. By the end of 2007, Huawei reported that it had deployed more than 100,000 green base stations, which saved 570 million kilowatt-hours, or 170,000 tons of coal.

Huawei Technologies has built a world-class enterprise, reaped tremendous profits in Africa over the last 10 years and is contributing to growth in Africa. In China, domestic media have heralded Huawei's success as a model for other Chinese companies trying to transform themselves from domestic entities into global players. Huawei has already profitably penetrated the European market, winning major contracts and servicing prominent clients such as Vodafone and Telefónica. As Huawei leads the way for home-grown Chinese corporations, the challenges its leaders face going forward include maintaining its growth and transferring the lessons learned in Africa to Europe and North and South America, all of which represent both enormous profit potential and new strategic challenges. ■

This article was written by Christine Chang, Amy Cheng, Susan Kim, Johanna Kuhn-Osius, Jesús Reyes and Daniel Turgel, members of the Lauder Class of 2010.

Published: April 20, 2009 in Knowledge@Wharton

"We Don't Eat Scones": Magic Johnson Proves He Has the Acumen for More than Hoops

Earvin "Magic" Johnson's basketball career included five national championships with the Los Angeles Lakers and a gold medal with the "Dream Team" at the 1992 Olympics. But domination on the court meant little when Johnson began approaching investors to launch his first business venture. "Everybody wanted the autograph, but nobody wanted to invest with me. At the beginning, I got turned down 10 times before someone said 'yes.' You know what they said? They said I was a dumb jock," Johnson noted during a recent presentation at Wharton.

Magic the businessman wasn't the proposal's only tough sell. Investors also doubted that there was any money to be made building high-quality movie theaters and restaurants in inner city neighborhoods. Over the past 20 years, however, Johnson has proven he has the acumen for more than hoops. Beverly Hills, Calif.-based Magic Johnson Enterprises now owns or operates gyms, Starbucks coffee shops, Burger Kings, movie theaters and other businesses in 85 cities across 21 states. His Canyon-Johnson Investment Fund has been behind nearly $4 billion in urban revitalization projects that resulted in the creation of 4.5 million square feet of retail and commercial space.

Johnson credits his success to having a concrete business plan that he felt passionately about—and an ability to help partners see the potential in urban, predominantly African-American and Latino neighborhoods. "You've got to knock on the doors of corporations who have the same mindset as yours, who have the same heart as yours," Johnson noted. "If I'm in New York, I can take [investors] to Harlem, I can take them to the Bronx, I can take them to Los Angeles, and I can take them to the South Side of Chicago. You're going to have to find a way to touch their heart and spirit."

Pound Cake and Sweet Potato Pie

When Johnson was trying to broker a partnership with Starbucks in the 1990s, he told CEO Howard Schultz that "the growth of his business would be in urban America. He already had [coffee shops] on every street and across the street from each other." But a boardroom pitch wasn't enough to close the deal. Johnson invited Schultz to spend a Friday night at one of the 6-foot-9 former point guard's movie theaters. The visit coincided with the opening night of the Whitney Houston vehicle Waiting to Exhale, and the theater's lobby and screening rooms were packed. "Our biggest screen had 500 women inside. All of a sudden every woman thought she knew Whitney Houston personally and started talking to the screen," Johnson recalled. "So Howard grabs me about 20 minutes in and says, 'Earvin, I never had a movie-going experience quite like this.' Guess what happened? That got me the deal."

Frappuccinos, lattes and Pike Place Roast are on the menu at a Magic Johnson-owned Starbucks, but there are subtle differences between the former basketball star's coffee shops and the chain's other locations. Instead of jazz standards and easy listening, R&B music plays on the stereo. There is extra space for meetings of community and church groups, and bulletin boards where local residents can post neighborhood news and events. "People said there's no way Latinos and African-Americans will pay $3 for a cup of coffee. Yes, we will pay $3, but we don't eat scones," Johnson stated. "I had to take scones out of my Starbucks and put in pound cake, Sock It to Me cake and sweet potato pie—things that resonate with the urban consumer. You have to know your customer and you have to speak to that customer every day."

The strategy to focus on inner city communities was developed by Johnson when he was still playing basketball. Riding high after winning back-to-back championships as a stand-out college, and then NBA, player in 1979 and 1980, Johnson recalled returning home to neighborhoods of crumbling storefronts, where residents had to travel long distances to shop or eat at chains that were plentiful in the suburbs. "Most of the people who own the businesses in urban America don't live in urban America, so they take the money to their communities and spend disposable income in their communities. We have trouble in our communities because we do not own the businesses," Johnson noted. "Now that we put Starbucks there, those same people that live in the community, they spend money there and Mom and Pop stores have more traffic. Now they don't have to close their doors because people have money to spend at those stores."

In addition to the Starbucks partnership launched in 1998, Magic Johnson Enterprises has also entered into agreements to develop T.G.I Friday's restaurants and 24 Hour Fitness locations in targeted markets. The company in 2008 entered into an alliance with Best Buy to help the electronics chain expand into urban areas and strengthen its appeal with multicultural customers. A deal with food service giant Sodexo includes contracts to feed employees of Toyota, John Deere and Disneyland, meaning "Mickey Mouse and all of them eat my food," Johnson said with a chuckle.

Johnson's investments are run through a partnership with Bobby Turner, managing partner of Los Angeles-based asset management company Canyon Capital. Over two years beginning in 1998, the Canyon-Johnson Investment fund raised an initial $300 million. But Johnson noted that he achieved a 30% return on the initial fund and that it took a shorter period to raise $600 million for a subsequent endeavor. "The returns are everything, and when we returned them 30% on money spent on urban America, when they did not want to invest it initially, it raised a lot of eyebrows," Johnson stated. "We just closed about a year ago on a billion in cash. It [required] a year because the economy is so bad....There's a lot of deal flow out there, but a lot of bad deals."

Earning His Nickname

Johnson retired from the NBA in 1991 after announcing that he had HIV. His company's interests also include a partnership with Abbott Labs to hold educational events and offer free testing in cities with high HIV infection rates. The business's nonprofit arm, the Magic Johnson Foundation, organizes job fairs, operates community "empowerment" centers and offers college scholarships to minority high school students. "There have already been people who have made millions, so you're not doing anything that anyone else hasn't done before," stated Johnson, whose net worth was estimated at nearly $500 million in a 2008 Los Angeles Times story. "But can you save and touch somebody's life? Can you help a community get back on its feet? That hasn't been done before. You can set yourself apart from everybody else if you can do something like that. That's why I love what I do."

As one of 10 children who "grew up poor" in Lansing, Mich., Johnson often arrived home from late basketball practices to find that his siblings had eaten all the food his mother had prepared for dinner. A high school standout, the athlete was given his nickname by a local newspaper columnist and went on to lead Michigan State to victory in the 1979 NCAA championship. As point guard for the Lakers, Johnson earned three Most Valuable Player awards, made nine appearances in the NBA finals, played in 12 All-Star games and still holds the league record for highest average assists per game. Johnson is the only basketball player to win championships at the high school, college, professional and Olympic levels. Those successes come with a responsibility to give back, Johnson said.

"Going down the street growing up, I knew if I turned left that trouble was there. Every time I would come to that street, everybody would say, 'You've got to go that way, young man. You've got to go right.' So I kept going right," Johnson noted. "Just think of all the ballplayers and entertainers of color—somebody told them to go right, too. So why don't you come back?... You've got to go back and you've got to help out. If you can touch and bring 10 people with you, then they bring 10 and then they bring 10 and now the community changes." ∎

Published: April 14, 2010 in Knowledge@Wharton

Cuil's Seval Oz Ozveren: Creating the Next Generation of Internet Search

As use of the Internet grows and changes, so has the ability of users to search for specific content or stories, photos and videos that relate to certain topics of interest. One of the companies trying to harness and expand the power of search is Cuil, which is developing Cpedia—an engine that promises less repetition, an encyclopedia-style summary for each search, results that integrate related topics, and input and recommendations from users' social networks. Cuil vice president of business development and finance Seval Oz Ozveren talked about the company's mission, the evolution of search and the creation of Cpedia— which is still in the "alpha" testing phase—with Knowledge@Wharton during the recent Future of Publishing conference in New York City.

An edited transcript of the conversation appears below.

Knowledge@Wharton: Tell me a little bit about Cuil, its mission, some of your current services and maybe some that are under development?

Seval Oz Ozveren: Cuil is a search engine that is differentiated from the other two search engines that crawl the worldwide web—the first being Google, the second being Microsoft—in that our mission is more about keeping the user on the [search] page. [Our goal is] enabling them to discover content—related content—and [creating a] visualization of content so that you can find things serendipitously that you didn't necessarily know you were looking for.

The second differentiator with Cuil is that Cuil has been searching and mining the worldwide web for intersections and long-tail queries in that we think that the next generation of search ought to be about intersections and finding more specific topics that are related to each other, such as, "osteoporosis, hypertension [and] side effects." That is also changing the way in which people use search because it is enabling the user to find more specific information about topics that they are querying.

Knowledge@Wharton: How is a contextual search different than if someone were to visit a traditional search engine, type in those three terms you just mentioned and get back a list of links? What's the difference between that and a more contextual search?

Ozveren: When you type in right now "osteoporosis, hypertension [and] side effects" what Cuil gives you, or tries to give you, is content that you can find on the Web that is percolating to the top, but also related [content, which appears] on the right hand side [of the results page]. [Contextual search] is categories that come up, maybe the actual nomenclature for the particular disease, maybe specific drugs that are attributed to that disease, maybe side effects in medications. The next generation of what we are doing is creating your social network inputs for that, so that if you are connected to Facebook, for example, you get your friends' or colleagues' or peers' views on those topics or related topics. It may not pick up—someone might not have said something specifically using the word "hypertension," but they may have said "high blood pressure." So our ability to mine the deep down Web enables us to draw inferences between the pages that exist on similar concepts and understand that those similar concepts are related. And I think the third part of the contextual search is really peer recommendations, which comes from having integrated search results from your social networks.

Knowledge@Wharton: So contextual search kind of bridges the gap between thinking about a topic and not being able to type the right words into a search engine to get results related specifically to that topic?

Ozveren: Exactly. And [discovering that] "Wow. I didn't know that there was a bad side effect [from] a particular drug when I took it for hypertension that might be [causing symptoms] like obesity and hair growth." So a lot of information that you may not expect, but serendipitously find there related to your query.

Knowledge@Wharton: How do you think the question of users' online identity creates opportunities for a search? How does it create limitations?

Ozveren: I think reputation isn't going to exist anymore on the Web. I think we are talking about a level playing field pretty much. Every piece of information that is out there on you is susceptible to being recorded and Tweeted about and coming up [in a search]. But I do think that it is important that people claim identities on the Web going forward. In as much as the Web tries to remain agnostic, you also need to try and claim who you are. And it really is a powerful tool for the individual because there is so much information out there. Your ability to [bring to the] surface information about yourself or your friends or your reputation or the work that you are doing is important to being able to control that channel.

Cpedia—I'll segway into that because it is a very powerful tool—is [Cuil's] next or third page of search. Now we are talking about content that is surfacing automatically through algorithms that generate Web-based content. So it is a summary engine. It is almost like a Wikipedia but the difference between Wikipedia and Cpedia is that [the results are] not user generated. It is allowing other points of reference, which Wikipedia doesn't do. Also, right now if you go to the Web and you search someone like me; I don't have a Wikipedia page.

There are only 200,000 active Wikipedia pages out there. That leaves a huge [opportunity to create profiles] for everyone else out there who you can't specifically read something about. Let's say you are going into a [meeting] and you want to read about someone that you are being interviewed by, or talking to. Unless you go to their LinkedIn profile or their Facebook profile, if you are in their network, there is very little information pertaining to them.

But this automatically generated summary [from] Cpedia enables you to find at a blink's notice all the information out there on a particular person. If [results that come up are] not the right person, [Cpedia] tells you it is not the right person. It disambiguates between that person and people with similar names so that you can find the right person. And that's also a problem with the Web right now, that there is so much information out there that people don't really know, "Is that the same Seval Oz that lived in Wilmington, Delaware in 1986?" Well, Cpedia, because it has information access to all that data, tells you that it is. And, in fact, we are finding that enterprise search is a very interesting part of this because now people, including credit report companies and the United States government, are starting to want to have background information on people. So there is other utility that is coming out from being able to mine this data and present this data.

Knowledge@Wharton: Is Cuil's Cpedia product available now, in beta form or for broader use?

Ozveren: Cpedia is a product of Cuil's, that is kind of [expanding on] what we have always been doing, which is data mining. We crawl a billion pages a day on a 120-billion page index. That gives us a huge scale of ability of being able to manage this data. It is a pretty powerful tool to be able to just algorithmically create or automatically generate summary pages.

[Right now] we call it alpha Cpedia because it is version one and like any other version one, it leaves something to be desired in terms of polish. It is a very, very difficult problem that we are trying to solve, so it takes time. It is not something that is clearly going to be out there as a branded ready product in two months. It is going to take time as people use it and come back with feedback. It works better in some verticals than it does in others. Like its people search is better than product search. There is a lot of information on the Web that doesn't necessarily surface to the top because maybe people don't want it to. I'm not throwing any jabs at any particular large U.S. conglomerates, but we have a right to know as the public if there are side effects with certain drugs that are being talked about, or if there are certain problems with certain car manufacturers. We want to engage in that conversation. We want to be a part of it. We want to watch what thought leaders are saying about that. We want to somehow feel a part of the experience.

That was the beauty of Facebook. Facebook really created the user experience. People went on to Facebook [because] they just wanted to watch what their friends were doing, feel a part of it and feel connected. And I think the Web going forward is about feeling connected. People use the word "engagement" and people are trying to monetize engagement, but I like to think of it in terms of not necessarily monetization but the connectability of every individual to another.

Knowledge@Wharton: What do you think the evolution of Internet search has shown publishers and companies about what people want to get out of these services? Were there some assumptions about users' habits that turned out to be incorrect?

Ozveren: I think people are finding the power of groundswell movements, especially in America. Every large civil movement in this country has been a grass roots groundswell—even the election of our President. And if you think about the election of our President, it was mainly done through the Web. His campaign was completely Web-centric. I also think there ought to be other applications like non-profit foundation search, so you can actually go and search on a search engine that relates to [environmental causes], that relates to the things that you believe in. One of our comments has always been "Let's create a blue and a red search engine for Republicans and for Democrats." Then the Democrats can find things that are related to their vision, and Republicans can find things related to their views. I see that potentially happening in the year 2020. So, yes, absolutely search is a powerful tool that people can aggregate ideas—like-minded ideas—around. But it also has danger in the fact that if it is not used carefully, if it is not used with a bit of concern over privacy, it can be misused. We need to have controls—regulatory controls—and I think you will see Facebook and Google and search engines like ourselves grappling with these tools and making sure that we are not infringing upon people's privacy. ■

Published: May 24, 2010 in Knowledge@Wharton

Aramex's Fadi Ghandour Unfolds His Roadmap for Budding Entrepreneurs in the Middle East

Fadi Ghandour needs little introduction, if any, in the Middle East. The founder of global logistics and transportation company Aramex is arguably the region's best-known entrepreneur, a mentor and role model for many young Arabs, an angel investor, and one who is more than happy to challenge traditional business and social values. Ghandour's accomplishments have been hailed by many, including New York Times columnist Thomas Friedman who wrote in his book, *The World Is Flat*, that every Arab should know the Aramex story.

Established in 1982 as an express operator for the Middle East and South Asia, Aramex became the first Arab-based company to trade its shares on Nasdaq in 1997. It returned to private ownership in 2002 and then went public three years later on the Dubai Financial Market as Arab International Logistics. It now has an alliance network of over 12,000 offices, 33,000 vehicles and 66,000 employees, providing freight forwarding, catalogue shopping, magazine and newspaper distribution and other services.

Ironically, 2009 was probably the best year ever for Aramex. At a time when most companies across the world were battling through the economic downturn, it opened new businesses and reported a 25% increase in net profit for the year. Ghandour's no-assets, no-debt policy helped as the the business environment changed rapidly. Ghandour spoke with Arabic Knowledge@Wharton in Dubai about addressing the region's weak business "ecosystem" and what needs to be done to help the next generation of innovators down the often bumpy road to entrepreneurial success.

Edited extracts of the conversation follow.

Arabic Knowledge@Wharton: What are the biggest challenges to entrepreneurship and innovation in the region? Are they purely economic or are there cultural, social and political reasons?

Fadi Ghandour: I don't think there are any cultural, political or social reasons. They are partly economic and partly developmental, like building a "softer" loan structure, [having an] an ability to easily register companies with very low capital, and securing intellectual property rights. On the other hand, clearly there is a need to have venture capital, angel capital and early-stage capital. There is a business culture, as you might call it, in the region that focuses on oil and gas, government contracts, and trading—representing overseas companies.

The story of entrepreneurship here is one without an ecosystem of capital, private-sector support and angel investors. There is also no mentoring, which is really important.

Arabic Knowledge@Wharton: You have been a mentor?

Ghandour: Yes, I do that. You are talking to me because I am an entrepreneur and I understand what they do. I am an angel investor and I find that while capital is important, what they need the most is advice. They need time. It is so much more important if you can tell them how to do things, what my experience has been—all that is not measured in terms of money.

Arabic Knowledge@Wharton: Did you get that kind of advice when you started?

Ghandour: I did and did not. The easiest way of getting a mentor is if your father understands what you are doing, understands business well and is willing to mentor you. I was mentored by a father who was an entrepreneur, but did not have time because he was a traveling man. You have to seek [out mentors]. Some of the networking events, some of the associations popping up for angel investors, etc., are a good step and helpful.

You need to make the private sector and businessmen aware of how important it is for them to give their time. It is like talking to your son or daughter. They need advice and eventually they will run, but you have to help them take those first few steps.

Arabic Knowledge@Wharton: How much time are you able to give them?

Ghandour: Just before [this chat], I was emailing a brilliant lady entrepreneur, telling her that I was traveling but will be in touch to do a conference call. You have to get back to them because they are young. If you believe in this, you have to give it time.

Arabic Knowledge@Wharton: Do you see a lot of young people in the region taking the entrepreneurial route these days?

Ghandour: Yes, I see a lot. The Internet has created all sorts of possibilities that people of earlier generations did not have. [Young people] see what the world is doing. They see the low cost of developing businesses online. They learn from others. There are some businesses that have already been developed in other places, but need to be customized and "Arabized." You will have the copycats and you will have the innovators. That is the nature of the beast.

Arabic Knowledge@Wharton: You once said the governments in the region are like mothers and the citizens are like their spoiled children. Do you see that changing quickly?

Ghandour: (Laughs) Yes, I stick to my position. An overprotective father is going to ruin the future of his child. He will not let him fail [and] he is not going to let him try or expose him to the world. It's a vicious world out there and you learn only when you fail. A mentor, father or mother can tell you a lot of stories, but the best way to learn is to fail. You have to stumble.

Arabic Knowledge@Wharton: But failure is not taken too kindly in this part of the world, is it?

Ghandour: No, it's not. Maybe it is in the U.S., the mother of all entrepreneurial countries. It has created that thing about an underdog. It is easy for people there to fail because that is seen as learning. If you tell people that it's fine to fail but to get [back] up and run, you have to create the ecosystem that helps. Mothers can never take failures, families can't.

An entrepreneur, who has just started, was telling us about what his family had to say about the Maktoob-Yahoo deal [in which Yahoo bought the Arab portal in 2009]. His mother or father said they did not know what Maktoob does, "but why don't you try and do something like that?" It catches on. It slowly becomes legitimate to try, which means that you don't work for the government or a big company that gives a secure job, but try something on your own. That, by definition, means that it might work or it might not, and possible failure means I am at least trying.

Arabic Knowledge@Wharton: Are people in the region averse to risk because of the fear of failure?

Ghandour: Entrepreneurship is something that is learned. I am a product of that process. Entrepreneurship is not something you are born with. You learn not only by doing, but also by having the skills—making financial statements, the discovery, logical thinking. This is stuff you have to learn in schools. That's where you get exposed to these things. You can throw somebody in the water and he can only become a good swimmer if he knows how to breathe. You have to give people the skill sets. You can teach people the rules of football and they can understand and enjoy it, but they can only play when they experience it themselves.

Arabic Knowledge@Wharton: How do you find the right idea?

Ghandour: A right idea is a product of exposure, learning and curiosity, which are essential for any entrepreneur. The status quo has to be unacceptable and that's what I keep saying in the organization. I tell people they need to question things. You can always do better by questioning anything that is in front of you.

You can do something that is totally different if you have a plan that is acceptable. A new product can change the face of an industry.

Entrepreneurship is all about questioning because that's where ideas come from. You also have to look closely at what is happening in your industry and learn from it. Any technological advancement in an industry can have a huge impact. For example, with the arrival of email, a whole industry around sending letters from one place to another almost vanished.

Arabic Knowledge@Wharton: Do you believe that entrepreneurs have only one good idea and tend to lose interest in innovation once they have achieved the first goal?

Ghandour: No, there are many serial entrepreneurs. They exit one thing and start another. It depends entirely on your skills, exposure and mind. I started my business 28 years ago, but I do a lot of intra-department entrepreneurship. But there are some who make their money and go on a vacation. Human beings make their own choices. You don't always have to be an entrepreneur.

Arabic Knowledge@Wharton: What are the better entrepreneurial stories in the region?

Ghandour: You have Orascom, which is a fantastic story, Maktoob, Consolidated Contractors Company - one of the biggest [diversified construction firms] in the world today—and Rubicon, one of the best animation companies. The region needs more but there are examples and role models. We need to document and celebrate them, and make people aware of them. There is nothing to be ashamed of in highlighting entrepreneurship stories in the region.

But the more relevant story to our youth is the small entrepreneur. You don't need to be worth hundreds of millions of dollars. At $2 million or $3 million, you can create jobs and value that is attainable. I don't want to scare people [by saying] entrepreneurship is about creating mega companies. It is about innovating the value and product you offer. You create wealth for the people who work for you, and [for] yourself.

Arabic Knowledge@Wharton: Are governments in the region doing enough to encourage entrepreneurship?

Ghandour: No, they need to do much, much more. They need to start with education, the regulatory environment and the enabling environment putting up seed money. The Arab world is facing a huge challenge of unemployment and the only way you can create jobs is by partnering with the private sector so that it becomes a public-private partnership. All those young people graduating from universities need to become job creators. That means creating companies and changing the tradition of working for governments.

Arabic Knowledge@Wharton: What are the three things you would tell a budding entrepreneur?

Ghandour: I would tell them they are in it for the long run, watch out for your cash and find a mentor. Finally, stop complaining. Don't worry about government regulations. Go and do it. I know it is an issue, but it should not stop anyone. Just do it, as Nike would say. ■

Published May 4, 2010 in Arabic Knowledge@Wharton

PART 6

Accelerating Innovation Through Inventive Management Practices

Putting a Face to a Name: The Art of Motivating Employees

Could a simple five-minute interaction with another person dramatically increase your weekly productivity?

In some employment environments, the answer is yes, according to Wharton management professor Adam Grant. Grant has devoted significant chunks of his professional career to examining what motivates workers in settings that range from call centers and mail-order pharmacies to swimming pool lifeguard squads. In all these situations, Grant says, employees who know how their work has a meaningful, positive impact on others are not just happier than those who don't; they are vastly more productive, too.

That conclusion may sound touchy-feely, but Grant has documented it in a series of research papers. In one experiment, he studied paid employees at a public university's call center who were asked to phone potential donors to the school. It can be grim work: Employees don't get paid much and suffer frequent rejections from people unhappy about getting calls during dinner. Turnover is high and morale is often low. So how do you motivate workers to stay on the phone and bring in the donations?

One relatively easy answer: Introduce them to someone who is aided by those dollars.

In his 2007 study, Grant and a team of researchers—Elizabeth Campbell, Grace Chen, David Lapedis and Keenan Cottone from the University of Michigan—arranged for one group of call center workers to interact with scholarship students who were the recipients of the school's fundraising largess. It wasn't a long meeting—just a five-minute session where the workers were able to ask the student about his or her studies. But over the next month, that little chat made a big difference. The call center was able to monitor both the amount of time its employees spent on the phone and the amount of donation dollars they brought in. A month later, callers who had interacted with the scholarship student spent more than two times as many minutes on the phone, and brought in vastly more money: a weekly average of $503.22, up from $185.94.

"Even minimal, brief contact with beneficiaries can enable employees to maintain their motivation," the researchers write in their paper, titled "Impact and the Art of Motivation Maintenance: The Effects of Contact with Beneficiaries on Persistence Behavior," published in the journal *Organizational Behavior and Human Decision Processes*.

Motivated Lifeguards

Motivating workers is a topic that interested Grant long before he became a professional academic. Prior to graduate school, he worked as an advertising director for the Let's Go line of travel guides. "We were producing travel guides and we had a couple of hundred people working in an office that would help travelers see foreign countries in a new way and travel safely," he recalls. "None of the editors had any contact with any of the actual readers." Grant suspected that the staffers would find more satisfaction in their work—and probably work even harder—if they could regularly interact with the readers whose globetrotting they enabled.

At the travel guide business, he never got a chance to put that hunch into practice. But as he moved towards his doctoral research at the University of Michigan, he returned to the subject, using call centers, sports facilities and classrooms as some of his early laboratories.

According to Grant, just being aware of the impact your job has on others can help with motivation. In a follow up study to the one he published in 2007, he focused on lifeguards at a community recreation center. Some of them were given stories to read about cases in which lifeguards had saved lives. A second group was given a different kind of reading material: testimonies from lifeguards about how they had personally benefitted from their work. The results: Those who had been reading about their ability to avert fatalities saw their measure of hours worked shoot up by more than 40%, whereas those who had merely learned that a lifeguard gig could be personally enriching kept working at the same clip. The results were published in a paper titled, "The Significance of Task Significance: Job Performance Effects, Relational Mechanisms, and Boundary Conditions," in the *Journal of Applied Psychology*.

Seeing Is Believing

Beyond awareness of job impact, face-to-face meetings with individuals who benefit from a job well done can dramatically improve workers' performance. In Grant's 2007 study, a second experiment looked at a group of students who were tasked with editing cover letters of fellow students who had contacted the university's Career Center in order to help find a job. One group of the student editors had the opportunity to see a would-be beneficiary who stopped by to drop off his letters and made small talk, purportedly unaware that the people in the room were the ones who would be tuning up his writing. Another group of student editors dug into the identical cover letters without having laid eyes on their author. The result? The people who had met the job-seeking student—even for a brief, apparently superficial conversation as he dropped off his paperwork— spent significantly more time on the editing task than those who hadn't.

However, there's more to know about contact than the simple idea that it is worthwhile to plunk workers down next to someone their daily tasks have aided. In a second run of the Career Center experiment, for instance, the alleged student job-seeker's biographical information was also manipulated. Again, both groups of editors worked on identical packets of cover letters. But they also saw a personal information sheet the student had submitted to the Career

Center. On one sheet, the student wrote that he desperately needed a job, saying he was having a hard time paying bills. For the other group, the personal statement did not contain any such language. Again, one group of editors met the student for the same few minutes of small-talk, and another group had no contact with him.

As in Grant's lifeguard experiment, reading the high-need personal statement—that is, learning that their work was very important—was crucial. But, the one-two punch of knowing the beneficiary's needs and meeting him in person generated the largest impact on motivation. Editors who didn't learn of the student's dire financial straits put in an average of 27 minutes of work. Editors who read of the student's money woes but never met him clocked 26 minutes apiece. Only those who had met the student and read of his worries worked significantly harder on the task of helping him, spending more than a half-hour on the task, or an average of 20% more time than the other editors.

Grant says this suggests that "task significance" is the key driver, and that face-to-face interactions, even seemingly superficial ones, can serve as a way of driving that significance home. In other studies, he has found that engineers, salespeople, managers, customer service representatives, doctors, nurses, medical technicians, security guards, police officers and firefighters who can directly see their impact on others all achieve higher job performance.

Over the course of several years' worth of experiments and surveys, Grant and his colleagues have spotted a few other nuances in how meeting beneficiaries affects workers. For instance, workers with a strong set of "prosocial values"—determined by those who say they agree strongly with statements such as, "It is important to me to respond to the needs of others"—are much more likely to be affected by reminders of how significant their work is. By contrast, generally conscientious workers, who presumably work hard whether or not their labors are beneficial, don't show nearly the same spike in performance upon being exposed to their beneficiaries.

Still, Grant says that in a wired economy where workers are increasingly likely to be physically isolated from end users, it's important for employers to build in systems that reinforce employees' awareness of whom they are helping. "Technology is this really fascinating double edged sword," Grant says. "On one hand, we have more and more ability to connect employees to end users from a different geographic region. But on the other hand, technology has also reduced the need for face-to-face interaction. A lot of organizations stop short of making this sort of connection because the work can get done without it."

That's a mistake, he says—one that many companies are now working to avoid. In fact, Grant is consulting with a number of organizations to establish these sorts of procedures on an ongoing basis. One of them, a pharmaceutical firm that does mail-order prescriptions, established a system where staff pharmacists occasionally rotate into regular pharmacies where they interact with customers.

They also began attaching photos of customers to their mail-order files, on the assumption that humanizing the names on all those medical forms would improve performance and minimize mistakes on the crucial, if sometimes mundane, work of pharmaceutical delivery.

Even in firms that are not focused on helping people as a core mission, managers might still look at increasing contact between workers and others in the organization who benefit from their labor, Grant says. "Everybody has an end user. In some cases, those end users are more inside the organization than outside. In some cases, the end users who managers want employees to focus on are coworkers, colleagues in other departments, or managers themselves." The question, he says, is: "How do we establish that connection as a regular routine, whether it's a weekly conference call with [co-workers] or a monthly check-in?"

Corporate charity might also have a productivity-boosting effect. "Some of my recent research on a Fortune 500 company suggests that, if you've got employees where the primary purpose of their job is not to help people, where there's no clearly defined group of end users, we can think about corporate philanthropy as a substitute. One option is to give people the chance to take responsibility for personally meaningful, important community service that can be sponsored by the company [so that they think], 'I make a difference by being here.'" ∎

Published: February 17, 2010 in Knowledge@Wharton

Borderless Innovation: Stretching Company Boundaries to Come Up with New Ideas

A few years ago, researchers at Cincinnati-based consumer goods multinational Procter & Gamble (P&G) made a breakthrough that could revolutionize how food is wrapped and stored. But there was one problem, as Chris Thoen, director of innovation and knowledge management at P&G, recounted during a recent conference at Wharton's Mack Center for Technological Innovation. Despite a portfolio of more than 300 products worth nearly $80 billion, P&G didn't have a strong presence on supermarket food-wrap shelves, and it would take millions of dollars of marketing, packaging and other costs to change that.

The good news was that one of the multinational's biggest rivals, The Clorox Company, did have that presence, thanks to Glad food wrap. So P&G approached Clorox with an offer to collaborate. Seven years later, Glad's Press and Seal—using P&G's technology, which embeds a kind of cement in small dimples in the cling film to increase its stickiness—is a top-selling product and Glad is now a joint venture of the two companies, with P&G owning 20%.

"Glad had a great name in marketing and in manufacturing, and we brought a product technology in," said Thoen, describing just one of several approaches to collaboration that have had a dramatic impact on how the company has become more innovative over the past decade.

P&G isn't alone. As the conference—titled, "Borderless Innovation: Management Practices, Promises and Pitfalls"—highlighted, many of the world's top multinationals have been leveraging the latest technological developments, their expanding global business networks and even competitors' expertise to change the way they harness new ideas. But while these tools may make global collaboration easier than ever, there's plenty of work left to do to make "borderless innovation" deliver, as the seminar's presenters noted.

Indeed, the seminar's keynote speaker, Michael Mandel of BusinessWeek magazine, said most companies—particularly in the U.S.—suffer from what he called an "innovation shortfall." Part of the reason, he noted, is that it's one thing to develop new products and quite another to get them to market and make them commercially viable. That certainly was the challenge faced by the companies behind many of the widely hailed breakthrough technologies of the 1990s, such as gene therapy and alternative energy.

The Sum of the Parts

Yet Mandel and other innovation experts also expressed optimism about the new wave of web-based collaborative innovation, which helps companies overcome shrinking R&D budgets and brings together like-minded and creative problem solvers from around the globe.

"The network really changes everything," said Mohan Sawhney, director of the Center for Research in Technology and Innovation at Northwestern University's Kellogg School and author of a recent book on the phenomenon titled, The Global Brain. Tightening of R&D budgets is a major driver behind the change, he noted. Western companies are looking toward Internet-based cooperation with technical experts in regions such as China and India because of the lower costs involved. Beyond costs, however, collaborative networks can develop superior products more quickly than the old "closed-loop," one-company model—such as what Bell Labs has used—"because the community is wiser than one individual."

As an example, Sawhney cited the success of Apple's iPhone, with an estimated 6.4 million units in use in the U.S. alone. The key, he said, was the ability of Apple staff members with different areas of expertise—including music, phone and camera—to work not only together, but also with outside innovators to develop more than 100,000 applications.

Success stories aside, however, "it's risky if you jump into [borderless innovation] and don't understand all the [internal] push backs," he said. Rather than racing to implement a program of borderless, networked innovation, companies should spend time understanding their culture, what they require from new products to deliver growth and the competitive landscape. To help companies get a better grip on their programs, he described several models that can be adopted to reflect their innovation needs:

- The Orchestra Model, which is highly structured and centralized. It is typically focused on upgrading an existing product or service that dominates a market, with tightly controlled ownership of intellectual property. Examples include the iPhone, whose developers have been releasing roughly 10,000 applications a month for use with it, or India's ultra-low-cost Tata Nano car, which uses a localized network to manufacture units from a fixed design.

- The Creative Bazaar Model, which is based on leading players in a particular market that want to acquire new ideas from small companies or individual inventors in order to broaden their range of products and market position. A case in point is Dial. The soap manufacturer aims to find 30% of its new ideas from outside the company through a program called "Partners in Innovation" that it launched with the New York-based United Inventors' Association, an organization founded in 1990 to foster education and support for inventors.

- The MOD ("MODification") Station Model, in which ideas come from a broad, global community, with the goal of coming up with new uses for existing products. One example is Mappr, a photo service developed by Stamen, a company in San Francisco. As users of Facebook and other social networking sites tag open-source photos, they help to build a database that

Mappr uses to create photographic guides to different geographic locations.
- The Jam Central Model has the loosest organizational structure and mission, often involving experts asked to solve problems that might not fit well into a large corporate profit strategy. For example, for the Tropical Disease Initiative, volunteer scientists are using open-source collaborative software to address Third World health problems, such as malaria and dengue fever. The medicine needed to cure these diseases does not have the recurring revenues that pills for chronic conditions have, so it attracts little attention from the big pharmaceutical companies.

Breaking News

As several speakers at the conference observed, borderless innovation has a variety of definitions, and in the case of General Electric (GE)—the world's largest company with 323,000 employees in businesses ranging from jet engines to TV news—it means breaking down internal "silos" to encourage collaboration. This is where Healthymagination comes in, said Trajan Bayly, director of the initiative launched by GE Healthcare in May 2009. It aims to lower health care costs and improve how patients are cared for by 15% in more than 100 fields by 2015. One area of focus is the poor or non-existent medical record-keeping in rural, Third World locations. By using hand-held electronic devices developed or improved by GE, record-keeping in these areas could be made more efficient and reduce medical errors.

Part of the strength of the initiative lies in its ability to tap into the expertise of GE's numerous business units that have not been focused on health care issues previously. "When you think about [GE-owned] NBC, it's always in terms of news or things like how do we sell more advertising for The Biggest Loser," Bayly noted. But since the launch of Healthymagination, GE's television units have been promoting and providing coverage of free health care clinics in America's inner cities operated by Remote Area Medical, an airborne corps of doctors that specializes in Third World and rural U.S. locations.

One of the trickiest challenges for borderless innovation, however, is making sure global innovators understand local customers. In the case of Vodafone, the world's largest mobile telecommunications company with 303 million customers worldwide, "innovating is where the customer is," said Paul Davey, head of R&D at the U.K.-based company. "Because if they live the problem, they'll [understand] the solution." That can at times mean coming up with very specific, tailored approaches to address consumer concerns. For example, in under-banked parts of Africa, Vodafone recently developed a novel system for paying rural health workers via their cell phones.

Customers have another role to play in borderless innovation. Several other speakers at the Wharton seminar remarked how such innovation requires a much broader, richer dialogue involving not only experts, but also rank-and-file consumers. That's clearly the case with P&G's well-documented Connect + Develop program. Launched in 2006, Connect + Develop offers a website for members of the public and employees to visit and submit ideas, which then undergo a technical review and weeding process.

According to P&G's Thoen, a surprisingly large number of ideas—about 4,000 in the last year alone—come via the site. "Most of them are not what we're looking for," he said. "But about 8% are substantial things that we need to look into. Every business unit is looking into one opportunity—some of them are things that we didn't even know we needed to figure out." ■

Published: February 17, 2010 in Knowledge@Wharton

Popularity Contests: Why a Company Embraces One Innovative Idea but Shuns Another

It's hard to imagine that any of the world's top multinational corporations (MNCs) have something in common with the angst-ridden, clique-driven drama of a high school cafeteria. But like the adolescent years we all remember, a multinational gets just as caught up with popularity contests and in-crowds as teenagers, especially when it comes to sharing ideas and best practices within their own organizations.

MNCs often have built up a rich store of knowledge over the years in ways that smaller companies can only dream of. MNCs use their vast global reach to tap different markets quickly and exploit their on-the-ground knowledge to sniff out new ideas or products being used at rival companies in other parts of the world. "The advantage of being a multinational is exactly this knowledge access on a global basis," says Felipe Monteiro, a Wharton professor of management whose recent research looks at how and why new knowledge spreads within firms. "What is equally interesting is the gap between the potential for that [access] and the actual use of such global knowledge."

At the heart of the issue is how an MNC manages to close that gap. And a lot of that hinges on behavior and cognitive factors. "If we look carefully at the patterns of knowledge flows, you see that not [all parts of a company are] participating in it and it's not every kind of idea that gets acted upon," says Monteiro. In other words, a company's success is ultimately less about the availability of innovative ideas and more about the human beings who need to share them.

Following Corporate Superstars

Monteiro's first analysis of the complexities of corporate knowledge flows appeared in a paper, published in the journal Organization Science in 2008, titled "Knowledge Flows within Multinational Corporations: Explaining Subsidiary Isolation and Its Performance Implications" (PDF). The paper, co-written with Niklas Arvidsson of Sweden's Centre for Banking and Finance and Julian Birkinshaw of London Business School, examined if, how and when MNC subsidiaries shared sales and marketing knowledge with each other. Based on questionnaires sent to the 171 subsidiaries of six Swedish global companies, including Ericsson and Volvo, about how the subsidiaries interact with other parts of the company, as well as follow-up interviews with personnel at peer subsidiaries and headquarters, they found a very uneven flow of knowledge.

According to the researchers, a subsidiary's willingness or ability to share know-how is influenced by its peers' perceptions—accurate or otherwise—about which of them are corporate superstars and which ones are not. The study found that subsidiaries perceived by others as being strong performers were, unsurprisingly, most frequently sought out as sources of help. What's more, the subsidiaries that perceived themselves to be high-flyers were also much more likely to seek advice. Subsidiaries that perceived themselves as underachievers, by contrast, shied away from seeking help, even though they presumably needed it the most.

"We suggest that subsidiaries with low group efficacy tend to be distracted by ruminations about perceived inadequacies and failures, which consume limited cognitive resources that are needed to process task demands effectively," the authors note in the paper. Self-confident and efficient, the strong performers are better at identifying problems and seeking solutions.

Behind the results of the research is a phenomenon that Monteiro says many executives and their management teams may be unaware of: isolated subsidiaries. From the vantage point of their corporate offices, executives back at headquarters may see a frenzy of knowledge sharing when, in fact, some subsidiaries are working in isolation and are not able to take advantage of the abundance of intellectual resources other parts of the firm have to offer, according to the research. Of the 171 subsidiaries surveyed, 22% learned about new product ideas or practices from their headquarters less than once a year, while 42% sent new product ideas and practices to their headquarters or to other subsidiaries less than once a year. More than 10% did neither.

What's the Big Idea

The findings of that study spurred Monteiro to re-examine the flow of new ideas through MNCs, but this time from a slightly different angle by asking why companies embrace ideas and abandon others when they first learn about them. Monteiro did this by homing in on organized efforts at what he refers to as "external knowledge sourcing." Such sourcing is prevalent at firms such as Procter & Gamble. Having introduced a program called Connect + Develop in 2000, the consumer goods MNC acknowledged that not all of its innovative ideas can, and should, be generated in-house. The C+D team uses technology and a series of on-the-ground networks to bring new ideas to headquarters, helping the company achieve its goal of acquiring 50% of future innovation externally by acquiring or working with smaller, nimbler firms.

Other companies have followed suit, recruiting teams of idea "scouts" who scour the world to identify and acquire cutting-edge ideas from outside the firm. In a working paper for Wharton's Mack Center for Technological Innovation titled, "Going Far for Something Close: Explaining Stickiness in the Initiation of the External Knowledge Sourcing Process," Monteiro looked at the hurdles of getting external ideas accepted within companies—or knowledge "stickiness," as it is sometimes called—from the perspective of the scouts. But unlike previous research from other academics, which has focused on new ideas that companies try to implement, Monteiro also examined external ideas that were never acted upon.

After sifting through a database containing more than 100 external knowledge-sourcing entries (that is, assessments of external technologies) of a large European telecom services provider, Monteiro identified two distinct groups of ideas: those that were embraced when they were introduced to the company and those that were ignored. According to his findings, which group an idea falls into does not necessarily depend on its strength or weakness, but rather on the people and organizations absorbing them.

Safety in Numbers

A critical hurdle to getting the initial buy-in for an idea from business unit managers is "dissonant knowledge"—knowledge that challenges a recipient unit's dominant logic. "The idea of [studying] knowledge dissonance is to try to separate the technical aspect—can you understand it?—from a more cognitive aspect—do you agree with it?" Monteiro says. "You're more likely to act on opportunities that confirm what you're doing rather than opportunities that challenge what you're doing."

To illustrate his point, Monteiro cites the hypothetical example of a telecom multinational scouting two types of Voice over Internet Protocol (VoIP) services. Using very similar technology, Skype and Vonage provide a service that telecom managers can easily comprehend. But the two function differently. Skype uses an application that customers download on to their computers and a novel business model that allows basic calls to be made free of charge. Vonage, in contrast, requires a modem or a router and has a revenue model based on customers' monthly payments. If asked to choose between the two services, business unit managers would lean towards Vonage's model, because it is very much like a traditional phone service compared with Skype's model.

Likewise, Monteiro says ideas that have already been successful at another company or market are more likely to be embraced elsewhere than those that have no track record. He adds that this isn't necessarily a bad thing—in the near term, at least. A certain amount of risk aversion, after all, can help as much as hinder a company. But because of the resistance at the beginning of the process—when the only thing that might be wasted is time—Monteiro's findings suggest that institutional inertia kicks in much earlier than previously believed. "This is not a story of failure," he adds. "What I'm showing is that it is easy for [a company] to import things that confirm what [it] already [knows]." Yet longer term, a firm that has trouble absorbing dissonant new ideas risks developing "core rigidities," Monteiro says.

"These findings suggest an intriguing paradox," he writes. "Even when scouting units are established thousands of miles from headquarters to access diverse knowledge, internal selection processes might be so strong that the organization ends up acting mostly upon market-validated opportunities consonant with its existing dominant logic."

What's important is to find a balance. "The paradox is that what's good in the short term, what's going to reinforce your business model, may not be good in the long term if a business is undergoing major changes," Monteiro notes.

Managing Knowledge Networks

Whether they have short- or long-term interests in mind, MNC executives and their teams can proactively manage knowledge-gathering processes. "It's [important] how you position [new ideas] internally," Monteiro says. His research findings indicate that the effort a scout makes looking for an external idea seems to matter less than how well she is able to sell the idea to a business unit. "Scouters' efforts to search within [the firm] for needs and constraints, translate the external technology into the MNC's internal language, and match the external opportunity to specific areas, all increase the odds of successful initiation," Monteiro writes.

Equally important, management teams can help ensure that some parts of the company aren't isolated from the knowledge-sharing processes. In their paper on isolated subsidiaries, Monteiro and his co-authors recommend setting up personal networks among subsidiary managers to improve contact and collaboration. A network could include a well-connected expatriate manager who is assigned to an underperforming foreign subsidiary to help it tap into resources in other parts of the company. MNCs also need to consider and compensate for language barriers—which could, for example, be preventing a subsidiary's manager from engaging colleagues locally and at headquarters. Finally, transparency is critical, for both the 'in' and 'out' crowd. Sharing information regularly about performance can address why subsidiaries' perceptions tend to vary wildly when it comes to knowing which of their peers are successful and which processes are valuable.

But the most important step, Monteiro says, is recognizing that the market for information isn't perfect. "Sometimes, you will see knowledge being shared, and you don't realize that some players are doing a lot of [the sharing] and some not at all. It's not evident that it's all being done by the 'in' crowd and that the 'out' crowd is not doing anything." ∎

Published: November 24, 2009 in Knowledge@Wharton

Eyes Wide Open: Embracing Uncertainty through Scenario Planning

As protests in Iran last month drew the world's attention, the top executives at a large global industrial goods company held a teleconference to consider their options. The meeting was hastily called, but the participants were not starting from scratch. In fact, the events unfolding in the country were strikingly similar to a scenario that they had developed, along with a handful others, in a 2008 offsite meeting focused on potential changes in their competitive environment.

The workshop, the output, and the eventual impact on decision making represents a perfect illustration of how so-called scenario planning techniques can be utilized to help managers navigate in complex and uncertain environments. In the meeting the industrial company held last year, executives had discussed each scenario they developed, the potential triggers for each of them, and how the company should respond to each of these situations if it were to arise. Pulling out the notes from these discussions, they already knew their options and had a view on how they would like to respond. In many ways, they were prepared—and already one step ahead of some other companies.

Paul J. H. Schoemaker, research director of the Wharton School's Mack Center for Technological Innovation, says such examples illustrate a continuing shift in how companies think about the future. He observes that when managers are facing the profound uncertainties increasingly seen today, they tend to adopt one of three strategic postures.

The first, Schoemaker says, is the "zero-future" option: Here, caution rules the day; no attempts are made to analyze, anticipate or predict anything beyond the short-term, and major decisions are put off until the fog lifts. The second choice is to bet strongly on one particular future. As Schoemaker describes it, the upside is that leaders are able to convey a clear message, reducing anxiety for stakeholders, and take bold action that may later be viewed as brilliant. The danger is that they could place the wrong bets or fall victim to wishful thinking.

The third option entails what Schoemaker describes as a deliberate attempt to separate what we do and do not know about the future, and to use that as a basis for exploring many possible futures—in other words, developing scenarios rather than predictions. This approach differs from the first two primarily in that it is a much more open mindset, with a focus on agility and options. Yet it also is in many ways the most challenging to adopt. "It takes courage to admit our collective ignorance," Schoemaker says, "because it conflicts with our common notion of leadership, which prizes omniscience. However, our world is too complex for the heroic leadership of the past where a great leader rides up on a white horse and points the way to the future. A better approach now is to embrace uncertainty and examine it in detail to discover where the hidden opportunities lurk."

Creating Options

Trying to gain a better understanding of the trends shaping the competitive environment has always been critical for managers. In the 1970s, scenario thinking first became relatively popular as a structured way to look ahead—to understand new growth areas, anticipate risks, spot opportunities and build a long-term vision. Perhaps most notably, Royal Dutch Shell used the approach to look more broadly at the trends and developments that could impact the price of oil and develop stories that could challenge management perceptions. Since then, however, companies of all sizes and in many industries have picked up the practice, particularly at times of crisis or dramatic change.

George S. Day, a professor of marketing at Wharton and co-director of the Mack Center, also has witnessed the recent rise in scenario thinking firsthand. "What has changed to make scenario planning so timely? Obviously uncertainty is way up. This is the main driver, because when conditions are stable it's easier to live with momentum and the projections we normally use," he points out. "The challenge is that when things are very uncertain we need to think differently, because what we project based on current momentum may be the least likely outcome. We need to start thinking about the unthinkable scenarios—and what's new today is people are finally figuring out how to do it well, in an environment with a huge amount of uncertainty."

Derrick Philippe Gosselin, who until recently was group senior vice president at French energy concern GDF Suez, offers a practitioner's perspective. Gosselin was responsible for introducing scenario thinking into GDF Suez's planning and investment processes, where the focus was on gaining strategic flexibility. "As someone thinking about scenarios, my job was to develop the capability in our company to anticipate things—to make sense of the environment before other companies," he notes. This is particularly important in capital intensive industries such as the ones in which Suez operates. "Once you are invested [in a massive project], you are locked in for years, and many of your strategic options are no longer valuable. So the traditional way of thinking about strategy also is no longer as valuable." In other words, it is nice to have strategic options, but they have no real value if a company will never be able to execute them.

The exception to this rule occurs when a company can sense changes before its competitors do. For instance, when a market shoots dramatically up or plummets, it is already too late to get in or out of an investment profitably. However, some companies, according to Schoemaker, Day and other experts, have developed a competitive advantage by leveraging scenario planning—first in stimulating discussion about potential outcomes arising from the swirling mix of trends shaping the world, and then in establishing monitoring mechanisms to identify which scenario is starting to unfold. In the end, the major objectives for these companies are to minimize surprises and to consistently anticipate— and act on—major emerging opportunities and challenges, ahead of competitors.

Gosselin, who is now a member of the Strategic Foresight Council at the World Economic Forum, believes that if he can get a company to start thinking about possible scenarios that could arise in the future, it means that "I create an awareness of these options, and each time they make an investment decision, they are aware of what could happen. It creates an early warning system, which is something I cannot get at all if we are all simply working with macroeconomic models. It also means we can operate extremely quickly. We have looked at the environment and potential developments, and now we can have a dialog on risk management, anticipation and investment options based upon that."

Thinking Differently

For many companies, the idea of scenario planning is not necessarily new, but often it is not practiced in a consistent or meaningful way. Most tend to follow key trends opportunistically and in relatively unstructured ways. Part of the challenge, experts say, is that the way organizations discuss and plan for the future is deeply rooted in the company's culture. This means it can take a great deal of time—or an extraordinary shock—to spark a change in approach. For instance, until recently, managers making a strategic recommendation to the CEO or board of directors often were expected to start by presenting a compelling opinion on what the future would be, and then offer a logical strategy or plan that, naturally, would emerge from that view of the future. Today, this kind of "linear" approach is increasingly being called into question.

At the same time, experts say, as planning discussions get closer to the top levels in a company, short-term financial concerns often rule the day. If there isn't strong backing by the CEO or other senior leaders to consider alternative views, then strategic planning discussions frequently default into financial exercises—and scenarios tend to get mixed with financial sensitivity analysis.

Wharton's Day says the solution is to involve senior management directly and actively in open, long-term oriented discussions. Consultants or teams in the organization can help, he notes, but the heavy lifting intellectually has to be done by the top management team. Indeed, at GE, he says, every one of the top management teams is required to go through a scenario exercise. "The leaders of an organization need to share mental models, challenge assumptions and basically learn from each other. Scenarios force managers to embrace uncertainty, and then figure out how to profit from it regardless of what happens. But first you have to get people out of their box. If they haven't participated in it, it is almost certain to fail. What you are doing is challenging assumptions that may have been tacit for years."

Kristel Van der Elst, who heads the scenario planning team at the World Economic Forum, has helped direct more than a half-dozen different exercises and seen the impact on participants' thinking. She emphasizes that it is crucial to have the right mix of people in the discussion. "It's important that you have different viewpoints," she says. "If you have people only from the same company, or even only from the business world, you may not get people who will challenge assumptions—people who will shake up the discussions and thinking a little bit." In addition, opening up the discussion can also help create new networks and partnerships, to discuss trends in a non-threatening manner and foster a sense of trust. "We have had people in workshops who would not talk openly to one another in the normal course of business, but the scenario process provides them with a safe environment to share views, creating mutual understanding, trust and respect."

Ultimately, Van der Elst adds, such discussions help create a dialog that enriches the capabilities of everyone involved. "You end up changing how people think," she says. "The long-term benefit is that you open up people's minds, which also is why it is so important that you have decision makers directly involved in the process. Of course, this is a challenge, because it requires a big time commitment, but when they are only involved at the end of the process, with a presentation being delivered to them, they will have their own picture of the future in mind and are likely toreject the alternatives. It is only by taking them through the process that you can open up their thinking."

Day agrees. "An interesting question is whether we should call this scenario planning, or what I prefer, which is 'scenario learning.' Learning implies an intense discussion that challenges the tacit assumptions and mental models of each member of the management team. This provokes tension that leads to reflection, which is essential to collective learning. Learning also implies an on-going process in which the results of actions taken leads to further reflection and insight."

Developing New Scenarios

Even with senior-level participation, however, the key question is how to proceed most effectively. Experts say many companies and organizations are now focused on building a more systematic process to identify and track emerging trends, feeding into discussions about the implications. Without it, the amount of potentially important information becomes overwhelming—impossible to assimilate or process well by using an opportunistic or essentially ad hoc approach.

Based on her experience at the World Economic Forum, Van der Elst offers some general guidelines on developing a scenario process within an organization. The first step, she says, is the identification of the "central question"—that is, the specific strategic issue that requires a decision in light of trends or potential developments. Making sure this central question is relevant for the stakeholders is essential for the exercise to be useful. It can be defined through research and discussion in the scenario team, but most importantly through interviews with the stakeholders.

Once the key question has been identified, the next step is the identification of the driving forces and systemic changes that are underway—the forces that will dramatically transform the playing field. Usually these are found in a variety of domains. A typical categorization used is STEEP: Social, Technological, Economic, Environmental, and (geo)Political. "It is important here to keep in mind you are thinking about the contextual environment in which you operate, not the transactional environment," Van der Elst says. "You look at forces beyond your control and influence that will impact you, as well as the industry you are in. You have to think broadly." These drivers are found in expert interviews and research, but most importantly through brainstorming with, again, a diverse, multidisciplinary group of people.

In doing so, according to Van der Elst, looking long-term is important: Engaging in a discussion about what the major drivers will be 10 or 20 years out can help people see things that they would never consider when looking only three or five years ahead. "The time horizon for the scenarios needs to be sufficiently long to avoid only conveying a creative description of the present, and sufficiently short for the scenarios not to lose focus and relevance." In addition, participants should not be looking only at things that are direct extensions of what is already happening, but instead at things that could happen. For instance, when the price of oil is soaring, thinking about a scenario of much lower prices is important because it is plausible, even if it is not an extrapolation of current trends. It is not being 'realistic' that matters; it is being plausible.

Out of the long list of potential drivers, companies can move on to determine the critical uncertainties. Simply put, these are the driving forces that are both extremely important and highly uncertain. "These are the things you need to think about and be prepared for," Van der Elst says. "For these critical uncertainties, you explore relevant, challenging, diverse, and possible outcomes." An effective mechanism to do this often is a workshop where the primary forces of changes are discussed and prioritized, with the results plotted on a 2x2 chart, usually with impact on one axis and certainty on the other. This helps management teams focus on what is important, and avoid what is just noise. It also begins to uncover implicit assumptions and beliefs—for instance, a lot of people think some things are certain, when it turns out they are not certain at all.

The biggest-impact uncertainties will be the key themes for the scenarios. "This is something we cluster," Van der Elst says. "During workshops, we explore different sets of drivers to find the scenarios that are most relevant. This depends on the audience. We always ask: What are the boundaries of possibilities? How would the world look like in this scenario and what does it mean to you?" The scenarios are often brought to life and communicated using story-telling techniques, which are effective ways to help decision makers understand the potential outcomes, easily remember them and challenge the current accepted wisdom.

As an example of the output from a robust scenario exercise, consider a recent paper by Schoemaker and co-author Rob-Jan de Jong from Europe. They offer four scenarios—titled Capitalism 2.0, Global Depression, Visible Hand and Obama World—that depict how Western economies might emerge from the global financial crisis that became visible in 2008. Looking ahead to the year 2012, these scenarios describe different futures that could define the next five years, including early warning signs. The scenarios are built around two pivotal uncertainties. The first concerns the deeper nature of the present downturn (i.e., will it prove to be cyclical as before, or deeply systemic and dislocating?) The second uncertainty concerns the role of government versus the free market in lifting economies out of the current malaise.

The final step is for participants and others to take the input back into their strategy decision-making process. In general, there are two different approaches, the experts say. One is to attempt to make a company's whole strategy completely robust against every scenario. This, however, can be difficult or even water down the strategy. A better option, the experts say, is to design a strategy that creates value in two or three scenarios—with a backup plan if other scenarios emerge.

Hidden in Plain Sight

Indeed, being prepared may be the single biggest benefit of scenario thinking. Otherwise, managers run the risk of engaging in overly linear thinking. This, in today's environment, can be devastating. As recent events have clearly shown, companies' positions in the future are not definitively linked to where they are today. Instead, more and more managers are being forced to think about alternatives.

Van der Elst sees this change already happening. "Companies had to get away from making decisions or arguments about what the future should be," she says. "One of the challenges we had until recently in the [World Economic Forum] workshops was to make the people in the room realize that there could be a slowdown in economic growth. They would say that is not possible, so each time we had to make sure people understood that the downside also was an option. As the participants went through the process, it opened their minds. Some CEOs told us afterward that they returned to work and changed their strategy. They had been completely banking on the high-growth option."

Gosselin voices a similar perspective. "The discussion of going from point A to point B is not the right one," he says. With more and more companies operating in turbulent environments, "you must be open to considering alternatives, and possibly an alternative that you do not agree with. When something shocking happens, afterward it always seems so obvious. People ask, 'Why did we not see it? Well, the answer is because there were lots of options for possible outcomes. But now, afterward, there is only one that we see.'" ∎

Published: July 22, 2009 in Knowledge@Wharton

Can Lean Co-exist with Innovation?

"Lean" has come to mean an integrated, end-to-end process viewpoint that combines the concepts of waste elimination, just-in-time inventory management, built-in quality, and worker involvement—supported by a cultural focus on problem solving. Can such practical principles be applied to innovation, or would lean's structure and discipline snuff out the creative spark that underlies the birth and development of great ideas? Can lean co-exist with innovation?

According to experts at The Boston Consulting Group (BCG) and Wharton faculty, lean and innovation can indeed complement each other, and it's about time they came together. Lean brings structure and predictability to innovation, and sharpens the distinction between idea generation and the development process, they say. Both share a common goal: to meet customer needs in a cost-effective manner. And lean can help empower researchers and reduce uncertainty in the innovation process itself.

"There is intense pressure to cut costs, and companies waste a lot of money on product development because the processes for accelerating the best ideas and terminating low-value ideas are often weak or non-existent," says Hal Sirkin, senior partner at BCG in Chicago and global head of the firm's operations practice. Companies would do well, he says, to reorient themselves toward "high-impact, high-value" innovations and to "be aggressive in cutting projects that are unlikely to deliver a payback from their portfolios."

Redefining the Individual and the Team

Hollywood animation company Pixar, the maker of blockbuster movies including the "Toy Story" series and "Finding Nemo," is a good example of how innovation and lean practices can enhance outcomes. Pixar has combined lean and innovation to good effect, according to Kartik Hosanagar, Wharton professor of operations and information management. Working within the movie industry "where lack of predictability is the norm," Pixar has created a set of processes that emphasizes team-based collaboration and continuous feedback loops to help overcome creative blocks and track deliverables, but without the stress that could go with a regime of control.

Pixar's record is proof that lean and innovation can coexist. "Pixar hasn't had a single failure as yet. All its projects have been successful," Hosanagar says, adding that unlike the rest of the movie industry, it has never bought scripts from outside; it develops all its ideas and scripts in-house. "I discovered that much of what the industry uses is madness; what Pixar uses is a method to the madness," says Hosanagar, who for the last year has been fascinated by the company while studying it along with Jehoshua Eliashberg, a Wharton professor of marketing, operations and information management.

Part of what helps Pixar succeed is a model of working in which the individual is as valuable to the team as the team is to the individual, says Hosanagar. To help structure fruitful interactions, Pixar has instituted a system of daily meetings where team members talk about what they have or have not accomplished each day and others provide feedback. The point is not to track people. "In a creative world you often hit roadblocks, and team-based collaboration is critical," he explains. "People might discuss work that is clearly in an incomplete stage; they don't have to feel embarrassed." The process involves cross-company teams, too, where one team working on a project might get feedback from another team working on a totally different project.

Filmmaker Woody Allen drafted a similar system years ago, according to Sirkin. "When people in the movie-making business know each other well and make movies over and over together, they get much better at knowing each other's strengths and weaknesses, and can improvise and collaborate far more effectively," he says of Allen's approach.

Separating Idea from Development

Coming up with good ideas is a very different process from developing and commercializing those ideas. Good ideas that don't generate a payback are ultimately of little value to a company, says Sirkin. Lean can bring the discipline needed to develop and profit from new product and service offerings. "Most people focus on ideas but not necessarily on what it takes to bring those ideas to market, and which ideas will make money," he says.

What will make money, of course, is an idea such as a new product or an improvement to an existing one that customers are willing to pay for, says Kim Wagner, senior partner and managing director at BCG and co-head of its bio-pharma R&D practice. Wagner sees lean concepts steadily making inroads into life sciences. "Listen to the voice of the customer," she says, explaining how "a scientist with an interesting finding" could answer the question of whether it has "any tangible value" for users.

Lean's focus on the customer can help reality-test an innovation, notes Wagner. It might seem like a great idea for a pharmaceutical company to replace a daily dosage with a once-a-week pill. But such an approach doesn't suit the needs of elderly patients. "If you're 75 years old, it's hard to remember that it's a Sunday and you have to take your pill," she says of a once-weekly dosage regimen, adding that pharmaceutical companies have to factor that market reality into their innovation process.

Listening to the Voice of the Customer

Lean approaches can help organizations take customer satisfaction to new levels. Ravi Aron, a senior fellow at Wharton's Mack Center for Technological Innovation who does extensive research on healthcare companies worldwide, cites the case of Bumrungrad International Hospital in Bangkok as an example. The hospital goes "well beyond" quality benchmarks in its industry, and owes that to "continuous and constant process improvements" on a range of metrics including recovery rates, time to recovery, length of stay and other patient satisfaction criteria, he says. "It goes beyond medical care to hospitality services, learning from feedback it collects from patients, physicians, clinicians and supporting staff."

Bumrungrad uses technology in innovative ways to maximize patient satisfaction, including continual electronic updates of patient records. Aron offers an example of how the hospital uses technology in administering medicines, avoiding the "spaghetti process that is prone to errors" and is common across the industry. A Swisslog pharmacy robot aggregates daily dosages for each patient into little rings that go on conveyor belts, get checked by RFID (radio frequency identification) and then by a nurse before they are handed over to patients. "It blew my socks off when I saw it," he says.

Lean is put to best use in process improvements like those at Bumrungrad, Aron says, and to a relatively lesser degree in product improvements that have longer gestation periods. "Lean is a natural fit for process innovation," he says. "Lean rarely comes into play in the first stage of product innovation," and really begins its journey when an organization attempts to "hear the voice of the customer." The third stage, where it orchestrates product innovation with delivery through constant improvements across its supply chain, "is where lean enters with a vengeance," as Aron puts it.

Orchestrating Supply Chain Efficiencies

Companies adopting lean concepts learn to integrate their suppliers more actively and earlier in the product development process. "Rather than waiting and testing out your products independently, you might integrate your suppliers—certainly of key components—so that they are already working on delivering it while you are figuring out the details of your innovation," says Sirkin. Even within the organization, lean has to be an enterprise-wide effort involving the functions of R&D, production, sales and so forth. "You need virtually every part of the company to make an idea come to life," Sirkin says.

Lean and its sharp customer focus can help companies explore innovation in areas that otherwise may have been overlooked, says Wagner. For example, a pharmaceutical company may decide to continue exploring treatments for hypertension even if half a dozen drug brands dominate that market, she says. Guiding that decision would be certain segments in the patient population that are not adequately served by the drugs currently available, and are willing to pay for alternative treatments that work for them.

Companies that embrace lean methodologies will reduce the risks inherent in their development processes, Wagner says. This is especially critical for pharmaceutical companies, where the drug development process is risky, expensive, and extremely time-consuming. "To shorten this process, many companies front-load activities or do them in parallel," she explains. "But when development efforts fail—as so many do—these activities end up wasting resources." Instead, companies should focus their efforts on the activities that increase the technical or commercial probability of a product's success. "This not only helps the team 'fail fast' and move on to the next opportunity, it also limits the amount of extra effort wasted on unsuccessful programs," she says.

In attempting to reduce waste and speed up processes in the product development process, pharmaceutical companies are also learning to de-layer their organizational structures. Wagner notes that many pharmaceutical companies tend to have very deep structures, with up to a dozen levels between the head of research and the researcher "at the bench," adding to costs, delays and other inefficiencies. Managers need to look at all the layers to see what value each adds to the product. "If you cannot articulate what value is added at each level of the organization, then you have to question why that level exists," She says. The de-layering exercise also "empowers scientists and makes the organization a much more exciting place to work. Productivity goes up."

Empowering Researchers for Stronger Innovation

At companies that have wedded themselves to inflexibility and regimented processes through Six Sigma programs, lean philosophies can liberate researchers and empower them to redouble their innovation efforts, says Hosanagar. He points to 3M Corp., the maker of innovative products such as Scotchgard, Post-it Notes and Scotch tape, which over the last four years has de-emphasized Six Sigma and the data-driven methodologies it brings to reduce process defects. It's a word of caution for those taking the notion of variability reduction to its extreme, he says. "Six Sigma clearly has its role in an organization, but excessive adherence to it will kill innovation; people are not going to deviate from the norm and you won't have innovation."

Hosanagar goes back to how Pixar marries the structure that lean brings with the freedom creative professionals crave. "They have worked out a golden solution: Nurture creative freedoms and yet reduce waste with the same process," he says. "They are able to create a situation where projects that are likely to be doomed are eliminated early on."

Much of what lean represents might seem like a no-brainer, says Sirkin. Yet it is an opportunity for companies that don't have lean development processes, he says. "Why the focus on lean now? In a downturn, cash-strapped companies are under a lot of pressure to cut costs," he explains. "The more stress there is on the system, the more people look for ways to relieve that stress, to increase their profitability. It's all about competition." ∎

Published: November 11, 2009 in Knowledge@Wharton

Running Faster, Falling Behind: John Hagel III on How American Business Can Catch Up

In the early 2000s, Silicon Valley-based business guru John Hagel III was involved in a high-tech start-up and hired Stephen Gillett, a young man right out of college. Less than a half dozen years later, Gillett was named a senior vice president and chief information officer for Starbucks—the youngest CIO of a Fortune 500 company at that time.

And Hagel thinks he knows a primary reason for his one-time employee's meteoric rise. Everything that Gillett needed to know, Hagel said, he learned while becoming a guild leader in the popular online game *World of Warcraft*.

The co-chairman of a tech-oriented strategy center for Deloitte LLP, Hagel told the annual Wharton Leadership Conference that Gillett—just like other top players on the massive online multi-player game, with an estimated eight million participants—reached out independently to build a large team of allies that solved complex problems and developed winning strategies.

Guild leaders in *World of Warcraft* "require a high degree of influence," noted Hagel, a successful author and longtime consultant. "You have to be able to influence and persuade people—not order them to do things. Ordering people in most of these guilds doesn't get you far."

The look inside *World of Warcraft* and its relevance for today's complicated business environment was part of a recent research project and book by Hagel and two co-authors—John Seely Brown and Lang Davison—that examines how companies re-invent and revive themselves by moving away from secretive, proprietary shops and toward a more open, collaborative business model. Their findings resulted in the recent publication of *The Power of Pull: How Small Moves, Smartly Made, Can Set Big Things in Motion*.

The bottom line, they found, is that American companies will continue to fall behind their counterparts in emerging markets such as China or India unless they move toward what Hagel called "the edge," which is where passionate, change-driven employees collaborate with others on the kind of innovations that prevent a company from seeing its core business model slowly erode. "The only thing that succeeds," Hagel said, "is to take those initiatives on the edge and pull more and more of the core out to those edges—rather than trying to pull them back in." He asserted that chief executives who stick to the conventional wisdom and cling to secretive proprietary business systems are doomed to fail.

Sustained Erosion

This year's Wharton Leadership Conference —titled, "Leading in a Recovering (and Even Rebounding) Economy"—came at a time of increasing focus on corporate executives and the role they play in defining a business's direction, its image and its accountability. The conference was organized by the school's Center for Human Resources, Center for Leadership and Change Management and Wharton Executive Education, in partnership with Deloitte. Hagel heads Deloitte's Center for the Edge, which studies emerging business strategies.

Hagel's more than 30-year career in the business consulting and high-tech industries also included a stint at iconic 1980s video game firm Atari, as well as launching the e-commerce practice at McKinsey. He said the bad news uncovered by his research team was that the erosion of American business leadership was not so much a function of the downturn beginning in 2008 as it was a systemic decline dating as far back as the mid-20th Century.

In trying to quantify the problems facing American industry, Hagel and his co-authors found little existing data to measure the overall performance of U.S. companies. So they worked up some measurements of their own—and even they were surprised at what they uncovered. Since 1965, they learned, the return-on-assets for all American firms has eroded by 75%.

"The erosion has been sustained and significant. There is absolutely no evidence of it leveling off, and there is certainly no evidence of it turning around," Hagel noted. Indeed, another measurement showed that survival is also an increasing problem for U.S. corporations. Firms in the Standard & Poor's 500 in 1937 had an average life expectancy of 75 years; a more recent analysis of the S&P 500 showed that the number had dropped to just 15 years. "When I'm in executive boardrooms, I hear the metaphor of 'the Red Queen' and the notion that we have to run faster and faster just to stay in place," Hagel said, referring to the character from Lewis Carroll's *Through the Looking-Glass*. "I would make the case, based on the analysis that we've done, that the Red Queen is actually an optimistic assessment of our situation, that we are running faster and faster and falling farther and farther behind."

What went wrong? Hagel argued that American companies and their leaders were essentially not prepared for a move away from a corporate model of "knowledge stocks"—developing a proprietary product breakthrough and then defending that innovative advantage against rival companies for as long as possible—and toward a more open and collaborative business model that he called "knowledge flows." The problem, he said, is that because of the increasingly global nature of business competition, the value of a major proprietary breakthrough or invention erodes in value much more quickly than in the mid-20th Century.

But in moving toward an economy based more upon knowledge flows, U.S. CEOs find themselves lagging behind their counterparts in rapidly emerging markets such as India or China, where businesses are much more adept at creating broad networks and finding innovation at "the edge" of their business rather than a proprietary core. "It's basically invisible innovation to most Western executives," Hagel asserted. "Most Western executives, when they go to China and India, are looking at products and technology and saying, 'What's going on?' They're not looking at this kind of institutional innovation so they don't see it—and I think we need to see it in order to be successful."

Indeed, in searching for examples as they researched *The Power of Pull*, Hagel and his co-authors looked far outside of traditional American corporations—at the highly competitive sport of large wave surfing, for example—to find places where teamwork, collaboration and skill in communication were bringing new heights of invention and success.

One conventional corporation that Hagel praised as an edge-based business is the German software giant SAP. He said the company's longtime CEO, Hasso Plattner, came to a decision that the firm was too hierarchical and too adverse to change; his solution involved buying a rival run by Israeli entrepreneur Shai Agassi. Plattner tasked Agassi with launching a venture called NetWeaver, an integrated technology platform. "Plattner said that [NetWeaver serves a function that is] not part of our core business, but it's a highly speculative new initiative," Hagel noted. "He said [to Agassi], 'I want you to use that product to create a very different set of relationships with our customers and with our third-party-channel partners of various types.' Shai Agassi used that mandate to go out and create this software user developer network which now has two million participants." The network, Hagel said, is currently helping SAP to develop both new products as well as new kinds of business relationships.

In that sense, Hagel thinks the teamwork and communication skills that SAP software designers have been gaining are quite similar to the talents that leaders among the millions of online gamers playing *World of Warcraft*—people like Starbucks CIO Gillett—have also been acquiring. In addition to the leadership qualities involved with becoming the head of a guild and assembling a problem-solving team from previously independent players, *World of Warcraft* enthusiasts, as noted by Hagel, conduct extensive after-action reviews of their performances as well as that of the leader. In addition, he said that game players typically customize their own dashboards to offer statistics and rate performance in areas they consider critical to their strategy.

Increasing the Perception of Opportunity

However, there's one important quality to success for the 21st Century business leader that cannot be measured by a dashboard, and that is passion. Hagel said CEOs typically don't understand the kind of passion that is necessary for a collaborative, edge-based emphasis. Ironically, Hagel said that American CEOs do place a premium on passion—but typically on the wrong type. "They say they want passion and I don't think they're being dishonest or disingenuous," he noted. "They really want passion but what they mean by passion is somebody who will follow instructions passionately [and] work nights, work weekends, to get the job done."

The type of passion that Hagel was describing involved what he called "a questing disposition"—that is, enthusiasm for pushing the work effort to new experiences and new frontiers, through activities such as attending conferences, meeting players from outside the company for lunch or getting involved in social media. Such workers are rare; Hagel asserted that no industry was composed of more than 20% of these passionate individuals, and the larger the company, the less likely you were to find them. Passionate employees are not always the happiest, he said, as many chafe at the corporate barriers to innovation. In fact, Hagel said he finds that most large American companies discourage passion among their workers. "Passion is extremely unpredictable in a world of 'push,'" he pointed out, referring to the older proprietary business models. "Prediction is everything. Passion is a very dangerous emotion. Passion is something you pursue outside of the workforce—not in the workplace."

Despite his somewhat pessimistic view of the U.S. business environment, Hagel said he believed that the potential is there for American business leaders and their companies to turn things around—providing that CEOs understand the pressures that they face are systemic, and not merely caused by the short-term economic downturn. Ultimately, success may mean defining a company in terms of its broader mission, rather than in terms of a specific product or products that it manufactures and it markets, he added. "I believe the opportunity for leadership in this regard is to flip the natural psychological reaction that we have to uncertainty," Hagel said. "All of us, when confronted with uncertainty, tend to magnify risk and discount reward, and that tends to lead us not to act but to stay on the sidelines, hoping that somehow, somewhere things will clarify and then we can move. The role of the leader, in making sense, is to increase the perception of opportunity and to diminish the perception of risk." ∎

Published: June 23, 2010 in Knowledge@Wharton

A Virtuous Cycle: How Managers Can Take the Lead in Building Trust at Work

At a time when business revenues are declining and corporate staffs are being dramatically cut in many countries, it is important to curb the growth of distrustful work environments that can affect the bottom line. Understanding how to build and communicate trust to employees is crucial for managers, say IESE professors Pablo Cardona and Helen Wilkinson in a recent study titled, "How to Create a Virtuous Cycle of Trust."

For their research, the professors drew from their experiences as business coaches, and an empirical study of 741 managers and 2,111 subordinates in 18 countries that was developed by IESE's Cross Cultural Management Network. That institution's goal is to promote intercultural research in the realm of human behavior in organizations. The study analyzed 2,848 responses and a series of qualitative interviews with managers in six different cultural regions: English-speaking countries, Western Europe, Eastern Europe, Latin America, Asia and Southeast Asia. The results of their research were presented at the 2009 Annual Conference of the Academy of Management.

In an interview with Universia Knowledge@Wharton, the authors analyze the keys for developing relationships between managers and subordinates that are based on trust and understanding. Healthy rapport between employees and their supervisors leads to a virtuous cycle: When a manager exhibits behavior that is deserving of trust, his or her employees not only feel more confidence in their superior, but also believe more strongly in their work and in the company as a whole. The strengthened bond between boss and subordinate makes it easier for the manager to maintain an attitude that is worthy of employees' trust.

Universia Knowledge@Wharton: What does trust involve within the business context?

Pablo Cardona: We have done several empirical studies that asked workers what trust means to them, [what it means] when they [really] trust someone. We obtained answers like these:

"I trust the sort of person who always responds to my expectations at work; someone loyal to his [or her] commitments. When he [or she] says that he [or she] is going to do something, he [or she] does it. And when he [or she] thinks that he [or she] is not going to be able to do something, he [or she] says that and explains why." [Comment from a 37-year old woman in the educational business sector.]

"I trust the sort of person who always responds to my messages, and who establishes a fluid exchange of information, and who is sincere in that exchange." [Comment from a 35-year old woman in the communications sector.]

"Trust is the feeling of security you have when you are sharing everything with a person who you know is going to respond to your expectations because he or she can take on commitments and fulfill them." [Comment from a 42-year old man in the consulting sector.]

Reciprocity, transparency, loyalty, responsibility and professionalism are the common denominators. These are the behavioral patterns that appear in our virtuous cycle of trust.

Universia Knowledge@Wharton: What are the behavioral patterns and characteristics that generate trust internally?

Helen Wilkinson: The behavioral patterns that generate trust are the following: Consistency and predictability, [or] not contradicting yourself and arguing about opinions; integrity based on ethical principles; open and fluid communication with collaborators—lying is never a good option; sharing and delegating (which leads to greater motivation and personal involvement); concern about subordinates—empathy is one of the competencies that help the most—and loyalty. Trust is based on the interconnection of these components.

Universia Knowledge@Wharton: Where does trust come from? Who originates it? How is it transmitted within the organization?

Cardona: Everyone in the company can begin to create trust, but managers play the main role. If they generate trust, it is easier for trust to spread to different levels within the organization. If they don't, workers can maintain trust in one another, but that is not necessarily something positive; it can be counterproductive because it can generate a defensive system "against" management.

How do you communicate trust? In the first place, you do that by setting an example, [such as] when managers do what they demand others to do, and when they do what they say they will do, and sustain behavioral patterns that they have previously laid out. Second, you need to enact policies of really evaluating workers: If managers assert values that they do not absolutely uphold when they evaluate other people, then there is no consistency in their real policies. Third, [managers are judged] by the decisions they make, day by day, within the company. Once again, people will realize the degree of consistency in these decisions. And, finally, [managers build trust] by communicating effectively the intentions and decisions of your company and the policies that it adopts to all levels of your organization.

Universia Knowledge@Wharton: What are the principal benefits of trust for the organization?

Wilkinson: People and departments can cooperate with one another like an integrated team. If you do not create trust, everyone devotes himself or herself to their own activities, not to the common good or the overall interest of the company or organization. When there is trust, there is fluidity, an exchange of ideas and pro-activity. Each worker thinks for himself [or herself] without waiting for instructions. They become the owners of their own work and they contribute initiatives that bring added value. They are not afraid that they might be penalized if they make mistakes, or that someone else is going to steal their ideas and contributions. These factors help the organization move forward, rather than get bogged down in behavioral patterns inherited from the past, which involve inertia. And, of course, this always has an influence on the development of the worker.

Universia Knowledge@Wharton: What are the warning signs of a working environment where distrust reigns?

Cardona: Depression, anxiety, medical leaves caused by stress, excessive mobility, team leaders who rule different areas within the company and the fact that information doesn't move easily.

Universia Knowledge@Wharton: Are there ways to measure the level of distrust in companies?

Wilkinson: Distrust is [something that takes place] between people. As far as the company as a whole is concerned, you have to measure the degree of unity and identification within the company, which is exemplified by the managers, their evaluation policies and the examples noted earlier. There are studies about how to measure business culture, such as, "Business Culture: An Empirical Study of Spanish and Portuguese Companies," [published by] IESE-IRCO in 2007. This study involves measuring the degree of unity, not just the labor climate.

Universia Knowledge@Wharton: Do companies get involved in measuring the level of trust, in some way?

Cardona: We are still very far from doing that. It is not enough that [companies] only do studies that measure the labor climate. Generally speaking, these sorts of studies measure the degree of satisfaction, not [the degree of] unity. They measure complaints. Nevertheless, some companies are already including questions directed at measuring unity, which is something tied to satisfaction. One example of this sort of question would be: "Do I feel proud that I belong to this company?"

Universia Knowledge@Wharton: Some factors that create trust are things we can barely influence. What are they and how can they be changed?

Wilkinson: Age, sex and race are factors that cannot be changed. In contrast, prestige and credibility can be [changed]. We can always increase trust through knowledge, networking and honesty—and we can therefore gain prestige and credibility. That has an indirect impact on those factors that we cannot modify. In China, for example, from the outset, a female manager finds it harder to generate trust merely because she is a woman. But she can lessen the negative handicap that stems from her sex—something that cannot be changed—through her knowledge and her professional prestige.

Another example involves age. You can compensate for age with the passage of time. It isn't always a negative handicap if you are [someone who is] younger. For example, in Eastern Europe, people immediately have less confidence in an older boss, rather than in a younger boss.

Universia Knowledge@Wharton: Do the dynamics of trust work the same way in Spain and Latin America?

Cardona: The basic dynamics, yes.

Universia Knowledge@Wharton: How do Spain and Latin America differ in that regard? How do the differences influence trust there?

Cardona: In Latin America, it is harder for managers to trust their subordinates. Managers there take it for granted that all workers must be completely devoted to their work. In Latin America, functions that have to be developed are not clearly outlined. In contrast, in the United States each job description is very rigorous and specific in such a way that when a worker excels, it is very easy to detect and it is easy for the boss to appreciate. It is easier to notice when someone excels than when someone is devoted [to his or her work].

UK@W: What are the practical implications of the results of this study?

Wilkinson: In the first place, generating ideas. Ideas can flow in an environment of trust. When distrust reigns, there are silos ruled by separate leaders; information is not exchanged and ideas are not generated [throughout the company]. There is stagnation and inertia. When there is no trust, there is no real commitment. Without trust, you can't be surprised by mercenary reactions, and you should be prepared to accept that the worker is not going to be concerned about the overall good of the company.

Second, trust is something that takes time to build and strengthen, but it can be destroyed very easily. Be careful about permitting certain kinds of attitudes during a crisis. You can create an atmosphere in which it becomes very hard to rebuild trust. The decisions that must be [made] must be [carried out] with consistency and integrity, by sharing information at the right moment and by maintaining genuine concern for people. Of course, the same holds at times when there is no crisis. ■

Published: May 19, 2010 in Universia Knowledge@Wharton

PART 7

Driving Social Change
Through Creative Leadership

"Greenomics": Making Cents in a Low-Carbon World

Seoul-based Hyundai Motor Company has good reason to be riding high. Its recent earnings reports have been turning rivals green with envy—including its first quarter 2010 net profit, which jumped fivefold from the year earlier to 1.13 trillion won ($1 billion), and sales that gained 40% to reach 8.4 trillion won. But while South Korea's biggest auto maker might be an industry pacesetter in many respects, it still shares the same big headache its rivals do: How to meet the growing demand for environmentally friendly cars in a way that's profitable for car companies yet affordable for consumers.

It's a tall order. Despite ever-more stringent regulations worldwide for a greener automotive industry, "the shift to eco-friendly vehicles is rather slower than we expected," said Hyun Soon Lee, head of corporate R&D and vice chairman of Hyundai Motor Company, during a keynote address at the recent Wharton Global Alumni Forum in Seoul. "The real problem is the cost." Despite years of research effort, auto companies still spend as much as $50,000 on the battery alone for each electric vehicle they manufacture. Without governments providing subsidies, "who can afford that?" asked Lee.

Welcome to "greenomics," or the economics of being environmentally friendly, which are leaving companies like Hyundai struggling to balance their eco-ambitions with hardcore business pressures. As experts gathered at the Wharton Global Alumni Forum for a panel titled, "Creating New World Greenomics," noted, greenomics isn't just about corporate profit and loss statements. Rather, it requires a symbiotic relationship between the public and private sector, non-profit and non-governmental organizations (NGOs), and consumers. Yet, observed Eric Bradlow, Wharton marketing professor and the panel's moderator, all these groups are a long way away from helping the business world reach the day "when we no longer need the term 'greenomics' because it's simply embedded into everything we do."

A "Green New Deal"

Until that day, the panel agreed that governments around the world can and should play a pivotal role in supporting greenomics. "Governments can create regulations, but also a market, even if it's through subsidies," noted Jong Hyun Chang, president and partner of management consultants B&MC (Booz & Company) in Seoul. What's more, they can also go as far as to influence major lifestyle changes among consumers. "Governments have a big role to play but I think they are afraid to," he said. "They think if people do a bit of recycling here and there so that they feel good about their lives, that's enough. But [environmentally friendly behavior] needs to get regulated."

There certainly has been no shortage of governments announcing national green initiatives and targets ever since the failed global push to combat climate change at the United Nations conference in Copenhagen last year. Among the more ambitious governments is South Korea. In November, the country volunteered to cut greenhouse gas emission 30% by 2020 from 2005 levels. It's a noteworthy pledge for several reasons. Over the past 60 or so years, South Korea's prosperity has been highly dependent on carbon-intensive industrial growth. The country has been one of the fastest-growing emissions sources among members of the Organisation for Economic Co-operation and Development, with the country's greenhouse gas discharges more than doubling between 1990 and 2005.

However, well before last year's Copenhagen talks, South Korea President Lee Myung Bak had ambitious climate change goals and unveiled his "Green New Deal," said Kang Nam Hoon, a panel participant and director general of energy policy at the country's Ministry of Knowledge Economy (MKE). In the summer of 2008, just weeks after beginning his five-year term as president, the former mayor of Seoul and Hyundai executive set up a committee dedicated to "green growth" initiatives. Months later, the Green New Deal was then melded into the administration's economic stimulus package to spur employment and business growth. For us, Kang stated, greenomics "means new jobs, new industries [and] new markets."

With a budget of $84 billion (about 2% of the country's GDP) to be allocated to environmental measures over the next five years, the South Korean government says it will generate as many as 18 million new jobs between 2009 and 2013. But the Green New Deal is not without controversy. For example, many of the new jobs will be part of the Four Rivers Restoration Project, which plans to construct or restore a number of dams, levees and reservoirs for an estimated cost of $13 billion. Many environmentalists say parts of the project could do the country's fragile ecosystem more harm than good.

There's more to the Green New Deal than ecology. While reducing its reliance on fossil fuels, the government also wants South Korea to become more energy self-sufficient, noted Kang. Korea currently imports 97% of its energy supply, with 84% derived from fossil-based fuel sources. "We have to make our best effort to develop renewable energy," said Kang.

Solar energy is one avenue that Korea is pursuing, but embracing the technology presents some challenges. According to consultancy Euclid Infotech, South Korea lags countries, such as the United States and Japan, when it comes to both R&D and price competitiveness in key solar power technologies. Currently, solar energy accounts for around 50% of South Korea's renewable energy output, yet nearly 70% of the solar modules needed for that output are imported.

Arguably, a more-promising source of energy for South Korea is nuclear power, said Kang. Less carbon-intensive than fossil fuel, nuclear energy could benefit South Korea's domestic and international energy ambitions as the country increases the exports of the technology it began commercializing some 40 years ago. The organizations behind a recent deal with the United Arab Emirates to export South Korea's nuclear know-how and technology say it will create 200,000 new jobs alone, while nuclear-related public bodies will recruit more than 2,000 employees this year.

The Weakest Links

With or without assistance from governments like South Korea's, there's plenty of greenomics that businesses can pursue independently, observed Chang of B&MC. That includes cleaning up their supply chains—from increasing the use of renewable energy and recycled materials to improving manufacturing efficiency and material yields. It can mean moving factories closer to logistic centers and customers to reduce travel time; partnering with suppliers to ensure goods are procured from more eco-friendly sources; or even investing in green manufacturing technologies, regardless of whether the return on investment is immediately clear.

The starting point for any of these measures is "to look at every link of a supply chain to understand what its carbon footprint is—that is, how much CO_2 each link is emitting," noted Chang. "Then you have to figure out how to reduce it, how to avoid it and how to take advantage of it, with [initiatives like] carbon credits." Addressing supply chain issues with "a thorough, fact-based analysis of CO_2 emissions" can bring surprises. For example, he said, a newspaper company using recycled paper could actually have a larger carbon footprint than a competitor that isn't printing on recycled paper but is using green energy to run printing plants and has eco-friendly trucks delivering its papers.

"It's very simple, once you understand where the energy is used and wasted," Chang added. "Each product has different CO_2 constraints. So management needs to run a product-by-product analysis to find a solution. But as long as we see the green issue as a cost, there is no way we'll make progress. If we see it as an opportunity, there is a chance."

The good news is that many green opportunities are within reach, according to Dong Sup Kim, president of SK Energy's Institute of Technology (SKEIT), the 30-year-old innovation center run by the Seoul-based energy and petrochemicals company. "The solution is very easy to me—on paper at least: Expand the supply of energy, increase efficiency and mitigate emissions," he asserted. "The 'how to' is the difficult part." To that end, SKEIT's mission has been to develop groundbreaking technologies that can be used to make products more environmentally friendly.

Consider GreenPol, a plastic SKEIT developed that is made up of 44% carbon dioxide, and can be used to manufacture products like cling film, food containers or car parts. "The question for us was how to turn CO_2 into a valuable product," recalled Kim. According to him, SK Energy is the first company to commercialize a CO2-based polymer. What's more, unlike with conventional polymers, GreenPol is "clean burning—there is no soot, no toxins." And its money-making potential is promising. "By 2025, the market for eco-friendly plastics such as GreenPol could be worth some $25 billion," Kim predicted.

Another big potential market that has captured SKEIT's attention is batteries for electric vehicles, to the delight of auto makers such as Hyundai. Since beginning commercial production of batteries that can be used in electric vehicles in 2005, SK Energy has won deals to supply both Hyundai and Mitsubishi. Citing research from the non-profit Electric Power Research Institute, Kim said the global market for such batteries could generate some $1.4 trillion of revenue by 2030.

Where's the Payback?

If companies need an additional incentive to develop greenomics, they should look no further than BP as it wrangles with the Gulf Coast oil spill, said Douglas Woodring, co-founder and director of Project Kaisei, a San Francisco and Hong Kong-based environmental non-profit focused on cleaning up plastic debris in the ocean. The environmental damage of the oil spill is devastating enough, he noted, but the U.K.-based oil giant also is facing potentially irreparable damage to its reputation among stakeholders as a worthy global citizen that is ecologically proactive. "Companies cannot hide, as the BP oil spill shows," he stated.

Looked at from another perspective, Woodring cited research from a global public relations firm showing that companies enhance their reputations among the general public by associating themselves with green projects, such as Kaisei. Launched last year, Kaisei (which means "ocean planet" in Japanese) brings together conservationists from around the world to focus on what the organization calls the "Plastic Vortex," a part of the Pacific Ocean containing an estimated four million tons of floating plastic waste in a mass nearly four times as large as Japan.

"National Geographic estimates that over 85 million plastic bottles are used every three minutes," Woodring noted. In many cases, plastic waste that is not incinerated or put in landfills ends up in the ocean. "Most plastics are something you use for a few minutes, but will last hundreds of years. There is a serious mismatch in the materials we're using and the way that we're using them." Moreover, he said, when plastic is dumped at sea, it does not biodegrade.

But it's a problem governments "are escaping," he said. "There is no ownership out there [in the ocean], no laws, no boundaries." This is where NGOs and the private sector come in. While the situation is a "nightmare," Woodring added, "it's also an opportunity." Project Kaisei is, among other things, developing a new way to treat ocean-based plastic waste, which uses low heat, no oxygen and allows for a variety of plastic waste to be processed into diesel fuel.

When it comes to greenomics in general, Woodring called for companies to put their money where their mouth is. "Companies need to invest in green technologies, otherwise we won't get the economies of scale to make them viable from a business sense," he said. "We shouldn't be afraid of these new technologies and processes. We can't forget that the economy is a 100% subsidiary of the environment. But who's going to take the first step? People always ask where the payback is."

Beyond corporate and NGO involvement, however, SKEIT's Kim, in the panel's concluding observations, said the "blame game" for damages to the environment needs to stop, and individual consumers might have the biggest role of all to play in greenomics. "I don't think its right to point the finger at [an environmentally unfriendly] product, especially if we don't change our lifestyles," he noted. "Do we really need all the energy we're using?" ■

Published: June 23, 2010 in Knowledge@Wharton

Nidan: Tapping into "the Wealth of the Poor" — Their Numbers

When Arbind Singh was named Social Entrepreneur of the Year for 2008 in India, one of the award's sponsors described Singh's non-government organization (NGO), Nidan, as "[building] profitable businesses and people's organizations led by assetless, informal workers."

"Social entrepreneurs embody excellence in creating disruptive technologies and ideas that empower the poor or the marginalized," said Don Mohanlal, president and CEO of the Nand & Jeet Khemka Foundation, which sponsors the annual award with the Schwab Foundation for Social Entrepreneurship in collaboration with the United Nations Development Program (UNDP). Nidan's "innovative techniques have fundamentally altered conventional development and business logic."

Based in Patna, Bihar, with additional operations in the states of Jharkhand, Delhi and Rajasthan, Nidan comprises "a range of cooperatives, self-help groups, trade unions, and individual and community businesses launched by Nidan that have positioned unorganized workers as legitimate competitors in India's globalizing markets," according to the Khemka Foundation's website.

In Hindi (and some other Indian languages), Nidan means "solution." "That's the difference between us and many others," Singh says. "We have focused on providing solutions rather than just complaining. Though advocacy has been a major plank for us, our advocacy has always focused on giving solutions rather than just raising issues of concern."

In 12 years, Nidan has launched and promoted 20 independent businesses and organizations that are governed and owned through shares by 60,000 urban and rural poor members, the foundation notes. "The enterprises include 4,618 self-help groups, 75 market committees, 19 cooperatives, two societies and one company, all envisioned and led by a complex of waste workers, rag-pickers, vegetable vendors, construction laborers, domestic helpers, micro-farmers, street traders and other marginalized occupation groups.

"Nidan taps into the wealth of the poor—primarily their numerical strength—and then aggregates them into economies of scale. This process of collectivizing generates social capital, representation and voice for the unorganized poor, which they then leverage to launch their own businesses and shift policy to be recognized as wealth creators."

The award recognition, Singh says, will mean increased support and the scope to bring more into the fold. The need is clear. An August 2007 central government report on working conditions in the unorganized sector says informal laborers make up 92% of India's workforce. These more than 340 million workers contribute 60% of national economic output, the report says. They constitute the poorest and most vulnerable segments of India's population.

"Reaching the Unreached"

The unorganized sector's potential is evident in Nidan Swachdhara Private Ltd. (NSPL), a Nidan enterprise. Set up as an urban waste management company with initial capitalization from 1,606 waste workers who collectively bid for business, NSPL has won multi-crore contracts from the Patna and Jaipur Municipal Corporations. Last year, NSPL recruited its first chief executive from the business sector, satisfying shareholder demands.

"Reaching the unreached" has been Singh's mission for years. After earning sociology and law degrees from Delhi University, "I appeared for the examination to enter the civil services," he says. "But even while preparing for the exams, I realized my heart did not lie there. I had a lot of exposure during my college days to societal issues. I happened to meet the late Viji Srinivasan, who was running a large NGO [named Adithi] on women's issues. I began working with her and she encouraged me to set up a separate organization. I realized that the development sector provides immense potential to impact lives of the poor."

The poor do not want charity forever, he says. "We want sustainable organizations based on ongoing revenue generation. This will provide efficient services. Only corporatization will ensure sustainability. This is the future direction. Nidan is gradually becoming an incubator and resource organization for such [ventures]."

Nidan's organizational structure is as complex as a medium-size company's. Its many layers include a general body at the top with an executive committee reporting to it. In education, for example, the academic facilitator reports to the executive director and finance manager. Below the facilitator come community coordinators, ward facilitators, teachers and, finally, the community. "All the operations have their own structure," Singh says. "We have 400 staff members and several volunteers."

While Nidan is a profit-making organization, it relies significantly on donations. Singh notes that donors include international aid agencies such as the United Nations Development Fund and UNICEF, national agencies such as the United Kingdom's Department for International Development, international NGOs such as the Ford Foundation, Indian NGOs such as the Sir Dorabji Tata Trust, state governments and district administrations. Revenue is also earned through services provided to government and local bodies. Residents and institutions pay for waste management services and purchase of handicrafts. "The spread from loan programs is also an important source of revenue," Singh says. "The commission earned from the insurance program constitutes another source of revenue. And there are occasional consultancies."

In 2007-08, Nidan earned Rs. 2.9 million (about US $60,000) from a program offering life, health, asset and property insurance to more than 35,250 members. It also received Rs. 45 million (US $925,000) in grants. Its own income was Rs. 8.6 million (US $175,000).

Individual units also contribute. NSPL, the waste management company, had a profit of Rs. 4 million (US $80,000). While that may not seem like much, consider that its capital base is made up of Rs. 100 (US $2) contributions from each of its 1,606 members—a total of Rs. 160,600 (US $3,212). The Wama Mahila Swablambi Sakhari Samiti, a cooperative that runs retail outlets, earned Rs. 133,269 (US $2,700). It has 351 members who have put in Rs. 10 (20 cents) each as share capital. The Gharunda Housing Cooperative made Rs. 134,851 (US $2,700). Its shareholding: 103 members chipping in Rs. 103 (US $2) apiece.

These minuscule numbers demonstrate the resource constraints of the people Nidan and Singh work with. But the numbers are far from small on another front. "Nidan reaches out to 60,000 poor workers, an equal number of middle-class households for waste management and 300,000 street vendors," Singh says.

Value Beyond Numbers

The impact on individuals has little to do with numbers. "An individual served by Nidan gets the opportunity to realize his or her potential," Singh says. "Nidan provides access to financial services, protection against harassment, legal aid when needed, insurance [coverage], help in getting children educated. For its members, Nidan has become an alternate home where they can come for any help related to their work, their children and gender issues."

"Nidan is a well-grounded organization with a deep insight on development issues within its operating region," says Tarun Vij, New Delhi-based country director of the American India Foundation (AIF). "We feel it has matured tremendously and is ready to take on additional responsibilities. We could in the near future look at an integrated programming approach with them, one that delivers education, health and livelihood simultaneously for the overall wellness of the community it works for."

AIF has supported Nidan for three years so far, and the NGO's success with waste workers in Patna and Muzaffarpur has prompted the foundation to extend the relationship. "Through a government-citizen-corporate partnership model, the second phase of the program will not only promote sustainable and scalable enterprises of waste-pickers and sweepers but also seek to actively project their occupation as a dignified livelihood," AIF said in a written statement.

Among the Nidan waste program's benefits, according to AIF:
- Significantly reduced vulnerability and insecurity for waste workers.
- Increased average monthly income for individuals from Rs. 1,500 to Rs. 2,800 (US $30 to US $56).
- Improved working conditions.
- Provided an effective solution for municipal waste disposal.

More waste workers want to get involved. In the next phase, AIF will provide a grant of Rs. 29.5 million (US $600,000) and a loan of Rs. 14.4 million (US $295,000). AIF's support will provide jobs to 2,306 people directly (in door-to-door waste collection and in composting and recycling facilities) and 3,468 indirectly (waste-pickers whose recyclables will be purchased). A total of 208,000 house-holds are expected to be served.

Critical Foundation Support

The high visibility AIF's support has provided has been critical for Nidan. AIF, founded in 2001 under the leadership of former U.S. President Bill Clinton, "is a bridge to channel philanthropy toward India," says Sanjay Sinho, AIF's New York-based chief executive. "Since inception, AIF has invested in nearly 100 high-quality Indian NGOs who are working on primary education, livelihoods and public health initiatives, including HIV/AIDs. AIF has worked in 21 states across India. Most of its funds come from Indians living in the U.S. and Indophiles. Among AIF's achievements are its ability to launch programs to scale, and the manner in which it has been able to bring corporates, government and civil society together to form meaningful partnerships that foster inclusion of those who are less privileged. A recent example is our Rickshaw Bank program that allows rickshaw pullers to [secure] loans from banks and eventually become owners of rickshaws."

Sinho says AIF is different in both "the way we view our work and the manner in which we carry it out. We identify local organizations of repute and handhold them throughout our association. We bring not only funds but valuable expertise and technical know-how to any partnership. On top of this we also provide linkages with other stakeholders to take the work to higher levels."

"The role of organizations like AIF is that of being a bridge between people who are willing to donate resources and people who need the resources," says N. Balasubramanian, chairman of the Centre for Corporate Governance and Citizenship at the Indian Institute of Management, Bangalore (IIMB). "There is need for this bridge. Very often donors have no way of assessing if their money and resources are going to an organization which will put them to good use. Organizations like AIF can do due diligence on the NGOs and their projects. They must, of course, first of all establish their own credentials and be completely transparent about their own operations: where they get their funds from, which are the units that they support and promote, and what is their process and criteria for evaluation of the NGOs."

Country director Vij highlights some of AIF's achievements. "AIF has sent 169 Service Corps fellows to serve for 10 months with Indian NGOs, and the Digital Equalizer Program has brought technology to touch the lives of over 570,000 students and 17,000 teachers in 1,400 schools across India. Many state governments have come forward to provide us with various kinds of resources."

The Award's Value

Through its awards, the Khemka Foundation has also played an important role in promoting social entrepreneurship. "We provide the winners with access to global platforms and showcase their work in national and international media," award program manager Payal Randhawa says. "Apart from the national recognition, the winner is included in the Schwab Foundation's global network of outstanding social entrepreneurs. Acceptance into global networks provides successful social entrepreneurs financial and technical support for their activities. In addition, the winner is eligible to be named a Khemka Fellow and receive a cash award of Rs. 800,000 (US $16,000) from the Khemka Foundation."

Do organizations such as AIF and the Khemka Foundation complement the government or simply fill gaps? "Actually, a bit of both," AIF's Vij says. "Most of our programs work in tandem with government initiatives like the Sarva Shiksha Abhiyan ("Education for All") and the national health missions. In many places across India we work with the government. But there are complex issues and concerns in India. No government can tackle these on its own, which is why the work of organizations like ours acquires relevance. The government recognizes this fact. So, yes, we are also filling gaps."

"The upliftment of the poorer sections of society is the duty of the government," says Balasubramanian of IIMB. "But it is also a fact that a vast majority of governments around the world are incapable of doing this. In such a scenario there is an important role for individuals, corporates and NGOs to do some of the things which were originally associated with government responsibility." To that extent, he says, initiatives such as Nidan "are valuable and need to be encouraged and appreciated."

Singh says the social entrepreneurship award has "dramatically raised the image of the organization. Being recognized by agencies outside Bihar, we expect we will have a better image with the state government, and this will improve considerably our access to government resources and officials. The award has given immense confidence to the members and staff of the organization. They now realize they are creating history." ∎

Published: February 26, 2009 in India Knowledge@Wharton

Coke on the Yangtze: The Corporate Campaign for Clean Water

Nearly half of China's sewage and industrial waste is discharged into the Yangtze River, the lifeline of millions of Chinese. As a result, the Yangtze now tops the World Wildlife Fund (WWF) list of the 10 most-threatened rivers in the world. In a project that reflects growing corporate concern over the sustainability of water, Coca-Cola, which operates 39 bottling plants in China, has joined forces with the WWF to improve the water quality of the upper reaches of the Yangtze. Coke is also working with the WWF to restore other rivers on the most-endangered list. Other companies, including PepsiCo, are also in partnerships with environmental groups to protect water resources. For the companies, it's a case of doing well by doing good. They need clean water, too.

The Yangtze River—the longest river in Asia and the lifeblood of millions of Chinese—was once said to be so clear you could watch a pen sink to the bottom. Today, as China's massive economic growth has taken its toll on the environment, it is at the top of the World Wildlife Fund (WWF) list of the 10 most threatened rivers in the world.

To help reverse the tide, the wildlife fund has joined forces with the Coca-Cola Company, which operates 39 bottling plants in China, to improve the water quality of the upper reaches of the Yangtze. Coke is working with rural farmers, for example, to reduce the runoff of animal waste into the river by turning pig waste into biogas for cooking and heating. It is also working with WWF to be more efficient in its own use of water and eventually to become "water neutral"— by reducing its so-called water footprint as much as possible while continuing to invest in projects to foster water sustainability.

The wildlife fund's partnership with Coke is part of a growing corporate awareness that water is a threatened resource, not just in the Yangtze but throughout the world. And that companies that require a lot of water to do business need to assess the risks they—and their customers—face on the water-supply front and to start doing something to reduce them.

To continue to grow in China, Coke recognizes that it must invest to strengthen what is coming to be called its water security. "It is not considered philanthropy, not even CSR," says Brenda Lee, vice president of Coca-Cola China, of the WWF project. "It is part of our business commitment. We can only prosper and thrive in communities that are sustainable."

Coke is now working with WWF to help clean six other rivers on the 10-worst list. It isn't the only multinational to add an environmental partner to its water-related efforts, which also involve industry groups. Indeed, Coke's chief competitor, PepsiCo, has been working for some time now with the China Women's Development Foundation, the architect of the Mother Water Cellars Project, which provides ways for people in the most water-scarce regions of China to have better access to water.

For the environmental groups, such alliances add clout to what they are doing. Coke's rural program "is really making a difference in the Yangtze," says Chris Williams, director of fresh water conservation at WWF. "If we could get this kind of involvement from a wider range of private-sector actors in the Yangtze, the results could be considerable."

For the companies, a key dividend is credibility. Undertakings like these by Coke and PepsiCo are critical to the companies' image and brand, according to Piet Klop, a senior fellow at the Washington-based think tank World Resources Institute (WRI). "The last thing a branded company would want," he says, "is to end up in a newspaper saying they are operating a bottling plant in an area where households cannot even access clean drinking water."

Coke is at a particularly sensitive point in China, eager to expand its business into the rapidly growing juice, dairy, and ready-to-drink tea markets. Its partnership with WWF is designed in part to build a relationship of trust that may help open doors to more consumers in China, according to Eric Orts, professor of legal studies and business ethics and management and director of the Initiative for Global Environmental Leadership at Wharton. China is increasingly important to Coke—its sales by volume grew 19% there last year while declining by 1% in North America.

Alliances like the Coke-WWF partnership don't come without challenges. Some environmentalists are critical of groups that work with companies that are seen as part of the problem. And in China, there are special issues, given that the government does not allow its citizens to freely organize into non-profit organizations and instead typically tries to micromanage projects itself.

"Companies need to be aware of the limitations that this reality imposes," Orts says. "They have to work with government and government-sponsored NGOs in China. At the same time, it's also important to work directly with people who are actually affected."

What's Wrong with the Yangtze
WWF has been working with Coke to help the people along the Yangtze for three years. It is also working with HSBC, the global banking giant, on conservation projects related to the river. (It has partnerships with other multinationals on a range of environmental projects around the world.)

The Yangtze provides China with 35% of its fresh water needs. Yet nearly half of the country's sewage and industrial waste is discharged into the river as its flows 3,900 miles from West China to the East China Sea at Shanghai. The river has also been affected by the construction of the Three Gorges Dam, the world's largest hydroelectric dam. Three Gorges, which went into operation over the last several years, weakened the river's ability to flush away pollution.

So-called non-point source pollution, including animal waste and fertilizer runoff, is as big a threat as industrial waste, or even bigger, says WWF's Williams.

The WWF-Coke partnership has run pilot projects to produce biogas with farmers at the upper reaches of the Yangtze in communities along the Minjiang and Jiangling Rivers. Another boost from the partnership has been Coke's program to educate communities along the river basin about environmental issues. The partnership also engages with the Chinese government, trying to affect environmental policy. "China now has tremendous resources they have set aside to invest in river basin management and water management," Williams says. "If they put some of those resources into replicating our pilot project, it could have a tremendous impact on water quality in the river."

Suzanne Apple, WWF's vice president and managing director of business and industry, helped set up the partnership with Coke, which amounts to a $24 million, seven-year commitment to support fresh water programs globally. With operations in more than 200 countries, Coke, the world's largest beverage company, uses more than 290 billion liters of water a year. The partnership provides for WWF's help to eventually make all of Coke's plants worldwide water neutral.

A former head of corporate social responsibility at home improvement retailer Home Depot, Apple says partnerships like this one are good for business because they help to guarantee supplies of water and other necessities. As for WWF, "it is a way for us to leverage funding from the government," she says. "When we say Coca-Cola is investing a certain amount of money, it is an incentive for the government to match funds." Put another way, "When you bring both of us together, two plus two equals five."

Coke's Growth Plans

Coke has big plans for China. The company already has more than half of the country's soda market, with rival PepsiCo a distant second, at 33%. And it thinks the market has plenty of room to grow, especially as it rolls out products tailored to Chinese consumers. For now, the average consumer in China drinks 32 Coke products a year, less than half the global average of 85.

Coke also has its sights set on China's fruit and vegetable drink sector, which grew by 20% last year, double the rate for carbonated drinks, according to *Euromonitor*. In what would have been the biggest foreign takeover of a Chinese company, Coke's $2.3 billion bid for China Huiyuan Juice was rejected last year. The deal would have given Coke a 20% stake in the country's juice market. The failed deal is hardly the end of Coke's ambitions in that area, however. The company has launched a three-year, $2 billion program to expand in China, in juice and other products. Eager to grow its food and beverage businesses, rival PepsiCo plans to invest $2.5 billion over the next three years as well.

Learning from the Past

Coke hasn't always gotten high marks for its environmental record. "Coca-Cola had an unpleasant reminder of the potential cost of ignoring the social and environmental foundations of consumer trust in India with respect to ground-water issues," says Wharton's Orts.

In 2004, Coke was forced to shut down one of its largest bottling plants in the southern Indian state of Kerala after community organizers blamed it for causing water shortages. (A year before, PepsiCo's plant in Kerala lost its operating license as local officials worried about its impact on the water supply.)
A state government panel recently recommended that Coke pay $47 million for damage allegedly caused by ground water depletion and the dumping of toxic waste between 1999 and 2004.

Coke has denied liability. In a recent statement citing "scientific evaluation," it said that its "plant operations have not been shown to be the cause of local watershed issues. It is unfortunate that the committee in Kerala was appointed on the unproven assumption that damage was caused, and that it was caused by Hindustan Coca-Cola Beverages."

The Sustainability Issue

Behind all of the environmental partnerships are worries about the growing vulnerability of big companies to water's uncertain future. Scarcity, flooding, and pollution pose serious risks to multinationals—particularly those whose operations rely heavily on a steady supply of fresh water, says Dan Bena, director of sustainable development for PepsiCo. Issues like these are "prompting investors to ask public companies to disclose how water shortages could hurt their businesses, and what companies are doing about it," he says. "In fact, the momentum around this concept of water accounting and risk has been at an unprecedented level these last few years."

One of the problems in assessing vulnerability is that companies tend to focus only on their own usage, says WRI's Klop. "What many companies do not have is the context around their footprint," he notes. Without knowing the competing factors for resources in a particular area, it is hard to assess the degree to which a company is exposed to water risk. One exception is Coke, according to Klop. "Context is key and Coca-Cola has a lot of that," he says. "They have a very good global model that is ahead of not only its competitors but of many governments and international agencies in thinking about modeling water risk management."

Klop and his team at WRI are working in partnership with Goldman Sachs and General Electric in developing a Water Index, which uses publicly available data on water quality and scarcity to create map overlays combining and comparing various risks. For example, along the Yellow River, China's second-longest, the index helps identify water "hotspots" so that government agencies and companies can avoid building what Klop calls another Phoenix, a city built in the wrong place, at least from a water perspective. "Aside from the index itself, it is absolutely crucial for companies to identify, understand, and manage their water risks, if they care about being successful long term," says PepsiCo's Bena.

Competitors Working Together

Coke's involvement helped WWF play a bigger role at the Yangtze River Forum, a bi-annual conference that brings together key stakeholders, says Chris Williams. Coke invited its industry peers to participate in a special meeting at the forum for the private sector. One result is that the companies agreed on a message to deliver to the Chinese government about how pollution regulation should be implemented. "Regulation of polluters in China is fairly uneven," Williams says. "It is such a nascent regulatory structure and there is some concern over how new laws could be applied." He adds that the forum has also been a good venue for companies to work together to develop joint solutions. "There has not been as much follow-through as there should have been," he says, "but we are working to make those commitments a reality."

Cooperation is essential, PepsiCo's Bena agrees. "Governments, NGOs, academics, and corporations—even competitors—have come to the realization that the nature of the water, climate, and food security crises we face are of such a magnitude that collaboration is the only way we will make a dent in them," he says.

For years, PepsiCo and Coke (as well as brewers, distillers, and other beverage companies) have been working together in a group called the Beverage Industry Environmental Roundtable. The group was formed to define what water stewardship means and to explore how a collective industry voice could be used to inform water policy and education. Each year, companies anonymously share water efficiency data to compare and improve their practices.

PepsiCo and Coke also work together as endorsers of the CEO Water Mandate, an offshoot of the United Nations Global Compact. Since its creation three years ago, says Bena, who serves on its steering committee, significant progress has been made in engaging leaders of the G-8 to take water policy seriously at the national level.

The Future

There is plenty of progress yet to achieve.

Coke is now working with WWF, for example, to reduce water use in its supply chains through the Better Sugar Cane Initiative. The company uses 4% of the world's sugar and one of the goals of the partnership in China is to figure out an entry point to work with the Chinese sugar industry. The goal is not to tell farmers or millers how to run their operation but rather to continuously improve production methods and reduce water use, according to Kevin Ogorzalek, the global coordinator of WWF's sugar cane program.

Overall, Klop is optimistic, arguing that efforts to improve water use efficiency have only just begun. The technology exists to do much better. But the economic incentive is not yet there, he says, because the cost to supply water to municipalities, irrigation authorities, and other users is nowhere near the point that it should be, based on factors such as scarcity.

"I am asked very often if water is the next oil," Klop says. "If only it were, because oil is at least priced according to its scarcity value."

Orts believes that if companies are seen as tackling these problems with government and other partners in a legitimate and public-interest fashion, they will not only help to find solutions but will also manage their reputational risks better. Klop adds, "When multinationals like Coca-Cola decide to get on top of a problem like water scarcity, they have the resources to quickly make them better informed than many government and international agencies are."

For their part, the environmental groups sometimes put their own reputations on the line when working with companies. Partnering with a large multinational such as Coke is not always well received, Ogorzalek admits.

"My fellow environmentalists can sometimes give us a hard time," he says, "but we're doing things with them that wouldn't be achievable without this partnership." ■

Published: August 18, 2010 in Knowledge@Wharton

The World Bank's Robert Zoellick: Countries Doing Badly Should Worry about Those Doing Worse

As Americans debated whether to spend nearly $800 billion to rescue their own economy from financial crisis this winter, World Bank president Robert Zoellick took to the pages of *The New York Times* to rattle the tin cup on behalf of far harder-hit countries. President Obama, he suggested, should promote "a stimulus package for the world." Zoellick argued that industrialized nations should devote 0.7% of their stimulus packages—around $6 billion in the case of the United States—to a "vulnerability fund" that would help stabilize the poorest of the poor. "Poor people in Africa should not pay the price for a crisis that originated in America," he wrote.

The initiative did not appear in the stimulus package signed into law last month—not even among the 9,000 earmarks. But, speaking recently at the University of Pennsylvania—where he headlined a moderated discussion as part of the Huntsman Program in International Studies and Business—Zoellick was still on the case, explaining why the crisis is so devastating well beyond the countries whose banks helped to derail the global economy. He argued that wealthier countries would find it in their best interests to prevent large chunks of the world from giving up on the free market. "I believe that globalization has brought a lot of benefits to people."

The World Bank's Robert Zoellick leads a panel discussion at Wharton on the global impact of the economic crisis

Zoellick, a former managing director of Goldman Sachs, was U.S. trade representative and then deputy secretary of state when President George W. Bush nominated him in 2007 to replace World Bank president Paul Wolfowitz. A graduate of Swarthmore College, Harvard Law and the Kennedy School of Government, Zoellick was a veteran of three Republican administrations. His announced plans upon taking office at the World Bank reflected the mood of the Bush years, with talk of increasing cooperation among countries in the name of spreading free-market economics.

Today, the theme of cooperation is especially important, as is tailoring the Bank's offerings to specific regions. "We are in a period of extreme uncertainty in the global economy," he said. "How do we customize [our] services for each of these groups and practices? The real need is to figure out how to mobilize other players."

Huge Challenge in Europe

Though his *Times* op-ed article argued passionately on behalf of strife-torn nations like Sierra Leone, Zoellick said the region most exposed to the global economic crisis is Central Europe, whose formerly Communist economies are in a uniquely vulnerable spot. Central European states are now sufficiently connected to the international economy that the past year's decline in trade and remittances has done major damage to their own markets. But the countries aren't wealthy enough to have some of the cushions that Western Europe, the U.S. or Japan enjoy—especially because, while transitioning to the euro, their currencies are in flux.

Zoellick noted that the World Bank is working with the European Bank for Reconstruction and Development "to put together a fund to support some of the key Western European banks that provide a lot of the banking structure for Central and Eastern Europe. But this won't work unless the European governments also provide the overall structure and framework." Keeping the region stable and free-market oriented would be important for all involved, he said.

Noting fears in the industrialized world that the global crisis might dissuade emerging countries from liberalizing their economies, Zoellick said: "It's a time of great flux with these issues. Given the diversity of the world, you get countries that are turning to different answers." Ecuador's recent imposition of import restrictions is not likely to succeed, he said. "But some of the East Asian countries are realizing that this may be a time to continue to move forward with reforms, to try to achieve greater flexibility of markets."

Towards that end, the World Bank will focus on lessons learned from the Asian financial crisis of 1997-98, Zoellick noted. Instead of reconfiguring entire economies, countries should focus instead on key pieces, such as social safety nets for the poor. About a dozen moderate-income countries had made advances in conditional cash-transfer programs, but still poorer countries in Sub-Saharan Africa lack the resources to expand welfare efforts. "We're trying to learn what has worked with food-for-work programs or school feeding programs that would send some food home to the family as well." Such efforts were more effective at reaching the needy than, say, increasing civil service salaries or trying to improve the overall wage structure, Zoellick pointed out.

The Bank is also encouraging poorer countries to focus on helping the small- and medium-sized business sector, because it is a driver of job growth and often the first victim during economic contraction. But the effort is a tricky one for the Bank, Zoellick said, because the issues of small businesses in Ukraine and those in Southeast Asia can be very different. "One of the challenges for us as the World Bank is to make sure the analysts see themselves as problem-solvers within this broader political and social context."

Relative Success in Africa

According to Zoellick, Africa has been a relative development success, with two-thirds of its countries growing at a significant rate. "The problem, in part, was the missing third"—often countries racked by civil war or other devastating conflict. Statistics show that countries with war-torn neighbors also see their own economic growth suffer. "One thing that would be a real tragedy of the crisis would be if we lose faith in African development," he said.

Still, he worries that African nations that have made the best strides may find themselves endangered precisely because they have successfully tied themselves to the global economy. Above all, he added, African states need help developing trade programs with each other and building laws and institutions to sustain their growth. "I would argue, in the case of Africa, that while you do want to provide targeted assistance—for example, in a social safety net—you don't want to lose the opportunity to build the future basis of growth." Some of that growth could be spurred by improving transportation across the continent, he said.

Asked which metrics he would focus on to determine whether the crisis was easing, Zoellick advised watching the impact of various countries' stimulus efforts. But the spending would be "like a sugar high" unless countries fixed their banking systems, recapitalizing the institutions, he warned. Credit markets must be sustained while banks remain in crisis, too. "The Federal Reserve has actually used its balance sheet to provide a secondary market by buying commercial paper, mortgages and other assets." He suggested other central banks follow the Fed's lead.

Zoellick noted that he is focused on other dangers lurking in the global economy. His top concern is the collapse of a major currency, which could send new shock waves around the globe. He called for doubling the resources of the International Monetary Fund, the Bank's sister institution which was established to intervene in such instances. Reiterating his faith in free trade, he also said he was worried about the return of protectionism, noting that countries look very closely at the U.S. and could view Americans as hypocrites because of recent policy overtures like the "buy America" proposal that was part of the Obama administration's original stimulus package.

Finally, Zoellick warned that when the economy operates on a global scale but governance remains national, the world's political system may not be able to coordinate responses to an unprecedented situation. "As we get further into increasing unemployment rates, do you start to see countries point fingers at one another as opposed to trying to work together? I think that's something that I would watch very closely during the course of 2009. As the leader of one of the international institutions, I can try to play a modest role in identifying these. But part of the challenge in the whole system is based on nation-states. That's the political basis. Those are where decisions are made. People still have to be responsible to the citizenry. But the issues are transnational. So how do you interconnect those things?" ∎

Published: March 18, 2009 in Knowledge@Wharton

Muhammad Yunus: Lifting People Worldwide out of Poverty

What began with a loan of $27 to 42 women in a small village 33 years ago has grown into a global microcredit movement that has changed the lives of millions of poor people around the world. Muhammad Yunus, founder and managing director of Bangladesh's Grameen Bank, was the guest speaker at Wharton's MBA commencement on May 17 and the recipient of an honorary doctor of laws degree during the University of Pennsylvania's commencement on May 18. Yunus spoke with Knowledge@Wharton about his successes, challenges and upcoming initiatives.

An edited version of the transcript follows.

Knowledge@Wharton: Our guest today is Muhammad Yunus, winner of the 2006 Nobel Peace Prize and founder of the microcredit movement—based on the idea of making very small loans to the world's poorest people, thereby giving them the opportunity to raise themselves and their families out of poverty. Thank you for joining us.

Knowledge@Wharton: People often associate good works and worthwhile causes with non-profit institutions. But you have emphasized that your model is a for-profit one, not a non-profit one. Can you briefly describe that model and tell us why the distinction is so important to you?

Yunus: We are not trying to create a non-profit. That was not our intention. Our intention was to persuade the bankers to lend money to poor people, so my struggle was always with the bankers. Initially, I offered myself as a guarantor, and then took the money from the bank and gave it to people. So it was an extension of the bank's activities. When we saw that it was working well and the banks were not as enthusiastic as we were, we thought maybe we should have a separate bank created for this purpose. Finally we did that in 1983—called Grameen Bank or the "village bank." So we became a bank because it is a bank's activity. We lend money to the poor. People sometimes refer to us as an NGO. We have to explain that we are not an NGO. It's not that we are belittling NGOs....I'm simply stating that people get confused, thinking that because we work with the poor, we must be an NGO. I say, no, we are a bank and it is owned by the poor people. The owners of the bank are the borrowers of the bank. That's the distinction that we want to make, to clarify what we are.

Knowledge@Wharton: Grameen Bank has grown dramatically since the time that you founded it. I've read that you now have operations in more than 100 countries, and you have seven million borrowers in Bangladesh alone. But your success with Grameen has led to a lot of other people entering the microcredit area. Some of them are commercial banks. Some are funded by venture capitalists. How has that changed the microcredit model, and can you explain some of the issues that have come up as a result of that?

Yunus: Just a little clarification: We work—or at least the main idea has been working—in almost all the countries of the world. So now it's not right to say 100 countries.

Knowledge@Wharton: So you're even more successful!

Yunus: At least the idea is that it's spread. Whether they are big or small—successful or not—there are presences in all those countries. Right now, we are nearly eight million borrowers within Grameen Bank itself. In that way, Grameen Bank has expanded within Bangladesh. Lots of organizations have come in [to do this] and we have encouraged them. NGOs have done that. Others have done that. When the word becomes popular and the idea becomes popular, many people want to join [in]. So the word "microcredit" became very popular. "Microfinance" became very popular. And [institutions] not using these words before, suddenly started using them—like agricultural banks around the world saying that they do microcredit. They never said that before.

Whether they are microcredit or not is a debatable subject because we define microcredit, microfinance, in a certain way. This is a credit and financial service to the poorest people without collateral, without guarantee and without any lawyers in the system. That has to be very clear in our work before we call it microcredit or microfinance. And this has focused more on women—the poorest women.

If you look at agricultural banks, for example, most of the agricultural banks around the world require collateral. Similarly, savings and loan associations say they do microcredit. Cooperatives say they do microcredit. Those who are giving agricultural loans—commercial banks—are saying they do microcredit. So we need to clarify what microcredit is in its pure form rather than everything else. Microcredit was always given to people for income generating activity. So whatever money you are taking, you are investing it to create an income source for yourself. There are many programs which give loans for buying consumer goods, and they say they are doing microcredit, they are giving money to buy a refrigerator or buy a television. We say, "No, sorry, that's not microcredit." So we have to sort this out.

Another aspect that I want to draw attention to—there are many microcredit programs going around advertising themselves saying, "Oh, this is a great opportunity to make money." And they encourage people who want to make money to join in and do that. Again, we say, "Look, our purpose is not to excite people about making money. Our purpose is to help people get out of poverty. The focus is not on profit making. The focus is on helping people to get out of poverty. Those who are seeing this as an opportunity to make money have to raise their interest rate to the extent that they make a lot of money. The interest rate issue becomes a sensitive one. We are saying interest rates should be kept as low as possible, preferably to cover costs. If you want to make a little profit on top of it, it should be a very modest profit, so that it doesn't look like this was your intention. Those who are doing that—using microcredit, microfinance, to make a lot of money—we keep saying that this is not microcredit in the sense that we do it. We came here to fight the loan sharks, not become loan sharks ourselves. This is their moving into the direction of loan sharks. We want to disassociate ourselves from them.

Knowledge@Wharton: So how do you tackle that? Is there some regulation required, and if so, what kind of regulation should there be?

Yunus: In Bangladesh, we have been talking about regulation. The Bangladesh government has created a microcredit authority, [based on] our suggestions. So they will be looking into the interest rate issue, the transparency issue. A lot of people quote their interest rate in many, many ways, hiding the actual fact of how much they are charging. We say it has to be very transparent. All interest rates should be expressed in a standardized form so that you can compare A and B. Who charges more or less? This is something that they have to clarify right away, and they also have to keep the interest rate as low as possible. This is an encouragement regulatory authorities should be putting in.

I, personally, have been promoting the idea that a true microcredit interest rate should be within a particular range—as a cost of fund at the market price plus 10%. This is the green zone of microcredit interest rates. You are legitimate. You are doing excellent work. If it is cost of fund at the market price plus 10% to 15%, we say your interest rate is in the yellow zone. You're on the high side, but still we will consider you a genuine microcredit program. We will encourage you to push yourself back into the green zone. If cost of fund is at the market price plus 15% and above, then we say you are in the red zone, meaning that you are too high and you are on the wrong side of microcredit. You are moving into the loan shark zone.

Knowledge@Wharton: You have spoken about the downside of a globalized economy, referring to it during the Nobel Peace Prize ceremony in Oslo as "a dangerous free-for-all highway whose lanes will be taken over by the giant trucks from powerful economies, even as Bangladeshi rickshaws will be thrown off the highway." I'm assuming you're referring to the one-dimensional profit mode of these giant trucks that focus more on money than on social good, but how do you think a global scenario could realistically be averted? Isn't globalization, in fact, desirable?

Yunus: I was giving an image of globalization as like a multi-lane highway. All the products are moving back and forth in many directions, and everybody on the road is getting their merchandise. Big countries, big economies, rich economies will have more merchandise to carry, and big trucks to carry [it in]. They are very powerful and take over the lanes. The small countries don't have space for themselves because it's all taken over by the big trucks and the big companies. I said if that image fits into the picture, then we should have traffic rules so that the little company in the little country in the little economy can move slowly and safely, and the big trucks don't take over everything.

If we accept the traffic rules idea, then we will need traffic police so that these rules are obeyed. The idea is to have a traffic authority that says, "This is the rule of globalization—that if you are a big company, you cannot come to a weak economy and say, 'I am taking over the whole economy.' They can, because they have the money power. That will be the wrong [kind of] globalization. In globalization, both sides must be the winner, and whatever gain in trade takes place, it should be shared equally. Just because I have the power—out of 100, I take 99.9% and give you 0.1% and say this is globalization—I don't think that would be tenable or sustainable. So we have to agree how much you should get and how much I should get, although I could have taken over everything. But by agreed principles, we don't do that. We give you some and we keep some. And what that participation would be—how the division would be—would be [up to] the traffic police or the traffic authority to decide. Otherwise, globalization will become an economic imperialism, with big economies taking over small economies.

Knowledge@Wharton: One affect of globalization we see right now is what's happening in the world banking industry. Why I find it very interesting is because if you were to look at Grameen's own borrowers, they are not just subprime, but sub-subprime. In spite of that, Grameen's repayment rates are 99% or so, and you have never required a bailout. From that perspective, I wonder how you see this global banking crisis and what advice you would give to the CEOs of institutions like Citibank or Bank of America about what they could do to salvage their operations.

Yunus: It's a paradoxical situation right now because 33 years ago—when I was trying to start this program in a city village with a few people and arguing with the bankers that it would be a good idea to give loans to poor people—their argument was that poor people are not credit worthy. They will never pay back and so on. Today, 33 years later, you can ask the same question. Who is credit worthy? It is the poor who turned out to be more credit worthy than the other category of people, because microcredit programs all over the world still function very well. Their repayment is very high, whereas the big banks and their big lending operations are [near] collapse. They are falling down.

Given the [situation] we have now, we have no other way but to redesign the whole system—recognizing the strength in non-collateralized loans for the poor people and the weakness in collateralized loans for the rich people. We have to find a ground where we can have an inclusive financial system where nobody will be thrown out of the system—not the poorest person, not the homeless person or a beggar person. Nobody should be thrown out. They have already created a long-time record of what they have done.

So this is one lesson [to be taken into account] when redesigning the financial system. Another point I would like to make is that this global crisis, financial crisis is the worst in our lifetime—the whole world is going through it. While we look at the crisis part of it, we forget this is also the greatest opportunity. When the system is not working, that's the time you unpack and redesign it so that it not only works, it works better than ever before. Unless we do that, we will be committing a big mistake. So I emphasize the opportunity part of it. The crisis will take time to [run its course], but we should be focusing our attention on redesigning, piece by piece, [those parts] that need to be fixed so that we don't have the same old system we had before.

Knowledge@Wharton: What qualities does one need to lead a microfinance institution and how are these different from the qualities needed for another type of organization?

Yunus: We came from the direction of wanting to bring financial services to the poor to help them generate income for themselves and gradually move out of poverty. Build confidence, build experience, and step-by-step, move on and get out of poverty. So we would like to keep microcredit in that [mode], not a profit maximization [mode], because then you are not looking at people's condition; you are looking at your own condition. You want to take out as much as possible to improve your financial strength and so on.

That is the number one requirement for microcredit—that you have the right kind of attitude when you get involved with it, that here I have come to use my talent, my creativity, my management skills to help people get out of poverty without losing money. Losing money pushes you into another direction. It pushes [you] into charitable kinds of programs. Microcredit is not a charity program. Microcredit is a business program—but business with a social purpose. In a separate way, I have called it a social business and defined in clear terms what a social business is like.

So ideally, I would like microcredit to be a social business where profit is zero for the person who is investing, but the company can make profit. Profit stays with the company with a social objective—in this case, to help people get out of poverty.

Knowledge@Wharton: But in terms of individual leadership skills, or organizational skills, how do you nurture these in individuals at Grameen Bank?

Yunus: With Grameen Bank, we just recruit people and let them learn by apprenticing with other, older persons in the branches. So it's not a classroom training, which makes all the difference. Classroom training is a very small part of our training. We simply introduce what we do and then let them figure out how it is done. When they join Grameen Bank, for them it's just a job. They are looking for a job. Not many jobs are available. They get the job. They are very happy. [They] will work and get a salary. So the intention of helping the poor was not part of the job.

But once you start working with poor people and get to know the system and its objectives, gradually you are taken by it. More and more you feel inspired by it. All these ideas that, yes, my work helps people, excites them. It's a wonderful experience to be able to touch other peoples' lives. It's almost an intoxicating experience. Once you have it, you cannot get away from it. You want to help more, because you see things are happening in people's lives. Their children are going to school. The kid you saw running around in the village—now you see that he or she is in school and doing very well, and talking about what she wants to be, what he wants to be. And you remember your own childhood—how difficult it was for you.

These kids are lucky kids. They are in school. Some of the older students are now going on to higher education. Grameen Bank gives them education loans. They say, "Nobody gave me an education loan. My education ended. After high school I couldn't proceed any further. The only job I could get is this one. But I'm happy. Through my job, I'm helping other kids to go on to higher education, become doctors and jurors and university professors and so on and so forth. That excites them, that yes, their service is useful."

Knowledge@Wharton: One of the really interesting aspects of Grameen's operations is the way you have been able to extend the concept of microfinance beyond just credit into areas such as health insurance. I wonder if you could explain some of those activities and how they have evolved? What have some of your challenges been?

Yunus: We do not consider micro insurance or health insurance as outside the financial service area. So we take it as a part of our activities—the bank's activity. We started with giving credit at the same time we were taking savings. So it's always together: Savings and credit formed our basic tool. Then we encouraged people to go into other directions regarding health and other issues. Gradually we introduced insurance programs. Life insurance was our first insurance program. Then we introduced the health insurance program. We saw that we can give health insurance, but then how do you ensure that people get the health service? The existing health service [system] is not very reliable. So we started creating health services through a separate company we created called Grameen Kalyan, or Grameen Well-Being.

Through that, we started setting up clinics in the villages with a professional doctor at the top of the clinic, and then paramedics and health workers with a pathological lab attached to it so that people don't have to go to the city for simple pathological testing and so on. Everything is self-contained. Today, we run about 51 such clinics. On an average day, they cover about 93% of the costs; another 7% we could easily cover if we could retain the doctors in these clinics. That became a big problem: Doctors don't want to stay in the kind of clinics that we operate in the villages. Most of the time, almost half or one-third of the doctors are missing.

That's where our popularity in the area is not as high as it should have been. Now we are trying to redesign it, do it in a different way [by] trying to set up a program at the village level—what we call Grameen Health Management Centers—where our focus will be on prevention. Our focus will be on the healthy people first and then on the sick people. For the sick people, we say this is where we will do early detection and early treatment without relying on the doctors in the village. So doctors can [stay] in the cities, wherever they are.

We are trying to link the doctor and the patients through information technology. The mobile phone in Bangladesh is everywhere, like many other countries. The mobile phone is a common phenomenon. Even in the poor families, you will see mobile phones. They are very cheap. And these phones are Internet phones. They also carry Internet service. Bangladesh can receive Internet services [everywhere] through the mobile phone. So we want to do the diagnostics and plug them into a mobile phone—transmit all the images and all the data to the specialist doctor in the city who can analyze it and decide what the problem is, talk to the patient on the mobile phone and [then] some intermediary who can go between the patient and the doctors to carry on all these services. This is the new idea that we are promoting. Health insurance is a very popular [concept] provided we can guarantee that [people] get the services.

Knowledge@Wharton: Is there a plan to extend this further with Google?

Yunus: We have been discussing it with many partners. Already we have created a social business with the Intel Corporation. It's called Grameen-Intel Company in Bangladesh. Through that company, we are bringing mobile phone services to the village with the health care software included in it.

The initial one that we are doing is a series of questions that we place before pregnant mothers designed in such a way that, by evaluating the answers, doctors can tell whether she has a risky pregnancy. So immediately, we have screened a risky pregnancy. Then you can concentrate on that one. Gradually we'll be moving into ultrasound. We will bring ultrasound to the family house to image the baby inside the womb and transmit it to the doctor. The doctor can then confirm that, yes, there is a problem. We can zoom in to that particular patient, and so on.

On this trip I'll be meeting with the Google people to talk about it. One other idea that I'll be discussing with them is how to capture all the patient data. Simultaneously, as we meet the people, talk to people, all this comes in a way that you can put in a central server through Google. You have global patient data available. You can analyze it. You can find out the incidents of diseases. [You can know] how the treatment is working, which treatment is working, how people are improving and so on. Lots of information can come out of that. There are many ways you can do that. It's very simple. Now that technology is available, it can be almost cost-free—but at the same time extremely valuable—information about health care. So we want to see Excite, Google and others get involved. Google already has a lot of health care related programs, but we are trying to see how to extend the service and collaborate with them.

Knowledge@Wharton: By basing your model on getting funds from the borrowers rather than getting, for example, money from international investors, does that give you enough money to make as many loans, offer as many services as you could? Or do you think that outside money actually could play a role as long it doesn't dilute the primary focus, which is social good and not making money?

Yunus: Within Grameen Bank, we are allowed to take deposits from everybody. It's not limited to the borrowers only. It's just like a bank. We can take anybody's deposits. So that's open within Grameen Bank. Each of our branches is required to mobilize enough deposits to carry on all the lending they do so that branches don't have to borrow from the head office and don't have to borrow from another branch. So they are self sufficient with their money.

On top of that, we encourage them to build up [an adequate] cushion of reserves of the deposits because of the problem of disasters. We have very frequent disasters. At times of disasters, you can't get your money back, but you need to lend more money than you did before to get people out of the problems they face. So we want to build up that cushion. Usually we recommend at least 30% or 33% reserves should be kept within that system.

Today, we have more than 30% reserves; 37% has been the level of our reserves in all of Grameen Bank. Some branches have more. Some branches have less. But the average is 37%. We have no problem with the deposits. We have enough deposits in the bank. So the question of borrowing outside never occurs to us because we have enough money. I keep telling people that literally no matter where we live, we live in an ocean of money. But the problem is that poor people cannot take a sip out of it. That's the problem. A shortage of money is not the problem. People have plenty of money to put in the bank. People are very happy that a Grameen branch came near their home because villages don't have bank branches. Banks are all concentrated in the cities. If people have to put the money in the bank, they have to go to the city in the town where the bank exists.

So Grameen Bank works in the villages. It's a very convenient place. People withdraw their money from the cities and put it near home because it's handy. They can go in any time they want to pick up the money. So we have enough of that money and we do not see any reason that it will ever dry up.

Having said that, what is the amount of deposits coming from the borrowers themselves? We lend out over $100 million a month through Grameen Bank today. Nearly half of that money comes from the borrowers' own deposits. So it's quite a substantial amount of money that the borrowers put in. That money keeps growing because everybody is putting additional deposits in every week. It keeps growing and growing. People have their own savings accounts. At the same time, other people can put in money there. Sometimes we see that, in a certain branch, we have too much money. We decide whether we should keep that level of deposits without expanding the business. We encourage [the branches] to expand the business rather than build up [excess] deposits.

Knowledge@Wharton: You had referred earlier to the idea of a social business and you explained how that differs from a conventional business. One example of that is Grameen Danone Foods. What I find remarkable is that you are able to produce a power yogurt called Shakti Doi for 5 cents for an 80 gram cup. Could you explain how the economics of that works and whether that model is scalable?

Yunus: Yes, very much, because it's a business and it [operates] according to business principles, [including] that you have to cover your costs and generate some surplus so that the business can keep running. But the idea of social business is that investors have invested the money not for their own benefit, but to achieve a social objective. In the case of Grameen Danone, the objective is to bring nutrition to malnourished children.

What we have done is put all the micronutrients, which are missing in the children, in the yogurt and make it very tasty. Children love it. They pay that 5 cents to buy a cup. If a child eats two cups a week and continues to do so for eight to nine months, he or she gets all the micronutrients back and becomes a healthy, playful child. That is the objective of the company.

That is how it is done. And others, it's a question of how much it costs. How much does milk cost? What are the processing costs, equipment and distribution costs and so on. Once you are in social business, lots of costs go down because you don't need to incur them.

For example, you don't do any elaborate or fancy marketing because people know what you are doing and they are interested in it. So you don't have to go on television and be in the newspaper. We are here. "Life is meaningless without eating Shakti Doi?" We don't say that. We explain what it is as the people come, and gradually this spreads. And that's it. So the marketing cost goes down. In our design, we made sure that extra costs are cut off. For example, we made it a very small plant so that you don't produce too much. Around our own plant, there are enough consumers to buy [the product so that we don't have] to move it long distances. The idea is to cut down on the cost of a cold train. If you are producing in a big plant, you have to carry [your product] long distances and you need a cold train. That is a very expensive item. So we eliminated that.

Our idea is to have many, many, many small plants all around the country so that you reach out to everybody. Our [first] plant is already operating. We are getting ready for the number two plant. We want to have about 50 plants to cover all the children in Bangladesh. Each one is self-contained. Each one makes money. Each will cover its costs and so on.

Sometimes we get through difficulties—like suddenly during the food crisis last year, milk prices jumped. We couldn't maintain the price tag that we had on the product. We were wondering what we should do. We came up with many kinds of alternatives to keep the prices down—without losing the micronutrients and so on. We quickly came out with the Shakti Drink [which uses] less milk but [increases] other [ingredients]—all without losing the good taste. We kept the price as low as before. We were lucky; milk prices went down again. So we have to cope with those kinds of fluctuations without losing the whole focus of the company.

Knowledge@Wharton: In addition to Grameen Danone and Intel, I think you have a relationship with BASF for anti-malarial nets. Do you have any other joint ventures or partnerships with companies in the works?

Yunus: Yes. Many companies are coming up with ideas to work with us for social businesses, and we are giving them ideas. One, already in operation, is a very important social business—Grameen-Veolia. Veolia is a French water company, one of the largest water companies in the world. Many U.S. cities are served by Veolia. We persuaded this giant company to create a tiny little water treatment plant in the villages of Bangladesh to serve 50,000 people, because our big problem in Bangladesh is arsenic in our water. There is a very high level of poison in the water.

About 75 million people—half the population of Bangladesh—drink water with a high level of arsenic. So we are putting up this company to supply clean Veolia-quality water to every household in the village. The people will be paying for it—a very small amount. Nobody will mind paying that, and it will cover all the company's costs. It will become a social business. Veolia is not there to make money out of it. But the fact [is] that people are drinking poison every day. We can work on that. Nothing is happening through any other program. So we said let's move on and do that. This becomes another example of social business.

Once you can do that successfully for 50,000 people in the village, you have developed a seed. Then all you need to do is plant the seed in other places. Because each one is self-contained. You can do as many as you want and cover all the people. So development of the seed is the most important thing in social business. Like Grameen Danone is a seed. You can now take it anywhere in any country. We have already been approached by India. We have been approached by China. They would like to have Grameen Danone in [these countries] because they have the same problem. Malnutrition is very common. So health authorities are saying that yes, this is a big problem, and this works. We have invited GAIN (Global Alliance for Improved Nutrition)—a big NGO based in Geneva that concentrates on monitoring the nutrition situation globally—to monitor whether this is really true, whether this is just a gimmick [or whether what] we do is real. Are the children benefitting, is their nutrition level increasing and so on?

So you have Grameen Danone, Grameen Veolia, Grameen Intel, and there are some others in the pipeline, very interesting programs like one shoe company. It's a very big shoe company. They approached us and said what can we do? I said, well, you have a theme. The theme or motto would be that nobody in the world should go without shoes. As a shoe company, it is your responsibility to make sure [of] that. So you come up with shoes that the poorest people can afford—a good quality shoe with your brand name so that it's not a second-class, third-class thing. You take ownership of that shoe and make it very cheap. The company likes that idea. I suggested that they start making shoes for under $1, so that they cover people who will never be able to use that brand name shoe in their lifetime, ever. But now, every kid, everybody will be doing that.

So there are many in the pipeline. BASF is one already who signed an agreement to do the mosquito nets, treated mosquito nets, and also nutrition sachets for pregnant women and malnourished women. Because women's nutrition is, again, another area where it is not as satisfactory as one would like it to be. This company will be making it possible for everybody to afford that nutrition. At the same time, while we are [offering] this nutrition supplement, we will be focusing on the diet itself. [We] can't forget about the diet. We will be also encouraging women to [eat the] right kind of food as they go on.

Knowledge@Wharton: You have been dedicated to the microcredit concept long enough to be able to observe the children of that first generation of women that you helped, going back to 1976 and the $27 that you loaned to 42 women in a small village. How are these children, who are now adults, doing? Are they creating jobs for other people? Are they starting their own companies? Are they adding societal wealth to the community? And just by the very fact that this new generation of people still needs help, does that suggest that you have a long way to go with microcredit? What does that say about the success of the movement?

Yunus: Microcredit is the first step. You build up step-by-step many other things like insurance programs, savings programs, and other programs around it. We have encouraged the borrowers of Grameen Bank to send the children to school because they themselves are illiterate. Their husbands are illiterate. Their parents are illiterate. So we said, let's break that circle here. Send the children to school so that they will be educated. They will be literate at least. And we succeeded at having all the children in school.

That was a very happy kind of experience for us—not only are we giving loans to the borrowers, but at the same time we have helped them to send the children to school. Then we saw that lots of these children are getting excellent results in the schools, some of them coming up at the top of the class. So we kind of got thrilled by the performance of some of these kids coming from poor, totally illiterate families. Now he or she is at the top of the class. We thought they should be celebrated. So we started introducing scholarships for all the top performing students. Grameen Bank gives over 30,000 scholarships every year. Now it's growing. It's 40,000 and so on every year because the number of children is growing.

Then we saw many of these children coming close to higher education. They have difficulty getting into higher education because they don't have the money to pursue it. But the quality is there. They are as good as anybody else. So immediately we introduced education loans so that they don't have to worry about money. The money is our problem. You can simply get an education. We started giving education loans and helping them through higher education. Right now, there are more than 35,000 students under education loans. We include medical schools, engineering schools and universities.

So in almost every single public university, public medical school and engineering school, there are Grameen children who are studying there as well. A whole wave of new children is going into that. When I meet them, they will always discuss [one] issue, which is that they worry about getting a job. They say: "After we finish our [education], can you help us find jobs?"

How am I going to find jobs for them? So I started thinking about it. I had the idea that maybe they shouldn't be thinking about jobs. We tell them: Look, you are children from Grameen families. You are Grameen children. Your thinking should be different than other children's. Other people, other children—they worry about jobs. You shouldn't be worrying about this. You should take a pledge and repeat this pledge every morning you wake up. And your pledge is: I shall never seek a job from anybody. I'll create jobs. This is my mission. So you are not job seekers. You are job givers. Think in those terms because your mother—you're the first generation child—your mother owns a bank. Not many children have that fortune. You have that fortune. Your mother's bank has an enormous amount of money. Money is not your problem. Your problem is what to do with your money.

Then, if you feel frustrated [because] you cannot come up with an idea, think about your mother and what she did. She didn't wait for anybody. She took the money and went into business herself. She's an illiterate woman. Along the way she was successful step-by-step. She went on and sent you to school. Now you're in higher education with her bank. And what good is your education if you cannot do better than your mother? If she can do it, you can do much better. That's the thing that you have to prove to yourself—that your mother gave you a chance and you will make use of it.

And the use is that you create a job for others. So start small and expand it as you grow and bring in more people to help you to grow. You don't have to wait to finish this school and get a certificate. In education, when you use it for getting a job, you need a certificate. You don't need a certificate when you go into business yourself. So when you're in school, you start a business at the same time. Continue with it. Some of them are taking this idea and have started borrowing from Grameen Bank and getting into business themselves.

Knowledge@Wharton: To link what you just said to what we were discussing earlier about social business, what kind of social businesses could you start around education, and is Grameen involved in any such activity?

Yunus: On the health side, what we have done this year—we are in the process of finishing it—is start a nursing college as a social business, because nursing is a good profession. We'll be giving nursing degrees to the young girls from Grameen families. They are coming from poor families and going to nursing college. Grameen bank will give them education loans so that they don't have to worry about money or where the money is coming from. The college will cover their cost and they will get the jobs. We will [train] the nurses in a way that there will be an internationally acceptable level of education. There is a big shortage internationally of nurses. There is a big shortage within the country. So each girl will have a choice whether she will work in the country or she will go outside.

This is a social business. As I said, I don't have to limit myself to one nursing college. I can have a series of nursing colleges. They are paying for themselves. Why can't you create as many as you want because there are millions of young girls waiting around, sitting around doing nothing because they have no opportunities? I can create some opportunities for them that will change their lives. They will change the society, because now, they go out of the village and they work in the hospitals , and go outside the country and learn languages, and so on. This is another example of social business. I also want to do a medical college on the same principle because medical colleges also can cover their own costs and produce doctors—doctors with a different kind of orientation than you normally have.

Normally doctors—student doctors—are planning, when they finish their education, to start their career and make a lot of money. That focus usually happens. So this orientation will be that when I come out, I want to make sure I can help the health situation in the country and focus on the poor families. So how do we do that kind of thing? By having a very high quality of education and not feeling that you're left out because you concentrated on a certain kind of thing. And you can get involved in researching health issues and so on. So another social business could come up. Even in education, you can use the idea of social business.

Knowledge@Wharton: Is there anything that's happened in the microcredit movement or in your own life as it relates to this work that has changed the way you view microcredit? Have you ever said to yourself I should have done this instead of that? Have any of your initial assumptions changed?

Yunus: The basic assumptions remain the same. We have expanded them. Lots of other things came. We thought, "Let's try this one." And we tried it and it worked. We felt happy about it. If I reflect on [this question], there is probably one area I would have done differently. When we began in 1982, there was a tremendous amount of enthusiasm among the donors to give us money because we had a small project. They wanted to help us. We were very reluctant to take money because we had plenty of money at that time. But they kept on pressuring us—the central bank with which we were working. Finally the central bank yielded because they thought, why not? If donors want to give money, let's take some money. It's a loan—not even a grant—from IFAD, the International Fund for Agricultural Development. So in 1982, we took the external money. Before that, we never had any external money.

Other donors came in. They wanted to give us more money. So we thought, why not? Once we have taken one, we can take two. We can take three. We started taking it and lots of money kept coming. We kept on expanding. Then one complaint kept coming, which was: Well, Grameen Bank works because it gets a lot of money and its donors are keeping it afloat. I said, no, that's not true. We didn't need the money. They gave the money so we took it. So in '95, we decided not to take any money at all, because we thought we can do it ourselves. From 1995 on, we never took any external money. It's entirely local money. If we could go back, I would have changed that 1982 decision.

Knowledge@Wharton: Never take any money?

Yunus: Never take any money. People said, "Well, a donor had to be there; otherwise they cannot survive. These are donor-supported programs." Which is a lie. I said that's a very wrong idea because that's not how we wanted to work, and we never worked that way. So that's one change.

Knowledge@Wharton: I have one last question. How do you define success?

Yunus: Just like any other case. Whatever your objective was, if you came to that, you are a success. It depends on what your objective was. In our case, we wanted to bring credit to poor people and savings services to poor people. People said it could never work. We hoped that it would work, and it did. And then [people would] said, "Well, it may work in one village, but it won't work for two villages." We did it. They said, "Maybe in 10 villages it won't work. If you grow big, it will collapse. You are stretching your luck too much." We did it. So that is a success, even beyond what we imagined. We never thought that we could continue with such a repayment record for years and years because organizations get weakened or, as you grow big, your management becomes a problem. This was a big worry for us.

As we grow, can the quality of administration, quality of management continue to grow with it, or deteriorate? Because you are not running it yourself any more, you are depending on hundreds and hundreds and thousands of young people who just came to know about it. We leave everything in their hands, [including] the decisions. But it worked. And then [people said], "It may work in Bangladesh, but it won't work outside." So now, as I said, it has worked all over the country, all over the world. In many countries, they said, "Well, our country is not like Bangladesh. We don't have such a huge density of population and not as much poverty concentrated in our population. So in our country it won't work." We said, "Well, you debate about your country and Bangladesh. Give the task to us. We will go and do it for you." Many countries accepted that, so we started doing it. We did it in Turkey. We did it in Kosovo. We did it in Costa Rica, Guatemala, China, India and many other places to demonstrate those kinds of things.

We started one in New York City last year. It's called Grameen America. We do the same kind of work that we do in the villages of Bangladesh and with beautiful results. We have more than 600 borrowers in New York City. All women. Five-member groups. Weekly repayment. Savings, $2 each week. We have given loans. The average loan is $2200. The repayment rate is 99.3%. No collateral, nothing. So it works. I would say the strength of the idea is that it's not country-specific or people-specific. It's global. It's a human thing. It's not something that works with one particular character trait or community. ∎

Published: May 27, 2009 in Knowledge@Wharton

African Aid Projects That Work: Partnerships on the Ground, Not Donations from a Distance

Not long ago, an unnamed global corporation decided that it wanted to help children in the southern African nation of Namibia—and so it spent millions to donate scores of new computers and television sets for the classrooms in a particular region of this poverty-plagued, mostly rural nation.

They should have talked to someone like Jonathan Johnnidis first. Currently pursuing his doctoral studies at the University of Pennsylvania with a focus on virology, Johnnidis recently spent time in rural Namibia working to improve healthcare with a non-governmental agency (NGO) called WorldTeach. The rural aid worker had information the large corporate benefactor apparently did not—that there is no electricity grid in that region.

Johnnidis drew a sharp contrast between that misguided project and another, more successful partnership between Namibia and the government of Germany, which was once colonial ruler of the African nation and now is helping to build miles of new roadways there.

"It was one of the best investments," said Johnnidis, who recounted his story during a panel discussion on new types of partnerships on the continent. The panel was part of the 15th annual Wharton Africa Business Forum, whose theme was "Africa Rising: The New Dawn of Trade and Investment." Germany "didn't provide money for drugs and it didn't provide money for computers. They just built roads." But the unglamorous, low-tech roads, he noted, will form the infrastructure that will eventually bring better healthcare and schools to these isolated regions.

The Wharton panel, entitled "New Partnerships in Business and Leadership Development," was focused on how a relatively new breed of NGOs—not just WorldTeach but newer, high-profile ones like the Bill and Melinda Gates Foundation and the Mo Ibrahim Foundation created by a Sudanese mobile-phone billionaire—are bridging the gaps between cash-strapped governments and traditional Western relief funds.

According to the five panelists, one way the new NGOs are achieving this is by placing more people like Johnnidis directly in the areas that need the most help, and by better identifying the initiatives that can make a difference right away. Too often, the panelists agreed, what Africans need are not glitzy high-tech items, but basic infrastructure as well as human capital, such as health care workers.

Donors "pour money into countries that don't have the infrastructure to support everything the initiative plans to do," said Brian Anderson, who raises funds for a program in his native South Africa called MaAfrika Tikkun, which seeks to help children in AIDS-ravaged families. "What is critical is to create structure, to create systems, to create ecosystems."

The panel was moderated by Emma Osong, a Maryland-based former engineer for the Federal Aviation Administration who now works as a consultant and actively promotes African development. She said she believes partnerships involving new-style NGOs are critical to Africa's future. "Investment opportunities remain on the continent," she noted, "but many are still cautious about investing."

The tenor of the discussion matched themes sounded by many who attended the Forum—that the long-troubled continent is now in a new period of economic revival with gross national product on the rise and the world's fastest growth in cellular telephones. At the same time, huge problems persist, from AIDS to abject poverty to corrupt governments that interfere with aid efforts.

It's this vast downside of the African story that has lured new players to the region, such as the Gates Foundation, which has spent a major part of its funds in Africa, or the Ibrahim Foundation, which seeks to support and reward good government. Increasingly, the panelists noted, this new breed is finding the gaps between inadequate government programs and slow-moving, poorly targeted, traditional aid programs.

Indeed, many of the African programs that the panelists are involved with have an economic development component, some directly and some more indirectly. An example of the latter would be the MaAfrika Tikkun program, established in the 1990s as the rate of AIDS infection in South Africa was soaring. MaAfrika Tikkun takes in hundreds of children whose parents have died or been rendered helpless by AIDS, and offers them schooling and nutrition while also seeking to empower the surrounding community. According to Anderson, the program helps economic development in several ways, both by training children from the poorest families for a future in the South African workforce, and by sometimes making it possible for an infected parent to work as well.

"We're focusing on children from infancy to age 20, when they can get jobs," Anderson said. "It's a very exciting opportunity because we are terrified that a whole generation is going to be lost. We have had moderate success." The MaAfrika Tikkun effort is backed personally by South African leader Nelson Mandela as well as the government.

Aid Money Never Spent

Throughout the Wharton panel discussion, a constant theme was finding new ways to put the considerable human capital of Africa to work—not only to spur new economic investment but also to reduce the drain of poverty on the region.

One of the most intriguing concepts was outlined by Jern Lyseggen, a Norwegian entrepreneur who recently founded a global business-to-business search engine called Meltwater News, which has a substantial presence in Africa. Through his start-up company, Lyseggen also helped to found the Meltwater Entrepreneurial School of Technology in Accra, Ghana. Its goal is to train young Africans to develop and market commercial software. "The reason we chose commercial software is that you don't need the infrastructure," Lyseggen said.

"You just need a few hundred dollars and a computer. If you get the right people and a computer, they can come up with all of these marvelous ideas."

Several panelists noted that the reason NGOs are thriving outside of governmental channels is that they operate relatively freely, outside the entrenched system of corruption. That corruption has led to the squandering of a significant portion of development and relief money.

Chris Odindo, CEO of International Development and Policy Corp., a global social enterprise venture, told the audience of his frustration when he learned, while playing squash with the minister of an African nation, of hundreds of thousands of dollars of aid money that was unspent. "That money could have been used more creatively for development," Odindo said. "That money could have been used for my passion in social enterprise. That money could have looked at how you can generate a new breed of entrepreneur."

Given the pervasiveness of corruption, it's not so surprising that many partnerships seek to sidestep governments and take a more direct, hands-on approach to specific projects. Johnnidis pointed out that one of those partners is the University of Pennsylvania. Penn's School of Medicine recently received a nearly $1 million grant from a U.S. government fund to combat AIDS in the African nation of Botswana, which has the highest rate of infection in the world. This initiative continues work that started in 2001 with private money from the Gates Foundation and the Merck Foundation.

As panelists noted, the AIDS epidemic also has had huge economic development consequences, because unlike most diseases, it tends to target adults who normally would be in the prime of their employment years. "You have all these qualified and motivated people who are being cut down," Johnnidis said, adding that the biggest problem is simply a stunning lack of health care. In all of Namibia, where Johnnidis worked, there were 500 health care workers serving about two million people. In some other nations, like Mozambique, the ratio is less.

Several of the audience members at the Wharton forum wanted to know what, if anything, these new relief partnerships were doing to address the so-called "African diaspora," the wide scattering of people of African descent around the globe. Although this process began during the slave trade centuries ago, there has also been a modern so-called "brain drain" as some of Africa's best-educated have departed the continent to work and raise families in the more stable environment of the West.

Odindo suggested that African nations take steps to encourage those of African descent who now live elsewhere to return—even if just for a week or two at a time— and assist in the redevelopment of the continent. He noted that Kenya already has such a program, allowing and encouraging Western physicians and health care professionals of Kenyan heritage to work in local hospitals. "That's one of the things we're working on," said Odindo, "to make it easier for people to go back."

The panelists all seemed to agree that Western-backed aid partnerships have the same goal—to solve problems up to a level where Africans can ultimately implement and run things by themselves, whether that involves training more African-born health care workers and software entrepreneurs or handing over control of the schooling for children of AIDS-ravaged families. "Most of all, we work from the ground up," said Anderson of MaAfrika Tikkun. "We are focused on establishing partnerships and embracing community leadership and developing community leadership—so that ultimately, we can leave the community." ∎

Published: November 28, 2007 in Knowledge@Wharton

From Soup to ... Corporate Social Responsibility: Campbell's Efforts to Lead the Way

Since 1869, Campbell Soup Company has transformed tomatoes, celery and carrots, among other ingredients, into mainstays of the American lifestyle. But as the culture wars in the U.S. have escalated, any company—even a seller of soup—can count on drawing fire from all sides of the political spectrum. When that firing starts, Dave Stangis, Campbell's vice president of corporate social responsibility (CSR), will be standing at ground zero.

By the time Stangis joined the company in 2008, it had already begun its rise in the CSR firmament. A global manufacturer with net sales of $7.5 billion in fiscal 2009 and 20,000 employees, Campbell has a presence in 120 countries with such brands as V8, Pepperidge Farm, Goldfish crackers and Franco-American sauces. Last year, it ranked second among American companies perceived by the U.S. public as the most socially responsible, according to the Corporate Social Responsibility Index of the Boston College Center for Corporate Citizenship and the Reputation Institute.

But earning a reputation as a solid citizen does not confer a mantle of sainthood on any company, as Stangis knows better than most executives. He spent 11 years at Intel, beginning in 1996, where he held several positions, including external affairs manager and senior engineer. Before his arrival, the company had weathered several crises of public confidence, including the discovery in 1994 of a tiny flaw in the company's Pentium microchip which the company failed to disclose to the public. Four months later, a professor of mathematics at Lynchburg College in Virginia discovered the flaw himself, posting the information online and sparking an Internet maelstrom that eventually reached the mainstream press, including *The New York Times*.

Although Intel fixed the flaw in later versions of the chip, the company took a financial hit—paying $450 million to replace the defective part—and a reputational one. But the tide began to turn, with Stangis' help. In addition to revising and publicizing the flaw, the company formed an issues and prevention management group, which earned the company positive marks for crisis management. Along with only Cisco and Starbucks, Intel has been one of America's "Best Corporate Citizens" on *CRO* (Corporate Responsibility Officer) magazine's list every year since its inception in 1999.

Food Fights and Gay-bashing

Campbell Soup has been no stranger to controversy, either. In 2000, a "food fight" erupted when U.S. consumer and environmental groups, concerned about the lack of safety testing on foods containing gene-altered crops, urged the company to stop using gene-spliced ingredients in its soups, breads and juices. Campbell drew fire because the company had licensed the first genetically modified food—

the Flavr Savr tomato—engineered for a longer shelf life.

Campbell replied that the Flavr Savr, like all ingredients it uses, is safe and meets all government requirements, including labeling. The U.S. Food and Drug Administration backed Campbell by stating that special labeling for these modified tomatoes was not necessary. (The Flavr Savr was sold for only a few years; production ceased when mounting costs prevented it from becoming profitable.)

More recently, Campbell Soup drew fire from conservative lobbying groups for, as one of the groups put it, "openly helping homosexual activists push their agenda." In 2008, the American Family Association (AFA) took notice when Campbell began promoting its Swanson line by purchasing two full-page advertisements in the nation's largest magazine for gays, *The Advocate*.

The ads depicted a lesbian couple and their son. "Not only do the ads cost Campbell a chunk of money," stated Donald Wildmon, founder and chairman of the AFA, "but they also send a message that homosexual parents constitute a family and are worthy of support." Campbell responded by explaining that the ads are simply an attempt to reach a wider audience. "For more than a century, people from all walks of life have enjoyed our products," a company spokesperson stated at the time. "We will continue to try to appeal to all people in ways that are meaningful and relevant to them."

Building Support for CSR

In his presentation at Wharton, Stangis focused on perhaps the most enduring challenge for CSR professionals: building and maintaining support within one's own company, especially in a recession, when indiscriminate do-gooding will invariably raise eyebrows among cost-conscious colleagues.

He pinpointed the challenge by discussing two global surveys conducted in 2008 by McKinsey, which canvassed 238 CFOs and investment professionals. "How Virtue Creates Value for Business and Society" stated, among other conclusions, that while investors often see CSR as part of the company's long-term strategy, fully 50% of the CFOs surveyed view CSR primarily as a compliance issue—that is, avoiding trouble—rather than a positive force for change.

To add to the challenge, many metrics and indices may now exist for evaluating the impact of CSR, according to the McKinsey surveys. However, with the exception of certification and accreditation standards, most CFOs and investors do not find these metrics and indices to be particularly convincing or useful.

When you're trying to build support for CSR within your own company, Stangis said, "You have to keep making it clear to your colleagues that CSR is not tree hugging. It's a way to improve the business." And to demonstrate the link between the business and its CSR, "you have to have metrics. If that's what drives the company's other goals, metrics have to drive CSR, too."

By far, the easiest "sell" for CSR remains environmentally based improvements to operations, because they can be shown to save money for a company.

At Campbell, sustainable packaging for frozen food, condensed soup and cracker cartons is expected to save more than 500,000 pounds of packaging materials and almost $1.5 million, Stangis told Sustainable Industries online magazine in 2009.

In addition, a freight optimization program is designed to eliminate more than 1,700 trucks in the Campbell network and save more than 225,000 gallons of fuel. A closed-loop water-and-heat recovery system at one soup plant is projected to save more than $1.2 million per year, while also saving millions of gallons of water per week.

Today, Stangis, who earned an MBA from the University of Michigan and a Master of Science in occupational and environmental health from Wayne State University in Detroit, is working to measure progress in areas of CSR where payback remains difficult to quantify. For example, Campbell is big on "employee engagement," reasoning that employees who are truly excited about their company will be more enthusiastic about volunteering for projects that improve their communities. "Our goal is 100% employee engagement," said Stangis. To measure that, the Gallup Organization has surveyed Campbell employees every year since 2001.

The survey began badly. The first year, the "engagement ratio" for the top 350 executives at Campbell was 1:1—among the lowest Gallup had ever seen in a Fortune 500 company. In other words, for every executive who was engaged in the company's efforts to build the business, one executive was actively disengaged. By 2008, however, the engagement ratio among top executives reached an all-time high of 77:1. Clearly, said the company's 2008 annual report, "we've come a long way."

Campbell recently launched a program called Reading Stars, where company volunteers mentor struggling readers in Camden, N.J., the site of company's headquarters. "We interview employees and demonstrate their increased level of engagement," said Stangis. "But more importantly, we can rigorously and quantitatively measure the improvement in reading literacy of the kids that come through the program. You can't expect your colleagues to become CSR experts," he noted during his presentation. "A large part of my responsibility is translating, so they don't have to become experts."

Stangis, who was recently named one of the 100 "Most Influential People in Business Ethics" by *Ethisphere* magazine, continues searching for new ways of demonstrating how the alignment of social and business forces directly affects the bottom line. He pointed to the company's efforts to "continuously improve the health and wellness profile of our products," by reducing, as one example, the sodium levels in its soups. Despite "the tough economy in 2009, we grew our sales across several product lines by 10%, while delivering better food to consumers and better choices for their health."

But no matter what you accomplish in CSR, he emphasized, "if you cannot tie your efforts directly to the business, you will lose support." Accordingly, one of his major campaigns today is bringing CSR metrics into employee compensation. The hours spent in volunteer projects are now a factor in determining pay for employees. "Companies everywhere are still struggling with CSR. We're all still learning how to make our case for it," he said.

The fact that CSR has become so visible can be an advantage to a far-sighted company, Stangis added. "It's not just activists and NGOs [non-governmental organizations] who want to know about our CSR. It's also long-term investors." ∎

Published: November 11, 2009 in Knowledge@Wharton

PART 8

Preparing for Succession and Executive Transition

CEO Succession: Has Grooming Talent on the Inside Gone by the Wayside?

The recent departures of two of the world's most prominent chief executives in the wake of major financial losses at their firms—Stanley O'Neal of Merrill Lynch and Charles Prince of Citigroup—have focused renewed attention on an important but often neglected component of corporate management: succession planning.

While the boards of both companies conducted internal and external searches to find successors, published reports speculated that they would hire from the outside. On November 14, Merrill Lynch did its part to confirm those rumors by announcing that John Thain, CEO of NYSE Euronext and a former president of Goldman Sachs, will become chairman and CEO of the firm effective December 1. Meanwhile, Citigroup has named former U.S. Treasury secretary Robert Rubin as its chairman while continuing its chief executive search, having tapped Sir Win Bischoff, a London banker who joined Citigroup when it acquired the investment banking operations of Schroeders in 2000, as the company's interim CEO.

According to Wharton faculty members, hiring CEO successors from the outside isn't surprising in cases like Merrill Lynch and Citigroup: The financial debacles that led to combined write-downs of more than $15 billion at the two firms, stemming from turmoil in the sub-prime mortgage market, mean that their boards may prefer to start fresh by hiring outsiders. But, they say, companies are increasingly looking to fill top spots with external candidates, while placing less emphasis on grooming employees to fill those roles.

Indeed, a November 26 Wall Street Journal article, citing a survey conducted by the Center for Board Leadership and Mercer Delta Consulting, noted that "only about half of public and private corporate boards have CEO succession plans in place...even at giant global companies that have thousands of employees and spend millions each year to recruit and train talent."

"The trend line from 1970 to 2000 shows a slow but steady increase in the number of companies that look to the outside in the case of a departing CEO," says Wharton management professor Michael Useem, director of the school's Center for Leadership and Change Management. "At the start of that period, one in seven new CEOs at major companies came from outside the firm; by the end, one in four."

The "Heir Apparent"

According to Wharton management professor Katherine Klein, bringing in an outsider for the top job poses risks. "If you go outside, there's a huge learning curve to understanding a company's strategy and culture," says Klein. "A CEO who comes in from the outside is very dependent on those left in the company for orientation, perspective and information. That's potentially problematic."

In general, Klein notes, given the complexities of running a major corporation, "what you would like in an ideal scenario is careful succession planning that grooms people internally. One reason is you want to maintain the intellectual capital of the organization. Another is that you want to motivate people in the upper levels of the company to stay and excel because they might get to lead the company someday. I'd rather see a company have a culture that welcomes newcomers at all levels to maintain freshness and new perspectives—but not bring in someone at the height of a crisis. As important as new perspectives are for a company's long-term survival, it's risky to bring in an outsider as CEO when the ship is listing because the learning curve is awfully huge."

Peter Cappelli, management professor and director of Wharton's Center for Human Resources, suggests that for many companies, there is "a huge disconnect" between the reality and the intent on the part of people engaged in talent management. And firms often undercut their succession plans by going outside to hire new CEOs when the going gets tough.

"A lot of companies don't do any planning, period," Cappelli says. "But in bigger ones, particularly the older companies, they develop people with the assumption that they will advance into top executive positions. I'm not sure all companies designate the heir apparent to the CEO job the way they did in the 1950s, but they're still plugging away at the process. Yet the odds on the process playing out successfully are so small you have to question why they're doing it. Every time a company appoints an external CEO, all that internal process is wasted."

According to Cappelli, a survey of CEOs at large companies found that only 25% had any kind of talent planning past two levels below the CEO—i.e., below the senior vice president level. It is not that companies have abandoned succession planning and other practices and moved to new approaches, he says. Instead, firms appear to have abandoned the systematic management of talent.

Ideally, Cappelli adds, it is not necessary for firms to groom specific people to become CEOs—or, indeed, for any other specific position. It is best for companies simply to "develop people so that their skills continue to improve.

"I don't think the idea ought to be to develop people for a particular job," Cappelli says, "because the odds of using them in that way are pretty small. Both the person and the job have to be lined up too exactly for that to happen. Boards of directors ought to be developing people who can fill the executive vice president jobs because there's some chance those appointments could be internal. Boards also ought to be developing general managers because CEOs sometimes come out of that experience."

It is true that General Electric, which is widely known for its talent-management capabilities, produced a handful of people who were publicly known to be in the running to replace Jack Welch when he retired as CEO in

2001. When Jeffrey Immelt got the nod, the others left the company to become chief executives elsewhere: Robert Nardelli first became head of Home Depot and is now head of Chrysler, while Jim McNerney went on to spend more than four years as head of 3M and is now CEO of Boeing.

But Cappelli says GE is unusual among large corporations in being able to groom specific successors for the CEO post. "GE is an anomaly because it's so big. Running a part of GE means running something larger than 98% of the companies in the U.S. The general managers at GE are ready to step into many other jobs elsewhere. GE does invest a lot in trying to develop people internally. One of the reasons for that is they're a big, diversified and reasonably stable company whose success has allowed them to be internally stable. If performance got bad at GE and they started bringing in outsiders, you'd have to wonder about" the company's ability to continue the kind of succession planning it has been doing.

John R. Kimberly, a Wharton management professor, agrees that succession planning is just one piece of the much broader endeavor of talent management. "If a company does it right, it's not just thinking of the top job but is looking down three or four or five levels. Bench strength is the key."

One company with renowned bench strength is Toyota. "Toyota has lost several very senior people recently, which is unheard of in Toyota. People are starting to raise questions about whether there are cracks appearing in the management structure there," Kimberly says. "But the CEO, Katsuaki Watanabe, has been very calm about the matter. He has said Toyota hates to lose these people, but that the company has real management depth and that this won't affect them."

Indeed, one of those senior executives, Jim Press, who left Toyota after 37 years to become vice chairman and CEO of Chrysler, was replaced within 24 hours by Shigeru Hayakawa, a 30-year Toyota veteran.

Shallow Talent Pools

While a decision by Citigroup or Merrill to hire outsiders as CEOs might send a positive signal to investors, it could have negative long-term consequences by depleting a pool of talent that may already be precariously shallow, notes Wharton management professor Lawrence Hrebiniak.

In looking outside to possibly replace O'Neal and Prince, the boards "realize they might not have the bench strength" to promote from within, he says. "They don't have people who are general-manger material, but by going outside they make it worse. They are giving signals to [internal] managers that the managers aren't ready to move into the CEO role. They are going to have even more problems in the future with managers leaving because a person from the outside is going to bring his own people. He's going to have his own way of doing things. The people inside are going to believe that their career paths are truncated by outsiders coming in."

Hrebiniak notes that the difficulty of running organizations as complex as Citigroup and Merrill means that their CEOs need to have strategic vision and wide experience. But such talent is often lacking on Wall Street, in Hrebiniak's view, because the chief executives of financial firms, while successful at trading or money management have little knack for managing large enterprises.

"When you look at firms like Citigroup and Merrill Lynch, for years all their top management people were finance people, numbers people, traders. Years ago, these companies were smaller, so you had a group of people who understood finance and everything was fine. But what's happened? With mergers and acquisitions and growth, Citigroup and other financial organizations need a whole new brand of management. They have to worry about M&A, integrating companies, building products across firms. They have to worry about general management, but they have had no training at that and aren't good at it."

Hrebiniak adds that Merrill and Citigroup, like all Wall Street firms, have been under intense pressure by investors to perform. "The Street has been killing them for lack of performance, so they start thinking short term. They have gotten rid of top people in the past year, or these people have left voluntarily. Why? Investor pressure. The CEOs don't know how to manage strategically and they are losing talent. The firms [lack] strategic thinking. They might want to find someone internally [to replace the departed CEOs] but now they can't because they haven't been grooming new people."

Finding a Fresh Perspective

Elizabeth E. Bailey, a Wharton management professor who sits on the boards of Altria and other companies, says that even if succession plans have produced insiders capable of being chief executive, the boards of Citigroup and Merrill would have little choice but to select outsiders for their new CEOs.

"The reason [O'Neal and Prince] were asked to leave is because they misestimated the risk of these new types of mortgage securities to a huge degree," according to Bailey. "My sense is that when there's a major failure in performance, then you don't want [to promote] the person you have groomed, even if you've done great succession planning. You want somebody with a fresh perspective."

"Boards go outside for CEOs in situations where things haven't been going all that well," agrees Cappelli. "The best way to let people in the investment community know that you didn't like the way things were going is to get rid of everybody associated with the old approach. In that context, an internal successor has got no prayer of becoming CEO. It doesn't matter how wonderful the person is; he or she is just tainted by their association with the previous regime. The directors feel the need to signal a change in direction, so pretty much anybody associated with the old regime can't be advanced."

Boards that hire outsiders to be CEOs feel that change is more important than continuity, says Kimberly, who is author of the recently published *The Soul of the Corporation: How to Manage the Identity of Your Company.* "If a board is looking for continuity in the way the firm is managed at the top, they look inside, where there's deep knowledge, presumably, of the organization's culture and identity among the heirs apparent. There's a high likelihood that the new person will build on the past. If the board feels a severe, substantial change of course is required, it makes more sense to go outside."

How can Citigroup and Merrill—and other companies in similar situations—retain the loyalty of the senior executives passed over for the top post? The Wharton experts say boards often do not worry about smoothing ruffled feathers with sweetened compensation because those senior executives, aware of how rough the game can be at the top, will look for work elsewhere.

In Bailey's view, the search committees at Merrill and Citigroup are asking themselves: Who is the person best suited to meet the future issues of our firms? "And the issue facing both firms is being able to handle risks well. No one inside had the sense to speak up against the risk that these companies took. The search committees—especially Citigroup's, which is a very complex company—will make a list of the three or four most important attributes going forward and make sure the successor has the attributes. One is that the successor knows enough about these new, complex financial instruments so that the company doesn't get sucked into the momentum" that caused their problems in the first place. ∎

Published: November 28, 2007 in Knowledge@Wharton

The Succession Question at Tech Firms: When's the Right Time to Go?

The recent resignation of Scott McNealy as CEO of Sun Microsystems, the company he founded 22 years ago, is another milestone in the succession process of a large technology company. But tech companies often pose unique succession issues, in part because of their unusually fast growth and young founders, according to Wharton faculty and technology experts. "If you look at the dominant companies in the technology industry, most of them are still led, or until recently were led, by a charismatic founder. By and large the companies that have made the transition have done a pretty good job of it," says Kevin Werbach, professor of legal studies and business ethics at Wharton.

In 2000, for example, Bill Gates turned his CEO position at Microsoft over to his first hire, Steve Ballmer, although Gates remains chairman of the company. Adobe Systems' founders John Warnock and Charles Geschke similarly turned over the CEO job to Bruce Chizen in 2000.

The industry is still young, however, and many of the best-known firms continue to be run by entrepreneurial founders, like McNealy, who have been in their jobs for decades and have grown to become corporate icons. Going forward, it remains to be seen what will happen at Oracle, which is still run by founder Lawrence J. Ellison after nearly 30 years, and at Apple, where founder Steve Jobs left the company once, but is now enjoying a second honeymoon with the success of the iPod and iTunes.

Celebrity Entrepreneurs

While succession is important at any company, it can be even more critical at a firm run by entrepreneurs, like Gates or Jobs, who are also celebrities. "In a situation where the CEO is also the founder, it's not just a succession event when he or she steps down," says Wharton management professor Peter Cappelli. "These people are closely identified with the organization and it can be extremely traumatic when somebody like that [leaves]. They have to think carefully about what kind of person could step in."

Young start-ups flourish with creative, charismatic leaders who have a deep passion for, and understanding of, technology. But as the organizations grow, they need chief executives with a different set of skills, including the ability to delegate and to operate in a highly structured management system, says Kartik Hosanagar, Wharton professor of operations and information management. "In the technology industry, you have entrepreneurs who have been running the show for a really long time. But as these firms start to grow, they need to be looking at seasoned managers who have broad-based management skills."

At the majority of technology firms, which never become household names, the transition from entrepreneurial founder to business-oriented CEO occurs early in the firm's evolution, often at the demand of venture capital investors, Hosanagar points out. For example, Larry Page and Sergey Brin founded Google in 1998, but by 2001 they had hired Eric Schmidt, the former CEO of Novell, as Google's chairman and CEO.

Only a handful of the largest firms have had founders with the ability to manage both the technology and business sides of their rapidly growing companies, Hosanagar says. "For the more successful companies, there was not a reason for the investors to make the intervention earlier. That's why you have some of the biggest companies—Microsoft, Sun, Apple—run by the same people for 10, 20 or 30 years."

The rate of innovation in the technology industry also allows entrepreneurial founders to remain in charge longer than their management skills might warrant because fast growth at the firms can mask management weaknesses, Hosanagar says. As the companies mature, those problems are not so easy to hide, making succession more urgent.

Many entrepreneurs are happy to turn over the chief executive job, notes Joseph Griesedieck, vice chairman of the management recruitment firm Korn/Ferry International. "There are those who have a tough time letting go, but then there are those who are smart enough to know what their limitations are. Sometimes they want to move on and start new things." He points to Jim Clark, a founder of Silicon Graphics and later Netscape, as an example of an entrepreneur who did not linger in the CEO position. At Microsoft, in addition to his chairman job, Gates now carries the title of chief software architect and has been largely focused on new product development and strategy.

Hiring from the Outside, or Inside

Once the decision is made to appoint a new chief executive, boards must wrestle with whether to hire from the outside or choose someone from their own ranks. "Clearly there's a preference for managers who are in the industry, but the challenge is that because the industry is so young, you can't find as many seasoned executives who can run the show. We are at an inflection point where this industry, which had been run by technologists, is going to increasingly look to traditional business executives to take on more important roles," says Hosanagar.

When McNealy stepped down, Sun promoted president Jonathan Schwartz to the CEO position. Schwartz joined Sun in 1996 and was long considered to be McNealy's successor. While Sun's shares rose 9% after the announcement, some questioned whether Schwartz has enough perspective to lift Sun out of its doldrums. In a research note, Toni Sacconaghi of Bernstein Research said Schwartz remains unproven as a leader, and he expressed concern that Schwartz's ideas were "eerily similar" to those of McNealy.

Wharton management professor Benjamin Campbell notes that McNealy had come under sharp criticism for his management of the company, although recently he appears to have turned the situation around. Choosing an insider gives Sun employees and investors a greater sense of certainty about what to expect, he says.

Sometimes, Campbell notes, companies should shop outside for chief executives, particularly if the company is performing badly and wants to signal it is headed in a new direction. "If it's clear the firm's business model is flawed and it needs to implement dramatic changes, then hiring externally is the right way to go."

The timing of the Sun succession is interesting because McNealy had been under pressure to step down years earlier, Campbell adds. It was not until the company appeared to be back on the upswing that he announced the change. "It looks as if the company is trying to create a situation where the new CEO can be quickly successful, which would help get buy-in with the external world. It seems like this is exactly the right time to switch CEOs—just when things are starting to perk up."

It has been difficult, Cappelli adds, for fast-growing technology firms to develop top managers internally. "The companies generally have not had a lot of systems in place, particularly for developing people, so that often makes it hard to find qualified people inside."

"Bill Is Back"

According to Werbach, the transition from Gates to his college buddy, Ballmer, was about as gradual as could be expected. The next succession, he says, will be a greater challenge for Microsoft. "There are a lot of great executives at Microsoft, but it will probably be a more traumatic transition from Steve Ballmer to the next CEO than it was from Gates to Ballmer. The next CEO, whoever it is, will not be someone who was around in the 1970s when the company got started."

Campbell suggests that Gates' celebrity will make it difficult for anyone else to occupy the chief executives' office. "Those are going to be extremely large shoes to fill. The probability that any CEO will lead the company with the success Bill Gates has had is extremely low." Yet according to Kendall Whitehouse, Wharton's senior IT director, one possible successor to Gates is Ray Ozzie, the principal creator of Lotus Notes, who joined Microsoft when the company acquired Groove Networks in 2005, a company which Ozzie founded in 1997. "Ozzie is clearly a tech visionary," states Whitehouse. "He may be just what Microsoft needs to lead it into the next generation of Internet-enabled software applications."

Meanwhile, Gates and Ballmer have been shaking things up at Microsoft lately. This week, the company announced it will introduce new initiatives for the Internet and Microsoft's game platform that will take on competitors like Google, Yahoo! and Sony. Announcement of the plans, which will cost the company $2 to $2.5 billion in the next year, sent shares down sharply.

Analysts say that the investment signals the beginning of a new era for Microsoft after a period in which the company was digesting the last decade's enormous growth, the maturation of the PC market and years of anti-trust litigation. "Bill is back. He's now thinking about the Microsoft that has to be built," Mark Stahlman, an analyst at Caris & Co. in New York, told *The Financial Times*.

At Apple, Steve Jobs has already passed through the succession process once. In 1983, Jobs and Apple cofounder Steve Wozniak selected a traditional business manager, John Sculley, then president of PepsiCo, to run the computer firm. By 1985, tensions had developed between Jobs and his hand-picked CEO. Sculley ousted Jobs, but 11 years later, long after Sculley had gone, Apple's board reinstalled Jobs after acquiring his new firm, NeXT Computer. "The change in environment certainly helped Steve Jobs," says Hosanagar. "He came back in with a very different approach to managing the firm. The years away brought a certain amount of energy and fresh thinking."

According to Wharton management professor Saikat Chaudhuri, Apple should be thinking about a successor to Jobs as the company celebrates its 30th anniversary. "Jobs is a visionary but, to his credit, after he left Apple the first time, he came back not just as a visionary, but he also implemented well. The iPod is the best example of that."

Even though Jobs is riding high now, the board should be careful not to become too comfortable with his ability to meld vision and execution. Sun may have fallen into that trap with McNealy, Chaudhuri suggests. "I think Sun got stuck. In some ways, the Sun succession should have come earlier. It could easily have come five years ago."

Oracle is another company that needs to be thinking about succession, Chaudhuri says. Ellison has recently become more hands-on at the firm, taking some aggressive steps in the company's Enterprise Resource Planning (ERP) systems and Customer Relationship Management (CRM) business, and has raised the possibility of acquiring a Linux provider, such as Red Hat.

Still, it will be difficult to meld Ellison's entrepreneurial vision with the business skills that will be necessary to carry out the strategy successfully. "It will be interesting to see [what happens] when Larry Ellison retires from Oracle, which may not be for another 20 years," says Werbach, adding that technology executives seem to stay on longer than executives in other industries because they were so young when they became successful. "What else are you going to do if you're Bill Gates and you're in your early 50s?" asks Werbach. "There's no other job for these people and they can live another 30 or 40 years. What would you expect them to say: 'I'm going fishing'?" ∎

Published: May 3, 2006 in Knowledge@Wharton

Job-less: Steve Jobs's Succession Plan Should Be a Top Priority for Apple

When Apple announced on December 16 that Philip Schiller, the company's senior vice president of worldwide product marketing, would deliver the keynote speech at this week's Macworld conference instead of CEO Steve Jobs, speculation swirled again about the future of the company—and Jobs's health. Jobs disclosed in August 2004 that he had a cancerous tumor removed from his pancreas. Observers at recent Apple events reported that the visionary technologist appeared gaunt. Adding fuel to the fire, Apple also announced that it would not be participating in future Macworlds, saying, "Trade shows have become a very minor part of how Apple reaches its customers."

Responding to questions about his health, Jobs said in a January 5 open letter that he was suffering from a hormone imbalance that was "robbing" his body of nutrients. He also noted that he is receiving treatment and will remain CEO of Apple. "I have given more than my all to Apple for the past 11 years now. I will be the first one to step up and tell our board of directors if I can no longer continue to fulfill my duties as Apple's CEO," stated the letter.

Meanwhile, the looming question of who would replace Jobs if he had to leave Apple remains unresolved for shareholders, analysts and customers. While the company maintains it has a succession plan, it has offered no details. Observers are left to question what Apple might look like without Jobs and whether the company can continue pumping out hits like the iPhone, MacBook and iPod.

A succession plan is critical for most companies, but especially so for Apple, according to Wharton faculty. They acknowledge that every company is different, but also point to established best practices for succession planning, including hiring from within, conducting an audition period, easing the successor into a leadership role and providing some level of succession disclosure to shareholders.

Companies with strong corporate cultures can usually count on continued success if they can seamlessly transfer power to an executive from a strong bench of managers. But selecting Jobs's successor will be challenging, given the degree to which he is tied to Apple's identity. As Wharton management professor Michael Useem puts it: "There are few companies where the top person has as much of an impact [as Jobs has had] at Apple."

Apple and Jobs seem almost inseparable in the public mind. Jobs cofounded Apple in 1976, left during a power struggle with corporate investors in 1985 and returned to Apple in 1997 after the struggling company acquired NeXT, another computer firm started by Jobs. Apple ousted CEO Gil Amelio, who had been at the helm a little more than a year. Jobs became interim and then permanent CEO, quickly establishing himself as the voice of Apple and launching a string of consumer electronics hits.

"He really is the face of the company," says Kendall Whitehouse, senior director of IT at Wharton. "When you speak to Apple employees, there is always a lot of talk about Steve and what Steve wants. It's palpable. That has generally been a positive thing for [Apple]. Jobs was the centerpiece for refocusing the company and brand" following his return.

But some Wharton faculty say Apple now seems eager to show that there is more to the company than the vision of Steve Jobs. At an October press event, Jobs appeared on stage with Schiller and chief operating officer Tim Cook, the latter wearing Jobs's trademark black shirt with jeans. "The strategy here appears to be showcasing different members of middle and upper management to illustrate that Apple, as an organization, is more than just a cult figure at the top," says Wharton management professor David Hsu.

Analysts agree. "Apple could have diffused speculation regarding Jobs's health by having him keynote this year's Macworld," Piper Jaffray analyst Gene Munster wrote in a research note. "While we do not believe that this change provides any indication regarding Jobs's health, we do believe that it is a sign we are in the early stages of changing roles in Apple's management structure."

Although Apple's succession plan for Jobs remains unclear, experts at Wharton offer a few tips to help guide the company's succession planning process.

Promote from Within

Apple has a strong bench of executives who could succeed Jobs, but major stakeholders, such as investors, customers and partners, don't know much about them, according to Wharton faculty. The first step in any succession plan may be illustrating that Apple is more than Jobs.

According to Wharton management professors Useem and Peter Cappelli, Apple's effort to highlight executives other than Jobs is a good test for any successor. Why? Part of Apple's mystique revolves around messaging and generating buzz. By putting executives like Cook and Schiller in the limelight, Apple can give other managers some practice introducing products and familiarize them with investors and customers. "It is important for any company to be developing talent internally. And it is also important to be promoting people from within," notes Cappelli. The board "should pay a lot of attention to the abilities and potential of their leadership team—always."

Wharton management professor Lawrence Hrebiniak also urges Apple to show off executives beyond Jobs. "Apple wants the world to know that it doesn't sink without Jobs. The company is addressing a common concern [that arises] when you have a powerful, well-known leader."

Useem suggests that a board of directors should be responsible for ensuring that a company has the right leader as well as the right leadership team—especially if there is any hint that the chief executive may step down in three to four years. He cites numerous research studies indicating that internal successors are more effective.

One related challenge is determining whether a company even has the talent to adapt to the new environment. If the decision is made to hire from the inside, then "a CEO and board should be looking at the top contenders" and analyzing what is known about each one, says Useem.

If a company develops its internal talent well, there should be a strong bench of executives who can lead under various scenarios, thus making succession planning easier. "Succession planning per se is a waste of time," says Cappelli. "It means trying to determine in advance who will take over a top job. But because the needs change so frequently, as often do the players, there is no real ability to plan. These plans take a lot of time and energy, they divert the attention of people in the company and they almost always get tossed aside because they are out of date." The solution: Companies need to develop talent internally so that they have multiple options when a successor is needed.

Useem notes that some companies turn to testing as a way to vet internal candidates. For example, they may hire third parties to interview executives who report directly to the CEO. More often, companies like GlaxoSmithKline pick internal candidates and then ask each of them to take on a CEO-level project and present it to the board. "This approach gives a company a better fix on how executives perform head to head. It can be awkward because these executives work together every day, but it is important to pick the right person."

What remains to be seen at Apple is whether Jobs would stay as a non-executive chairman with a new CEO. While these arrangements are rare in most American industries, says Useem, there are many examples among technology firms. Intel, Microsoft and Dell have all had CEOs become chairmen as day-to-day management was transferred to a new executive. Such an arrangement is more likely if a company founder—such as Michael Dell or Microsoft's Bill Gates—is involved, Useem adds.

Meanwhile, a company also has to prepare for the inevitable mop-up duty that follows the appointment of the new CEO. It is unlikely that executives who lost out on the top job will stay. For example, when General Electric transitioned leadership from Jack Welch to Jeff Immelt, the other top candidates for Welch's job—Robert Nardelli and James McNerney—departed to become the chief executives of Home Depot and 3M, respectively. Nardelli is now CEO of Chrysler and McNerney is chief executive of Boeing. "Having successors just waiting in the wings is not a good idea," Cappelli says. "If they're good, they won't stay."

Transparency Is Key

Generally speaking, companies in the midst of succession planning need to deliver some kind of transparency to customers and investors. In Apple's case, disclosure—or lack of it—about Jobs's health and future plans appears to be a sore point with some analysts. Wharton faculty agree that Apple needs to disclose more about its succession plan, but how much detail is needed is open to debate.

Wall Street is clearly worried about Apple's future post Jobs. Any rumor about Jobs's health can move the stock. Following Apple's announcement that Jobs would not be the keynote speaker at Macworld, Oppenheimer analyst Yair Reiner downgraded Apple shares because the company would not disclose details about the state of Jobs's health or a succession plan.

In general, having a succession plan is a good idea since it minimizes uncertainty, but how much a company discloses depends on culture, says Hrebiniak. If a company is too transparent, "every would-be CEO would leave if he or she was not a finalist," and performance would suffer.

Cappelli agrees. It "isn't obvious" that Apple needs to outline its plans. "Whatever [Apple] outlines today will be irrelevant as soon as circumstances change, and that will happen in months. Apple probably will go through three or four plans before Jobs steps aside, so what's the point?"

Meanwhile, it's unlikely that Apple will fall apart without Jobs, suggests Cappelli. "Investors get worried if they think the future of an entire company depends on a couple of key individuals. In fact, that is almost never the case. This bias—attributing the success of organizations to individuals—is pretty common. Several studies have looked to see what happens when CEOs die unexpectedly. All the studies show that, rather than collapsing, share prices in fact actually go up. The current leaders are not that crucial. Companies don't collapse when the leader departs and there is some time to fill the job."

Whitehouse, however, says Apple "needs to articulate something." If the company needs a disclosure blueprint, he adds, it doesn't have to look any farther than its long-time rival—Microsoft.

In January 2000, Bill Gates signaled the beginning of a transition of power at Microsoft. He named Steve Ballmer, who became president of the company in July 1998, as CEO. Gates said he was stepping down to focus on long-term strategy, but he remained chairman and added a new title—chief software architect. At the time, Gates said making Ballmer CEO was a "very good transition" for Microsoft. Over the next eight years, Microsoft gradually put other executives in the spotlight. In June 2006, Microsoft announced that Gates would transition out of his day-to-day role to focus on the Bill & Melinda Gates Foundation. The biggest change for Microsoft was appointing Ray Ozzie, then chief technology officer, to be the chief software architect working side-by-side with Gates. Gates' last day as an executive was June 27. He remains chairman and advises Microsoft on "key development projects."

"Microsoft had been about Gates for so long. But he scheduled a long, phased wind down. You can see the way that the succession was comfortable for the company, customers and shareholders," Whitehouse notes.

Preserve Corporate Culture

What remains to be seen is whether a post-Jobs Apple will retain the corporate traits that made the company successful with its iconic leader at the helm. The conventional wisdom is that Jobs's control has influenced everything from marketing to design at Apple, says Hsu. After a decade of leading Apple, he argues that it's quite possible Jobs's imprint is permanently etched on the company. "No one could move up in the organization without Jobs's approval. Eventually, management fits the mold Jobs wants."

Hsu says the secret sauce for all successful companies is having a corporate culture that transcends any individual. "You want a culture to be so ingrained in the rest of organization that it [provides a] competitive advantage."

Useem agrees. "You cannot overstate how important corporate culture is—if it's a good one—in sustaining and carrying on a company." Some companies, such as Wal-Mart, Mary Kay Cosmetics and Southwest Airlines, support strong cultures that have lasted well beyond their founders' departure, Useem notes. "A strong culture will transcend the exit of leaders. At Wal-Mart, pictures of Sam Walton keep the company thinking about the values that were used to create the company."

The problem for Apple is clear: No one will know until after Jobs leaves how thoroughly his imprint permeated the company. Useem acknowledges that developing a corporate culture is not clear cut. "Culture is one of the great mysterious aspects of company business. It is very important, but poorly understood. You can try to copy a company like Southwest, but rivals can't get their hands around what it is that makes these companies so successful." ∎

Published: January 7, 2009 in Knowledge@Wharton

Carol Bartz's Challenge at Yahoo: Choose a Path, Build a Team and Do It Fast

New Yahoo CEO Carol Bartz has a long to-do list—chart the company's strategy, weigh a potential search partnership with Microsoft, boost morale and round out her management team—and not much time to deliver amid a weak economy that is hurting online advertising, say experts at Wharton.

On January 13, Yahoo named Bartz, a Silicon Valley veteran, to be Jerry Yang's replacement as chief executive although Yang will remain as "Chief Yahoo" of the company he co-founded in 1994. In addition, Yahoo president Sue Decker said she would resign. Until the announcement last week, Bartz, 60, was the executive chairman of Autodesk, a computer-aided design software firm where she was CEO for 14 years before stepping down in April 2006. Bartz also worked at Sun Microsystems, Digital Equipment and 3M.

Yahoo chairman Roy Bostock, who, along with Yang, declined merger overtures from Microsoft throughout 2008, said in a conference call that Bartz is "a seasoned ...and highly regarded technology executive with a decisive leadership style and proven track record."

This past month has been a busy time for Silicon Valley leadership changes. In addition to the news about Bartz, Apple CEO Steve Jobs announced that he would take a six-month leave of absence to address health problems that have drawn media attention in recent weeks. The companies' situations contrast sharply: Apple is led by a dominant and respected personality who may, or may not, be planning an exit strategy; Yahoo is looking for the type of leader that Jobs represents. As Wharton management professor Lawrence Hrebiniak puts it: Yahoo needs someone with "spunk. Bartz has to come in and take action."

Analysts overall have been positive about Bartz's appointment although many suggest that she lacks online media experience. Bernstein analyst Jeffrey Lindsay said in a research note that Bartz "has been a good CEO," but is "not a natural choice for Yahoo." Citi analyst Mark Mahaney agreed that Bartz "brings to Yahoo organizational chops, a fresh perspective and substantial technology industry experience," adding, however, that she would need to hire a lieutenant with extensive media industry experience. Gartner analyst Allen Weiner characterized Bartz as a "solid and safe choice" who will need Yahoo insiders for media expertise.

Taking the Deep Dive

Wharton observers say Bartz could infuse Yahoo with a trait much needed at the company: decisiveness. Yahoo's biggest problem, they contend, is lack of focus. Is Yahoo a media company? Is it a technology outfit? Does it need to be in search? Who are Yahoo's biggest competitors—Google or established media companies? Bartz's job will be to answer those questions.

"I don't think people know what Yahoo is right now," says Wharton management professor Keith Weigelt. "Yahoo's core product requires technology, but it's really a media company. Yahoo [has many] positive characteristics, but Bartz needs to bring in a strategic focus. Yahoo is way too broad."

That complaint comes up frequently among Wharton experts, analysts and shareholders. "Yahoo is this odd company that is part search, part technology and part media," says Kendall Whitehouse, senior director of IT at Wharton. "Bartz needs to pick one or two of those parts. The focus has shifted as Yahoo has changed leaders."

According to Whitehouse, Hrebiniak and others, Bartz's biggest decision will be whether to outsource Yahoo's search service to Microsoft, which wants to take market share from Google. Google accounted for 63.5% of search queries in December, according to research firm ComScore. Microsoft, which accounts for 8.3% of the more than $30 billion search market compared to Yahoo's 20.5%, has expressed interest in buying Yahoo's search business, which generates revenue by linking ads to specific queries. Experts at Wharton suggest that outsourcing search to Microsoft could make sense for Yahoo by boosting revenues, cutting costs and giving the company a focus. The move could enable Yahoo to become a next-generation media company, says Whitehouse.

If Bartz has a strategy for Yahoo, she isn't making it public. Her immediate goal is to meet with Yahoo employees and gather information for future moves. "It's no secret that Yahoo has had challenges over the past year, but as I look around I see a powerful global brand with a great collection of assets, strong technology, good cash flow and talented employees," Bartz said on the conference call introducing her as CEO. Regarding the well-publicized questions swirling about Yahoo's strategy, Bartz did not divulge any specific thoughts. "I have a lot of ideas on these subjects, but it would be very presumptuous to discuss them on my first day on the job. I'm first going to do a deep dive to meet the great people of Yahoo before I start speaking about how I plan to lead the company," she stated.

For now, Bartz said everyone needs to "give this company some breathing room." How much breathing room Bartz gets remains to be seen, but her challenges are clear, say experts at Wharton.

Employee Morale and Shareholder Confidence

Her first mission is to calm the waters at Yahoo. The company has angry shareholders, a restive board member in Carl Icahn, who is itching for a search deal with Microsoft, and employees in need of a leader. In addition, employees have had to endure a year of dour media reports about Yahoo's future. And then there is the financial crisis that's hurting online advertising—the mainstay of Yahoo's business.

According to Wharton management professor Rahul Kapoor, Bartz needs to make a few early moves to address the short-term concerns. The biggest of those, he believes, are employee morale and shareholder confidence. "The present economic crisis won't make addressing those challenges any easier."

Perhaps Bartz's more significant contribution to Yahoo will be in developing the company's long-term strategy, Kapoor adds. Bartz alluded to this during her introductory news conference by noting that "It has been too crazy. That is going to stop. This is a company with enormous assets that frankly could use a little management."

Hrebiniak suggests that Bartz first needs to get stakeholders together in an offsite meeting to assess strategy and build consensus to move forward with a plan. "She's under pressure to act. [Microsoft CEO Steve Ballmer] is seeking action on a search deal. The economy is bad. Investors want action. She knows she has to act and, as basic as it seems, you start with getting key players together, talking and laying out strategy."

Creating a coherent strategy for Yahoo will be a formidable task. Yahoo is a complex company that breaks down to three primary parts: Media and content, technology development and ad-funded search. Of those three legs, search is the item most in question. "Strategically, a Microsoft deal looks like a good move," says Hrebiniak. "Ballmer wants to get this deal done and go against Google. Yahoo should take the money and find other opportunities." Weigelt agrees. "Yahoo is losing the battle with Google slowly," he says. "I'd seriously consider the Microsoft search deal as a way to focus the company."

Yahoo would still have significant assets even if it sold the search business. The company "has done some intriguing work on the technology side," notes Whitehouse. Yahoo Pipes, a technology that aggregates web feeds to create new applications, and a venture with Intel to create TV "widgets," or on-screen software that complements television programming, are two examples of innovative technology from the company.

Meanwhile, Yahoo also has been busy rolling out the company's "Yahoo Open Strategy" intended to make it easier for developers to create software programs that work across the company's various web sites. Adding that technology to Yahoo's proven ability to aggregate users—the company attracted 146 million unique visitors in December, just behind Google's 149 million, according to ComScore—could create a powerful combination, argues Whitehouse. "A technology-focused company that understands media could be powerful."

The other option for Yahoo would be to become solely a media company. Yahoo has numerous properties—Yahoo News, Flickr and Yahoo Finance—that are among the category leaders. Various press reports have detailed talks between Yahoo and Time Warner about a deal to have Yahoo take over AOL, which was No. 4 in overall Internet traffic in December with 110 million unique visitors, according to ComScore.

During her conference call, Bartz acknowledged the complexity of Yahoo, but said the main goal is to get focused on executing well. "The important thing is being best in all of our markets," she said.

Ultimately, Bartz's success will be judged on how she reshapes Yahoo's competitive position, Kapoor suggests. "Yahoo's big puzzle is how to create more value for its enormous user base especially in the wake of an ever-expanding threat from Google. Strategic reconfigurations will be the key to how Bartz affects Yahoo. This is a multiyear effort and she has her work cut out in the short term."

As Bartz addresses strategy and short-term challenges, she must also build a management team. Wharton observers say that she needs a mix of insiders and long-time colleagues she can trust. From there, she can focus on rebuilding Yahoo's management talent, which has been eroded due to turnover and layoffs.

Weigelt expects Bartz to hire a few outsiders, as she did at Autodesk. "You look back at Autodesk where she moved pretty quickly, fired underperformers and brought in her own lieutenants." But she will also need the help of Yahoo insiders—the most important of whom may be Yang. Weigelt expects Yang—who knows Bartz well, in part because they both serve on the board of Cisco Systems—to step back and let Bartz run the company. Meanwhile, given the departure of Decker, Bartz will have to hire a No. 2 executive to carry out her plans. Analysts such as Mahaney expect Bartz to hire someone with media experience.

Wharton management professor Peter Cappelli suggests that Bartz "find an insider, someone with expertise in the media side, to help understand the ins and outs of the company and provide some balance as to what is possible." The rationale for such a move is clear, he says: Bartz needs to move quickly. "If the top two people are outsiders, they are both trying to learn how things work at the same time. Also, you don't need two different outside perspectives."

Hrebiniak agrees. Given some level of discontent within the company, Bartz will need "a No. 2 who can facilitate internally. She will need a peacemaker who can get consensus and carry out her strategy." ■

Published: January 21, 2009 in Knowledge@Wharton

One Former Investment Banker's Take on Restoring the "Financial Quality, Integrity and Soundness of Our System"

At the recent World Economic Forum in Davos, Wharton management professor Michael Useem talked with Suzanne Nora Johnson, vice chairman of Goldman Sachs until 2007, about the global crisis, executive compensation, the Goldman Sachs culture and CEO succession, among other topics. Johnson currently serves on a number of for-profit and non-profit boards, including AIG, Intuit, Pfizer, Visa, Women's World Banking and the American Red Cross.

An edited transcript of the conversation follows.

Michael Useem: Suzanne, thank you for taking the time to talk with us today. I'm going to begin with a question about your background. You worked for Goldman Sachs for 22 years, but left the company before the crisis really hit in full force. Goldman has been one of the investment banks that people thought would survive and yet it has faced its own meltdown in recent months. When you were there, did you see any signs in the financial services industry that we were headed for the type of global disaster we are experiencing now?

Suzanne Nora Johnson: Mike, thanks very much for the opportunity to speak with you today. I think that the most important warning sign was the fact that if you look back several years ago—and even as late as 2007—the only undervalued asset class that you could find was risk. Literally, you could go to traditional asset classes, whether it was real estate, commercial/residential, whether it was emerging market debt or equities, whether it was private equity alternatives from venture capital to private equity—clearly the risk premiums were mispriced.

Why I say they were mispriced, literally, [is that] there were no differentials from one very sterling credit to one lousy credit. That was a warning sign. You also had the warning sign that volatility was at an historic low. There were, again, no differentiations on the volatility front. The flipside of it was that we were going through an extraordinary period of time when the globalization revolution actually had created quite [a lot] of profound change—meaning many countries around the world were part of an active trading regime. Around the world, you saw many people pulled out of poverty. The two kinds of macro trends that were positive were that you were going through a period of historically low inflation around the world and also low interest rates—which, again, for the average man or woman around the world, was a positive in terms of their standard of living. That said, this produced profound imbalances. Those imbalances really were the underpinning of the asset pricing problem that I referred to when I first answered your question—which really was kind of a tip off that something was probably amiss.

Useem: We have often heard it said that J.P. Morgan Chase and Goldman Sachs had taken more steps [than others] to protect themselves, especially from the subprime mortgage meltdown when it did come. We've often heard it said that at Goldman in particular, a management culture had developed over many decades which helped people in the ranks bring bad news up to the top. So therefore the CFO and CEO at Goldman, in effect, had more early warnings than might have been the case at other firms.

Johnson: Goldman Sachs was extraordinarily lucky and fortunate that, in fact, it had come relatively recently from a partnership culture. If you remember, the firm went public in '99. But there was still a large number of people—both in the partnership and non-partnership ranks—who had grown up with a partnership structure. That partnership structure meant that there was relative transparency from one division to another, from one desk to another. People could ask questions about what was going on. And you knew the real live individuals there who had everything on the line. It wasn't just their own personal capital, it was the livelihoods of thousands of employees.

That was a great foundation going into both the expansionary period at the beginning of the decade, and then the problems toward the end. You don't lose that overnight. Also, there was a view in [recent] years that we didn't need to be biggest. We wanted to be "Best in Class," and we wanted to be very good at what we were doing. So there was extraordinary accountability inside. In terms of— were you good at what you were doing? What kinds of risks were you taking to get there? How high-quality were the activities that you were exercising? I would also say that, just from a diligence perspective...it was fortunate that you had ...market share leadership positions in so many businesses. You didn't have to stretch everywhere. And, again, if you look at many people in the financial services industry, it was clear that they were stretching very, very far afield.

Useem: When you joined Goldman, you were the inheritor of a culture, a way of doing business that had put Goldman on top for many, many years. But as you rose up through the ranks—as you became vice chair—you were also the maker of the culture. So, thinking back about how you and other executives helped create and sustain a culture that you just described very tactically—what does it take to create that kind of ownership, of everybody taking responsibility, everybody feeling they are a leader, wherever they may be in the bank? It's a cultural statement, but that was the mindset created. The question is, how do you create and sustain that kind of a culture of ownership and responsibility?

Johnson: I know this sounds too simplistic an answer, but at the end of the day, it comes down to: Do you walk the walk, not just talk the talk? In an organization as large as Goldman Sachs—it was several thousand when I joined and close to 25,000 when I left—when you have that large an enterprise, everyone who's in a leadership position is watched very, very closely to see what their actions are. So starting with Hank Paulson, he put in some very formalized what I'll call "ethics training programs," or kind of "true north programs," that were cross-firm, cross-divisional, where they were taught by both Hank and the other members of the management committee and then other partners. Again, there was formal training with real live situations discussed. But also, in everyday business, people felt comfortable talking about kinds of moral dilemmas—not just compliance dilemmas or legal dilemmas, but really, "Were there ethical issues?" I can think of a number of situations where people celebrated if someone turned down a piece of business, or decided not to go all the way on it....Once you could celebrate or reward non-revenue generation—or risk-avoidance, is another way of looking at it—that helped reinforce the messages.

Useem: Given that culture, given that mindset, given that dominance of the markets, the last 12 months have not been kind to Goldman—along with everybody else. I realize you have now been gone for a couple of years, but looking back on the company, what do you think has happened that led it to become officially, now, a commercial bank? Just comment on the events of the last 12 months, as Goldman, along with everybody else, has struggled to get through them. What happened at Goldman?

Johnson: Again, ..ith the very fair caveat that I haven't been there formally in the last two years, the observation I would make is that, historically, the business's success was highly correlated to what global GDP looked like and how active the capital markets were. As you know, in the last 12 months, we've seen a significant reduction in global GDP growth, and also a real quieting of the markets, a lack of market activity. So, that being kind of the soup, if you will, from which they fed, it being greatly reduced also made it much more challenging for them. One, you just have to understand, as a market participant, that this single issue was the biggest one. Again, I really credit the leadership, over many years, of having risk management systems that were quite thoughtful and rigorous—for example, Goldman Sachs looked at liquidity VAR [value at risk] as well as VAR—for many, many years to get a feel for what would happen in the case of a true liquidity crisis. But we've had events now that are at the tail [the unlikely extreme of a probability distribution]. If you had tried to probability weight—how likely is it that we would have the kind of meltdown—most people would have commented that it would have been a very, very low probability that you would have this kind of interconnected meltdown. Did certain commentators absolutely see it coming? No question. But I think the kind of depth and magnitude of it was hard for even the best minds, and the most rigorous risk management systems, to understand.

Useem: Arguably, one of the problems that we're all now working to overcome is a mindset that did not see the tails, that did not anticipate the once-in-a-century kind of event. Other factors, though, we need to be mindful of as well—which include the relatively short-term thinking that seemed to dominate many financial decisions in the financial market. Picking up on all of the above, as you think about the culture of American business, not just financial but beyond—do we need a change in mindset? Do we need a cultural shift? Is it a matter of tweaking, or should we really be rethinking our business model? And then, to add one last quick, final question to that long question, if a culture shift of some kind is required, who's going to make that happen? How difficult is it going to be to push through?

Johnson: I've actually thought a lot about this question because so many thoughtful people I know have said, "I'll never take a management position in a public company. I'll only do it in a private company." When they say that, I always ask them: "What is it that's motivating you?" And they generally come back with something that says, "I want to be able to do the right thing." Then I say, "Well, what does that mean?" And they say, "Well, I want to be able to balance the need to optimize shareholder equity with other constituencies, to do it somewhat under the radar screen."

And, again, I always look at the radar screen as a double edged sword. "Are you doing that because you don't want to be transparent? Or are you just doing it because you want to find a way to do some of the difficult decisions that might be challenging?" The other element of that which is relevant is that the U.S. and much of the Western world—and much of Asia—has a public company model that still is very short-term focused in terms of what institutional investors are rewarding. So, as I think about ways to change a culture, often it revolves around compensation structures. Again, I think compensation structures will likely be more transparent, rather than less, going forward. To the extent that those compensation structures are more long-term focused, that isn't necessarily always in line with what your shareholders—particularly your more active shareholders—are demanding. For example, I can see compensation structures making incentives multi-year. And I don't mean stock vesting. I literally mean that your revenue targets—your earning targets—are multiple years, not single years. I could see clawbacks. I could see looking at internal rates of equity—meaning how much differentiation is there from the top to the bottom. All those things would have significant culture changes.

But to go back to the beginning—of private company versus public company—I think a lot of people sense that they would have a lot more flexibility in a private company setting to do some of those things, which means doing the right thing, making longer-term incentives, having clawbacks, having the kind of thing that helped justify a culture of "one for all," not "all for one."

Useem: As a non-executive director at Pfizer, AIG, Intuit and Visa, you're in kind of the hot seat on this very question right now.

Talk through a little bit what it means to move compensation towards more long-term. Are we talking three years out? Are we talking five years out? How would you structure it? Be as concrete as you can here—to ensure that the top people, say at Pfizer, Visa, or you name the company—are ready to look at what those companies need [in long-term executive compensation].

Johnson: I actually like seeing kind of multi-year timeframes. Clearly, you need to have some annual timeframes, because often budgets and investors are on that timeframe, at the very least. So you obviously have to have some annual metrics. But I think two, three, five-year metrics can be very, very healthy protocols to go through. It generally lets you live in and out of business cycles. It gives you a sense of who performs particularly well in adverse conditions. And hopefully there's a high correlation in the longer term of companies that do this with their shorter-term earnings, although, again, I think that's the billion dollar question. Can you make it somewhat consistent with those shorter-term expectations of public shareholder growth?

Useem: Suzanne, you joined the board of AIG, attended your first meeting, when AIG was really in the process at that very meeting of deciding it had to be, in effect, nationalized. What was it like to have joined the board of AIG at that particular moment?

Johnson: I would compare it to Ed Liddy's experience. Ed Liddy—as people probably know—is the CEO of AIG, who was brought in by the (U.S. Depart-ment of the] Treasury to replace the then-current CEO. Liddy had been the CEO of Allstate. When he was asked to take on the job, he was told, "This is really an act of public service. It's a very difficult, challenging situation." I think that's the way that you have to look at these situations—it's critically important that we restore the financial quality, integrity and soundness of our system. Again, I view our whole economy—both domestically and globally—being very closely correlated to the strength of our financial institutions. I view it as, "Can you help make it right at this point," recognizing that you're having to balance public and private sector constituencies?

Useem: I'm going to change focus here. Thinking back on your own career—you were trained as a lawyer, you clerked for a judge—you've seen many law students as they have come out of law school over these years. You've seen many graduates of business programs as well. Do you think that the men and women coming out of law schools and business schools these days should have a different skill set, so to speak, a different orientation, than those who came out 20 or 30 years ago? And now, looking back at the schools themselves, are there some changes that law schools and business schools ought to be thinking about?

Johnson: Mike, it's a great question. I'll tell you, I've really seen the recruiting landscape change. When I joined Goldman Sachs over 20 years ago—and I had practiced law for a number of years at that point—most of the questions they asked were very broad, global, macro, thoughtful questions that would test my insight, my judgment, my common sense, my ability to deal with difficult questions. Over the last number of years, I have found that we gravitated much more toward asking people, "What was their experience in the business?" meaning at a summer job or as an analyst. "Why did they want to be an investment banker?" "Why did they want to be a trader?" "Why did they want to be an analyst?"

It's not that I don't think those questions are important, but I'm hoping we will get back to much broader gauged individuals who really do have extraordinary qualities of accomplishment, leadership and integrity—that manifest themselves more broadly. Because I really do think people who understand the world—no matter what situation they're in, whether that means globally or even in a domestic context—are being more broadly gauged. It's not that I don't want people with quantitative aptitude who can do the rigors of a financial job. But I think those other qualities are more important at the end of the day [in terms of] how successful we will be and how successful your institution will be by having that cohort of people.

Useem: Suzanne, to put you on the spot here. If I'm a newly-minted graduate of a law school, a newly-graduated MBA holder—I'm in your office, you're considering me for a position—let's say at a Goldman Sachs or a Pfizer. What would be a question you might pose, now—to get beyond the more particular issues that you said are more typical—to gauge my ability to think broadly, to work effectively, longer-term, within the enterprise?

Johnson: Well, one very simple question I always ask is, "What's the most difficult situation you've had in your life, and how did you overcome it?" Just because I want to try to understand what level of adversity someone has actually really had, or how they think about adversity. Again, what was their game plan for changing it. And then I always ask people, too, to rank certain personal attributes, worst to best. If you can imagine all the very accomplished people I interview, they always answer it, first, best to worst. Then I force the other way around. And I find that by having them rank their worst to their best, in terms of core attributes, I get a lot more thoughtful answers in terms of how they think about those personal traits.

Useem: When you were still with Goldman Sachs, a couple of years back, the media often described you as one of the most influential women on The Street. Looking back on your own career—think about the glass ceiling; you helped break it along the way—talk a bit, if you would, about your own experience with the glass ceiling. Reference what it was like when you began, to what you think it is now, for women coming into investment banking.

Johnson: I think the single biggest change for women is that generationally, people think about differences more broadly [and] very differently. The cohort in business school today thinks about gender differences—ethnicity, racial differences, global differences—much differently. They're much more used to dealing in a very diverse world and understanding what the benefits of that are. That has changed in mindset. What hasn't changed—and we have to still continue to push—is you get very different cultural norms and very different value judgments, depending on how diverse a group you get. I find that whenever any one group tends to have a preponderance of influence, or concentration, that always skews the answer—on questions or on modes of behavior. For part of my career at Goldman Sachs, I ran a group in investment banking with another partner—who was an African American, but of African descent. His father actually was an African, from an African country. We had a group that was almost evenly balanced on any metric—gender, ethnicity, race, nationality. I found that our group actually got the best and the brightest, in terms of questions being answered and addressed, problems being addressed, alternative methods of marketing, having insights. I really was still taken by that experience—it clearly had a different cultural vibe than any other group I had worked with at Goldman Sachs.

Useem: [From your vantage point] as an independent, non-executive director on four major boards—it's often said that for non-executive directors, the single most important decision is picking an executive successor as CEO. As of today, what would you look for when there is a succession event—a CEO stepping down. Maybe you asked the person to step out or maybe that person has come to the end of their natural tenure. If you wouldn't mind walking us through the three or four criteria—in light of the events of these past 12 months—that you think would be vital to get the right strategic fit between the person you're looking at, and what one of these companies—or maybe all four of them—would be looking for, going forward.

Johnson: Again, not commenting on any individual company, but just as a general observation, I still find that companies that do the best are the ones where there is a very strong sense of succession planning, and there are multiple internal candidates who could assume the role. Because I do think understanding the culture, having been part of it, having paid your dues, having done the right thing, being rewarded, has incredibly powerful commercial impact—and also has very powerful incentives inside, organizationally. That's not to say that, at times, you don't need to go outside and find the best, because there are circumstances where you need to do that. But on the margin, where you can go inside, I think it's very powerful. In terms of leadership attributes, first and probably most importantly, are they someone who has the kind of strategic vision and articulation—literally, communication capability—to motivate the troops to deliver to that common vision and understand that vision. And to external constituencies, can they make a very compelling enunciation of what the company is all about.

That, again, is reflected in their products, services and people—but that is something that is true north, for both the inside and the outside.

It almost goes without saying that [it should be] someone of impeccable integrity. Related to that is their character. And do they have judgment? Do they have ability to take very tough topics, and, again, 99 out of 100 times, come out in the right place? I say 99 out of 100, because I assume there's always some gray areas where you could go either way. And then do they have courage? Can they do things that other people can't?

Useem: Let's assume you have three—maybe even more—great candidates in the ranks. A chief executive working for you as a non-executive director is about to step down. Or maybe you've got a six-to-12 month notice. People in the ranks at the senior level—they're not there if they're not very good. But you want to find out who is the best. It's often a more difficult challenge than I think we sometimes appreciate. And let's assume that, as a non-executive director, you don't see them day to day—could you offer up a couple of thoughts on how, as a non-executive director, you can cut through the images? Cut through reputations? Help identify, of three final candidates, which of those three best exemplifies the kinds of qualities you've identified?

Johnson: I'd say, first of all, the thing that I don't like that a lot of companies do is they set up horse races for internal candidates where they make it very clear that two, three or four people are in the running. And everybody knows it. I actually think that often causes more damage than it does good. You find that people are play acting for you more than anything else. But I do think [it's important to] find ways to make sure that your pool of potential candidates gets some face time, in a formal sense, presenting to boards, so that you see them over a period of time, [and can] interact in a formal setting. I've also found that, on some boards—where if you make it a constant practice that every time you have a formal board meeting, you're having lunch or breakfast with a different member of the management team, getting to know them kind of one on one, or in a small group with a couple of board members—you get a very different perspective than seeing them in a smaller setting. [You see] how they think about the world. Also, seeing their 360s—and really understanding what the organization thinks about them, not just what the CEO thinks about them—is critically important.

Useem: Suzanne, a final question. As the public looks in on, not just Wall Street, but large corporate compensation packages at the very top, there is a public revulsion—maybe that's too strong a word—but certainly a strong public criticism that for too many people at the top—as their company is going south, their compensation is going north. Aside from that, aside from the poor correlation between pay and performance, many people think that the top people on The Street, the top people in industry in general, are, simply put, overpaid. What's your thinking on that one?

Johnson: That's interesting, Mike. I was with Lester Crown, at the Aspen Institute, maybe 10 or 12 years ago—before executive compensation became a hot topic. He was saying how distressing he found it, as a board member, because clearly the way it was justified is you would look at employment comps of outsiders. And often when you would bring outsiders in, it would raise the whole comp level. He was very disturbed about this practice. I think you can use internal equity as a good touch point, and what I mean by internal equity is really looking at the differentials, from top to bottom, in an organization. I do think no matter how good somebody is at the top, if you see that stratification getting too significant, it is a warning signal to you. It is a red flag. And the other thing I have found—and there's a fair amount of academic literature which absolutely supports this—is that the more unequal you make your compensation structures, the more you pay, in total. Because often people are willing to take lower pay, if they think there is real equity, parity and fairness. The more they think there's unfairness in the system, the more they are chasing somebody who has a higher comp level who they are perceived to be a lot like. Again, I think we do this to ourselves sometimes.

Useem: I'm going to close with an extra question. The next 12 to 18 months are vital in the U.S., vital in Europe—really, the world—for getting through this enormous crisis that we've managed to walk ourselves into. It's sometimes said now that the private sector has helped create some of the problems, but many other forces are responsible, as well. But to dig out of this crisis, [some say] it is a time for government, for agencies, such as Treasury, for regulators, such as the SEC and their equivalentsaround the world, to not get the upper hand, but to take a strong hand in the months ahead. What's your cut on that one?

Johnson: It's clearly important for the government—the public sector—to provide a substrate for the conditions for reform and basically for rejuvenation of the system. But by providing a substrate, I think they need to make a very healthy, functioning private sector because that is where you still are going to have job creation over the longer term. You're going to have people build competitive advantage. And you'll have much healthier systems. So, again, they provide the substrate, but to think that they, alone, could solve this problem would be a mistake. There really does have to be a partnership with the other sectors of the economy. ■

Published: March 18, 2009 in Knowledge@Wharton

PART 9

Key Lessons from the Multinational CEO

From CEO to Senate: Why Some Executives Make Better Politicians than Others

Growing numbers of top business executives appear to be running for political office. Among others, former CEOs Meg Whitman and Carly Fiorina recently won California primaries for governor and senator, respectively, while promising to use leadership skills and financial acumen honed at private corporations to solve thorny public problems. But experts on leadership and politics say that the leap from one world to the other is fraught with challenges. They warn that the ability to rise through the corporate ranks doesn't always translate into an ability to campaign for office. And managing a city or state, let alone entering a legislative body, has challenges and responsibilities that are much different than those of managing a for-profit business.

Michael Useem, a Wharton management professor and director of Wharton's Center for Leadership and Change Management, says some business-leadership skills translate well to the public sphere. "If you have held a prominent role in a substantial business you have learned how to mobilize, motivate and align the work of a lot of people. That ability is a learned skill. It's not natural for most people," he notes. "Equally importantly, as you've risen up in larger firms, you've had to learn how to communicate. You have to communicate persuasively with vision and mission and strategy in your voice." Adds Peter Cappelli, professor of management at Wharton and director of the Center for Human Resources: "General management skills help a lot in running anything, even a political campaign."

Business people who run for public office naturally maintain that their backgrounds are an asset in helping them understand how to run things, create jobs and work within financial constraints. Executives making the switch hope to benefit from the current economic environment and voter anger at traditional politicians. Connecticut Senate candidate Linda McMahon, former CEO of World Wrestling Entertainment, is typical. Her campaign's website boasts: "She isn't a career politician, but she is an outsider with 30 years of real life business experience who understands how to balance a budget and create jobs."

The strong record of New York Mayor Michael Bloomberg inspires many executives to believe that applying business skills to public management can make government work better, experts say. Many are motivated by a desire to give something back to society, and some who have left top corporate jobs crave a return to the spotlight. Business leaders are frequently embraced as candidates by political parties because they usually have substantial fortunes of their own or networks of wealthy potential donors to help fund campaigns. Whitman spent $71 million of her own money to fund her record-sized $81 million Republican gubernatorial primary campaign.

While precise statistics aren't available, it appears that business leaders are increasingly common among the ranks of would-be political leaders. Whitman, who was formerly eBay's chief executive, and Republican nominee for the U.S. Senate Fiorina, former CEO of Hewlett-Packard Co., are only the most prominent new entrants in the field. In Massachusetts, Charles Baker, a health insurance company CEO, captured the Republican nomination for governor. In Colorado, John Hickenlooper, a brew-pub founder who is now mayor of Denver, is running for governor as a Democrat. Ski resort entrepreneur Les Otten recently lost a bid for the Republican nomination for governor of Maine to a candidate backed by the Tea Party movement.

In Florida, Rick Scott, former CEO of health care giant Columbia/HCA, is surging in the polls against an establishment Republican in the race for the party's governor's nomination. Scott has spent more than $15 million so far, and is now regarded as the front-runner in the race. His success comes despite a scandal at the health care chain in the 1990s that resulted in $1.7 billion in company payments to the government over charges of Medicare fraud and payments to doctors. Scott was forced from his job at the time by the company's board of directors, but never faced any personal charges. On the Democratic side in the Sunshine State, investor Jeff Greene (a Harvard MBA) is strongly challenging for the Senate nomination.

Some business leaders have higher ambitions. Bain Capital co-founder Mitt Romney is a front-runner among Republicans eying a presidential campaign for 2012, following a largely successful term as governor of Massachusetts. Romney also sought the presidency in 2008. If he wins this time around, he would become the nation's second president with an MBA, following fellow Harvard Business School alumnus George W. Bush. Bush himself ran the Texas Rangers baseball club before becoming governor of Texas.

The American political system depends on constantly attracting new participants, experts note, but most elected officials have backgrounds in law or as political aides before they start running for low-level offices. Business executives generally plan to short-hop the process by running for top state or national offices. "All these business leaders shoot pretty high," says Marc Meredith, a political science professor at University of Pennsylvania. "You don't see them trying to become lieutenant governor or a state legislator."

At a time of economic pressure, business leaders may have skills that appeal to voters. Wharton insurance and risk management professor Kent Smetters, a deputy secretary in the Treasury department during the George W. Bush administration, says: "It's good to have people who we think of as running public institutions under private sector principles. They're used to thinking about benefits and costs, particularly marginal costs."

Kathleen Hall Jamieson, a professor of communication at the University of Pennsylvania's Annenberg School of Communication and co-author of the forthcoming book, *The Obama Victory: How Media, Money, and Messages Shaped the 2008 Election*, says that experience as a business leader can be a strong credential. "In tough financial times, the assumptions are that a CEO brings skills that are helpful in managing a state," she notes. Meeting a budget and managing to a bottom line both look attractive to voters. Many executives also boast success at creating jobs, an appealing claim at a time when many states have double-digit unemployment.

A Double-edged Sword

But Jamieson says such accomplishments can be a double-edged sword. "The question is: Can you manage an image of efficiency while still showing you're humane?" She notes that almost all executives have laid off workers at some point. Inevitably, some of those laid-off workers will pop up in opponents' commercials to counter the job-creation theme. Jamieson adds that there are many differences between the life of a business leader and the life of a government leader. "First of all, the corporate CEO is largely insulated from the public." Even in a consumer products company, top executives seldom deal with the consumers the way politicians, particularly during a campaign, must interact with voters. "There are layers and layers of communications and marketing people who manage the brand and the image of the CEO."

Moreover, the brand and the person are usually separate. Nobody judges the president of Caterpillar Inc. by how well he operates a back hoe. The CEO of Kmart doesn't have to buy clothes there. But in politics, "the brand is the candidate," Jamieson points out.

Even though CEOs are used to speaking to big crowds, and many have polished their communications skills during years of making presentations to investors and encouraging subordinates and sales forces, those abilities don't always translate to politics. "As a corporate CEO, you can control everything unless some scandal occurs," Jamieson says. Even CEOs who have faced severe criticism during their business careers—like Fiorina, who was ultimately forced to resign from Hewlett-Packard—always had the comfort of "talking to a highly educated group of people about a value they share. The audience brings assumptions about what is good—like making a profit." CEOs running for public office can't assume that voters share the same set of values.

Leadership experts note that the disaster of the BP oil spill in the Gulf of Mexico has illustrated the risks well-meaning executives take when they speak to the press or Congress. Useem points to the angry reaction to the statement by BP chairman Carl-Henric Svanberg: "We care about the small people." While acknowledging that English is a second language for Svanberg, Useem says that politicians "have to be extremely savvy about the nuances." When running for office, he adds, communicating "requires a high emotional intelligence factor. You have to understand how you express your own emotions and understand how people react to what you say."

According to Jamieson, women executives benefit more from their business background than male executives do, because women suffer from a perception that they can't run large operations and don't understand finance. For a candidate for public office, a background as a business leader overcomes that perception. Jamieson's 1995 book, *Beyond the Double Bind: Women and Leadership*, explored the way women leaders are viewed. Women as candidates "benefit from the stereotype that women are more compassionate," she adds. Male CEOs have a harder time proving they care about people—especially when they have a history of layoffs or ruthless takeovers.

Still, even for women, a long history as a leader may contain negative issues. For example, Whitman's compassion has been called into question as a result of reports of an altercation in which she forcefully shoved a subordinate. The parties involved have acknowledged there was an incident but have declined to detail the event. Jamieson notes that stories about "being harsh or rude to subordinates [are] more damaging to women executives." Whitman's campaign has featured commercials with enthusiastic subordinates endorsing her.

Even in areas where business skills look similar to those needed to run a government, politics can make things difficult. Meredith notes that CEOs running for mayor or governor may assume that working successfully with a board of directors gives them the experience needed to work with a legislator or city council. Not so, he says. "The board and the CEO have pretty similar goals" of growth and raising profits. "The legislative body will have a substantial number of people with different goals. It's a much more adversarial relationship." Business leaders, Cappelli says, "are used to telling people what to do—when that's their leadership style—and may do poorly in politics where the goal is to persuade voters to your cause." Legislators also need to be persuaded or negotiated with rather than ordered around.

One former CEO who became a governor says there is little similarity between the roles. Former New Jersey governor, Jon Corzine, who was once CEO of Goldman, Sachs, told Newsweek in February that politicians "don't have the flexibility you imagined. There's no exact translation." He pointed out that states are much bigger than any business. "It's 20,000 people versus nine million. I don't think candidates get the scale and scope of what governing is." Corzine was defeated for reelection for governor last fall by an anti-tax Republican, Chris Christie. Smetters, who followed the race, speculates that if Corzine "had come across as a fiscally conservative guy, trying to protect the taxpayer, he probably would have done a lot better. He under-utilized his business background."

Measuring Success

Measures of success are also different. The metrics for a CEO are fairly clear—such as boosting the stock price, at least faster than rival companies do. Government "is a more ambiguous world," Useem notes. For a strong leader, that can be good. "There's a lot of research that when the world is more ambiguous, the value of effective leadership is stronger. It puts a premium on the art of leadership."

Executives who struggle with the tyranny of a "quarterly report card" on earnings may welcome the longer-term focus that comes with four or six-year terms, Useem says. But the counterpoint is that "you don't have good interim measures of success." Indeed, some business people who go to work for politicians are frustrated to find that their operations are focused largely on daily issues driven by newspaper headlines rather than longer-term plans. In politics, CEOs also lack tools they are used to wielding. Useem notes that "you can't motivate people with payroll." Government salaries generally are set independent of a governor or mayor. While appointed officials may serve at the pleasure of the politician, most employees can't be fired, and legislators can only be threatened with opposition in the next election cycle.

Judging by the polls, many voters are growing increasingly frustrated with professional politicians. And examples like Bloomberg and Indiana governor Mitch Daniels, who once worked as a senior executive at pharmaceutical giant Eli Lilly, appear to demonstrate that some business people can lead significant change. Still, Meredith notes that "businesspeople who think they can just go in and shake things up will be disappointed." ■

Published: June 23, 2010 in Knowledge@Wharton

Wipro's Azim Premji: "Ecology Is One of Our Big Bets for the Future"

Wipro chairman Azim Premji believes that just as the past few decades have been the "Information Age," the next few decades will be the "Ecological Age." And just as he transformed Wipro from a small oil and soap business into a US $6 billion IT and FMCG (fast-moving consumer goods) powerhouse, Premji is now betting on ecology as the next big business opportunity for the group.

Wipro Water and Wipro Eco-Energy were set up in 2008 and 2009 as part of Wipro Infrastructure Engineering (WIE). In a recent company reorganization, Premji has appointed two of his top executives to head these fledgling businesses. Wipro Eco-Energy has been spun off as a separate business unit under the leadership of T.K. Kurien, who was formerly president of Wipro consulting, global programs and strategic initiatives. Pratik Kumar, executive vice-president (human resources), has been given additional charge of WIE, which includes the group's hydraulics and water businesses. In an interview with India Knowledge@Wharton, Premji talks about ecology as a social and business imperative, the vast opportunities that it holds, and Wipro's foray and plans in this space.

An edited transcript of the conversation appears below.

India Knowledge@Wharton: When did you first start thinking of ecology as a business proposition? How did you zero in on the areas of water and eco-energy, and how do these fit in with Wipro's overall gameplan?

Azim Premji: Ecology and economy are becoming inextricably entwined and the world is becoming more conscious of this fact. Despite widely differing perspectives and agendas, there seems to be a remarkable global consensus that has built up over a fairly short period of time that climate change and ecology is one of the truly defining issues for humanity. This is not a 'few quarters trend'; this is something that will build over the next few decades and will become the defining force for all of us. We think that if the past few decades can be characterized as the "Information Age," the next few will be the "Ecological Age."

One of the simplest ways to address this at Wipro—simple, because in a way [that] was within our control—was to try and implement methods and policies which resulted in a positive impact in each of these areas: economy, ecology and society. Hence the idea was that Wipro should go green internally. Next was the question of how we influence our other stakeholders: employees, partners and customers. All of these questions led us to an incremental business opportunity we could create in our existing businesses.

Around January 2007 we narrowed down on ecology as the key strategic socio-economic dynamic that we would invest in. We finally decided on water and renewable energy as two areas within the ecology domain we would evaluate and enter. The choice of ecology has a double benefit: in itself ecological considerations will dramatically change and drive opportunities across the world and secondly, a lot of these factors will also leverage infrastructure growth. Our focus on water and eco-energy does not only make ecological sense, but underlines business sense, as well.

India Knowledge@Wharton: How big do you expect these new businesses to become in the long term for Wipro? Is this Wipro's big bet for the future?

Premji: According to a U.N. report, the global market for environmental products and services is expected to be more than $2 trillion by 2020. Together both the businesses [Wipro Water and Wipro Eco-Energy] currently employ around 300 people and in the last year and a half we have done several key projects for large organizations in the country. We have big plans for this business and believe that it has the potential of becoming a significant business in the next five years. Yes, in that sense, it is one of our big bets for the future.

India Knowledge@Wharton: How much have you invested till now in Water and Eco-Energy and what kind of investments are you looking at making over the next three to five years?

Premji: We have made and will make adequate and significant investments. Whatever investments are required to make these businesses fulfill their promise, we will do.

India Knowledge@Wharton: What areas are you focused on at Wipro Water?

Premji: We have a methodical, step-by-step approach. We are not in a hurry. We are focused on segments where customers value engineering, technology and execution capability. We are in high-purity water segments where we can deliver complete solutions for large and small- scale industrial water treatment, effluent treatment and reuse solutions. We offer desalination solutions also. Over a longer period we will be across multiple segments and geographies.

India Knowledge@Wharton: What is Wipro Eco-Energy focused on and how do you see it evolving?

Premji: We can offer a range of clean energy and energy efficiency technologies customized for specific client situations and integrated with a lot of system intelligence. We consult, engineer, implement, integrate and manage these systems.

In simple terms, we can help build green facilities and infrastructure for you, make your factories green or help manage your service operations to become green. We can do this for a bank, a telecom services company, a steel plant, an airport operator, a tire manufacturing firm, etc. We can do this at a very large (utility) scale or at the scale of smaller facilities.

India Knowledge@Wharton: What is your business model in these two new areas?

Premji: Our business model is primarily that of consulting, engineering, system integration and managed services.

India Knowledge@Wharton: What are the current strengths within the Wipro Group that you believe you can leverage in these two new businesses?

Premji: We understand how to build and manage businesses that involve technology, engineering and people at a large scale on a global platform. Added to this is our focus on process excellence. We also have expertise in systems integration and high-precision manufacturing.

The fact that Wipro has implemented what it preaches helps. By addressing our own energy problems first, we have sharpened our learning in this area. Wipro's 22,000-people campus at Electronic City [in Bangalore] has turned into a test bed. Besides this campus, we have the largest number of LEED (Leadership in Energy and Environmental Design) Gold and Platinum level "green buildings" in India.

India Knowledge@Wharton: Can you share some more details of how you are addressing energy and water issues within Wipro itself?

Premji: Everything that we are offering to customers, we have done ourselves. For example, extensive water treatment in combination with rainwater harvesting ensures that 32% of our total water requirements are met through recycling and harvesting. Implementation of waste-to-energy conversion at our biogas and paper recycling plants in our Electronic City facility are important milestones. [The latest sustainability report is available at http://www.wipro.com/corporate/investors/sustainability-wipro.htm.]

India Knowledge@Wharton: What are the green initiatives within the other businesses of Wipro? What are the key priorities and challenges?

Premji: All of our businesses have their own green offerings. There are three aspects of green in the IT business. We think that 'IT for Green' is far more important than 'Green IT'. IT in itself or IT infrastructure has less than 2% contribution to greenhouse gases or other ecological concerns. The big opportunity for IT is to help mitigate the effect of the other 98%. We will work with customers to create opportunities for their businesses, in the "Ecological Age," using IT. This is where IT can play a real role and this is what we are trying to build on.

Let me give two examples. One, technology-enabled energy management services is integral to intelligent buildings and intelligent buildings are going to be one of the key battle fronts for climate change. We have made significant investments in a smart energy grid along with our technology partners. Two, IT is the heart of "intelligent" devices which can use less or more energy from the grid based on load or other factors. Say you had a refrigerator that would use power based on a combination of the food inside the refrigerator and the load on the grid. This can dramatically increase energy efficiency. Simply put, IT can help improve efficiency of all assets. We will help our customers with this and build on this opportunity.

Our innovation program combines the rigor of process with widely spread (across employee and partner base) sparks of creativity. We have built it over the past seven years. We are now [promoting] 'green' as a big theme in our innovation program. This is a long-term and fundamental investment theme for IT.

In our PC manufacturing business, we have made significant progress on the Green PC on all three dimensions: energy efficiency, RoHS (Restriction of Hazardous Substances Directive) and Take-Back [recycling] program.

In our lighting business, we have the entire range of LED lighting solutions. Already, 70% of LEED-certified buildings in India are lit by Wipro Lighting.

India Knowledge@Wharton: What are your key priorities for Wipro Water and Wipro Eco-Energy?

Premji: [We want] to prepare a sound platform of engineering ability and technology so that we can scale this up over the long term; we are very clear that we are in it for the long haul.

India Knowledge@Wharton: What do you see as the key challenges for Wipro in these new businesses?

Premji: The regulatory environment must execute the policies well and with stability. Also, technology is rapidly evolving in certain segments and we must keep pace with that.

India Knowledge@Wharton: Do you plan to get into equipment manufacturing in these two businesses?

Premji: No plans as of now; however, in the very long view that we have of the businesses, we won't rule anything out completely.

India Knowledge@Wharton: Do you plan to take these businesses global? If so, when?

Premji: Yes, we will. But we will do that after a while.

India Knowledge@Wharton: You have recently spun off Wipro Eco-Energy as a separate business to be headed by T.K. Kurien. What was the thinking behind this move? Will the Water business also be spun off as an independent unit?

Premji: Eco-Energy is a key area of growth and requires that degree of leadership attention. This structure enables the same leadership attention on Water as well. ∎

Published: June 17, 2010 in India Knowledge@Wharton

Roger Farah's Strategy for Polo Ralph Lauren:
Weaving "Left Brain" Discipline with "Right Brain" Creativity

The recession and pullback by American consumers have dealt serious blows to the retailing landscape. Yet while some big names have gone under, Polo Ralph Lauren has emerged unscathed from the wreckage, according to company president and chief operating officer Roger Farah, who recently spoke on campus during the University of Pennsylvania's Fashion Week, an event co-sponsored by Wharton. "Where others were groaning under the weight of loans and borrowed money and working capital constraints, we continued to invest during the last crisis. We did not take our foot off the gas pedal at all."

To hear Farah tell it, Polo Ralph Lauren's ambitions have hardly been dampened by the turbulence of the last two years. The $5 billion company is now making a major push into the Asia-Pacific region. After buying back licenses to the company's products in Japan, China, Hong Kong, Singapore and the rest of Asia, Farah is preparing to build a powerful operation there that he expects will generate one third of the company's revenues in 10 years. "We are on a 10-year path to reinvent ourselves in Asia," Farah stated.

Succeeding will require the perfect union of what Farah called "left brain/right brain creativity." And in many ways that is what Farah's partnership with founder Ralph Lauren has been all about. Started 43 years ago when Ralph Lauren began with a simple line of ties, Polo Ralph Lauren evolved into a mega-brand that represented an almost Great Gatsby-like American lifestyle. The company went public in 1997 but immediately stumbled, missing earnings estimates. The stock, which hit the market at $33, was mired in the teens when Lauren hired Farah in 2000.

Farah brought a heavy dose of left brain business acumen to Polo Ralph Lauren. Fresh off his job as chairman of Venator Group, the company that would eventually become Foot Locker, Farah began upgrading the less sexy but critical aspects of the business, including supply chain management, technology and distribution. He also began the process of reclaiming control of the Ralph Lauren brand, buying back licenses for the company's products in Europe and other markets. "We had 1,000 employees when I joined in 2000, and now we have 18,000," Farah said in an interview with Knowledge@Wharton before his speech. "We developed the management, and we have the balance sheet and talent to run all these businesses now."

Polo Ralph Lauren today is an amazingly complex machine, he noted. "It is manufacturing, transportation and logistics; currency hedging and financial controls, as well as all the things that go into what the customer actually sees." The company has what Farah described as a pyramid of brands, with Ralph Lauren's expensive runway collection at the top. That collection, which includes handmade products using the best materials, has limited distribution. Suits, sportswear and other premium items occupy the middle of the pyramid, and products designed for Kohl's and JC Penney are on the lower rung. The company produced 175 million products last year in 45 countries and shipped them to more than 9,500 different points of distribution around the world.

On top of that, Polo Ralph Lauren handles advertising and store design in-house, requiring a large internal advertising team and an army of architects and design professionals who not only design the stores and displays for the company's products, but also scour the world for antiques and flea market finds to make those settings unique. "I can stand here with great confidence and tell you nobody who has stood here before me has ever [handled] that kind of complexity," Farah told the crowd.

The level of intricacy will only grow as the company begins its offensive in Asia. Farah is hoping to replicate the success Polo Ralph Lauren has had in Europe. After buying back some core apparel and accessory licenses there 10 years ago, the company pumped hundreds of millions of dollars into its operations and built a business that had been just a couple hundred million dollars into a nearly billion dollar operation. On April 15, the company opened a 13,000 square-foot flagship in an historic district in Paris. The progress came despite skepticism that Lauren's distinctly American image would play well overseas. Farah noted that the brand now portrays less of an American-centric ideal and more of an "aspirational lifestyle" in general. Still, he acknowledged the company is wrestling with how to penetrate the Asian market, a push he said will require customizing some products, from color to fit, for clients in that region.

Of all the challenges Asia presents, however, finding the right people to lead the charge is one of the greatest, Farah stated. To build and manage the business he envisions there, Farah calculates that Polo Ralph Lauren will need an army of thousands of people. "We talk about attracting and developing talent, [but] it is easier to talk about than to do." That's one reason he advised students in attendance to think about what the growth of Asia means for their own careers. "When I talk to young people at our company, I say part of our strategy is global, and that may mean over time an opportunity for you to work internationally. They all say 'Great, I'd love to go to London or Paris'. Well yes, but there may be other parts of the world that have opportunities as well."

Riding Out the Recession

Polo Ralph Lauren's ambitions for Asia aside, Farah also acknowledged that the recession has had an impact on the company. Net revenues for the first nine months of fiscal 2010 were down 4% to $3.6 billion, due in large part to the broad drop in consumer spending. Still, the company's financial footing is solid with $1.3 billion in cash and short term investments on hand. In February, the company announced full year revenue would decline by a low single-digit rate— better than the mid single digit figure expected earlier.

The turmoil of the last two years is certainly impacting how people spend their money, Farah added. "I think the real change in this is not the wealthy customer spending money differently. It is the customer who was operating on borrowed resources. Whether it was excessive credit card debt or home equity loans, [spending by] the segment of the population that was spending today because tomorrow was going to be better has changed. I think people will spend more in line with what their real income and prospects are." And that, he said, will be a long-term positive factor for the U.S. economy. "The U.S. savings rate will go up. I think it had gone negative in 2007 and 2008, which means people were spending more than they were making. The U.S. was the only developed nation in the world [in that position]."

Farah suggested that the reach of Polo Ralph Lauren's brands from high end couture to mass market retailers, like Kohl's, positions the company well for that shift. "We were already balanced in a way that allowed us to capture changing consumer sentiment," he noted. "We did not change prices and we did not change marketing or distribution strategies. We obviously managed our balance sheet and our expenses carefully. And we probably shifted some capital to international opportunities. So we are spending proportionally more internationally and less domestically."

While Farah considers himself the left brain discipline to founder Ralph Lauren's right brain creativity, he also has a true love of the retail world. He told the crowd that back in 1974 when he left Wharton for a job at Saks Fifth Avenue (he finished his studies early but returned in 1975 for the formal graduation ceremony at the urging of his mother), most of his fellow students were headed to Wall Street or consulting jobs. He figures his starting salary—$8,600 a year—was one half to one third of what others in his class were earning. "A lot of people thought I was crazy. I took a path that was unproven and untested." But Farah said he knew it was the right road for him. "One of the things that was clear to me was I wanted a diversified day. And over the course of my career what has been particularly satisfying to me was I had a hand in marketing, finance, design and distribution."

He insisted that retail was also a great place to test yourself. "Retailing at the time was one of the few businesses where you could operate a fully integrated [company] at 23 or 24 years old. You had product, marketing, distribution and a P&L [profit and loss] statement. Here's your name and here are your results. I thought that was important." He started out at Saks and was president of Rich's/Goldsmith's Department Stores by the time he was in his mid-thirties. After years with Federated Department Stores, including some of that time running Macy's, Farah left to head up struggling retailer F.W. Woolworth. In 1997, Farah shuttered the remaining Woolworth stores, focused the company on its Foot-locker franchise and renamed the business Venator Group. In 2000, he made the leap to Polo Ralph Lauren.

Having witnessed the end of a once great retailer like Woolworth, Farah noted that Polo Ralph Lauren's longevity is a rarity. "I was a student here in the mid 1970s, and unfortunately most of the brands that were important then are no longer in business. Part of the reason for that was they did not properly control the distribution and pricing of their brand." As for the greatest challenge facing Polo Ralph Lauren today, "Our risk is really in the execution," Farah said. "While we have executed well to this point, we are looking to do some pretty big things. And as a company I think one of our in-house challenges is [asking whether] we are taking on too much at once." ■

Published: May 12, 2010 in Knowledge@Wharton

Hu Xiongqing, President of Akiyama International, on How to Manage a Multinational Company

Amid China's rapid economic growth and the increasing trend toward globalization, more and more Chinese companies are eyeing overseas acquisitions. But mergers and acquisitions represent a complicated process, and post-acquisition integration often proves difficult. Along the way, many Chinese companies—from electric appliances giant TCL to automaker Shanghai Auto— have learned important lessons about how to map out a global strategy, adjust to the international legal environment, overcome obstacles to reform, bridge cultural differences and allocate resources.

Shanghai Electric Group (SEG) is the largest industrial equipment manufacturing group in China, with more than 60 core firms, net assets of 152 billion RMB and more than 40,000 employees worldwide. Printing Machinery is one of its six business units. Faced with heated competition home and abroad, SEG identified advanced technology and international market experience as part of its acquisition strategy. In 2001, SEG's $9 million acquisition of the Tokyo-based Japan Akiyama Printing Machinery Company received significant attention, largely because of its successful integration of the acquired entity.

Hu Xiongqing, a Chinese native and CEO of the printing machinery business unit of SEG, was heavily involved in the deal and was appointed president of the new company, which was renamed Akiyama International Co., Ltd. after the acquisition and remains based in Tokyo.

In the five years since the deal, the new Akiyama International has booked $500,000 in sales per person, up from $250,000; profit margins have exceeded 20%; and, most importantly, morale among the Japanese employees at Akiyama has risen to what it had been before the acquisition. Hu Xiongqing is a well-known turnaround expert in the domestic printing industry. Akiyama International was the fourth printing enterprise he has helped during the last 20 years, following one in the city of Wuhu and two in Shanghai. Hu now spends his time between Shanghai and Tokyo. In an interview with Knowledge@Wharton, Hu talked about his experience in managing a multinational enterprise.

Knowledge@Wharton: Why was Akiyama picked as the acquisition target?

Hu: Founded in 1948 as a family business, Japan Akiyama evolved into the No. 6 manufacturer of printing machinery in the world and No. 3 in Japan. At its peak, it employed 460 people and generated 18 billion yen in sales. Although its scale was still small-to-mid-size, its technology was among the best in the world. It had more than 50 patents. In 1995, Japan Akiyama invented a double-page, color printer and that printer has had a stable market share ever since. The technology and markets enjoyed by Japan Akiyama can complement what

Shanghai Electricity Group has, and that's why it makes it an ideal target for us.

Knowledge@Wharton: Had Shanghai Electricity Group already thought about becoming global?

Hu: Our plan is to build in Shanghai an internationally recognized manufacturing base for printing machinery and to build in Japan a R&D center and a global sales center. To realize these goals, the company needs to invest a lot in R&D and to hire top management talent. Going forward, Akiyama International's strategy is this: The Japanese and the Chinese will gradually move toward producing mid-level printing machines together, while the Japanese headquarters will retain its leading position in R&D. Continued investment in R&D and the advantage associated with "made in Japan" will guarantee Akiyama International's global strategy.

The goals set by Akiyama International are, first, to continue expanding its market share in Japan; second, to develop China's and other markets, and third, to develop products that are high quality but low cost. If the combination of "China's low-cost advantage" and "Japan's high-quality advantage" can prove very competitive, Akiyama International is right on track to establish an international standard. In addition, the continued inflow of talent will constitute the core of its sustainable development.

Knowledge@Wharton: What kind of changes did you make after taking over Akiyama International?

Hu: We reformed the way employees get paid. Instead of looking at how long they have been with the company, we advocate looking at how big of a contribution they make to the company. After the reform, though some employees have seen their salaries decrease, overall their salaries have gone up. Those measures have greatly motivated employees to improve their efficiency and competency levels.

We then reformed the personnel function. We made some adjustments to Japan's traditional "life-long employment" system and reviewed the performance of all the employees at Akiyama International. Some of them were let go due to their poor performance. For instance, we fired a manager responsible for procurement. At the same time, we promoted some young people to key posts. The average age of the managers at Akiyama International used to be 60 years old. Post-acquisition, through internal training, promotion and hiring, [we now have] a group of managers in their 30s.

We also took measures to reduce production costs. Akiyama International had long pursued technological advancement at the expense of costs, thereby leading to persistently high production costs pre-acquisition. At that time, the company didn't shop around for materials and never did comparison shopping.

After the acquisition, lowered production costs helped drive up profit margins from a negative number to 20%.

Knowledge@Wharton: Have you encountered any obstacles while making those changes? And how did you deal with those obstacles?

Hu: Initially, there was some resistance on the part of the Japanese employees. The most effective way to overcome that is "communication." We made it clear to them that their own opportunities lie with Akiyama International and that they are not only employees of the company but also its owners.

At the same time, we made sure that everything we do is fair and objective, which helped us establish management's credibility. Lastly, the very fact that Akiyama International turned profitable proves the strongest evidence of our reforms' effectiveness.

Knowledge@Wharton: What do you think are the key cultural differences between Japanese companies and Chinese companies? Have those differences in any way affected your ability to run the company? And how do you deal with it?

Hu: Key to us is to pay enough attention to the cultural differences and to understand the Japanese culture, which centers on perfection and excellence. The biggest difference between the two cultures lies in the way we go about doing businesses and the degree of seriousness.

Of the 170 employees at Akiyama International, only three are Chinese, with the rest Japanese. So the Chinese managers have to do their best to respect and recognize their culture without appearing weak or too compromising. We stick to our principles, as evidenced by the measures we took to reform the personnel system. At the same time, we emphasize communication as a way to reduce any resistance to our reform efforts.

Knowledge@Wharton: How did you manage to retain and motivate the Japanese employees?

Hu: Shanghai Electricity managed to both retain existing employees and encourage those who had already left to come back. There were only 53 employees remaining at Akiyama International under the acquisition contract. But on the first day of operation, the number of employees exceeded 70 and the company has been hiring employees back ever since. The number of employees has reached about 160 so far. To expand further, Akiyama International plans to hire more locally, including both Japanese and the Chinese who are studying here.

Knowledge@Wharton: How have you allocated resources to achieve efficiency?

Hu: The efficiency is first reflected through costs. After Akiyama International was bought by Shanghai Electricity, it naturally adopted China's low-cost advantage. The reduction in supply costs has helped its profit margin. In the meantime, the combination of Shanghai Electricity's cost advantage and Akiyama International's technology advantage positioned the company to compete better in China's printing business.

A second measure of efficiency is human resources. Post-acquisition, there has been greater cooperation between Shanghai Electricity's own printing unit and Akiyama International. With its relatively advanced core technology, Akiyama International periodically sends its engineers to the Chinese unit to share their technological know-how. The Chinese unit also periodically sends people to Akiyama International to be trained there. The parent company also organizes frequent communication between the two, with the Japanese appointed as chief technology officers and the younger Chinese working with them.

A third measure of efficiency is production management. While we thoroughly reduced the production costs at Akiyama International, we also improved our management skills by learning from the [employees there]. For instance, the Japanese employees have demonstrated a greater level of professionalism than the Chinese. So we enhanced our evaluation of Chinese employees' performance and better motivated them to improve their efficiency.

Knowledge@Wharton: How do you define success?

Hu: As a professional manager, career for me tops everything and I'm very loyal to my career. My success will be reflected in the company's position in the industry, its recognition by customers, its return to shareholders and its contribution to employees' lives.

Knowledge@Wharton: What kind of advice would you give other Chinese managers of foreign enterprises?

Hu: They must be willing to learn and work hard. There are enormous things for a Chinese manager to learn when he or she faces managing a multinational company, but the time for learning is also very limited. Meanwhile, a company's success depends on teamwork, and it's especially true when it comes to a multinational company. So the manager must have the ability to bring everybody together. It's management, and art, too. Lastly, I want to repeat my own management philosophy: There is no lackluster employee, only a lackluster manager. ∎

Published: May 23, 2006 in Knowledge@Wharton

Bill George's "Authentic Leadership": Passion Comes from People's Life Stories

Bill George, probably best known in the business community for his former position as chairman and CEO of Medtronic, is also an author. In 2003 he published a book called, *Authentic Leadership: Rediscovering the Secrets to Creating Lasting Value*. This month he published his second book titled, *True North: Discover Your Authentic Leadership*, described by George and his co-author Peter Sims as a way to "locate the internal compass that guides you successfully through life." George is also a professor of management practice at Harvard Business School. He has been recognized as Executive-of-the-Year by the Academy of Management, Director-of-the-Year by the National Association of Corporate Directors and was included in a book by Knowledge@Wharton called *Lasting Leadership: What You Can Learn from the Top 25 Business People of Our Times*. We asked him and Michael Useem, director of Wharton's Center for Leadership and Change Management, to talk with us about authentic leadership, both the book and the concept.

Knowledge@Wharton: How is this book different from the hundreds and hundreds of other leadership books out there?

George: This is a book on leadership development that results from the largest study ever done on how leaders develop. We had about 3,000 pages of transcripts that came out of 125 interviews with people who we deemed to be successful and authentic leaders. We were very surprised by what they were telling us, because we thought that going in they were going to tell us the traits, characteristics and leadership styles that made them successful.

And, instead what they told us was that their passions came from their life stories. It took a little while for this to sink in. At first it seemed like mush. But the more we got into it, it was so consistent that people wanted to talk about how they captured their passions from a crucible life experience, a transforming experience or just a "growing up" experience.

An example of that is Dick Kovacevich, the chairman and CEO of Wells Fargo and arguably the most successful commercial banker in the last 20 years, in terms of his record. He didn't want to talk about that. He wanted to talk about what it was like growing up in a saw mill town, where people are losing their jobs and no one had ever gone to college. He played sports three hours a day and he said that he learned a lot more about leadership on the athletic field and working in a corner grocery store where he also worked three hours a day, than he ever did at Stanford Business School.

He has tried to take that model and translate it into Wells Fargo. In other words, he saw the idea of trying to make Wells Fargo the most consumer friendly bank in every small town; not just to "be big at global banking" but to be very friendly and to also create an executive team with people much stronger than he was. He has said, "If you had 11 quarterbacks on your football team, you would lose every game." And so he has tried to create a team of people who are really good in every other position, and I think he has been quite successful.

Useem: Bill, I like the phrase that you just used which is that leadership does emerge out of a life story. You referenced moments that are like crucibles of experience. As you listened to the 125 people tell their story and talk about those formative moments, is there a common pattern to what really seemed to stand out? Or are there a couple of themes that stand out when people begin to talk about those moments, when they really made in a sense that self-discovery and came to appreciate where they were heading in life?

George: I can't help but think it's a situation that causes you to go deep inside yourself and say, "Who am I? Who am I in this world? Where do I fit? Do I matter?" And then from that, you can find your passions to lead and that's where the passions to lead come from. At least that's what we learned.

Andrea Jung had this incredible passion for empowering women in her life, because of coming out of this very strict Chinese family. And, you know one time she was destined to be CEO of Neiman Marcus. At 31 she got the Executive V.P. job; she quit cold turkey, four years later, and went off without having another job. A year later she joined Avon because she said she didn't want to just provide luxury goods to the upper 1/10th of 1% of American women.

As soon as she went to Avon and made it to the top, she changed the mission from cosmetics to empowering women. This was her passion. So now, you listen to her talk [she came to my classroom] about having a million people who work for her in Brazil and how exciting it is to go down the Amazon and everyone waits for the retail store to come to them. You see her passion. She said, "If I don't have the passion for this business, I can't be an authentic leader."

Useem: Let me make this personal here. You led Medtronic for 10 years. Medtronic, as I recall, in revenue was 10 times the size when you stepped down after 10 years as chief executive compared to when you began. So, surely in your own background, there is one of those crucible moments. What is the essence of your life story that helped you prepare for those 10 years at Medtronic?

George: Mike, I talk in the book about my life as a "series of crucibles." It started out, I guess as a 3-year-old, when my father saw himself as not successful and wanted me to be CEO of a big company, but said "don't be like me son." So, I was carrying that forward for the next 20, 30, 40 years. It's very hard not to be like your father, but thinking that I wanted to be CEO of a really big company.

And, I remember running for office in high school and college—seven times and losing every time. This was because it was all about me; it was all about my ambition and getting ahead. And finally, a group of seniors [I went to Georgia Tech] pulled me aside and said, "You know, Bill, there's a reason why you're losing these elections and it's because no one wants to follow you because you're not interested in them." That was easy to understand intellectually. It was much harder to internalize and to try to develop myself.

In my mid 20s, I had two very traumatic experiences that brought me to the marrow of life. One was my mother's death at 24. I was very close to my mother, not my father. She died suddenly and I never got the chance to say good-bye. I'm an only child and I was very much alone. Eighteen months later, I was engaged to be married and happy as can be and thought I had the world made. Three weeks before my wedding date, my fiancée died of a malignant brain tumor. It was totally unexpected. She had been having headaches, but it was diagnosed as something else. She was gone and again, I felt very much alone.

But this also caused me to reflect deeply about what life is all about and what I want my leadership to be about. Even so, I still had this propensity to go off and track this goal of being a CEO.

I remember going to Honeywell, a great global company and being on course to be CEO and taking on a series of turnarounds. Finally, I looked at myself in the mirror, one day, coming home on a beautiful day like today; it was in the fall, and I was miserable. 'Why am I miserable, when I think I'm supposed to be happy?' I went and talked to my wife about it and she said, "Well, I've been trying to tell you this for a year. You just didn't want to listen." And I realized that I was just chasing my ego of having the CEO's title of a major global corporation.

Three times I had passed up the opportunity to go to Medtronic, to be president of the company. This was because I thought that it was maybe too small for my ego. And I went back and talked to the folks at Medtronic. I talked to Earl Bakken, the founder and realized that this was a wonderful company, with a mission that I can embrace and values that I can embrace. I remember walking into Medtronic for the very first day in April of 1989 and I felt like I was coming home.

As my favorite folk singer John Denver says, "I was coming home to a place where I've never been before." It just felt like a place where I could be me. I can be alive and I can be who I am and people appreciate who I am. I don't have to be something different than what I am. I can be the authentic me. And, it never changed for the next 12 to 13 years. I feel blessed to have been there. It was just a thrill to have the opportunity and the company did far better than I ever anticipated it would.

Knowledge@Wharton: Maybe I could ask a very obvious sort of question. What is an authentic leader and how do you become one?

George: I think that it is very straightforward. You have to be yourself. You have to be the genuine person and you have to recognize that 'I'm a unique person and so I'm not trying to be like you. I'm trying to be who I am'. But you have to develop yourself as a leader. And that is why we wrote True North, because my first book Authentic Leadership did not tell people how to develop themselves. If you want to understand the purpose of your leadership, you have to gain a deep level of self-awareness. You can't just, as we say at Harvard, "follow the herd" and everyone is going into this profession or that one. You have to decide what it is you want.

Knowledge@Wharton: They say that at Wharton, too.

George: Good.

George: And you have to test your values under pressure. You know, anyone can tell you that they have good values. They can even practice good values when everything is going well. That's pretty easy. It's when you are really under pressure and you deviate from your "true north." Why? Because you're getting so much pressure from Wall Street, or you get seduced by big stock option gains and keeping your stock prices up. Do you hang in there and stay true to what you believe in under pressure?

It has to do with how do you lead? Do you lead from the heart or purely from the head? Are you chasing money, fame, power and glory? Or, can you balance those motivations, which all of us have to some extent, I certainly do, with the intrinsic motivations of making a difference in the lives of others, helping to develop people —and maybe changing the world. You know, like Bill Gates is trying to change the world with his contributions to Third World/developing countries with diseases.

And so I think it is really important, not that we should eschew the values or the motivations of extrinsic [forces], but we also need to have something at the end of the day that makes a difference. I think it's about how you build relationships.

Useem: So, Bill, once you have the place that you want to be in, that you've come to understand who you are, authenticity is a great phrase to capture the essence of being who you are, bringing out the best and using the best of the talent that you bring to a setting. You also write, though, about the importance of helping people in a setting to understand the significance of what they're doing and the meaning for which they come to work every day.

At Medtronic, not that it was easier there than anywhere else, but there was an advantage that you had there. This was that people working for you did take pride in the fact that people on earth are walking around alive today and this is because they have an Medtronic pacemaker. The meaning was pretty obvious there.

As you get away from medical products, maybe from medicine in general, could you talk a bit about how people in your kind of position can infuse the workplace with that kind of meaning to help people appreciate the significance of what they are doing, when it's not obvious that there is that kind of meaning or significance to the work that they are engaged in?

George: One of the people that we interviewed is Dave Dillon, the chairman and CEO of Kroger. Dave told us about his desire to and how he leads to bring people together around a common purpose of making everyone's life a little bit better that day in the Kroger Store. And that sounds really simple, almost simplistic.

But you know it gets carried out when you go and approach the stock boy and he walks you four aisles down to help you find what you want rather than just say, "It's over there." And it's that caring thing that he makes his employees—they are minimum wage employees, many of them—feel like they made someone's day a little bit better. That's a rallying point.

Howard Schultz has that rallying point at Starbucks by creating a safe place for people to come and where you can establish a relationship between the employees and the customers. You know they aren't saving any lives. It's $3.50 for a cup of coffee. But they really feel like they're creating that kind of environment. So, I think that it can be translated into everyone.

Back to my first example, Dick Kovacevich. He feels like "When people come to our bank, we don't want to just give you that home loan. We actually want to talk to you about, have you thought about building up a savings account for your kids so that they can go to college?" He feels that they are doing them a favor by helping them build a secure financial future.

So, I think it's not limited to the more dramatic things like saving lives, but I think that is the leaders' job in this century. It's not telling people what to do; it's bringing them together around a shared context, a shared set of values and then empowering them to lead. I think far too often we've had the idea of people in organizations taking direction or following the leader's guidance. I think today the great leaders are figuring out that context, but then being able to empower other people to lead at all levels of their organization and even people who have no direct report.

Useem: You know in your observation of people that you worked with at Medtronic, you serve on a couple of boards now at major U.S. firms, as you work with MBA students, everybody is drawn to work because of the need for a salary, good compensation, promotion opportunities and getting ahead. You're saying though, I think if I hear it correctly, at the end of the day, or maybe even at the beginning of the day, ultimately people do come for purpose and significance. Is that a fair summary?

George: They're looking for meaning and significance. And frankly, they have options to work somewhere else. They aren't locked into work for your organization. And, most of them are never going to be millionaires. We think about all of the people, when you are around business school students, they all think that they are going to be wealthy. But the vast majority of people working at organizations are never going to be wealthy.

But they want to feel like, "Hey my time was well spent. It wasn't just a job." You spend more time at work than you do at anything else in your life, including sleeping. Don't you have a right to meaning and significance? So, at the end of the day, whether you've made a billion dollars, or you've put away just enough for your grandkids' college education, what are you going to leave behind?

Useem: Let me ask a two-part question here. Near the end of the book you say, "The hardest person to lead is yourself." And then you also add a piece of advice which is, "Don't wait to be asked to lead." So, could you expand on both of those statements?

George: In my study of leaders who have failed—and I've studied a lot of the leaders and I've known a lot of the leaders that have failed—in every case, it wasn't that they lacked the ability to lead others; they lacked the ability to lead themselves. A guy like Dick Grasso could have been a great leader, but he got so caught up with needing the money, not because he needed the money to live on. He didn't live on it. He needed it for prestige. He couldn't lead himself. It's just a tragedy to see this happen to people who are otherwise excellent leaders, but they just get so caught up in that.

But I think you never learn about yourself until you get into the game. Maybe you can do it through college leadership experience; maybe you do it through an outward bound experience. But you got to get in there in business and do it and not just stand on the sidelines and wait to be tapped on the shoulder or do brilliant analysis. I'm really encouraging people to get down there, get roughed up a little bit and make some mistakes. The game looks a lot different when you're in it and you get a bloody nose. And so, learn to fail early rather than fail at the top. Fail early and bounce back—and learn from that. Failure is not a bad thing. It's an opportunity to learn from your experiences.

Useem: So if a young person working for you says, "I hear what you are saying. I should get into the game. I shouldn't wait to be asked to take on a leadership responsibility. What does that tangibly mean in the office or on the floor of the company?"

George: Well, it depends on how you see your role. I mean if you're a creative, innovative person, go and innovate and say, "Hey, I have this great idea. Will you give me money to fund it for the next six months, just to get it going?" You know maybe you're out working with your customers and you have an insight about that or how to develop that customer base. Or maybe you're a manufacturing person and you see why the quality is repeatedly a problem in this product and you take the initiative.

I think we need organizations where people are rewarded for that kind of initiative, not punished because they're the ones who know the most about the work. The reality today is that the people doing the work know a lot more about their jobs than their bosses ever will.

And so, it's not up to the boss to tell them how to do it; we don't have an apprenticeship system anymore. But how else are you going to learn until you can make some mistakes and learn that it's really okay? The world didn't come to an end. 'It's not because I'm a bad person that we made mistakes—no. We tried out this new product, we put it out to market and it didn't work. Hey, maybe we can go out and learn why it didn't work'.

Earl Bakken, the founder of Medtronic, has a philosophy and he calls it, "Ready, Fire, Aim." Get ready, do your plan, but then jump into the market, fire off, get out there, get feedback from your customers and then adjust your aim. In other words, adjust your plan. If it didn't work, how can we adjust it to do a lot better, rather than plan, plan, plan or aim, aim, aim for years—and then by the time you get into the game, like when many big companies do, the market has passed you by.

I mean look at the products coming out of Silicon Valley. A lot of those are quite imperfect when they first come out. But they have Rev 1, Rev 2. You know they're continually being improved and they just get better and better. And, if you get into the game late, you never know quite where to get in, because the leader keeps getting ahead of you.

Knowledge@Wharton: This book seems to be doing well and is getting good reviews. Why do you think that it resonates so much with readers?

George: I think that people want to be authentic and I think they want to know how. And, unlike my first book which didn't tell them how, this book has a whole series of exercises and I think it gives them the opportunity to take responsibility for their own development. Too often we thought of leadership as something that you're born with and I reject that idea. Of course you're born with gifts, but you have to develop yourself.

To me, it's much like a championship athlete or a great cellist who wants to play at Carnegie Hall. These days, you can qualify to play at Carnegie Hall if you're 15 years old because they have the screen, so they can't see how young you are or you're a female or that you're a minority. You get selected on the basis of your own playing ability. But you wouldn't think about going there unless you practiced every day, would you? You wouldn't think about riding in the Tour de France unless you practiced every day.

Well, it's the same thing with leaders. They need to practice leadership. I think for too long we've been going off to company training programs and they tell us how to do it. All they are doing is socializing us and trying to bring us in line to conform to the company's norms. And, you will find that most of the great leaders are standard deviations outside the company's norms because they don't conform. And so by forcing people to conform, we get a nice happy social place—but nothing ever happens.

And so I think we need to empower people to develop themselves. Now that needs help. You need a mentor. You need a support team around you. You need to avail yourself of the resources out there, either the academic resources or the educational resources in your company. You need to ask for the experience to get into the game. But until you do that, I don't think that you can really test your leadership and learn whether you can lead and learn from your experiences.

Knowledge@Wharton: One of the things I have found very interesting about your book is that you went out and talked to people who are leaders at different ages. I wondered when you spoke to people who were in their 60s and 70s, whether they approached leadership differently than people who are in their 20s and 30s and who were also leaders.

George: We looked at a minimum of 15 people per decade. And actually the differences were less than we thought because there was clearly a context. But I think that the leadership journey is now widely appreciated as changing. In the old days, in our parent's generation, they were darn glad to have a job. They had come out of a Depression and two World Wars. So they went to work for a company when they were 22, became loyal to the company picked up their pension at 62 or 65 and the 40-year-pin—and they went off and retired and probably died before they were 70.

Today all of that has changed. People are going to change jobs/change companies seven to eight times during their lifetime. But the journey is different. Most people, here at Wharton and other places aren't starting their real career until they are about 30. They're getting great experiences. They may work for Morgan Stanley or Goldman Sachs or Bain or McKinsey or private equity—but they aren't really plunging into their real career until they are 30.

So, they have 30 years as we see it and then we have Phase 2. The first 30 years is preparation and the next 30 years is you are actually leading and generally it is with one organization. But many of these older people now are no longer retiring and going to Florida. They're going into a period of wisdom and generativity—so they want to continue to keep giving back.

But typically they leave their principal career leadership post and have the opportunity to spread that leadership across many different fields. This is whether it's through teaching or through a community service organization or whether it's serving on boards, whether it's through investing in companies or whether it's through writing and sharing their wisdom. I think it's a wonderful thing.

We had John Whitehead the other day, the former chairman of Goldman Sachs, at one of my kick-off events. He has been in every field that you can imagine. He's been head of 12 non-profits. But John, who is going to be 85, is still going strong. He's still taking on assignment after assignment because he is so passionate about trying to change leadership.

Knowledge@Wharton: In 2003, when you published Authentic Leadership, you wrote an article in Fortune Magazine, in which you said that "The business world had run off the rails, mistaking wealth for success and image for leadership". You said "My generation of CEOs began listening to the wrong people, Wall Street analysts, media pundits, economists, compensation consultants, public relations experts and hedge funds—all the players in what I call the game." Isn't this even truer these days than it was four years ago?

George: It's true that those pressures are stronger than they were four years ago, certainly with hedge funds, the power of private equity and the shortening of holding periods of stock. But I think the new group of CEOs who I call the post-Enron CEOs—people like Sam Palmisano at IBM or Anne Mulcahy at Xerox or Jeff Immelt at GE—these people have a totally different view. They know that if they play that game, by somebody else's rules, that they will lose. And so, they are steeling themselves to say, "No, we're going to do what we want to do. Here's the way we are going to run our company. And, we hope that you'll buy the stock, because it's going to be a great long-term investment."

A good example of this is Jeff Immelt at GE. He was just ranked and his company is the most admired company. And yet, for the five to six years he has been in office, the stock price hasn't moved. But everyone sees the wisdom in which he is developing people, restructuring the business, putting emphasis on innovation, technology, new businesses like Ecoimagination and focusing on customers. There's a general acceptance that this is a very wise thing to do and he gets the admiration of a lot of people, myself included.

I think that this is true of a lot of this new group of CEOs—not my generation; it's the new generation. So I'm very encouraged by the kind of leadership that they are providing. Look, there are always going to be the bad actors. They are the people who I would call the takers as opposed to givers. Immelt and Mulcahy, these people are givers. They see leadership as service and building a great organization that can serve people. If you were to offer Immelt a bundle of money to go to private equity, there is no way that he would do it. He wants to build a great organization that can serve society and humanity.

But, you have the takers; they just want to get as much out of it as they can. They flip from one company to the next. They go get a big fancy contract and they blow out of their companies and pick up a $100 million termination and severance. And I don't know why we are choosing them as leaders. They are not the kind of people that we should choose. They don't help the employees; they don't help the customers and they don't help the shareholders.

And in the end, it's all a facade, this talking about shareholder value. It's really their value that they are trying to build. So, I have a real concern that boards often still don't do their job of internal succession and they wind up being forced to go outside. They'll hire someone with a contract, a no cut contract for failure. That is why the public is so upset by executive compensation. If we don't get on top of this, there are going to be laws passed regulating compensation and we're going to have more and more problems. And so, we in the business community—and that's one reason why I wrote the book—need to step up and lead. ■

Published: March 28, 2007 in Knowledge@Wharton

Mundivox's Alberto Duran: "My Biggest Problem Is Creating Middle Management."

Alberto Duran, founder and CEO of Mundivox Communications of Brazil, has seen the world of telecommunications from various perspectives. He worked in the telecom sector for J.P. Morgan in New York, and Bain & Company and Monitor Company in Boston and London. He specialized in the development of strategies for major industry players worldwide, including privatizations and M&A in North America, Europe, and Asia. In 1999, Duran founded Mundivox Communications in Brazil. In an interview with Knowledge@Wharton, he talks about the troubled environment in the wake of the slowdown and the key issues in managing a company that is growing at an astonishing 100% a year.

An edited transcript of the conversation appears below:

Knowledge@Wharton: What has been the impact of the global financial crisis on Brazil?

Alberto Duran: That depends [on if you're asking about the] short term or long term. In the short term, it has been incredible what has happened with the [real-dollar] exchange rate. Some say it is good—that it is a natural path, because the real was overvalued. The real was at 1.60, 1.55 during the summer [though it went up to 2.4 by December]. These are incredible numbers that we have not seen for so many years. Remember that right before Lula [President Luiz Inacio Lula da Silva] was elected for the first term, the real was four to the dollar. It has been an incredible shift, historically.

In the long run, I believe that Brazil is very solid. Why? Brazil has a rich population, and a growing middle class to manufacture, to produce. They are incredibly aggressive and ambitious. And you have poorer people who, despite the social issues, want to come back into a market, want to go into a market. And finally, a lot of people, and I see that in my employees, are looking for the steps they have to take in order to make money, in order to be able to work.

I travel around the world. I go four or five times to Asia every year. I am in the U.S. every month. I am in Europe three or four times a year as well. I see huge changes in what is outside the so-called "developed market." These markets consist of incredibly rich countries. But they have not been able, throughout history, to tap into opportunities for their population. So I am extremely positive about Brazil. Obviously, you have to go through the shifts of a developing country, which is still very bound to market forces like everyone else. But you have the fundamentals, something that I do not really see in Europe, for example.

Knowledge@Wharton: Do you see any impact on the telecommunications sector?

Duran: The telecommunications sector is interesting. In my case, we build networks and we have products for companies—voice and data. We have not seen any changes whatsoever. We have not seen any change in the past month in sales. We have not seen any change in productivity. However, we obviously have to see the impact on the banks. We have not seen any impact on credit—for example, short-term credit from banks in Brazil. I do not know if it is going to happen. A lot of people are actually guessing that it may happen, but let us see.

Knowledge@Wharton: It is, of course, true and a very positive sign that the market has been going up in the U.S. as well as in Brazil and in Asia. Do you see this as volatility, or do you think that things are back on the upswing again?

Duran: The question for me would be: Why is the market driving all this? The managers of a company and the board of directors are in charge of the long-run situation, [but] the health of a corporation is measured mostly by the stock market. That was supposed to be for the long-run growth of the company and to align [it] with the shareholders and their interests. In reality, what I have seen is companies taking short-term decisions to create short-term mini-bubbles or to please the expectations of bankers who often do not understand exactly what they are doing. I have seen it in my industry. I see the major telecom companies acting like banks. I do not see them acting like telecom companies. I benefit greatly from that. I do not know about society, but personally I could not be more pleased because I actually compete with banks instead of competing with telecom companies.

Knowledge@Wharton: Speaking of the telecom industry, I had a question about one more aspect of the economy. As you know, the real was fairly strong against the dollar, but as a result of this financial crisis there has been depreciation in value. Some companies import equipment from overseas, and I understand you import some equipment from China. In what kind of position does this put importers in Brazil?

Duran: It is a good question, but it is not as relevant as one would think. I manage the company in such a way that I try to maintain my costs. My industry is very local, because most of my cost is actually digging the streets, it is construction. And construction is cement. Construction is PVC. Construction is cable. Construction is fiber optics. Construction is people, local people. Today, after nine years, I have more than 1,000 people in the company. Equipment is significant, and the high end of my equipment comes from overseas—the U.S., obviously, China and India. But in reality, it is only 7% of my cost. So if the real devalues 25%, I can absorb that with no sweat.

Knowledge@Wharton: Perhaps you could help put what you just said into context for our listeners by explaining what exactly Mundivox is and how your business model has evolved.

Duran: Mundivox is a telecom company that began in 2000. I came up with the idea in 1999, and in March 2000 we started operations, building networks and providing data and telephone services for corporations. Now, we are expanding. Late last year, we started to expand to the residential market as a separate unit of the company. But Mundivox is 90% based on corporations. This year, we will be growing 100% in revenues. Our strategy is to recreate modern infrastructure to connect clients. When I started the company, everybody was talking about unbundling. So you do not need another infrastructure company, everybody will share infrastructure. But the fact of the matter is that unbundling did not work. I said it at the time; not too many people believed me. Being a small company I had to do what people did 70 years ago when the telephone industry started, which is building infrastructure on a city-by-city basis. So I focused on geographic growth. And I believe in a BCG framework, which is relative market share drives profitability. I use that consistently. I go to one neighborhood. I go to one city block. I build infrastructure there. I maximize sales. I move to another city block. One by one, I optimize logistics, my capex [capital expenditure] and my people, performing better in terms of services. And so we are going to complete a decade.

The industry is very small compared to the huge banks I compete with but we can have the benefit of looking at the client in the eye. And hopefully responding better than the other companies do and increasing revenue. And, interestingly, I have not spent one cent in marketing.

Knowledge@Wharton: That is interesting because Brazil has such a large and growing telecommunications market. There are huge telephone companies, Telefónica and others, who are quite active here. Could you help explain your competitive strategy? How do you compete in this environment and how is that you are able to grow at a time when other companies seem to be struggling?

Duran: First, Brazil is divided into three major areas. Let us forget about Brazil and let us think about three different countries: the south, which is dominated by a company called Brasil Telecom; the northeast and the Rio area where there is Telemar; and Telefónica in the state of São Paulo. Those companies bought the rights and they are natural monopolies. It used to be the Telebras system. On top of that you had long distance deregulation. One company—Embratel—was allowed everywhere, but it did not have local networks. What I saw was that the monopolies would continue to be monopolies. They are going to act like better monopolies, but they will continue to be monopolies. [But] you have a long distance network Telmex, which is owned by Carlos Slim, which is coming. He is going to have to build networks and he will not be able to do it everywhere. So let us find niches.

In the beginning, everybody told me go to São Paulo, which is the biggest city in Brazil. And I thought why São Paulo if I can go to a second city, which is half the size, and has huge opportunities. The fact of the matter is that it takes a long time to build infrastructure. And it is not a question of money. You can have all the money in the world [which I did not have]. But the government will never allow you to break and destroy the whole city at once because you have money. You have to do it by tranches, which means you may have an opportunity to start small.

The financial crisis of 2001-2002 and the telecom and internet meltdown, hit me. I went virtually bankrupt three times and I sold my house to be able to fund the company. I could not believe that the large companies were not going to look at me for such a long time. It is probably a big question they still have. But the fact of the matter is that we continued growing. We focus on a niche which is small-and-medium sized companies, which is very difficult for a big corporation to focus on. The main reason for that is the small-and-medium sized company thinks like a big company, makes demands like a big company, but does not have the revenue to be attractive to a major corporation.

In 1995, when I was working for Bain & Company and AT&T in New Jersey was one of my clients, they acquired a company called Unitel in Canada, which became AT&T Canada. I was business director for a year in Toronto. Every time that I tried to create a strategy and I used every tool to attack small-and-medium sized businesses, the answer from my boss was always: You are fighting too much with little crowds. Come with me, play golf, I will introduce you to six people and you will have a much better bonus at the end of the year. He gave me an understanding of how these companies think.

The year before I had spent time working with the Mexican government on how to deregulate the market and privatization. I was a kid out of Wharton, but I actually saw how the forces influenced the government of Mexico. That is how I came up with the idea of building a micro [but full-sized] telecom company that builds infrastructure, goes to buildings, puts fiber and builds the infrastructure in the building. I would have my own technicians, because otherwise I lose contact with the client. If I do not understand the infrastructure and problems happen, as they always do, I will not have the knowledge of where or how to fix them. I will not depend on third parties. That works for big companies.

Knowledge@Wharton: You went from being a consultant to becoming an entrepreneur.

Duran: Yes.

Knowledge@Wharton: What did you have to learn to make that transition and how did you learn it?

Duran: I remember a partner at Bain & Company taught me a very big lesson. He came and said: "Look, the difference between being a consultant and being a manager in a big company is that we have the benefit of not dealing with normal people. We usually deal with very interesting, highly-educated, self-motivated people making good money and thinking big. You are now going to be dealing and struggling with the difficulties that a normal person and a normal worker face every day."

It is very hard and very important because, at the end of the day, as an entrepreneur you end up providing a lot of jobs. You have to think of the reactions of your employees. We were very lucky in getting the benefits of higher education and dealing with very interesting people around the world. But we very often forget the real people, the majority of the people in the streets. And that is a disease that all of us who come from great schools face and must try to cure, because that is where the real growth and the real creation come from. I am not talking about creating money. I am talking about creating things that this world still needs.

After nine years we are close to 1,000 people now. I do not see my company stopping until we drive 100,000, perhaps 200,000. Maybe I will do it. Maybe I will be in charge; maybe not. But what is interesting is having the model that is going to continue growing. Hopefully we will find a way to continue motivating people to work hard, to make more money, and to bring more money and knowledge to the next generation.

Knowledge@Wharton: What are your top two or three priorities for the next couple of years?

Duran: The first priority, believe it or not, it is creating new management in the company. I find the biggest problem is to create middle management. They are extremely smart; they are extremely capable in their field technically. But their view of the world and their view of what is right and what is wrong may be sometimes different. Diversity to me is not in race, it is in the way you think. And that is where the biggest focus and the biggest challenge lie, because without those managers we cannot grow to have 10,000 people. I need more managers to move into different areas, to lead more people and to influence those people like I would.

I had an interesting meeting with Craig Barrett from Intel seven years ago. Everything was going down (in price) and Intel was looking at companies. I was not a "sexy" company for Intel at that time because I was infrastructure based. I was not going to help Intel. But everybody was asking questions about money and capital and Intel capital. I was struggling to survive at that time but I did not ask that question. [I did not look to them for money.] I came in and asked: How did you make this a company with so many thousands of employees. That to me represents how you have grown. That is what I am concerned with;

growth—economic growth, healthy growth—is everything. That is how companies become rich. And that is how countries become richer.

And Barrett said I had asked a very interesting question. The answer is culture—it depends on the culture. That is when I started going back to my books
and my management theories. I said, "Okay, that is what it meant." I started
paying more attention to the soft issues and to psychology, than the tools that I
had learned to use at the beginning of my career.

Knowledge@Wharton: What are some of the things you are doing to shape
the kind of culture you want at Mundivox?

Duran: It is very difficult to structure a program when you are growing at 100%.
At 100% the fact of the matter is that we change every year, we change everything,
every system, every procedure. Everything that we had a year ago is basically non-
existent today. So we have to be constantly changing. And to constantly change,
the biggest problem that I find is that people think in their boxes. They forget to
share with others those boxes and perspectives—right or wrong—for the company to grow as a whole.

So to me it is constantly being together, being in the field. Twice a week I
am with my people and I go to visit every construction site. I take my supervisors
to lunch, not my directors. I go with employees to a site for an hour or two to
understand their lives and to talk to them as much as possible. The one thing
that we are doing is trying to create some retreats and some parties where you
share on a day-to-day basis.

If there is a mistake or if I have a different opinion, I go and tell them. And
I tell them it is not just your right to criticize me; you have to criticize me. But
please bring me two pieces of data. Only with the two pieces of data to justify
your statement can you convince me that you think mathematically and I can
try to understand what you are trying to say. It is very easy to criticize; everybody
can be a critic. But positive criticism is what it is all about.

Knowledge@Wharton: What are some of the risks that keep you up at night?

Duran: The biggest one is having an accident or security problems. We had an
incident some months ago in Leblon. At 3:00 a.m. we were installing the fiber
optics. [The workers] were probably making too much noise. Suddenly, someone
came down with two machine guns and said, "You stop now; otherwise, I will
kill you." That is something that really concerns me. Companies have to learn
how to deal with it and people have to learn, so we are putting more and more
security into the company. We are growing, so we have to structure all that
within the company.

The other [risk] is losing the best talent. But that has become easier because

I always pay my people better than the competition. It is very simple. They work harder, but I pay much better. And it is not easy to work in my company because growing at 100%, you are not going to have an easy day. I do not care where you come from. I do not care if you are a man or a woman. All I care about is your creating value. And the way we define creating value is doing what we decide together to do. We have clients to connect and we have to be much better than the rest. So it is incredibly aggressive and we make lots of mistakes. But I believe that the winner is he who corrects the mistakes faster.

Knowledge@Wharton: In your career, whether as a consultant or as an entrepreneur, what is the biggest mistake you have made? What did you learn from it?

Duran: Underestimating people is very easy. You sometimes become too arrogant. Companies are people; the leaders are very smart. I never underestimate my competition, I never underestimate my employees, I never underestimate anybody. I am very clear about it. I believe that we live in a world based on people, not based on markets. I am a finance major. But finance to me is a consequence which sometimes becomes a leading edge. But it should not be the purpose, unless you are a bank. It should be a measure.

Knowledge@Wharton: When entrepreneurs think about the future, at some point there is an exit strategy, sometimes through an IPO and in other cases by being acquired. Do you give any thought to such issues today, and if so what is your thinking?

Duran: I did at the very beginning. When I started Mundivox, I had a reputation and I raised easy money from investors [who I still have]. I sold 27% of the company. I kept the rest. Everybody asked me why I did not sell more. And I said no. I need to be in control. I cannot let bankers or investors decide. If I am not the right guy, I have to go away and someone else should take command. But there has to be a leader. It is a family corporation owned by shareholders. It is nothing else but a family corporation. When the capital structure of a company dictates results, it is very damaging. Strategy starts being driven by [the need for better short-term] financial results.

Many entrepreneurs do not have a choice. They have to sell the majority and become an employee with an upside. But then you change the rules. You become an employee. You do not remain an entrepreneur. To be an entrepreneur is to have the biggest burden of the risk. And it is very distracting to think about exit strategies. You have to think about creation of value for the enterprise. It is not only the money that should lead you to become an entrepreneur, because that is not what it is all about. To be an entrepreneur is to be in creation. You are an architect, you are creating, you are leading people. In the long run it is hopefully going to bring you profit and wealth. I do not know what I would do with that afterwards, which is a bigger problem.

Knowledge@Wharton: How do you define success?

Duran: You have to look at yourself. Success is different for everybody. It is like truth, that depends on the glass that you are looking at. Dante said that a long time ago [in The Divine Comedy]. My definition of success at this moment is growth. It is seeing people being influenced and having the life I always wanted to have. It is a combination, having time to spend with my family as well and trying to influence other people to have 25 years of growth. I do not want to have five years of stellar growth. Success is seeing something being realized and seeing something continue to be realized. More and more success is having something being realized by my directors, my employees, and not by me. That is a big shift that I had to do two years ago. If it continues based on me looking at every client, I am not building a company, I am being a consultant.

And so it is my definition of success. Economics is nice. It is part of life, but it is not my driving force. I believe I am creating a lot of wealth, but it is just a measure to fulfill the rest. ∎

Published: December 18, 2008 in Knowledge@Wharton